WHO'S WHO
THE STAGS
1902 - 1995

FROM WESLEYANS
TO
MANSFIELD TOWN

By Jack Retter

Published by:
Yore Publications
12 The Furrows, Harefield,
Middx. UB9 6AT.

© Jack Retter 1995
....

British Library Cataloguing-in-Publication Data.
A catalogue record for this book
is available from the British Library.

ISBN 1 874427 90 9

Yore Publications specialise in football books, normally of an historic theme.
Newsletters (which detail all current and new titles) are posted free, three times per year.
Please send a S.A.E. for your initial copy of the latest Newsletter.

Printed by 'The Book Factory'

THE AUTHOR

JACK RETTER was born at East Kirkby, Nottinghamshire in 1927, but the family moved to Mansfield when he was barely three and he saw his first "Stags" match as a seven year old when his father took him to Field Mill to see Harry Johnson play. His business career commenced during the war at the now defunct William Hollins' works at Pleasley Vale from where he joined the Royal Navy in 1944, serving in a variety of ships and shore establishments, reaching the rank of Supply Petty Officer. Returning to Hollins' as a management trainee, he moved to Leicester in 1951 to take up a position as Yarn Buyer with a major hosiery manufacturer and ten years later this led to him setting up his own schoolwear manufacturing business. Due to business and other commitments, he was a Town exile for almost 30 years, seeing only a handful of games each season until he returned to the county upon retirement in 1984, and now rarely misses a match.

He became interested in the historical and statistical aspects of the club during the war years and extensive research, particularly during the last few years has culminated in this publication. He possesses a fine collection of Mansfield Town memorabilia.

A shareholder in the Club, Jack Retter was educated at High Oakham School and gained an economics degree at university. He is also an Associate of the Textile Institute, a Member of the Institute of Purchasing and Supply and an Associate of the Institute of Certified Accountants.

Now living in retirement in the North East of the county and a member of the Association of Football Statisticians, he is a regular contributor to the "Stag's" match day programme.

Jack Retter is now working on a comprehensive history of Mansfield Town from 1897 to date and this will be published in 1997 to commemorate the Club's Centenary.

Inevitably errors, hopefully not significant ones, will creep into any statistical production such as this and whilst a number of people have been involved in much of the information revealed herein, I take full responsibility for any errors and I accept them as mine and mine alone. I must also be held accountable for any opinions expressed.

Completeness is a comodity which of course no statistician can ever achieve - but one must try as future generations may consider these historical works as their bible, so accuracy is vital. All too often in my researches I have discovered long accepted "facts" that are simply not true and these, where applicable, have been incorporated in this work.

The Author would welcome comments from any reader who has good reason and/or documentary evidence, to challenge any of the information within these pages, or has additional information to offer and I can be contacted through the publisher.

Publisher's note: A number of photographs have been taken direct from newspapers, very old team groups (of variable quality) and/or have required considerable enlargement from original team groups. Consequently, in some cases, the quality of reproduction has inevitably suffered to a degree.

INTRODUCTION

This book is the culmination of many years research into the personal details, playing records, etc. of every traceable player who has made at least one appearance at senior level with Mansfield Wesleyans, Mansfield Wesley and Mansfield Town from 1902 to 1995. Regrettably it has not been possible to cover the first five years of the club's existence as no records or newspaper accounts of the club's activities were reported until 1902, and sadly there is no one left alive who can go back that far. However, I have been fortunate enough to be able to interview several older fans who were able to recall seeing the club play before the First World War!

Also regrettable, it is inevitable that some omissions will have occurred, although no effort has been spared to make this record as comprehensive and accurate as possible.

Therefore I apologise in advance to relatives of former players who may feel aggrieved that any of their ancestors have been overlooked and I would welcome hearing from anyone who may feel that this is so, thus enabling corrections to be made in any future edition.

I hope this volume will take its place in the soccer archives as a tribute to the 1,160 players featured in this book, who have all made a contribution, no matter how small, to the 98 year old history of one of the many clubs which has played its part in the structure of the Football League.

Many questions can be answered from within the following pages and if supporters find enjoyment from this work, it will all have been worthwhile.

JACK RETTER,
Tuxford, Nottinghamshire.
June 1995.

ACKNOWLEDGEMENTS

My special thanks to Paul Taylor, with his excellent knowledge of all things concerning Mansfield Town and with an unbelievable amount of of information stored in his computer files. Several times he proof read the original draft - and this revealed a number of errors. He has my eternal gratitude for his work and assistance in this direction and if the book achieves its place in soccer history, then in no small measure is it due to him.

Another person who must receive my very special thanks for his help and for throwing his home open to me on more occasions than I could possibly remember, as well as providing copious supplies of food and refreshment, is Raymond Shaw. His collection of football books, Who's Who's and club histories must be one of the finest in existence, and through his kindness this was ever available to me in my search for completeness.

Steve Emms, who was working simultaneously on a comprehensive Who's Who for the Association of Football Statisticians, was immensely helpful in providing information on "Stags" players during the 1919-39 period, for which he has my heartfelt thanks. Dave McPherson, whose frequent visits to the Football League's headquarters at Lytham St Annes to check on registrations, dates of birth, etc., was of tremendous assistance. Special thanks too must be given to Jeremy Plews (editor) and Roger Grayson (chief photographer) of the *Mansfield Chronicle Advertiser*, for the valuable assistance extended to the author over a lengthy period.

Amongst the great number of other people who gave their help in various ways, I must include Lou Smith, Hedley Hill & Nicola Wilcockson of Mansfield Town Football Club - the staff of Mansfield Central Library for their help, kindness and consideration - Geoff Sadler of Chesterfield Public Library who has been researching the history of the original Shirebrook Football Club - Marshall Gillespie for information on Irish born players - the many authors, too numerous to mention who have produced Who's Whos and histories for so many clubs that have made my task immeasurably easier - relatives and friends of many ex Mansfield Town players - and, several octogenarian supporters for their time, hospitality and above all, reliving of nostalgic moments. A most delightful letter from nine year old Richard McGarry, giving information regarding his great grandfather, Jack Bellas, was most touching and made my day. A lady who has resided in Australia for over 40 years gave me valuable information concerning her father, who played for the Wesleyans in the last season before the club changed its name to Wesley. A number of ex "Stags" players have also been consulted. To all of them, my most grateful thanks.

If I have inadvertently omitted to thank anyone who may feel that they should have received a mention, please let me assure them that whilst it was not possible to acknowledge every person who has helped individually, these contributions, no matter how small, have all played their part in the production of this book and are deserving of my gratitude.

Lastly, but by no means least, a very special tribute must be given to Jean who suffered many lonely hours and took it all stoically, particularly when research problems must have made me very hard to live with - to her my love and eternal thanks.

Jack Retter

PHOTOGRAPHIC CREDITS:

Mansfield Chronicle Advertiser, J A Retter collection, Albert E Wilkes & Son, Chris Bradshaw, A C Vallance, George S Ellis, Chris Smith, Le Butt Studios, Sheffield Telegraph & Star, Provincial Press Agency, Evening News & Hampshire Telegraph, Central Press Photos, R Clements Lyttle Studios, P.Turton, Doug Salter,

BIBLIOGRAPHY

Mansfield and North Notts. Advertiser, Mansfield, Sutton and Kirkby Chronicle, Mansfield Reporter and Sutton in Ashfield Times, Mansfield Chronicle-Advertiser ("Chad"), Derbyshire Times, Numerous Who's Who's, Numerous Club histories, Gamages Football Annuals, Athletic News Football Annuals, Post Football Guides, The Football League Competitions (W M Johnston - T W Pegg & Sons), Football League Players Records (Barry J Hugman - Tony Williams Publications 1992), Soccer at War 1939-45 (Jack Rollin - Willow Books 1985), Soccer in the Dock (Simon Inglis - Willow Books 1985), History of the Welsh Cup 1877-1993 (Ian Garland - Bridge Books 1993)

CONTENTS

A BRIEF HISTORY
OF MANSFIELD TOWN FOOTBALL CLUB

As with many football clubs which sprang up in the early days of organised football, these were formed with a church background and the roots of Mansfield Town are no exception.

The origins of the club go back to 1897 when the Bridge Street Wesleyan Chapel formed its first football teams associated with the Boys' Brigades which it organised. For the juniors these were created for different companies and at least three such teams operated, being known as Mansfield Wesleyan Boys Brigade No 2 Company, for example. The senior male members of the church community also formed their own team and this was known as the Mansfield Wesleyan Guild (or Bible Class), soon simplified to Mansfield Wesleyans. Only friendly matches were played initially and as the club became more ambitious, membership of the Mansfield & District Amateur League was sought and in the 1903-04 season competitive football for the team started in earnest.

Within three years this enthusiastic bunch of players aspired to bigger things and joined the Notts & District League which was semi-professional. When the church elders discovered that the club was paying at least some of its players, and what was perhaps more distasteful to Methodist principles, using a public house for its meetings, the chapel disowned them and forbade them from using the name *Wesleyan* in their title. So for the 1906-07 season, the club made its appearance under the modified guise of Mansfield Wesley and by 1909-10 had entered the F A Challenge Cup competition for the first time.

Burning ambition to make the club into the premier club in the town and take this distinction away from its bitter rivals, Mansfield Mechanics, brought about a further change of name in 1910 to the far more impressive Mansfield Town. This was evolved mainly to upstage their arch enemies and at the same time the club declared its intention of aiming ultimately for admission to the Football League.

This was not the first time that this title had been used by a football club in the town - indeed a club had been formed as early as 1871, and by 1892 playing in the acclaimed Midland League plus the F.A. Cup competition, was known by this title. This club merged with the other leading team in the town - the Greenhaigh's (formed in 1861) - during the summer of 1894, as Mansfield F.C. until their demise in 1901.

So, the following season (1911-12), a further move was made in the progression of the club by becoming founder-members of the more prestigious Central Alliance, but this advance in status received a severe check when the Alliance voted the Town out at the end of the 1913-14 season. Their exclusion was due not only to their finish at next to bottom, but more important was the appalling state of their ground, quaintly known as "The Prairie", which was located in Ratcliffe Gate. The conditions there must have improved considerably, for a mere twelve months later the club was re-admitted to the Alliance after an absence of only one season.

With the conclusion of hostilities at the end of 1914-18 war, the club resumed in the Alliance by 1919 at a new ground, the Field Mill, the former home of Mansfield Mechanics (who were by now moving into oblivion, finally folding in 1923), and promptly won the championship. But grander things were yet to come!

In the summer of 1921, the club's application for membership of the Midland League was accepted and for the first time it became necessary to employ full time professionals. This astute move brought quick results, the championship being won in 1923-24 and again the following season. The 1920's was a purple period for the "Stags", for one season later, 1925-26, they finished runners up. 1926-27 saw the club invited to join the newly formed Midland Combination, ostensibly formed for the reserve sides of Football League clubs, many of them First and Second Division sides, so the opposition was getting tougher. Most creditably, the "Stags" finished as runners up, also winning the Combination Cup competition.

Due to Football Association opposition to a non league club playing in a league specifically originated for the reserve sides of Football League clubs, 1927-28 saw them back in the Midland League. In 1928-29 they won the championship for the third time and had a wonderful F A Cup run in which they disposed of League clubs Barrow and Wolverhampton Wanderers on their own grounds before succumbing to the almost invincible Arsenal at Highbury to two goals scored in the last eight minutes. Mansfield missed a penalty in the first half, that no one wanted to take! This brought national acclaim to the club and probably helped towards achieving their avowed goal - Football League membership, for which they had been applying annually since 1924 without managing more than a handful of votes.

At this time, the "old faithful" were generally re-elected year after year in the Northern Section.

As the club's geographical position was favourable to the move, it was decided to change tack in 1931 by applying to the Southern Section.

So, following much lobbying by manager Jack Hickling and others, completely without the knowledge of one of the relegation candidates - Newport County - and much to their chagrin, the "Stags" were elected and the Welshmen were out. The final goal at last!

Mansfield Town have enjoyed membership of the Football League ever since - 65 continuous years, and are one of the few regular members of the lower divisions who have not had to apply for re-election more than once, and that was at the end of the first post WW II season when things were far from normal. Due to the special circumstances prevailing at this time - the war had only recently ended, many players were still awaiting demobilisation and were not always available to their clubs. Some clubs were only re-starting again after complete closure during hostilities, and the Football League recommended that the four unfortunate clubs be re-elected unopposed - the only time this has ever happened in the League's 106 year history. Therefore the record number of election hopefuls that year, some 27 in number, went away disappointed.

In 1997 the club celebrates its centenary and on solid foundations, with the prospect of a new ground and much ambition, the future looks decidedly rosy.

KEY TO TEXT

Details appear in the main text of every player who has made at least one appearance or been used as a substitute in matches played by Mansfield Town in the Football League from 1931-95, (excluding play-offs,) but including matches played during the Second World War by players on the "Stags" books, of which details are excluded from official records. Also encompassed on the same basis, are games played from 1919-31, before the club was admitted to the Football League - this includes matches played in the Central Alliance (1919-21), Midland League (1921-26 and 1927-31) and Midland Combination (1926-27). Players are also covered who have not appeared in a league match, but have made at least one appearance in a cup competition - and this includes F A Challenge Cup, Football League Cup, Associate Members' Cup, Watney Cup, Anglo Scottish Cup, Notts F A County Cup, Notts F A Senior Cup, Notts Benevolent Bowl and Mansfield Hospital Charity Cup. All other matches including friendlies, benefit games and pre season fixtures are excluded. Appearances relate to league matches only - all other first class matches are additional to the figures shown. It may be assumed that all appearances/goals are for matches played in the Football League - alongside individual seasons - unless indicated otherwise.

The basic information given for each player shows - full name (the name by which he was known has been bracketed where the player had more than one first name), years at club, position played, height, weight (year this was taken is shown in brackets), clubs played for, signing dates, transfer fees, appearances (substitute appearances bracketed), goals scored and honours gained during career. Note that appearances and goals are only those achieved with the "Stags".

Where clubs' names have changed, the actual name used at the time is shown, e.g. Leicester Fosse became Leicester City in 1919, Stoke became Stoke City in 1925 and The Wednesday became Sheffield Wednesday in 1929. These are examples of three of the more famous clubs, but there are many other lesser known ones too. Similarly, the present League of Ireland was, until 1936, known as the Free State League and this title has been used where appropriate.

A single year has been used to denote the date of players' honours. In all cases this refers to the last year of the season concerned - e.g. 1925 represents the 1924-25 season. Inclusion of a player's name under a League award generally implies a minimum of 14 appearances were made in the competition that season.

Match reports up to 1916 tended to be sketchy and incomplete - generally only goalscorers were recorded, so prior to 1919 it has not been possible to list with any degree of accuracy the players' appearances, so only the goalscorers have been shown. Unlike the WW II period, when the Club continued playing in the regional war leagues, the "Stags" closed down at the end of the 1915-16 season until the end of the war and did not resume playing again until August 1919.

ABBREVIATIONS USED IN TEXT

actg	=	acting				N K	=	not known
am, amat	=	amateur	F A	=	Football Association	OL	=	outside left
app	=	appearances	FB	=	full back	OR	=	outside right
appr	=	apprentice	F C	=	Football Club	perm	=	permanent
approx	=	approximately	F L	=	Football League	p/exch	=	part exchange
(also depicted by an asterisk *)			F.T.	=	free transfer	P F A	=	Professional Foot-
assoc	=	associated	G	=	goalkeeper			ballers' Association
asst	=	assistant	gls	=	goals	physio	=	physiotherapist
B C	=	Boys' Club	IF	=	inside forward	pro	=	professional
b	=	born	IL	=	inside left	res	=	reserve
c	=	circa (about)	IR	=	inside right	RFB	=	right full back
C/C	=	contract cancelled	jnr, jr	=	junior	RHB	=	right half back
CF	=	centre forward	K I A	=	killed in action	sch	=	schoolboy
CHB	=	centre half back	LFB	=	left full back	snr, sr	=	senior
c/s	=	close season	LHB	=	left half back	temp	=	temporary
D	=	defender	loan	=	loan transfer (temp.)	v	=	versus (against)
d	=	died	M	=	midfield	W	=	winger
d.o.b.	=	date of birth	N A B C	=	National Association of	WHB	=	wing half back
exch	=	exchange			Boys' Clubs	WW I	=	World War One
F	=	forward	N/C	=	non contract	WW II	=	World War Two

PLAYERS 1902 - 16

MANSFIELD WESLEYANS 1902-06   MANSFIELD WESLEY 1906-10
MANSFIELD TOWN 1910-16

LEAGUES
Mansfield & District Amateur League 1903-06
Notts and District League 1906-08
Notts & Derbys District League 1908-11
Central Alliance 1911-14
Notts & Derbys District League 1914-15
Central Alliance 1915-16

	Seasons Played	Pos	d.o.b.	Previous Club	Subsequent Club	Goals
ABRAHAM George	1902-06	IF				* 15
ALLISON	1910-11	IR				
ALLSOP	1914-15	CHB				
ALTON	1915-16	WHB				
ARMISON	1904-05	LHB				
BAGNALL	1911-12	CF		Clowne Red Star		2
BAILEY John (William)	1908-10	OL			Mechanics	
	& 1913-14			Shirebrook		
BALL Alfred	See entry in main section.					9
BARNETT	1912-14	IR		Pinxton		12
BARNETT Thomas	1912-14	IF	c 1882	Notts Olympic	Pinxton	12
BARRINGTON	1907-08	FB				
BARROWS D	1904-05	RHB			Mechanics	
BARSTON F	1914-15			Sheffield		
BASSETT	1913-14	IL				
BENSON Samuel #	1902-03	OR				
BELSHAW	1915-16	IR				
BELTON Thomas	1907-11	WHB				1
BEXON Samuel	1903-10	CHB				
BINGHAM William	1914-15	IF		Mechanics		5
BLACKNELL William	1912-13	CF	c 1892	Pinxton	Shirebrook	29
("Fatty")	& 1914-15			Shirebrook	Shirebrook	
BLAND	1913-14	CHB				
BOCOCK	1904-05	LHB				
BONSALL Thomas	1914-15	RHB		Shirebrook		
BOSTOCK	1908-11	WHB			Mechanics	
BOWLER Thomas	1914-15	OL		Nottingham		
BOWLES W	1907-11	FB				1
BRAMLEY F	1914-15	LHB		Ilkeston		
BRAWN	1913-14	G				
BRETNALL Oliver Charles	1912-13	CF		Portsmouth	Stamford	
BROTHERHOOD	1913-14	IR				
BROWN	1909-10	CHB				
BROWN Arthur	1915-16	WHB				
BROWN George †	1915-16	IR		Gresley Rovers		8
BRYAN John Joseph	See entry in main section.					3
BURGIN	1911-13	CF				2
BURTON	1911-12	G				
BUTLER	1914-15	LFB				
BUTLIN	1909-10	LHB				
CARTER	1910-11	CHB				2
CARTWRIGHT	1909-10	LFB				
CHAFFIN	1906-08	F				
CHAPMAN	1912-13	IL				
CLARE	1906-07	FB				
CLIFFE	1914-15	RFB		Mechanics		
COALWOOD	1911-12	FB		Worksop Town	Shirebrook	
COLEMAN Frederick	1902-12	RFB				
COLEMAN James	1903-05	RHB				
COLLINS	1914-16	IF				16
CONGRIEVE Frederick	See entry in main section.					11
COOK	1906-07	WHB				
COOPER †	1914-16				Sutton Town	1

	Seasons Played	Pos	d.o.b.	Previous Club	Subsequent Club	Goals
DALEY	1906-07	IR				* 10
DEXTER Luther	1913-14	OR	7/1895	Moore's Ath		1
DEXTER George	1915-16	FB	5-8-96	Preston N E	Mechanics	2
DOUTHWAITE J	1914-15	CF		Sheffield		
DOVE	1903-04	OR				
DUDLEY	1910-11	CF				
EARDLEY	1907-08	G				
EVANS	1911-12				Mechanics	
EVANS A	1906-07	OL				
EVANS J	1904-06	WHB				
FARNSWORTH	1913-14	G				
FEARNEY	1914-15	CF		Southwell		
FEEBERY H	See entry in main section					
FELL	1911-12	IR				
FLANDERS George	1913-14	CF				4
FLETCHER	1907-08	OL			Mechanics	
	& 1913-14			Mechanics		
FOSTER W	1910-11	OR				
FOSTER B B	1913-16	OL		Newhall		14
FOX	1906-08	CHB				
GADSDEN	1915-16	G				
GADSDEN Ernest †	1915-16	FB	22-12-95	Bulwell	Nottm. Forest	
GELSTHORPE G	1910-11	CF			Shirebrook	1
GOAD	1914-15	G				
GODBER	1913-14	RHB				
GOODE	1911-12	LFB				
GREEN Arthur	1912-16	RFB	1885	Lincoln	Grantham	
GREEN Thomas	1913-14	IR		Cleethorpes Tn		1
GREGORY Thomas	1912-13	IL	1892		Notts County	
GRUNDY	1905-06	LFB				
GUNN	1911-12	G		Millwall		
GUNTHORPE R	1902-04	IF				
	& 1907-08					
HAGUE	1913-14	IR		Mechanics		
HALL	1904-05	G				
HALL	1910-11	WHB				
HANKIN	1913-14	OR			Mechanics	1
HARDY Harry	1907-15	WHB	c1880			1
HARDY W	1904-05	CF				
HARRIMAN	1908-11	OR				
HARRIS	1905-06	OR				
HARRISON	1909-10					
HARRISON †	1915-16					1
HART	1913-14	LFB				
HARVEY	1910-11					
HEMSTOCK J	1913-14	FB		Mechanics	Shirebrook	
HEXTALL	1905-06	CF				* 25
HILL	1911-12	RFB				
HOLDEN Jack	See entry in main section.					5
HOLLINGSWORTH	1914-15			Sheffield		
HOLMES Thomas	1903-04	IR		St Peters		
HOLMES Albert	1903-08	W			Chesterfield	* 35
HOPKINSON	1905-06	CHB				
HOPKINSON	1912-13	OL				
HORSMAN Frederick	1910-12	FB	c1891		Watford	1
HOUSLEY Herbert	See entry in main section.					16
HOWES	1909-10					
HUGHES	1908-10	LFB				
HUMPHREYS Caleb('Cabby')	1914-15	FB		Mechanics		
HUNT	1910-11	FB				
HURT	1913-14	RFB				
IBBOTSON	1911-12	IR		Mechanics		
JACKSON S	1905-07	CF				* 20
JAMES	1907-11	IF				6
JOHNSON	1908-10	RFB				
JONES	1907-10	G				
JONES A	1911-13	CF		Mechanics	Mechanics	5

Name	Seasons Played	Pos	d.o.b.	Previous Club	Subsequent Club	Goals
KING George	1912-15	RHB		Mechanics		2
KING H	1913-15	G				
KIRK	1909-10	IR		St Peters	Mechanics	
KIRKMAN	1914-15	LHB				
KITCHEN	1914-15	RFB				
LEE	1905-06	CHB				
LINTON	1906-07	FB				
LOVATT	1912-13	LHB				
LOWE	1907-08	WHB				
LYNALL	1906-07	WHB				
McKEE George S	1902-03	CF				
MAHON Lawrence	1911-12	CHB			Shirebrook	
MALTBY P	1910-11			St Mark's		
MAUDE	1911-12	G				
MANSELL	1910-11	RFB				
MARPLES James	1903-07	G				
MARPLES Wilfred	1902-11	G				
MAPLETOFT	1907-08 & 1910-12	G		Sutton Tn	Sutton Tn	
MARSHALL	1909-10					
MARSHALL A	1913-15	OL				
MARSHALL George	1914-15	OR		Sutton Tn		1
MASKREY (Harry) Mort	1914-15	G	8-10-80	Mechanics	Celanese Derby	
MASON W	1905-06	IR				
MEAKINS	1907-08	FB				
MEE Herbert N	1912-14	OR				4
MIDDLETON Alfred	See entry in main section.					* 15
MILLER	1912-14	G				
MILLS	1907-08	IL				
MORTIMORE E	1913-14			Crystal Palace		
MORTON	1914-15	F				6
NASH	1911-12	OR				
NEAL	1909-10	CF				
NEEDHAM John ("Jack")	1907-09	IF	1891		Birmingham	* 50
NEWBURY	1914-15	G		Mechanics		
NUTTALL	1905-06	WHB/IF				* 10
OLTON †	1915-16					1
ORTON Josiah ("Jo")#	1902-03	OL	c1879		Mechanics	
OSCROFT William	1905-06	OR	10-3-88	M Woodhouse R.M	Woodhouse R. d:19-2-42	
PAGE	1905-06	LFB				
PARKER	1913-14	LHB				
PARKES	1907-10	RHB				
PARNELL G (Frederick)	1913-14	OR	1886	Sutton Junction		3
PEACH	1914-15	G		Chilwell		
PEARCE	1913-14	CHB				
POOLE Henry ("Harold")	1913-14	CF	22-6-93	Coventry City	Sutton Town	
POPE	1909-10	IR				
POWELL	1903-04	CF				
QUIBELL Charles	1904-05	OL				* 10
QUIBELL Harry	1903-05	IL				* 45
RADFORD J	1904-05 & 1908-10 & 1911-13	IF/WHB		Langwith	Langwith }	* 10
RANDALL Reginald	1912-13	OR		Mechanics		
RANSOME	1910-11	CHB		Heanor Utd		
RAWSON F	1910-11	CHB				
RAYNOR	1905-07	IR				
READ	1903-04	IR				
REYNOLDS	1906-08	IL				* 10
RILEY	1913-14					
ROBINSON F	1914-15	IL		Alfreton		
ROBINSON Peter	1906-10	CHB				
ROBINSON W	1906-10	OR				
ROWSTON	1913-14	OR				

	Seasons Played	Pos	d.o.b.	Previous Club	Subsequent Club	Goals
SADLER H	1902-04	LHB				
SAXTON	1914-15	CHB		Sneinton		
SCOTT	1910-11					
SCRIMSHAW Harold	See entry in main section.					
SEVERN	1908-10	G				
SHEPHERD H	1914-15	OR		Nottingham		
SMEDLEY	1910-12	RHB		Sutton Tn	Mechanics	3
SMITH A	1905-07	IL		St Mark's		
SMITH Alec	1912-15	LHB		Mechanics		3
SMITH E	1903-04	G				
SMITH George	1902-03	RHB				
SMITH George W	1914-16	OR		Watford		14
SMITH J	1906-08	G				
SMITH Thomas	1905-06	IL				
SMITH Thomas	See entry in main section.					3
SMITH Walter	1913-14	IR				
SMITH	1910-11					
SOMERTON	1912-13	IL				
SPALL J	1906-07	CF				
SPRIGGS	1913-14	CF				2
STALEY	1910-11	G				
STALEY	1911-12	OR				
STATHAM W	1902-04	G		St Peters		* 20
STATHAM	1909-10	OR		Ripley		
STATHAM	1912-13	IL			Mechanics	1
STEVENSON	1908-10	CF		Mechanics		
STOKES F S	1902-04	CHB				
STRINGFELLOW J Frank	1912-13	IF	c1888	The Wednesday	Portsmouth	1
SYKES	1911-12	OL		Worksop Tn	Mechanics	
SYLVESTER Thomas	1910-13	RFB				
TATLEY	1903-04	OL				
TAYLOR	1906-08	LFB				
TEMPLE	1910-11	OR				1
THOMAS A	1905-07	IR				
THOMPSON	1911-13	CHB				1
TIMMINS	1913-14	LHB			Eastwood	1
TIVEY	1909-10	CF				* 35
TOMLINSON	1908-10	CF		Mechanics		* 15
TREMELLING Elijah (Soloman)	See entry in main section					
TREMELLING Richard (Daniel)	1914-15	G	12-12-97	Langwith W W	Shirebrook	
VARLEY	1914-15	CF				
WAKEFIELD	1905-06	IL				* 15
WALKER	1910-13		(d: K.I.A. France WW I)			1
WARD A	See entry in main section					
WATSON	1908-10	IR				
WEST	1909-10 & 1914-15	RHB		Long Eaton	Long Eaton	
WESTON	1909-10					
WHEATLEY James	1910-12	CF		Mechanics		31
WHEATLEY William	1910-12	IF		Mechanics		10
WHEELIKER	1912-13	LHB		Pinxton		
WHITBY	1909-10					
WHITEHEAD	1912-13	IR				1
WHYSALL William (Wilfrid)	1915-16	G	31-10-87	Shirebrook		
WILDEY	1914-15	IR		Southwell		
WILSON F	1902-08	LFB				
WILSON Strawson L	1915-16	CHB		Mechanics		
WILSON	1906-08	FB				
WOOD	1914-15	OL		Matlock Tn		
WOODCOCK	1903-04	LFB				
WOOLLATT George	1913-15	CHB				
WOOLLATT L I	1913-14	IF				4
WRIGHT F	1909-11	G				
WRIGLEY	1906-08	LHB		Mechanics		

The two players, Benson and Orton, marked #, were with the club from it's inception in 1897. Both served on the Committee and Benson also acted as trainer, from 1909-16. Honour for players marked † - Central Alliance Subsidiary Competition Championship in 1916 whilst with Mansfield. The figures marked with an asterisk (*) are approximate figures only for the period 1902-10. All unmarked figures are accurate.

LEADING PRE-WORLD WAR ONE PLAYERS

In the author's opinion, the following are the most prominent players who played for the Club before the First World War. Some had made their reputations in the Football League before joining the "Stags", whilst others did so after leaving Mansfield. Many achieved neither and spent their entire careers in the district.

ABRAHAM George 1902 - 06   Inside Forward. With Wesleyans from the time when they were only involved in playing friendly matches. He spent four seasons with the club, scoring c 15 goals.

BARNETT Thomas 1912 - 14   Inside Forward. b: c 1882
Clever, scheming, inside right, who was almost a veteran by the time Town obtained his services. Had enjoyed a long career in Midlands football, joining from Notts Olympic and moving on to Pinxton.   Scored 12 goals for Mansfield in two seasons.   Had played for Mansfield Mechanics c 1904 - 06.

BELTON Thomas 1909 - 11   Wing Half Back. Apparently a constructive wing half, with the club for four seasons.

BEXON Samuel 1903 - 10   Centre Half Back. From contemporary reports, Sam Bexon was a fine attacking centre half who served Wesleyans well for seven seasons.

BLACKNELL William ("Fatty")
1912 - 13 and 1914 - 15   Centre Forward. b:1882 d:France, 8 April 1917, K I A.
"Fatty" Blacknell came to Ratcliffe Gate from Pinxton although he was born and lived in Scarcliffe. A butcher by profession he was a most effective goalscorer, netting 36 from 27 appearances in his first season here. Joined up with Shirebrook the following term and his tally of goals helped them to win the Central Alliance Championship in 1913-14. Rejoined Mansfield the following season, but only stayed a few weeks, playing in three matches and scoring one goal before rejoining the "Magpies" for the remainder of the season. Joined the Yorks & Lancs Regiment in May 1916 and was killed in action in Flanders 8 April 1917, less than a year after volunteering and after only six months in France. Could well have had a great career in front of him.   Honours: Central Alliance Championship 1914 & runners up 1915 (both Shirebrook).

BOSTOCK 1908 - 11   Wing Half Back. Three seasons with Wesleyans before transferring to the Mechanics.

BOWLES W 1907 - 11   Full Back. This strong kicking full back was with the club for four seasons.

BRETNALL Oliver Charles
1912 - 13 Centre Forward.
Joined Town from Southern League club Portsmouth, moving on in turn to Stamford, Rotherham County and The Wednesday. Member of the Wednesday's First Division team which was dumped out of the F A Cup at Hillsborough in Jan 1920, at the hands of non-league Darlington by 2 goals to nil.

COLEMAN Frederick 1902 - 12 Right Full Back. Bedrock of Wesley's defence for 10 years, Fred Coleman had been with the club from the "friendlies only" period.

COLLINS 1914 - 16   Centre Forward. Only with the club for a couple of seasons immediately prior to WW I, but he scored a lot of goals.
Honours: Central   Alliance   -   Subsidiary Competition Championship 1916 (Mansfield).

DEXTER George 1915 - 16   Full Back. b: Hucknall, Notts., 5 August 1896.
In the Southern League with Coventry before spending a season at the "Prairie", followed by Second Division Preston's promotion season.
Honours: Division 2 runners up 1915 (P.N.E). Central   Alliance   -   Subsidiary   Competition Championship 1916 (Mansfield).

FOSTER B B 1913 - 16   Outside Left. The first of a long and illustrious line of players bearing this name who have graced the colours of the "Stags".   Came to Mansfield from Newhall Swifts, the club which discovered Leeds and England star, Ernie Hart, later to serve at Field Mill. Also the birthplace of the famous Tremelling brothers. Three seasons with the club. Honours: Central   Alliance   -   Subsidiary   Competition Championship 1916 (Mansfield).

GADSDEN Ernest 1915 - 16   Full Back b: Bulwell, Nottingham, 22 December 1895 d: St Albans, Beds., 6 January 1966.
After leaving Mansfield, went on to serve Forest, Norwich, Portsmouth, Blackpool and Halifax, retiring in 1928.
Honours: Central   Alliance   -   Subsidiary Competition Championship 1916 (Mansfield).

GREEN Arthur 1912 - 16   Right Full Back. Regular member of the first XI for four seasons.

Honours: Central Alliance - Subsidiary Competition Championship 1916 (Mansfield).

HARDY Harry 1907 - 15 Wing Half Back b: 1880. For eight seasons a stalwart of the defence.

HORSMAN Frederick 1910 - 12 Full Back b: Nottingham, c1891.
Enjoyed a fine career following two seasons at Mansfield. Transferred to Watford and subsequently Doncaster, playing regularly in the Football League until 1925.

HUMPHREYS Caleb ("Cabby")
1914 - 15 Full Back.
"Cabby" Humphreys had enjoyed a long and successful career with Mansfield Mechanics before he joined Town towards the end of his playing days.

JAMES 1907 - 11 Inside Forward.
He claimed 6 goals in his four seasons with the club.

KING G 1912 - 15 Right Half Back.
Recruited from Mansfield Mechanics, King served Town for three years.

MAHON Lawrence 1911 - 12 Centre Half Back.
One of three brothers who all played for Shirebrook. Mansfield released him to the "Magpies" and he went on to serve Watford and Blackpool.

MARPLES James 1903 - 07 Goalkeeper.
The name Marples is synonymous with the club. Joe served Wesley as goalkeeper (and outfield positions when the need arose), and Club Secretary for a number of years. Perhaps less notable than his brother, he nevertheless played a very important part in the early days.

MARPLES Wilfred 1902 - 11 Goalkeeper.
Brother of Jim, Wilf Marples really was "Mr Mansfield Town", at least before the last war. Associated with the club from it's very inception, he served it tirelessly from 1897 until the mid-1930's. In that time he was player, committee member, groundsman, trainer and general factotum. He went on to serve as trainer after WW I right through to joining the Football League, until he finally retired from active participation in the Club's affairs in the 1930s - 40 years of loyal service! He was the only survivor from the inauguration of the club who saw it through to achieving League status 34 years later!

MAPLETOFT 1907 - 08 and 1910 - 12
Goalkeeper. Career: WESLEY (1907), Sutton Town (1908), TOWN (1910).
Two separate spells with the club - three seasons in all.

MASKREY (Harry) Mort 1914 - 15
Goalkeeper b 8 October 1880 d 21 April 1927.
Harry Maskrey had a fine career in the First Division with the "Rams", making a total of 202 League appearances for them and gaining an England cap and Football League recognition along the way. Aging somewhat when he played for the two Mansfield professional teams towards the end of his playing days. Played till he was turned 40. Other clubs included Ripley Athletic, Ripley Town, Bradford City and Mansfield Mechanics.
Honours: England International 1908 (Derby).

MEE Herbert N 1912 - 14 Outside Right.
After his playing career ended Bert Mee became a Football League referee and gained an excellent reputation, ultimately handling international matches and running the line at an F A Cup Final. Became a Town director in 1945 and acted as Hon. Secretary to the club until Joe Eaton's appointment in 1956 following Mee's retirement. A fine cricketer with Mansfield Amateurs in his younger days; was 'Mine Host' at the Railway Inn for a number of years.

NEEDHAM John ("Jack") 1906 - 09 Inside Left
b: Newstead, Notts., 1891.
After scoring some 50 goals for Mansfield Wesley after making his debut as a sixteen year old, Jack Needham spent a season with Birmingham followed by a great spell at Molineux, both before and after WW I, where he played in 187 matches, scoring 57 goals. Played as a guest for Coventry City during the Great War and finished his playing days with Hull City.

PARKES 1907 - 10 Right Half Back.
A stalwart of the half back line for three seasons.

QUIBELL Harry 1903 - 05 Inside Left.
Harry Quibell's goalscoring contribution in two seasons at Newgate Lane was a most creditable 45. His brother Charles also played at outside left for the club during 1904-05, scoring 10 goals.

RADFORD 1904 - 05, 1908 - 10 and 1911 - 13
Inside Forward/Wing Half Back. Left sided wing half/inside forward who had two spells away from the club, but returned each time to Mansfield where he spent five seasons in all.

ROBINSON Peter 1906 - 10 Centre Half Back.
Four seasons at the centre of the defence.

ROBINSON W 1906 - 10 Outside Right. Also performed for the club for four years.

SMITH (George) William 1914 - 16
Outside Right. This nippy right winger moved on to Southern League Watford after two seasons at the Prairie.
Honours: Central Alliance - Subsidiary Competition Championship 1916 (Mansfield).

STRINGFELLOW J Frank 1912 - 13
Inside Forward b: Annesley, Notts., c1888.
Locally born forward who played a season with Mansfield after refusing terms with Wednesday, before the "Owls" transferred him to Portsmouth. Gained representative honours with "Pompey" and ended his career with Hearts in the Scottish First Division. Leading scorer for Portsmouth 1912-13, 1919-20 and 1920-21. Started his career with Ilkeston United.
Honours: Southern League Championship 1920, Southern League XI 1920, Division 3 South 3rd 1922 (all Portsmouth).

SYLVESTER Thomas 1910 - 13
Right Full Back. Full back for three seasons at Newgate Lane and Ratcliffe Gate.

TIVEY 1909 - 10 Centre Forward.
Scored some 35 goals in his one season with Wesley.

TOMLINSON 1908 - 10 Centre Forward.
Well known local player who spent seven years with the Mechanics, for whom he scored a lot of goals, before joining the Wesleyans for a couple of seasons. May have also played for Shirebrook 1913-15.

TREMELLING Richard (Daniel) 1914 - 15
Goalkeeper b: Newhall, Derbys., 12 December 1897 d: Birmingham, 15 August 1970.
Although Dan Tremelling was born near Burton on Trent, the family moved to Mansfield Woodhouse when he was quite young. Started his career as a full back with Langwith Waggon Works, becoming a goalkeeper when he deputised during an emergency. Played for Town at the Prairie before he was 17 years old, moving on to Shirebrook and Lincoln, before reaching Birmingham for whom he played for 14 years before being displaced by the up and coming Harry Hibbs. Made 382 appearances for Birmingham and won a Division 2 Championship Medal, International Cap and Football League appearance during his stay there. Wound his playing career down with Bury for three seasons before joining their training staff, followed by 5½ years in a similar capacity at St Andrews.

Had three brothers who played professional football and all appeared for Mansfield at one time or another. Honours: Division 2 Championship 1921, England International 1927, Football League XI 1927 & 1928 (all Birmingham).

WALKER 1910 - 13.
The first Town player to be killed in France whilst serving in the Army during the Great War. He had previously served the club for three seasons.

WHEATLEY James 1910 - 12 Centre Forward.
Sharpshooting centre forward who joined Town after a spell with the Mechanics. Netted some 31 league goals for the club, plus 15 in cup ties, in two seasons. Brother of William (below).

WHEATLEY William 1910 - 12 Inside Forward.
Bill Wheatley was a hard grafting inside forward who joined Town along with his brother Jim (above) from the Mechanics. Scored 10 league and 1 cup goal in his two years with the club.

WHYSALL William (Wilfrid) 1915 - 16
Goalkeeper b: Woodborough, Nottingham, 31 October 1887 d: Mansfield, 11 November 1930.
Wilfrid Whysall was far more famous as a cricketer than a footballer, playing for Notts and England, at the former for 22 years, and scoring 51 first class centuries. Met his death at only 43 when septicaemia set in following a fall at the Palais de Dance in Leeming Street late in October 1930 and he died at Mansfield General Hospital within a fortnight. Lived in the town and had a sports shop in White Hart Street at the time of his death. Also played for Clay Cross Town, Mansfield Mechanics and Shirebrook.
Honours: Central Alliance Championship 1914, runners up 1915 (both Shirebrook). Central Alliance - Subsidiary Competition Championship 1916 (Mansfield).

WILSON F 1902 - 08 Left Full Back.
Member of the Wesleyans defence for six seasons.

WILSON Strawson L 1915-16 Centre Half Back
b: c1888 d: K I A, France, c1917.
Strawson Wilson was the first player with a Mansfield club to receive international honours, albeit at amateur level, winning England Caps with both Mansfield Amateurs and Mansfield Mechanics. This talented player sadly lost his life towards the end of WWI, the third Town player to do so.
Honours: England Amateur International 1911 & 1912 (Mansfield Amateurs & Mansfield Mechanics). Central Alliance -Subsidiary Competition Championship 1916 (Mansfield Town).

PLAYERS 1919 - 1995

**Post First World War
Leagues:**

Central Alliance 1919-21
Midland League 1921-26
Midland Combination 1926-27
Midland League 1927-31
Football League 1931 to date

ADAM Charles

1952 - 55 Outside Left 5' 8" 11st 2lbs
b: Glasgow, 22 March 1919
Career: Strathclyde, Leicester City (Sep 1938), TOWN (July 1952), Corby Town (1955)

A tricky winger who had a long career with Leicester before joining Mansfield for three seasons. During WW II was a "guest" player with Leeds United. After his playing career was over he became briefly a Leicester City scout and was for 16 years coach to Leicester County F A. Made 158 appearances, scoring 22 goals for the "Filberts".

1952-53 40 apps 4 gls
1953-54 36 " 2 "
1954-55 17 " 0 "
Honours: F A Cup Finalists 1949 (Leicester)

ADAM James

1954 - 55 Inside Forward 5' 5" 9st 12lbs
b: Paisley, 22 April 1931
Career: Penlee United, Lossiemouth, Leeds United (Jun 1951), TOWN (month's trial - Aug 1954, F. T. Sep 1954)

Leeds reserve who joined Town on a "free" after a month's trial.

1954-55 39 apps 10 gls

AKERS William (Walter) George

1939 - 46 Outside Right 5' 6" 10st 7lbs (1939)
b: West Auckland, Co Durham, c1916
Career: St Lukes, Preston North End (1932 - am), Wolverhampton Wanderers (c/s 1934), Bournemouth & Boscombe Athletic (May 1935), Newport County (Aug 1936), Chelsea (c/s 1937), TOWN (May 1939), Gillingham (c/s 1946), Corby Town (c/s 1948, 1949 - manager to 1953)

Wally Akers had travelled around various clubs before joining the "Stags". He had a reputation of being a speedy winger who could cut in from the wing and score goals, although his only previous league appearances had been with Bournemouth in 1935-36 when he managed 15, scoring 4 goals. After the war he had a successful spell with Gillingham in the Southern League helping them to a Championship win. He finished his career with Corby Town, eventually as manager. During WW II also assisted Notts County.

1939-40 3 apps 3 gls Leading Scorer (Joint)
WW II 29 " 8 "
Honours: Southern League Championship 1947 & runners up 1948 (both Gillingham)

ALDREAD Paul

1963 - 67 Forward 5' 9" 10st 7lbs
b: Mansfield, 6 November 1946
Career: Bentinck Welfare Juniors, Queens Park Rangers (am), TOWN (Sep 1962 - am, Dec 1963 - pro), Sutton Town (1968)

A good servant to the "Stags" albeit in a supporting role as he spent his first two seasons entirely in the reserves, then deputised when Bill Curry was not available.

1963-64 0 apps 0 gls
1964-65 0 " 0 "
1965-66 10(1)" 3 "
1966-67 1(0)" 0 "

ALEXANDER Keith

1994 - 95 Forward 6' 4" 12st 7lbs (1993)
b: Nottingham, 14 November 1958
Career: Notts County (am), Worksop Town (am), Clifton (Sep 1975), Ilkeston Town (1976-77), Kimberley (Sep 1978), Alfreton Town, Stamford Town (Mar 1979), Boston United (Aug 1980), Kings Lynn, Spalding United (1982-83), Kings Lynn (1983-84), Grantham Town (Aug 1984), Kettering Town, Wisbech (loan), Barnet (July 1986), Grimsby Town (£11,500 - July 1988), Stockport County (£8,500 - Sep 1990), Lincoln City (£7,000 - Dec 1990, Mar 1992 - youth team coach, May 1993 - manager to May 1994), Malta, TOWN (Aug 1994 - youth team coach), Cliftonville (Jan 1995 - loan)

Appointed Youth Team Coach at Lincoln in 1992, Alexander thought his playing days were over, particularly when he was appointed Team Manager of the "Imps" following Steve Thompson's dismissal in May 1993. After losing his job during the close season, he joined Mansfield as Andy King's no. 2 in August 1994. In September, when the "Stags" squad was particularly depleted, he was pressed into service on the field again, albeit as a substitute and this was repeated in the Auto Windscreens tie with Crewe in November when he scored two goals, coming on after 59 minutes. No other Mansfield substitute has scored two goals in a match - and in 31 minutes too - quite a remarkable achievement for a man within six days of his 36th birthday! Scored a goal in Stamford's F A Vase triumph at Wembley 1n 1980, when they ran out winners against Guisborough by 2 - 1. Loaned out to Irish League club Cliftonville in Belfast during early 1995, he earned a fine reputation there as a goalscorer, but the main reason for this arrangement was for him to weigh up talent in the Irish League with a view to bringing players to Field Mill for trials.

1994-95 0(2) apps 0 gls
Honours: St Lucia International, F A Vase Winners 1980 (Stamford)

ALLCOCK Kenneth

1946 - 47 Centre Forward
b: Kirkby in Ashfield, Notts., 24 April 1921
Career: Notts County (am), TOWN (Apr 1947)

1946-47   1 app   0 gls

ALLEN Frank

1953 - 55 Wing Half Back   5' 9"   11st 0lbs
b: Shirebrook, Derbys., 28 June 1927
Career: Chesterfield (Mar 1951), TOWN (July 1953)

1953-54   4 apps   0 gls
1954-55   2 "   0 "

ALLEN John

1984 - 85 Forward   6' 0"   11st 9lbs
b: Mancott, Chester, 14 November 1964
Career: Chester (Nov 1981), TOWN (Aug 1984)

1984-85   1(1) apps   0 gls
Honours: Welsh Schoolboy & Youth International
(Chester)

ALLEN Joseph

1928 - 30 and 1935 Inside Left   5' 8½"   11st 4lbs (1934)
b: Bilsthorpe, Notts., 30 December 1909
d: Rainworth, Notts., 29 November 1978
Career: Bilsthorpe Colliery, TOWN (Aug 1928 - am, Aug 1929
- pro), Bilsthorpe Colliery (c/s 1930), Tottenham Hotspur (Aug
1932), Northfleet, Queens Park Rangers (Apr 1933), TOWN (Aug
1935), Racing Club de Roubaix France (Nov 1935)

Had two spells at Field Mill. Made one appearance
in Spurs first team, but was a regular in the
successful Q P R side of the mid 30s. "A scheming
grafter and provider" was how he was described by
a contemporary writer and after his return from
France in 1939, he "guested" for the "Stags" from
time to time whilst working in the mines. A useful
cricketer with Bilsthorpe Colliery for many years.

1928-29   8 apps   0 gls Midland League
1935-36   8 "   5 "
WW II   14 "   0 "
Honours: Mansfield Hospital Charity Cup Winners
1929, Byron Cup Winners 1930 (both Mansfield).

ALLEN Russell P

1978 - 81 Forward   5' 9"   11st 7lbs (1980)
b: Smethwick, Birmingham, 9 January 1954
Career: Arsenal (appr), West Bromwich Albion (May 1971),
Cambridge United (1972 - loan), Tranmere Rovers (July 1973),
Chicago Stingers U S A (Jun 1977), TOWN (£20,000 - July
1978).

Son of Ronnie Allen the former W B A and England
forward. Now a Senior Group Manager with the
Abbey Life Insurance Group and based in
Nottingham.

1978-79   26(10) apps 5 gls
1979-80   38 (6) "   4 "
1980-81   35 (1) "   9 "   Leading   Scorer
Honours: Smethwick Schoolboys, Staffordshire
Schoolboys.

ALLEN

1926 - 27 Left Full Back
Career: TOWN (1926)

Only first team appearance was in the winning
Byron Cup team of 1926-27.
Honours: Byron Cup Winners 1927 (Mansfield).

ALLSOPP

1926 - 27 Right Half Back
Career: TOWN (1926)

Only senior appearance was in the Benevolent Bowl
final.
Honours: Notts Benevolent Bowl Winners 1927
(Mansfield)

ANDERSEN Nicholas J

1986 - 89 Midfield   5' 10"   10st 10lbs (1990)
b: Lincoln, 29 March 1969
Career: TOWN (1985 - appr, Jan 1987 - pro), Lincoln City (Aug
1989), Nuneaton Borough (Sep 1989), Grantham Town (Oct 1991
- trial), Leek Town (Oct 1991 - trial), Bedworth United (Dec
1991), Tamworth (1993), Bedworth United (Mar 1994)

Youngster who failed to make the grade in league
football and joined his father's building firm near
Newark when he left Lincoln
1986-87   5(2) apps   0 gls
1987-88   3(9) "   0 "
1988-89   1(0) "   0 "

ANDERSON Geoffrey T

1964 - 66 Outside Right   5' 8"   10st 8lbs (1964)
b: Sheerness, Kent, 26 November 1944
Career: Canterbury Schools, Ramsgate Town (July 1960),
Birmingham City (Dec 1962), TOWN (F.T. May 1964), Lincoln
City (July 1966), Brentford (Aug 1967 - trial), Hastings United
(Sep 1967 - trial), Port Vale (Nov 1967 - trial)

Joined Mansfield having made but a single league
appearance with the "Blues", Anderson moved on to
Lincoln after a season and a half, where he obtained
regular first team football again. It was to be his

swan song however, as he drifted out of League football after just one year at Sincil Bank.

| 1964-65 | 14 apps | 4 gls |
| 1965-66 | 29(0)" | 9 " |

Honours: Division 3 - 3rd 1965 (Mansfield)

ANDERSON (George) Russell

1936 - 37 Inside Forward   5' 9"   10st 3lbs (1936)
b: Saltcoats, Ayrshire, 29 October 1904
d: Cambridge, 9 November 1974
Career: Dalry Thistle, Airdrieonians (1925), Brentford (May 1926), Chelsea (May 1927), Norwich City (May 1929), Carlisle United (Aug 1930 - trial), Gillingham (Sep 1930 - trial), Cowdenbeath (Oct 1930), Yeovil & Petters Athletic (July 1932), Bury (Jun 1933), Huddersfield Town (Nov 1934), TOWN (Jan 1936), Ayr United (c/s 1937), Saltcoats Victoria.

A much travelled player who nevertheless must have been reasonably successful with all his clubs as Gillingham, where he played a trial, was the only one where he did not make the League side - managing appearances in the First Division with both Chelsea and Huddersfield and Scottish First Division with Airdrie and Cowdenbeath. He was one of the principal suppliers of passes to Harston during his record goalscoring performances. Retired during WW II.

| 1935-36 | 17 apps | 8 gls |
| 1936-37 | 19 " | 8 " |

ANDERSON (Robert) John

1956 - 60 Outside Right   5' 4"   9st 7lbs
b: Portsmouth, 23 February 1936
Career: Chesterfield Tube Works, TOWN (Jun 1935 - am, Sep 1956 - pro)

Robbie Anderson was signed on professional forms after performing well in a pre season trial match and stayed at the club four years, but never quite made the breakthrough that had been hoped for. Son of John Anderson, Portsmouth centre forward pre WW II, who won an F A Cup Winners medal v Wolves in 1939, scoring one of the winning goals.

1956-57	15 apps	2 gls
1957-58	4 "	0 "
1958-59	18 "	1 "
1959-60	3 "	1 "

ANTHONY Charles

1927 - 29 and 1932 - 33 Right Full Back 5' 9" 12st 7lbs (1928)
b: Mansfield Woodhouse, Notts., c1903
Career: Oxclose Lane School, Sherwood United, Sutton Junction, Army - Royal Field Artillery (1921), TOWN (Mar 1927 - am,

May 1927 - pro), Northampton Town (£300 - Jun 1929), TOWN (c/s 1932), Ollerton Colliery (Aug 1933).

"Pop" Anthony was an aspiring outside left in local football in the days after the end of WW I, but after he joined the Army for seven years in 1921, he became a very solid full back who represented various Army teams at the highest level all over Europe when he was stationed with the Army of Occupation on the Rhine. He even "guested" for Guildford United when he was stationed at Aldershot for a short time. Played in the famous "egg and milk" team during the F A Cup run of 1928-29 and refused to take the penalty against Arsenal even though he was the regular spot "king" at the time. A great admirer of Herbert Chapman, the Arsenal manager who he met at Highbury, he named a son after him - Herbert Chapman Anthony! Had the unusual experience v Chester in December 1932 - of scoring for both sides! He netted for Town at one end and put through an o.g. at the other.

1926-27	1 app	0 gls	Midland League	
1927-28	9 "	1 "	"	"
1928-29	44 "	2 "	"	"
1932-33	39 "	2 "		

Honours: Notts Benevolent Bowl Winners 1927, Mansfield Hospital Charity Cup Winners 1928 & 29, Midland League Championship 1929 (all Mansfield)

ANTONIO (George) Rowlands

1949 - 51 Inside Forward   5' 9½"   11st 5lbs
b: Whitchurch, Salop, 20 October 1914
Career: Oswestry Technical College, Oswestry Town, Stoke City (£200 - Feb 1936), Derby County (£5,000 - Mar 1947), Doncaster Rovers (£7,000 - Oct 1948), TOWN (Oct 1949), Oswestry Town (July 1951 - player manager), Wellington Town (July 1954 -

player coach, Jan 1955 - player manager), Stafford Rangers (Sep 1957 - player manager), Oswestry Town (July 1958 - player coach, Jun 1959 - player manager), Berriew (1963 - player manager to 1964)

Was born George Rowlands, but adopted the surname of the Italian family who brought him up. A skilful and scheming inside forward who had consid-erable experience in the First Division with both Stoke and Derby. Assisted Doncaster to their second Division 3 North post war title, before joining Mansfield. Obviously had a great affection for Oswestry Town from the number of times he played for them, Pre war was once selected for Wales until it was realised that he was born the wrong side of the border - the rules were much stricter then than today! During WW II "guested" for Nottingham Forest, Wrexham, York City, Notts County, Aldershot, Leeds, Clapton Orient, Ipswich Town and Norwich when he was serving in the Army. Refused Town's terms in 1951 and moved back to Oswestry as player manager. Still living in Oswestry, aged nearly 81, and in July 1995 believed to be the oldest ex-Stag

1949-50   29 apps   1 gl
1950-51   38   "   1 "
Honours: Division 3 North Championship 1950 (Doncaster), Division 3 North runners up 1951 (Mansfield)

ARMITAGE
1923 Outside Left
Career: Cammel Laird Sports, TOWN (Feb 1923)

1922-23   1 app   0 gls Midland League

ARNOLD
1920 - 22 Outside Left
Career: TOWN (1920)

1920-21   1 app   0 gls Central Alliance

ARNOLD Rodney
1971 - 84 Goalkeeper 5' 10"   11st 4lbs (1974)
b: Wolverhampton, 3 June 1952
Career: Warstone's Youth Club, Wolverhampton Wanderers (1968 - appr, Jun 1970 - pro), TOWN (Feb 1971 - loan, Mar 1973 - loan & Jun 1973 - permanent)

An offer of £10,000 for Rod Arnold's services after his first loan spell at Field Mill was rejected by Wolves, but after a second loan period two years later, the "Stags" obtained him on a free transfer. In a brilliant career lasting 14 years at Mansfield he

went on to become the club's holder of the highest number of appearances - 440. Was an ever present during his stay at Mansfield apart from when he suffered cartilage trouble and a broken arm. Settled in the area when his playing days were over and became involved in local football, until recently being assistant manager of Ashfield United and in addition establishing his own goalkeeping school, *Shotstoppers*. Among the players he is currently coaching is Northern Ireland international, Alan Fettis of Hull City. As well as soccer, he played rugby during his schooldays, winning a place in the Staffordshire Schools side.

1970-71	17 apps	0 gls	(Loan)
1972-73	13 "	0 "	(Loan)
1973-74	29 "	0 "	
1974-75	46 "	0 "	
1975-76	39 "	0 "	
1976-77	46 "	0 "	
1977-78	42 "	0 "	
1978-79	28 "	0 "	
1979-80	43 "	0 "	
1980-81	38 "	0 "	
1981-82	45 "	0 "	
1982-83	43 "	0 "	
1983-84	11 "	0 "	

ASHALL Thomas
1934 - 35 Inside Left
Career: TOWN (c/s 1934), Nuneaton Town (c/s 1935).

1934-35   2 apps   0 gls
Honours: Bass Charity Vase Winners 1935 (Mansfield).

ASHLEY John (Albert)
1933 - 35 Full Back
b: Clowne, Derbys., c1912
d: December 1992
Career: Clowne Welfare, Notts County (1931 - trial), Shirebrook (1931 - am), TOWN (Feb 1933 - am, Jun 1933 - pro), Sheffield Wednesday (£1,100 - Sep 1935).

Played both full back and centre half for Mansfield before being transferred to Wednesday after only one match at the start of the 1935-36 season, for what was at the time, Town's record transfer fee. Made a great career with the "Owls" appearing in 106 matches before the outbreak of war in 1939. Made six appearances at centre forward during the relegation season of 1936-37 and scored in three of them as Wednesday struggled to find a goalscorer. Retired in 1945 after playing in 126 wartime matches.

1933-34	30 apps	0 gls
1934-35	38 "	0 "
1935-36	1 "	0 "

Honours: Football League North War Cup runners up 1943 (Sheffield Wednesday).

ASKEY Colin
1962 - 64 Outside Right   5' 9"   10st 7lbs (1957)
b: Milton, Stoke on Trent, 3 October 1932
Career: Port Vale (juniors, Oct 1949 - pro), Walsall (F.T. July 1958), TOWN (F.T. Jun 1962), Wellington Town (c/s 1964), Stafford Rangers (c/s 1965)

One full season with the "Stags", only managing five appearances during his last term there. Had slowed down considerably from his successful and younger years with Port Vale.

1962-63	25 apps	2 gls
1963-64	5 "	0 "

Honours: Division 3 North Championship 1954 (Port Vale). Division 4 Championship 1960 (Walsall).

ASPINALL (Brendan) James
1994 onwards Defender   6' 0"   12st 2lbs (1994)
b: Bloemfontein, South Africa, 22 July 1975
Career: Huddersfield Town (1991 - appr), TOWN (Mar 1994 - trial, July 1994 - permanent).

Young defender who managed to break into the League XI at the beginning of the 1994-95 season, but was given a free transfer in May 1995.

1994-95	13(6) apps	0 gls

ASTON John Jr
1977 - 78 Outside Left   5' 9½"   11st 6lbs (1979)
b: Manchester, 28 June 1947
Career: Manchester United (Jun 1963 - appr, Jun 1964 - pro), Luton Town (£30,000 - July 1972), TOWN (£15,000 - Sep 1977), Blackburn Rovers (July 1978)

A good old fashioned style winger, John Aston was the son of a famous father who was a full back in United's 1948 F A Cup winning team and the 1952 Championship side.   Junior won his place in the Manchester first team in April 1965 and became the regular left winger until he broke a leg in 1971 and afterwards could not regain a regular place, moving on to Luton in 1972.   Like his father before him, John Jr won both a League medal (1967) and Cup medals (F A Youth Cup 1964 and European Cup in 1968).   Sadly, the winger was going out of fashion when he joined the "Stags" but he commanded a fee when Blackburn signed him up the following season. He failed to save Town from relegation.

1977-78	24(7) apps	4 gls

Honours: England Under 23 international, F A Youth Cup Winners 1964, F A Charity Shield - shared 1966, Division 1 Championship & F A Charity Shield - shared 1967, European Cup Winners 1968 (all Manchester United).

ATKINSON George (Arthur)
1934 - 37 Outside Right   5' 9"   11st 0lbs (1935)
b: Goole, South Yorks., 30 September 1909
d: 20 July 1980   ? or 14 July 1983
Career: Goole Juniors, Lincoln City (Dec 1930 - am, Jan 1931 - pro), Hull City (F.T. Jun 1933), TOWN (Jun 1934), Southport (May 1937), Thorne Colliery (c/s 1938).

A skilful winger who also played inside forward for Mansfield. His goal haul was more than useful for an outside right and he played no small part in Ted Harston's successful seasons at Field Mill. Retired at the outbreak of war. A fine vocalist too apparently.

1934-35	40 apps	12 gls
1935-36	40 "	10 "
1936-37	40 "	10 "

Honours: Division 3 North Cup Winners 1938 (Southport).

AUSTIN Terence W

1979 - 80 Centre Forward   6' 1"   12st 7lbs (1980)
b: Isleworth, Mssx., 1 February 1954
Career: Crystal Palace (1970 - appr, Jun 1972 - pro), Ipswich Town (May 1973), Plymouth Argyle (Oct 1976), Walsall (£25,000 - Mar 1978), TOWN (p/exch £30,000 + Syrett - Mar 1979), Huddersfield Town (£125,000 - Nov 1980), Doncaster Rovers (Sep 1982), Northampton Town (Aug 1983), Stamford Town (c/s 1984)

Highly successful as a goalscorer with Mansfield, he could not prevent the team being relegated to Division 4. Ian Greaves, who was managing Huddersfield at the time, lured him away to Leeds Road in November 1980. Later spells at Doncaster and Northampton did not reveal the scoring prowess he had shown at Walsall and Mansfield. Still living in the town ten years after his playing career ended, he is currently working as an independent financial advisor. Terry Austin was leading scorer with his clubs on four occasions - Plymouth 1978, Walsall 1979, Town 1980 and Northampton 1984.

1978-79	16(0) apps	5 gls	
1979-80	46(0) "	19 "	Leading Scorer
1980-81	22(0) "	7 "	

AYRE William

1982 - 84 Defender   5' 11"   12st 10lbs (1983)
b: Crookhill, Consett, Co Durham, 7 May 1952
Career: Scarborough, Hartlepool United (Aug 1977), Halifax Town (Jan 1981), TOWN (Aug 1982, Jan to Feb 1983 - acting manager), Halifax Town (July 1984, Jan 1986 - coach/asst manager, Dec 1986 - manager to Mar 1990), Blackpool (Nov 1990 - manager to May 1994), Lincoln City (May 1994 - asst manager), Scarborough (Aug 1994 - manager to Dec 1994), Southport (Apr 1995 - manager).

A solid defender of the stopper variety, Billy Ayre has since made rather a penchant for managing clubs struggling to avoid relegation. After Stuart Boam was sacked, acted as caretaker manager at Field Mill for a few weeks until Ian Greaves was appointed. Gained promotion via the play-offs for Blackpool in 1991-92, winning the Manager of the Month Award during the first month of the season.

| 1982-83 | 42(0) apps | 3 gls |
| 1983-84 | 25(0) " | 4 " |

BACON (Arthur) Everitt

1925 Outside Left
b: Bulwell, Nottingham, 12 March 1895
Career: Basford United, Gedling, Norwich City (Mar 1920), Sutton Junction, TOWN (Mar 1925), Sutton Junction.

| 1924-25 | 1 app | 0 gls | Midland League |

BAINES

1927 - 28 Wing Half Back
Career: Army, TOWN (1927 - am)

| 1927-28 | 2 apps | 0 gls | Midland League |

BAIRD J A (Gordon)

1946 - 48 Wing Half Back
b: Basford, Nottingham, 14 January 1924
Career: New Houghton, TOWN (Nov 1946), Sutton Town

"Dixie" Baird was a promising wing half who should have gone to Arsenal as part of a package when Calverley was transferred to Highbury, but recurring illness prevented the move. Served in the Royal Navy during the war.

| 1946-47 | 8 apps | 0 gls |
| 1947-48 | 1 " | 0 " |

BALL Alfred

1910 - 13 and 1921 - 22 Outside Left 5' 7" 11st 0lbs (1914)
b: Clowne, Derbys., 1890
d: 3 October 1952
Career: Creswell Athletic, Clowne Rising Star, TOWN (c/s 1910), Lincoln City (Jun 1913), TOWN (Jun 1921), Ilkeston United (c/s 1922)

A very fast winger with a powerful shot, Alf Ball had his most successful period with the "Imps" in the Second Division and during WW I. A regular with Mansfield before the war, joining them when they had just changed their name from Wesley to Town, he only played in the reserves during his second spell with the club in 1921-22, when he had lost much of his speed.

1910-11 N.K. apps 8 gls Notts & Derbys League
1911-12 N.K. " 7 " Central Alliance
1912-13 N.K. " 2 " " "
1921-22 0 " 0 " Midland League

BANKS (George) Ernest

1947 - 49 Centre Forward 5' 8½" 11st 5lbs
b: Wednesbury, 28 March 1919
Career: Clayhanger Villa, Brownhills Albion, West Bromwich Albion (Jun 1933 - groundstaff, 1935 - am, Jun 1938 - pro), TOWN (£1,250 - Nov 1947), Hereford United (c/s 1949), Dudley Town, Darlaston.

Gained first team place at the Hawthorns towards the end of the 1938-39 season, scoring a brace on his debut and retaining his place in the first three matches of the aborted 1939-40 term, netting one goal. Served abroad for most of the war period and could not regain a first team place upon demobilisation from the Army in April 1946. Successful and thrustful leader with Town and finished his career playing non league soccer in the Birmingham area.

1947-48 27 apps 14 gls Leading Scorer
1948-49 36 " 7 "

BARACLOUGH (Ian) Robert

1994 onwards Full Back 6' 1" 11st 10lbs
b: Leicester, 4 December 1970
Career: Leicester City (1986 - appr, Dec 1988 - pro), Wigan Athletic (Mar 1990 - loan), Grimsby Town (Dec 1990 - loan, Aug 1991 - permanent), Lincoln City (£10,000 - Aug 1993), TOWN (May 1994)

Strong attacking full back who likes to come through and support his forwards. Opened his scoring account with one of the most remarkable goals ever witnessed at Field Mill - a free kick from fully 50 yards!

1994-95 36(0) apps 3 gls
Honours: Leicestershire Schoolboys. England Youth international (Leicester City)

BARKE John (Lloyd)

1937 - 47 Wing/Centre Half Back 5'10½" 11st 12lbs (1937)
b: Nuncargate, Notts., 16 December 1917
d: Kirkby in Ashfield, Notts., 7 March 1976
Career: Nottinghamshire Boys (1931), Annesley Colliery, Chesterfield (am), East Kirkby Welfare, Bleakhall United, TOWN (trial), Scunthorpe & Lindsey United (trial), Sheffield United (May 1933 - groundstaff, Dec 1934 - pro), TOWN (£80 - Jun 1937, Aug 1944 - caretaker manager to May 1945), Denaby United (1947 - player manager), Sutton Town 1950 - player manager), Ilkeston Town (1951 - player manager), Belper Town (1952 - player manager), Heanor Town (1953 - player manager to 1954)

Lloyd Barke must have been one of the "Stags" best servants. He joined from the "Blades" for a paltry £80, of which £40 was his accrued share of benefit, so for 10 years of excellent service, this has to be one of the bargains of the century. He also acted as temporary manager after Jack Poole went to Notts County and until Roy Goodall was appointed to the post after his Army demob. As his career ran down post war, he managed a succession of non league clubs before finally hanging up his boots in 1954 at the age of 40. "Guested" for many clubs during WWII when Mansfield did not have a match.

1937-38	42 apps	0 gls
1938-39	40 "	0 "
1939-40	3 "	0 "
WW II	212 "	9 "
1946-47	32 "	0 "

Honours: Nottinghamshire Schoolboys. Notts F A County Cup Winners 1938 & 1939 (both Mansfield)

BARKS Edwin

1949 - 55 Wing Half Back   5' 10½"   11st 5lbs (1949)
b: Ilkeston, Derbys., 1 September 1921
Career: Heanor Town, Nottingham Forest (Apr 1939), TOWN (Jan 1949).

A wholehearted and hardworking wing half who gave sterling service to the club for six years. As a 17½ year old youngster, he was the first signing made by Billy Walker after his appointment as Forest manager in March 1939. Served under four managers at Mansfield for who he made 213 League appearances.

1948-49	16 apps	2 gls
1949-50	32 "	0 "
1950-51	36 "	3 "
1951-52	45 "	1 "
1952-53	28 "	0 "
1953-54	33 "	0 "
1954-55	23 "	0 "

Honours: Division 3 North runners up 1951 (Mansfield)

BARKS Wilfred

1934 - 35 Inside Forward   5' 10"   11st 8lbs (1935)
b: Dinnington, c 1912
Career: Dinnington, Chesterfield (c/s 1932), TOWN (c/s 1934), Mexborough Athletic (Jan 1935), Rotherham United (c/s 1935), Denaby United (c/s 1936), Rochdale (c/s 1937)

Made little impact at Mansfield when deputising for Harry Johnson.

| 1934-35 | 4 apps | 0 gls |

BARLOW George (Arthur)

1934 - 36 Right Full Back   5' 8½"   11st 4lbs (1935)
b: Langwith Junction, Derbys., c1914
Career: Langwith Welfare, TOWN (Mar 1934 - am, Nov 1934 - pro),

His only opportunities came when deputising for Dransfield in 1934 and a few matches after Ashley was transferred to Sheffield Wednesday the following season. Released April 1936

| 1934-35 | 4 apps | 0 gls |
| 1935-36 | 7 " | 0 " |

Honours: Bass Charity Vase Winners 1935 (Mansfield).

BARNETT Charles

1920 - 21 Goalkeeper
b: Derby, c1887
Career: Derbyshire juniors, Newark Town (1907), Leicester Fosse (Apr 1913), TOWN (Sep 1920), Alfreton Town (Oct 1921)

Played in 19 matches for the "Fossils" in the last pre WW I season.

| 1920-21 | 21 apps | 0 gls Central Alliance |

Honours: Central Alliance runners up 1921 (Mansfield)

BARROWCLOUGH (Stewart) James

1983 - 85 Midfield   5' 9"   10st 5lbs (1984)
b: Barnsley, 29 October 1951
Career: Barnsley (Mar 1967 - appr, Nov 1969 - pro), Newcastle United (£33,000 - Aug 1970), Birmingham City (£150,000 - May 1978), Bristol Rovers (£90,000 - July 1979), Barnsley (£35,000 - Feb 1981), TOWN (F.T. Aug 1983)

Earned a reputation as a fast direct winger during his spell at Newcastle, capable of both attacking and defending and he gained five U/23 caps for England whilst there.

1983-84   36(2) apps 10 gls
1984-85   14(2) "   0 "
Honours: England U/23 international. Football League Cup runners up 1976 (all Newcastle).

BARTLEY (Phillip) James
1935 - 36 Centre Forward   5' 8"   11st 4lbs (1935)
b: 1915
Career: Norwich City (1933), Rochdale (c/s 1934), TOWN (c/s 1935).

After being reasonably successful with his previous club, Phil Bartley only played in a couple of matches for Town when Harry Johnson was out of action for the first two games of the 1935-36 season.

1935-36   2 apps   0 gls

BATES Brian F
1969 - 70 Forward
b: Stapleford, Notts., 4 December 1944
Career: Loughborough College, Notts County (July 1963), TOWN (July 1969), Boston (c/s 1970).

Had four fruitful seasons at Meadow Lane but was not the hoped for success at Mansfield and moved into non league football at the end of his first season here.

1969-70   20(0) apps 3 gls

BAXTER (Thomas) William
1926 - 27 & 1931 - 32 Outside Left 5' 6½" 10st 6lbs (1928)
b: Warsop, Notts., c1905
Career: Warsop, Newark Town (c/s 1923), Worksop Town (c/s 1924), Mexborough (c/s 1925), TOWN (May 1926), Wolverhampton Wanderers (c/s 1927), Port Vale (c/s 1929), TOWN (c/s 1931), Carlisle United (c/s 1933)

A small speedy winger who was particularly effective in his earlier years, but was past his best when he came back to Field Mill for a second spell in 1931. Was in the Wolves team beaten by the "Stags" during their famous F A Cup run of 1928-29 and toured Algeria with the North Notts League party in May 1923. Cricketer with Welbeck Colliery during the summer months.

1926-27   27 apps 13 gls Midland Combination
1931-32   14   "   1 "

Honours: Midland League Championship 1926 (Mexborough). Midland Combination runners up, Notts F A Senior Cup Winners, Notts Benevolent Bowl, & Mansfield Hospital Charity Cup Winners 1927 (all Mansfield). Division 3 North Championship 1930 (Port Vale).

BAYLISS Leonard (Richard)
1921 - 25 Left Half Back   5' 9"   11st 7lbs (1924)
b: Alfreton, Derbys., 28 April 1899
d: Coventry, 5 April 1947
Career: Alfreton Town, Luton Town (c/s 1920), TOWN (c/s 1921), Southend United (500 - May 1925), Shirebrook (c/s 1927), Coventry City 1931 - scout to 1939, Jun 1945 - manager to Apr 1947).

Dickie Bayliss was one of the stalwarts of the Mansfield teams during their successful years in the early 1920s when two Midland League titles were won in successive years. Had only made one appearance in Luton's first XI when he joined the "Stags" and signed for Southend at the same time as Dickie Donoven who proved much more successful there - Bayliss only managing 8 appearances in two seasons before returning to Midland League football at the White Swan Ground. After his career was terminated by injury in October 1928, he became a scout for Coventry until the outbreak of WW II. In June 1945 he accepted the managership of Coventry and was building up a most promising side when he caught a chill which in turn led to kidney failure and he died at the early age of 47 whilst still in office. Oddly enough he was succeeded by another ex "Stag" in Billy Frith.

1921-22	32 apps	0 gls	Midland League	
1922-23	33 "	2 "	"	"
1923-24	38 "	1 "	"	"
1924-25	35 "	0 "	"	'

Honours: Mansfield Hospital Charity Cup Winners 1922, Notts F A Senior Cup Winners 1923, Midland League Championship 1924 & 1925 (all Mansfield)

BEASLEY Andrew

1984 - 93 Goalkeeper 6' 2" 12st 2lbs (1985)
b: Sedgley, Worcs., 5 February 1964
Career: Luton Town (1980 - appr, Feb 1982 - pro), TOWN (Aug 1983 - loan), Gillingham (Nov 1983 - loan), TOWN (July 1984), Peterborough United (July 1986 - loan), Scarborough (Mar 1988 - loan), Kettering Town (Oct 1989 - loan), Cheltenham Town (Nov 1989 - loan), Kettering Town (Nov 1992 - loan), Bristol Rovers (Mar 1993 - loan), Doncaster Rovers (F.T. July 1993), Chesterfield (F.T. Aug 1994)

Although Andy Beasley spent nine seasons as a Mansfield player, he only managed regular appearances from 1990-91 and was loaned out to various clubs on many occasions both in and out of the League. Had a bad run of injuries latterly with Town and it was thought that his career was finished, but it seems to have revived with both Doncaster and Chesterfield, where he is still a regular performer. Had the misfortune to miss the 1995 Play-off Final at Wembley, due to facial injuries received in the semi final 10 days earlier, when he collided with one of his own defenders.

1983-84	0 apps	0 gls	(Loan)
1984-85	3 "	0 "	
1987-88	8 "	0 "	
1988-89	6 "	0 "	
1989-90	26 "	0 "	
1990-91	42 "	0 "	
1991-92	9 "	0 "	
1992-93	0 "	0 "	

Honours: Division 3 promotion - via play-offs 1995 (Chesterfield).

BELL Ernest

1938 - 39 Inside Forward 5' 8" 10st 7lbs (1938)
b: Hull, 22 July 1918
d: 8 December 1968
Career: Blundell St O B, Hull City (Nov 1935), TOWN (May 1938), Aldershot (July 1939), Hull City (Aug 1944), Scarborough (Aug 1947), Hessle O B.

Although a clever ball player, Ernie Bell was not a great success at Field Mill and was not retained at the end of season 1938-39. After joining the Army he had the unusual experience of being reported "missing believed killed" at Dunkirk in 1940, but he later resurfaced to play a number of games for Aldershot during the war, being in the team that beat Southampton 10-1 on 27 February 1943. Rejoined Hull after hostilities ceased but made only 5 appearances before moving into the Midland League with Scarborough.

1938-39	28 apps	1 gl

Honours: Notts F A County Cup Winners 1939 (Mansfield)

BELL (Ian) Charles

1981 - 83 Forward 5' 9" 10st 10lbs (1983)
b: Middlesbrough, 14 November 1958
Career: Middlesbrough (1974 - appr, Dec 1976 - pro), TOWN (F.T. July 1981).

Made occasional appearances in Boro's first team for four seasons before joining Mansfield where he was a regular for two seasons before being given a free transfer in May 1983.

1981-82	45(0) apps	5 gls
1982-83	37(2) "	7 "

BELL (William) John

1925 - 26 Outside Left 5' 8" 10st 10lbs (1925)
b: Backworth, Nr Newcastle on Tyne c1904
Career: Blyth Spartans, Chopwell Institute, Leadgate Park, Aston Villa (Dec 1923 - trial), Lincoln City (Aug 1924), TOWN (May 1925), Leicester City (£425 - Feb 1926), Torquay United (July 1930)

A number of League clubs were anxious to sign this clever winger when he was released by Lincoln, but Willie Bell preferred to stay with his friend, Jim Heathcote who had thrown in his lot with Town. This was indeed fortunate for Mansfield, as they not only had excellent service from him for almost a season, but also collected a tidy sum of money when Leicester recruited him on 24 February 1926 and he went straight into their First Division XI. Son of a former Glasgow Rangers goalkeeper.

1925-26   25 apps   12 gls Midland League
Honours: North Eastern League Championship
1923 (Leadgate Park). Midland League runners
up 1926 (Mansfield).

BELLAS John Edward

1923 - 25 Right Full Back   5' 10"   11st 6lbs (1924)
b: Bishop Auckland, Co Durham, 16 September 1895
d: Pleasley, 23 August 1977
Career: Shildon, The Wednesday (Sep 1920), TOWN (Jun 1923), Coventry City (£500 - Jan 1925), Heanor Town (c/s 1926), Sutton Town (c/s 1927), New Houghton Church (c/s 1929)

A strong dependable full back from Mansfield's "glory years" of the early 1920s, Jack Bellas joined the "Stags" after enjoying considerable first team experience at Hillsborough. Coventry paid a good fee when they secured his transfer on 17 January 1925 even though he was then almost 30 years of age. He served them well for two seasons before easing off in the confines of local non-league football. Having settled in the area, he worked at Pleasley Colliery and played for them at cricket for many years. A keen darts enthusiast, he served in the Army in WW I. His feat of winning three consecutive Midland League championship medals is without parallel. When he died, his ashes were scattered on the Field Mill pitch.

1923-24   38 apps   1 gl Midland League
1924-25   19 "   0 "   "   "
Honours: Midland League Championship 1923 (Wednesday). Midland League Championship 1924 & 1925 (both Mansfield)

BENTLEY David A

1972 Midfield   5' 8½"   10st 0lbs (1977)
b: Edwinstowe, Notts., 30 May 1950
Career: Rotherham United (1966 - appr, July 1967 - pro), TOWN (Sep 1972 - loan), Chesterfield (Jun 1974), Doncaster Rovers (F.T. Aug 1977), Gainsborough Trinity (1989 - manager to 1991).

Dave Bentley had a long and distinguished career with Rotherham with just the one loan spell at Mansfield. Became the Stag's Football in the Community Organiser in 1991, which is of tremendous benefit to local youth. Managed Gainsborough Trinity on a part-time basis prior to this.

1972-73   1(3) apps   1 gl   (Loan)

BERESFORD Joseph

1926 - 27 Inside Forward   5' 7"   10st 9lbs (1926)
b: Chesterfield, 26 February 1906
d: Birmingham, March 1978
Career: Askern Road W M C Doncaster, Mexborough (1924), TOWN (May 1926), Aston Villa (£750 - May 1927), Preston North End (Sep 1935), Swansea Town (Dec 1937), Stourbridge (c/s 1938)

Possibly the best and certainly the most successful footballer the club has ever produced in terms of achievement.

Joe Beresford was the old fashioned inside forward "par excellence". A superb dribbler and passer of the ball, he was fast and could score goals - at Mexborough he netted 60 in two seasons. Often described as "a real bundle of tricks" he was always a potential match winner and very much a crowd pleaser. Mansfield paid a fee to Mexborough to secure his services, (and that was a rarity for non league clubs in those days,) but it was money well spent. In early May 1927, an Aston Villa representative went to run the rule over the Stockport goalkeeper who had been getting rave reports. The County were entertaining Mansfield that day but the Villa observer had eyes for no-one but the little inside left who "was running rings round the Stockport defence and causing them all sorts of problems". The player in question was Beresford and immediately the Birmingham club stepped in and signed him for what was by far Mansfield's biggest fee to date. It is not recorded what happened to the Stockport goalkeeper, but it was obviously his unlucky day!

Beresford went straight into the Villa first team and his career with them was distinguished. He won a place in the Football League XI in 1931, followed by a further selection in 1934 and an England cap the same season. Moving to Preston in the twilight of his career, he won an F A Cup winners medal in 1937 at Wembley, in a team which included another ex "Stag" in Billy Tremelling, the centre half. Joe Beresford retired during the war in 1941, but he came out of retirement to make just one appearance for Hartlepools United during 1943 in an emergency.

1926-27   35 apps   18 gls
Midland Combination Honours: Midland League Championship 1926 (Mexborough). Midland Combination runners up, Midland Combination Cup Winners, Notts F A Senior Cup Winners, Notts Benevolent Bowl Winners, Mansfield Hospital Charity Cup Winners 1927 (all Mansfield). England International, Football League XI, Division 1 runners up 1931 & 1933 (all Aston Villa). F A Cup Winners 1937 (Preston). Welsh Cup runners up 1938 (Swansea).

BERRY James
1924 - 25 Outside Right
Career: Stalybridge Celtic (1922), TOWN (1924)

A winger who made one appearance for the "Celts" during their last season in the League, before he joined the "Stags".

1924-25   3 apps   0 gls Midland League

BERRY William
1956 - 57 Inside Forward   5' 8"   11st 0lbs
b: Mansfield, 4 April 1934
Career: Langwith Colliery, TOWN (Mar 1956)

1956-57   10 apps   1 gl

BETTS Eric
1946 - 47 Outside Left   5' 10"   11st 0lbs
b: Coventry, 27 July 1925
d: Rochdale, March 1990
Career: Mansfield Villa, Nottingham Forest (July 1943 - am), TOWN (Feb 1946), Coventry City (Aug 1947), Nuneaton Borough (c/s 1948), Walsall (May 1949), West Ham United (Apr 1950), Nuneaton Borough (c/s 1951), Rochdale (Oct 1951), Crewe Alexandra (Feb 1953), Wrexham (Oct 1953), Oldham Athletic (£350 - Feb 1956), Bangor City (late 1957)

A much travelled player whose longest spell with any club was 2½ years at Wrexham. A good reliable winger with a fair turn of speed and a powerful shot, Betts was somewhat handicapped by being completely one footed. As a young amateur with Forest during WW II, he "guested" for Crystal Palace and Mansfield, before he signed pro for the "Stags" in February 1946.

WW II   7 apps   2 gls
1946-47   19 "   5 "

BIDDLESTONE Thomas (Frederick)
1939-40 Goalkeeper 5' 11½"   12st 0lbs (1937)
b: Pensnett, Worcs., 26 November 1906
d: Great Barr, Birmingham, 7 April 1977
Career: Bilston B C, Hickman Park Rangers, Moxley Wesleyans, Wednesbury Town, Sunbeam Motors, Bloxwich strollers, Walsall (Apr 1929), Aston Villa (£1,750 - Feb 1930), TOWN (Aug 1939)

Fred Biddlestone had a distinguished career with Villa, culminating in a Division 2 championship medal in 1938 when he missed only three matches. After playing in 25 games in 1938-39 he was signed by the "Stags" on the eve of the 1939-40 season when it became apparent that Jack Hughes' back injury would keep him out of the team for a long time and the young and inexperienced Dennis Wright was not considered ready for regular first team action. When he moved from Walsall to Villa, the fee was a huge one for a goalkeeper and was possibly the highest ever paid at that time for a custodian "Guested" for Walsall during the war until 1942 when he retired. Nicknamed "the Councillor" at Villa Park.

1939-40   3 apps   0 gls
Honours: Division 1 runners up 1931, Division 2 Championship 1938 (both Aston Villa)

BIGGS Kenneth
1930 - 31 Inside/Outside Left
b: c1912
Career: Staveley Town, TOWN (Mar 1931)

1930-31   1 app   0 gls Midland League

BILLINGTON (Charles) Royston

1958 - 59 Centre Half Back   6' 3"   13st 7lbs
b: Chesterfield, 8 November 1927
Career: Chesterfield (am), Aldershot (Dec 1944), Norwich City (£3,000 - Jan 1956), Watford (Jun 1957), TOWN (Jun 1958), Burton Albion.

Somewhat "over the hill" when he teamed up with the "Stags", after 12 very successful years at Aldershot, he managed just one appearance.

1958-59	1 app	0 gls

BINGHAM John G

1970 - 72 Winger   5' 9"   11st 4lbs (1971)
b: Ripley, Derbys., 23 September 1949
Career: Charlton Athletic (1966 - appr), Manchester City (Oct 1967 - pro), Oldham Athletic (July 1969), TOWN (Aug 1970 - 1 month trial, F.T. Sep 1970 - permanent), Chester (Mar 1972 - loan), Stockport County (F.T. July 1972).

Could only muster a few games with each of the clubs he served.

1970-71	4(1) apps	0 gls
1971-72	14(2) "	0 "

BINNIE Laurence

1946 - 47 Wing Half Back
b: Falkirk, 17 December 1917
Career: Camelon Juniors, Chesterfield (May 1939), TOWN (Nov 1946)

The only appearances Laurie Binnie made for the "Spireites" were one in 1942-43 and five in 1945-46, even though he was signed before the war. He was thus on the club's books for 7½ years without getting a full League game!

1946-47	20 apps	0 gls

BIRD Kevin

1972 - 83 Defender   5' 11"   12st 0lbs (1982)
b: Armthorpe, Nr Doncaster, 7 August 1952
Career: Doncaster Rovers (1971 - am), TOWN (July 1972 - 3 month's trial, Oct 1972 - pro - permanent), Huddersfield Town (F.T. Aug 1983).

After not being re-signed by Doncaster, Frank Marshall, ex Rover's and by this time, Town's assistant manager, lured Bird to Field Mill where his career really took off and he became one of the "Stags" longest serving and most reliable player. Had 11 full seasons with Mansfield, making 377 appearances and scored a lot of

goals for a defender. Still resides in the town, being currently involved with the building trade. A truly great clubman.

1972-73	26(0) apps	2 gls
1973-74	44(0) "	8 "
1974-75	28(0) "	7 "
1975-76	26(2) "	6 "
1976-77	37(1) "	8 "
1977-78	34(0) "	4 "
1978-79	44(0) "	4 "
1979-80	38(0) "	7 "
1980-81	42(0) "	5 "
1981-82	25(1) "	2 "
1982-83	28(1) "	2 "

Honours: England Youth International. Division 4 Championship 1975, Division 3 Championship 1977 (both Mansfield).

BISBY Clarence (Charles)

1935 - 36 Left Full Back   5' 9"   12st 0lbs (1935)
b: Mexborough, South Yorks., 10 September 1904
Career: Denaby United (c/s 1922), Notts County (c/s 1926), Coventry City (Jun 1932), TOWN (Dec 1935), Peterborough & Fletton United (c/s 1936)

A dependable full back who joined Notts when they were relegated from the First Division in 1926 and was a regular for them for six seasons before assisting Coventry to the Third Division title. They placed him on the transfer list because he transgressed club rules - what his offence was alleged to be was never stated. Moved out of League football when he left

Mansfield. Had his first taste of professional football as a 17 year old with Denaby United in 1922 in the Midland League.

1935-36   9 apps   0 gls
Honours: Division 3 South Championship 1931 (Notts County) & 1936 (Coventry)

BLACK Daniel
1936 - 39 Goalkeeper 6' 2"   12st 7lbs (1936)
b: Whitehaven, 1913
Career: Kells, Carlisle United (1932), Rotherham United (c/s 1935), TOWN (Mar 1936), Peterborough & Fletton United (Mar 1939)

A great favourite with the schoolboys, Danny Black joined Mansfield from reserve team football at Rotherham, although he had held the first team slot at Carlisle earlier. Came straight into Town's team after Fawcett's unfortunate spell and held the position until challenged by Welsh International Jack Hughes from 1937 onwards, when he had to largely play "second fiddle". It was rather ironic that he was released to join Peterborough in March 1939, for he would have been the obvious choice when Hughes' injury ruled him out of contention some five months later.

1935-36	10 apps	0 gls	
1936-37	28 "	0 "	
1937-38	3 "	0 "	
1938-39	5 "	0 "	

BLACKBURN (George) Frederick
1931 - 32 Left half Back   5' 11'   12st 7lbs (1931)
b: Willesden Green, London, 8 March 1899
d: Handsworth, Birmingham, 3 July 1957
Career: Pound Lane School Willesden, Willesden, London Schools, Willesden Juniors, Army (1917 to 1919), Hampstead Town (am), Aston Villa (Dec 1920 - am, Jan 1921 - pro), Cardiff City (Jun 1926), TOWN (£250 - Jun 1931), Cheltenham Town (July 1932 - player coach), Moor Green (Aug 1934 - coach), Birmingham (July 1937 - trainer, Aug 1946 - coach to 1948)

One of the experienced players that Jack Hickling brought in for the "Stags" first season in League football. His experience was undoubted, but his legs were failing and he only managed a handful of games here. His long and distinguished career with Villa and Cardiff brought him an England cap, an F A Cup Final appearance at Wembley and two Welsh Cup winners medals.

1931-32   14 apps   0 gls
Honours: London Schoolboys. England International, Football League XI, F A Cup runners up 1924 (all Aston Villa). F A Charity Shield Winners - Cardiff v Corinthians 1928, Welsh Cup Winners 1927 & 1930, runners up 1929 (all Cardiff).

BLACKHALL Raymond
1982 - 83 Defender   5' 10"   11st 7lbs (1983)
b: Ashington, 19 February 1957
Career: Newcastle United (Aug 1974), Sheffield Wednesday (£20,000 - Aug 1978), S K Tord Sweden (F.T. c/s 1982), TOWN (F.T. Nov 1982) Carlisle United (c/s 1984).

An experienced defender with Wednesday, Black-hall spent a few months in Swedish football before joining Mansfield for one season.

1982-83   15(0) apps 0 gls

BLAIR John
1986 - 87 Midfield   5' 8"   11st 0lbs (1986)
Career: TOWN (1986)

Young midfielder who made a single appearance when brought on as substitute for Tony Lowery in a Freight Rover Trophy tie at York in January 1987.

BLISSETT Luther L
1993 - 94 Centre Forward   5' 11"   12st 3lbs
b: Jamaica, 1 February 1958
Career: Watford (July 1975), A C Milan (£1,000,000 - Jun 1983), Watford (£550,000 - Aug 1984), A F C Bournemouth (£60,000 - Nov 1988), Watford (£40,000 - Aug 1991), West Bromwich Albion (Oct 1992 - loan), Bury (F.T. Aug 1993), TOWN (Dec 1993 - loan), Southport (Mar 1994 - loan), Fakenham Town (F.T. Aug 1994).

Sadly Luther Blissett was well past his best when he had a loan spell at Field Mill and was not a success. Had earlier developed a wonderful career with Watford, followed by a year in Europe when A C Milan paid a seven figure sum for his services. Apart from all the football that Watford got out of Blissett, they also did very well financially by him too, signing him on no fewer than three occasions, for considerably less than they sold him for. Now languishing in non-league soccer at the age of 37.

1993-94   4(1) apps   1 gl   (Loan)
Honours: England U/21, B & full international, Division 4 Championship 1978 (all Watford).

BOAM (Stuart) William
1966-71 & 1981-83 Centre Half Back 6' 0" 12st 0lbs (1971)
b: Kirkby in Ashfield, Notts., 28 January 1948
Career: Kirkby B C, Nottingham Forest (trial), TOWN (July 1966 - am, Jun 1967 - pro), Middlesbrough (£50,000 - Jun 1971), Newcastle United (£140,000 - Aug 1979), TOWN (July 1981 - player manager to Jan 1983), Hartlepool United (Mar 1983), Guisborough (July 1983 - player manager).

Made "Stags" debut whilst still a teenager and carved out a re-markable career in seven seasons with the club, before being snapped up by the Teessiders who he captained to the Second Division title in 1974. Moved on to Newcastle for an even bigger fee, returning to Field Mill as player manager in July 1981. His stay this time was not a happy one for him, as after only just avoiding re-election in his first season and being in a lowly position in the League early in the New Year of his second, he was dismissed. After just one more match as a player with Hartlepool he moved into non-league football.

1966-67	1(0) apps	0 gls
1967-68	44(0) "	0 "
1968-69	46(0) "	1 "
1969-70	46(0) "	1 "
1970-71	38(0) "	1 "
1981-82	4(4) "	1 "
1982-83	7(0) "	0 "

Honours: Division 2 Championship 1974 (Middlesbrough). Giant Killers Cup Winners 1969 & Notts F A County Cup Winners 1971 (both Mansfield).

BONER David
1963 - 64 Outside Right   5' 7"   11st 0lbs (1963)
b: Queensferry, Edinburgh, 12 October 1941
Career: Juniors, Dundee United, Everton (Oct 1958), Raith Rovers, TOWN (F.T. July 1963)

Did not make the first XI at Everton and returned to Scotland from where the "Stags" recruited him in July 1963.

1963-64   12 apps   1 gl
Honours: Scotland schoolboy international.

BONSER L
1926 - 27 and 1931 - 33 Goalkeeper 5' 11"   12st 0lbs
b: 1910
Career: TOWN (Feb 1927 - am), New Houghton, Luton Town (trial), TOWN (c/s 1931)

Amateur player in 1927 when he was called in to play a single game, signing pro in 1931, but he failed to make the League side during his second spell with the club.

1926-27   1 app 0 gls Midland Combination

BOOK Kim
1971 Goalkeeper
b: Bath, 12 February 1946
Career: Frome Town, Bournemouth & Boscombe Athletic (July 1967), Northampton Town (Oct 1969), TOWN (Sep 1971 - loan), Doncaster Rovers (Dec 1971)

Borrowed from the Cobblers" as cover when Graham Brown was injured.

1971-72   4 apps   0 gls   (Loan)

BOOTH
1920 - 21 Goalkeeper
Career: TOWN (1920)

1920-21   4 apps   0 gls Central Alliance

BOOTHROYD (Adrian) Neil

1993 to date Full Back 5' 8"   10st 12lbs (1989)
b: Bradford, 8 February 1971
Career: Huddersfield Town (1987 - appr, July 1989 - pro),
Bristol Rovers £30,000 - Jun 1990), Heart of Midlothian (c/s
1992), TOWN (F.T. Dec 1993)

Strong tackling full back who likes to get forward, "Aidey" Boothroyd joined Town from Scottish Premier League club Hearts and immediately obtained regular first team match experience.

1993-94	22(1) apps	1 gl	
1994-95	35(1) "	0 "	

BORROWS John Edward

1939 - 40 Full Back/Winger 5' 10"   11st 0lbs (1939)
Career: Manchester North End, Chelsea (£1,000 - c/s 1937),
TOWN (May 1939)

Joined Mansfield ostensibly as a reserve, but played in one match during the ill-fated 1939-40 season. "Guest" with Fulham during WW II.

1939-40	1 app	0 gls	
WW II	1 "	1 "	

BOWATER George

1931 - 33 Outside Left   5' 6"   11st 0lbs (1931)
b: Shirebrook, Derbys., 26 April 1911
Career: Sherwood Lads Club Shirebrook, Shirebrook (c/s
1928), TOWN (c/s 1931), Bradford P A (£375 - May 1933),
York City (c/s 1934), Burton Town (c/s 1935), Frickley
Colliery (c/s 1936), Peterborough & Fletton Utd. (c/s 1937)

A clever, fast, diminutive winger, Georgie Bowater made his professional debut at the age of 17, oddly enough against the "Stags" at Christmas 1928 at the White Swan Ground, Shirebrook in the Midland League. He was an excellent performer for Mansfield, who he joined when the "Magpies" folded, before moving up the scale to Second Division Bradford. Had an appetite for goals, being Town's second highest scorer behind Harry Johnson in 1932-33. Retired during the last war.

1931-32	22 apps	10 gls	
1932-33	38 "	18 "	

BOWMER

1922 - 23 Outside Left
Career: TOWN (1923)

1922-23	1 app	0 gl

BRACE Stuart C

1966 - 67 Winger 5' 8"   10st 0lbs
b: Taunton, 21 September 1942
Career: Taunton Town, Plymouth Argyle (Nov 1960),
Watford (Sep 1965), TOWN (F.T. July 1966), Peterborough
United (£5,000 - Nov 1967), Grimsby Town (£4,000 - Oct
1968), Southend United (£6,000 - Oct 1973), Falmouth Town
(c/s 1976)

A much travelled winger who was quite successful at Mansfield with a good scoring rate and was similarly accomplished at Grimsby and Southend. Pipped by Bill Curry by just one goal for the leading scorers spot at Field Mill in his first season there.

1966-67	44(1) apps	21 gls	
1967-68	11(1) "	4 "	

Honours: Division 4 Championship 1972 (Grimsby)

BRADLEY Donald J

1949 - 62 Left Full Back   5' 11½"   10st 8lbs
b: Annesley, Notts., 11 September 1924
Career: Clipstone Colliery, West Bromwich Albion (Sep
1943), TOWN (Aug 1949)

An excellent servant to Mansfield, Don Bradley had signed for West Bromwich during the war, but did not make a senior appearance for them and he joined the "Stags" six years later.

Immediately going into the first team, this tall but lithe defender was not displaced for 13 seasons, apart from injuries, playing his final match for the club in October 1961, when he was 37 years of age. His long standing partnership with Sammy Chessell will be affectionately remembered by older Town supporters and was one of the best in the club's history, being at least on a par with Bellas and Brelsford, Anthony and Jackson, Toon and Humble or Pate and Barry Foster. He made a total of 385 League appearances for the Amber & Blues, the highest number by a player for the club until surpassed by Sandy Pate some 16 years later. As a youngster, played for Dukeries Schoolboys in goal! Made a couple of "Guest" appearances for the "Stags" during the 1944-45 season, when still a "Throstle".

WW II	2 apps	0 gls	
1949-50	36 "	0 "	
1950-51	42 "	1 "	
1951-52	46 "	0 "	
1952-53	32 "	0 "	
1953-54	32 "	3 "	
1954-55	43 "	1 "	
1955-56	29 "	1 "	
1956-57	23 "	0 "	
1957-58	5 "	0 "	
1958-59	23 "	0 "	
1959-60	35 "	0 "	
1960-61	29 "	0 "	
1961-62	9 "	0 "	

Honours: Division 3 North runners up 1951 (Mansfield)

BRADLEY Leslie S
1925 - 26 and 1927 - 28 Inside Left 5' 10" 11st 6lbs (1927)
b: Pleasley, Mansfield, c1905
Career: Warsop Rovers, Sutton Junction, TOWN (1925), Burnley (Apr 1926), TOWN (Jun 1927)

Had an excellent scoring record during his two spells at Field Mill but failed to make the senior team at Burnley.

1925-26	5 apps	4 gls	Midland League	
1927-28	10 "	13 "	"	"

Honours: Mansfield Hospital Charity Cup Winners 1928 (Mansfield)

BRADLEY
1930 - 31 Outside Right
Career: TOWN (1930)

1930-31	1 app	0 gls	Midland League

BRAMLEY Arthur T
1949 - 53 Goalkeeper 6' 1½" 11st 10lbs
b: Mansfield, 25 March 1929
Career: Bentinck Colliery, TOWN (Sep 1949 - am, Oct 1949 - pro), Spalding United (Aug 1954).

Reserve 'keeper who had a fiery baptism into League soccer when he was on the receiving end of a 3 - 6 thrashing at the hands of Chester in the final game of the 1949-50 season. His opportunities were rare due to the consistency of Dennis Wright. 1952-53 season provided his only decent run of appearances when Wright broke his wrist and was sidelined for four months.

1949-50	1 app	0 gls	
1950-51	1 "	0 "	
1952-53	17 "	0 "	

BRAMLEY Ernest
1938 - 47 Outside Left/Full Back 5' 9" 12st 3lbs (1946)
b: Mansfield, 29 August 1920
Career: Bolsover Colliery, TOWN (Jun 1938)

Originally a full back, converted to winger, then back to full back again. Ernie Bramley was a strong tackling defender who gave no quarter and asked for none. Played before, during and after the war for Mansfield.

1938-39	13 apps	0 gls
1939-40	2 "	0 "
WW II	61 "	4 "
1946-47	28 "	1 "
1947-48	4 "	0 "

BRAMLEY John

1919 - 21 Centre Half Back
b: c1898
Career: TOWN (c/s 1919), Welbeck Colliery (c/s 1921), Bradford City (May 1922), Rotherham County (Jun 1924).

Strong centre half who, when moving into League football, made a useful contribution with Second Division Bradford City and Third Division Rotherham, who changed their name to United during Bramley's second season there.

1919-20	19 apps	0 gls	Central Alliance
1920-21	27 "	0 "	" "

Honours: Central Alliance Championship 1920, runners up 1921 (both Mansfield)

BREEDON J H

1925 - 26 Inside Forward   5' 10"   11st 6lbs (1925)
b: 1903
Career: Newstead Colliery, TOWN (c/s 1925 - am)

1925-26	4 apps	1 gl Midland League

BRELSFORD Charles

1923 - 27 Left Full Back   5' 10½"   11st 6lbs (1924)
b: Darnall, Sheffield, 1890

Career: Buxton, The Wednesday (Aug 1911), South Shields (c/s 1919), Castleford (c/s 1922), TOWN (c/s 1923)

Formed one of the famous Town early full back partnerships with Jack Bellas and was a regular in the two successive Midland League Championship sides. Broke a leg early in the 1926-27 campaign and at the age of 36, this accelerated his retirement from the game.

1923-24	42 apps	0 gls	Midland League
1924-25	38 "	1 "	" "
1925-26	39 "	0 "	" "
1926-27	1 "	0 "	" "

Midland Combination Honours: Midland League Championship 1924 & 1925, Midland League runners up & Notts F A Senior Cup Winners 1926 (all Mansfield)

BRIGGS Roy

1936 - 41 Outside Left
b: c1920
Career: Mansfield Shoe Co, TOWN (c/s 1937 - am)

Roy Briggs was a teenage left winger playing for the Shoe Company team when he caught the eye of the "Stags" who signed him on amateur forms in 1936. Playing largely in the reserves, he was given his chance the week after Cyril Poole played in the first team - this was immediately after Jack Roy had been transferred to Sheffield Wednesday and the left wing slot was causing problems. He was only 16 years old upon making his debut and although he stayed with the club for some time, his only other appearances in the first team were in September 1940 when he appeared in a South Regional game at Northampton and April 1942 in the North Region at Lincoln, where he scored his only goal for the "Stags".

1936-37	2 apps	0 gls
WW II	2 "	1 "

BROOME William Henry

1931 - 33 Inside Forward   5' 8"   12st 0lbs
b: Chorlton cum Hardy, Manchester, 16 April 1904
Career: Altrincham, Bury (May 1926), Colwyn Bay United (July 1927), Bangor (Aug 1928), Caernarfon Town (Nov 1928), Crewe Alexandra (Jun 1929), Accrington Stanley (July 1930), TOWN (July 1931)

Harry Broome had done the rounds of a number of non league clubs before he reached the exalted heights of the Football League, albeit the 3rd Division North. Described as a constructive "box of tricks" type of player, it was probably the case that his scheming play was somewhat out of place in the hurly burly of Division 3. He did however survive four seasons at this level, two of them at Field Mill and also had the distinction of scoring twice in Town's first ever match in the Football League.

1931-32	34 apps	8 gls
1932-33	14 "	1 "

BROWN Albert (Roy)
1947 - 48 Winger   5' 5"   10st 0lbs
b: Sneinton, Nottingham, 14 August 1917
Career: Sneinton, Nottingham Forest (Feb 1936), Wrexham (Jun 1939), TOWN (July 1947)

Was a regular in Forest's Division 2 team in the last two pre-war seasons before moving to Wrexham a couple of months before the outbreak of hostilities. After completing the first post-war season with the "Robins", Roy Brown came to Field Mill for one season before dropping into non league football.

1947-48	17 apps	2 gls

BROWN Alexander
1946 - 47 Inside Forward
b: Seaton Delaval, Co Durham, 21 November 1914
Career: Chesterfield (Dec 1933), Darlington (Jun 1935), Shrewsbury Town (c/s 1938), TOWN (Nov 1946)

Only second to Cyril Poole, in that he managed a gap of 10 seasons between consecutive Football League appearances, Darlington 1936 to Mansfield 1946, albeit with seven wartime seasons in between!

1946-47	5 apps	0 gls

BROWN Alfred
1936 - 37 Wing Half Back   5' 10½"   11st 7lns (1936)
b: Chadderton, Lancs., 22 February 1907
Career: Chamber Colliery, Oldham Athletic (Mar 1927), Northampton Town (July 1933), TOWN (Feb 1936).

Gave excellent service to the "Latics" during his six year stint there. Contemporary reports quoted him as "a strong tackler good in the air, quick and powerful". Served the "Stags" for a season and a half.

1935-36	14 apps	0 gls
1936-37	32 "	0 "

BROWN Graham C
1968, 1969 - 74 & 1982 Goalkeeper 5' 11" 12st 0lbs (1972)
b: Matlock, Derbys., 21 March 1944
Career: Millwall (Dec 1964 - trial), Crawley Town, Brighton & Hove Albion (Feb 1966 - trial), Crawley Town, Watford (Aug 1968 - trial), TOWN (Aug 1968 - trial), Crawley Town, TOWN (Aug 1969), Doncaster Rovers (F.T. July 1974), Portland Timbers U S A, Swansea City (Sep 1976), Southport (Dec 1976), Portland Timbers U S A, York City (Aug 1977), Rotherham United (Feb 1980), TOWN (Jan 1982 - N/C)

Graham Brown had a long career in football and played for a great many clubs too. He had to vie for the custodian's berth at Field Mill with the likes of Hollins and Arnold, but held off the opposition for a time. Joined the "Stags" on three separate occasions, the final one on a non-contract basis, before retiring. Now a salesman.

1969-70	33 apps	0 gls
1970-71	19 "	0 "
1971-72	40 "	0 "
1972-73	33 "	0 "
1973-74	17 "	0 "
1981-82	1 "	0 "

Honours: Notts F A County Cup Winners 1971 & 1972 (both Mansfield)

BROWN (Roy) Eric

1975 Goalkeeper 6' 1"   12st 10lbs (1964)
b: Hove, 5 October 1945
Career: Tottenham Hotspur (1961 - appr, Oct 1962 - pro), Reading (July 1968), Notts County (July 1970), TOWN (Nov 1975 - N/C)

Had a very good career at Meadow Lane and was released in May 1975, joining the "Stags" six months later as a non-contract player for just one game.

Season	Apps	Goals
1975-76	1 app	0 gls

BRYAN John Joseph

1922 - 28 Wing or Centre Half Back 5' 9" 11st 8lbs (1924)
b: Langwith, Notts., 22 August 1897
d: 1978
Career: Langwith Red Rose, Mansfield Swifts, Shirebrook (am), TOWN (1915 - am), Lincoln City (May 1919), TOWN (May 1922), Worksop Town (c/s 1928), Mexborough (c/s 1929)

Jack Bryan first played for Mansfield as an amateur during WW I, joining the "Imps" after the war on professional forms. Was a regular in their relegation season of 1919-20 and Midland League Championship side the following term. After one more season at Lincoln, he joined the "Stags" in May 1922. At this time he was a wing half, but soon developed into probably the best attacking centre half in the Midland League, providing many goals for Chris Staniforth.

Captained the team to successive Midland League titles, but was less effective after the change to the offside law in 1925 when "stopper" centre halves became the vogue and he was replaced by Bernard Chambers, who was the stopper type. Bryan moved on to Worksop and Mexborough, where he finished his playing days. He was a useful cricketer for Langwith during the summer months. Played for Notts County and Lincoln City during WW I.

Season	Apps	Goals	League
1922-23	38 apps	2 gls	Midland League
1923-24	38 "	3 "	" "
1924-25	36 "	3 "	" "
1925-26	35 "	1 "	" "
1926-27	29 "	1 "	Midland Comb.
1927-28	31 "	1 "	

Midland League Honours: Midland League Championship 1921 (Lincoln). Central Alliance - Subsidiary Competition Championship 1916, Midland League Championship 1924 & 1925, runners up 1926, Midland Combination runnersup & Midland Combination Cup Winners 1927, Notts F A Senior Cup Winners 1923, 1926 & 1927, Mansfield Hospital Charity Cup Winners 1928 (all Mansfield).

BRYANT Eric

1946 - 48 Centre Forward
b: Birmingham, 18 November 1921
Career: Gillingham (c/s 1939 - am), Army, TOWN (May 1946), Yeovil & Petters United (F.T. c/s 1948), Plymouth Argyle (£3,000 - Oct 1949), Clapton Orient - July 1951)

Picked up by manager Roy Goodall from Army football, Eric Bryant made a useful impact in a very mediocre "Stags" side by averaging over a goal every two games in his first season, but had little opportunity the following term after George Banks had arrived from W B A and was released at the end of April 1948. He became one of the stars in the Yeovil team which had such a wonderful F A Cup run in 1948-49, reaching the 5th round, which no doubt prompted Second Division Plymouth to pay the not inconsiderable sum of £3,000 for him - probably a non league record at the time.

Season	Apps	Goals	
1946-47	28 apps	15 gls	Leading Scorer
1947-48	7 "	2 "	

BUCKLEY Walter

1926 - 27 Right Half Back   5' 8½"   11st 0lbs (1932)
b: Eccleshall, Sheffield, 30 April 1906
Career: Sheffield Schools, Birley Carr, Arsenal (Apr 1923 - am), Bournemouth & Boscombe Athletic (Aug 1926 - trial), TOWN (Sep 1926), Bradford P A (May 1927), Lincoln City (May 1930), Rochdale (Aug 1933), Runcorn (Aug 1936)

Joined Town as a 20 year old after failing to impress sufficiently to be offered terms at Dean Court. Bradford paid a fee to secure his transfer less than a year later and he appeared in their Second Division side during their championship campaign. Later played for Lincoln and Rochdale.

1926-27   32 apps   1 gl Midland Combination
Honours: Sheffield Schoolboys, England Schoolboy international 1920. Midland Combination runners up, Midland Combination Cup Winners, Notts F A Senior Cup Winners & Mansfield Hospital Charity Cup Winners 1927 (all Mansfield). Division 3 North Championship 1928 (Bradford). Division 3 North runners up 1931 & Championship 1932 (Lincoln).

BULLOCK A

1926 - 27 Right Full Back
Career: TOWN (1926 - am)

1926-27   2 apps   0 gls   Midland Combination
Honours: Byron Cup Winners 1927 (Mansfield).

BUNGAY (Reginald) Harold

1936 - 39 Utility Player   5' 9"   11st 0lbs (1936)
b: Reading, 5 February 1911
d: October 1986
Career: Oxford City, Tottenham Hotspur (1931), Plymouth Argyle (c/s 1933), Bristol City (c/s 1935), TOWN (c/s 1936), Clapton Orient (c/s 1939)

Reg Bungay was the utility player supreme - he occupied no less than five positions during his spell at Mansfield, although he was mainly used in the inside left and left half berths. Spurs was the only team he played for where he did not secure a first team place.

1936-37   28 apps   1 gl
1937-38   32 "   1 "
1938-39   27 "   3 "
Honours: Notts F A County Cup Winners 1939 (Mansfield)

BUNTING John B

1925 - 26 Goalkeeper 6' 1½"   11st 9lbs (1925)
b: Nottingham, 1903
Career: Grantham, Boston (c/s 1922), Brighton & Hove Albion (c/s 1924), TOWN (c/s 1925).

Had some League experience with Brighton, making eight appearances during 1924-25.

1925-26   8 apps   0 gls Midland League

BURNS Neil J

1965 - 66 Inside Forward   5' 7"   10st 0lbs
b: Bellshill, Lanarkshire, 11 June 1945
Career: Aidrieonians (1964), Bethesda (1965), TOWN (Nov 1965)

Perhaps his greatest claim to fame was the fact that the place where he was born and the first team for which he played, were both the same as the great Hughie Gallacher.

1965-66   5(2) apps   0 gls
1966-67   2(1) "   0 "

BURROWS (Adrian) Mark

1979 - 82 Defender   5' 11"   11st 12lbs (1987)
b: Sutton in Ashfield, 16 January 1959
Career: TOWN (May 1979), Northampton Town (F.T. Aug 1982), Plymouth Argyle (£10,000 - Sep 1984), Southend United (Sep 1987 - loan), Saltash (c/s 1994)

The youngest son of ex "Stag", Horace Burrows (below), who gained fame later with Sheffield Wednesday and England, Adrian signed for Town as a 20 year old and later had an illustrious career with the "Pilgrims" for 10 years. Married to an Exeter girl and now living in that city, he is currently playing for Saltash in the Western League and captaining the Cornwall County team.

1979-80   17(0) apps 0 gls
1980-81   19(1) "   3 "
1981-82   41(0) "   3 "
Honours: Division 3 runners up 1986 (Plymouth)

BURROWS Frank

1974 Defender 6' 1"   12st 8lbs (1970)
b: Larkhill, Scotland, 30 January 1944
Career: Raith Rovers (1961), Scunthorpe United (Jun 1965), Swindon Town (July 1968), TOWN (Mar 1974 - loan), Swindon Town (Feb 1978 - asst manager), Portsmouth (1978

- coach, May 1979 - manager to Mar 1982), Southampton (Aug 1983 - coach), Sunderland (1986 - coach), Cardiff City (May 1986 - manager to Aug 1989), Portsmouth (Sep 1989 - asst manager, Jan 1990 - manager to Mar 1991), Swansea City (Mar 1991 - manager to date)

After giving many years service to Swindon, Burrows entered the administrative side of football as Assistant Manager with them in 1978 and has been employed in various capacities with several clubs since then, including two spells at Portsmouth. He is currently manager of Second Division Swansea City.

1973-74   6(0) apps   0 gls   (Loan)
Honours: (as player) - Football League Cup Winners 1969 (Swindon).   (as manager) - Division 4 runners up & Welsh Cup Winners 1988 (both Cardiff)

BURROWS Horace
1930 - 31 Left Half Back   5' 9½"   11st 11lbs (1935)
b: Sutton in Ashfield, 11 March 1910
d: Sutton in Ashfield, 22 March 1969
Career: Sutton Junction (c/s 1929), Coventry City (Feb 1929 - trial), TOWN (c/s 1930), Sheffield Wednesday £350 - May 1931)

A rising star, Burrows moved to Wednesday just a month before it was learned that Mansfield had gained election to the Football League. Won a place in the "Owls" premier side in December 1932 and helped them to third place in Division 1 that season. In 12 very successful years there he won three England caps in 1934-35 and an F A Cup Winners medal in 1934-35 when W B A

were vanquished 4 - 2 at Wembley. Retiring during the war years in 1942, he was the father of Adrian (above) who played for the "Stags" in the late 1970s, but sadly he passed away before he could see his son make a successful career in League football.

1930-31   44 apps   0 gls Midland League
Honours: Notts F A Senior Cup Winners 1931 (Mansfield). England International, F A Cup Winners 1935 & F A Charity Shield Winners 1936 (all Wednesday)

BUTLER Edward (Leslie)
1932 - 34 Centre Half Back   6' 2"   13st 0lbs (1933)
b: 1910
Career: Derby County (am), Southend United (1930), TOWN (c/s 1932), Ollerton Colliery (c/s 1934)

Leslie Butler, more generally known as "Tiny" amongst his team mates, for obvious reasons, was a commanding pivot who joined Mansfield after failing to make the first team at Southend. He gave Town very good service, particularly during his last season with them.

1932-33   14 apps   0 gls
1033-34   32 "   5 "

BUTT Leonard
1947 - 48 Inside Forward   5' 6"   11st 3lbs (1947)
b: Wilmslow, Cheshire, 26 August 1910
d: Macclesfield, June 1994
Career: Wilmslow Albion, Ashton National, Stockport County (Jun 1928 - am, Aug 1929 - pro), Macclesfield Town (May 1932), Huddersfield Town (May 1935), Blackburn Rovers (Jan 1937), York City (Jan 1947), TOWN (Oct 1947), Mossley (Jun 1048 - player coach).

A diminutive inside forward who took Town's penalties by standing over the ball and just rolling it into the net with expert placement an inch or two inside the post and along the ground - he never missed. Sadly, that was one of his few achievements with the club as he was 37 years old by then and his former skills had deserted him. In his Blackburn days he had been a scheming goalscoring inside forward who was verging on international honours, but the war put an end to that. However, he did play a major part in them winning the Division 2 title in the last pre-war season. He is the second oldest player to turn out for the "Stags" in a League match - the occasion being v Hull City at Field Mill on 10 April 1948, when he was 37 years 228 days old. During WW II he "guested" for Manchester United, Huddersfield, Wrexham, Manchester City, York City, Chelsea, Aldershot and Stockport.

1947-48   15 apps   4 gls

Honours: Cheshire County League Championship 1932 & 1933, Cheshire Senior Cup Winners 1935 (all Macclesfield). Division 2 Championship 1939, Football League War Cup runners up 1940 (both Blackburn).

BUTTRELL Charles E

1922 - 23 Centre Forward
b: Sheffield, c1900
Career: Chesterfield Town (1921), TOWN (Sep 1922)

A centre forward who made 9 appearances and scored 3 goals for Chesterfield in Division 3 North the season prior to joining Town.

1922-23   2 apps   0 gls Midland League

BUXTON H

1924 - 25 Wing Half Back
b: New Hucknall, Notts.
Career: TOWN (1924 - am).

An amateur reserve wing half who made his only league appearance at outside right due to injuries to Berry and Harrison.

1924-25   1 app   0 gls Midland League

BYTHEWAY (George) Samuel

1933 - 36 Outside Left   5' 9"   11st 0lbs (1935)
b: Shuttlewood, Derbys., March 1908
d: Chesterfield, October 1979
Career: Mansfield Woodhouse Comrades, Mansfield Labour Club, Seymour F C, Staveley Town, West Bromwich Albion (£600 - Oct 1927), Coventry City (£100 - May 1933), TOWN (£100 - Dec 1933), Guildford City (c/s 1936).

Quoted at the time as, *one of the fastest wingers in the game who cuts in from the wing and makes for goal*. Suffered numerous injuries during his career including three broken legs, two broken ankles, one broken collarbone and one broken wrist - rather vulnerable it would

seem. When he moved from Staveley to W B A it was for a very large fee indeed for a Midland League club to receive. "Guested" for Grimsby Town late in the war when he was nearly 36 years of age.

1933-34   24 apps   7 gls
1934-35   31   "   12   "
1935-36   32   "   4   "

CALDERWOOD Colin

1981 - 85 Central Defender   6' 0"   11st 9lbs(1987)
b: Stanraer, 20 January 1965
Career: Scottish Juniors, TOWN (1981 - appr, Mar 1982 - pro), Swindon Town (£27,500 - Tribunal + £2,500 after investigation + half sell-on fee, July 1985 making total of £655,000), Tottenham Hotspur (£1,250,000 - half to Stags, July 1993).

Signed by Mansfield from Scottish Junior football as a 16 year old, becoming a full time pro just after his seventeenth birthday. A strong dependable player, he developed quickly and was snapped up by the "Robins" for a miserly, arbitration-dictated fee which was later adjusted, but in a still ungenerous manner. Was at the core of Swindon's run through to the Premier League in 1993, before joining Spurs for a seven figure fee. He was one of a number of players who were arrested during the investigations into the illegal payments scandal at Swindon in May 1990, but was released without charge, although his club were ordered to be relegated two divisions, later just one, by the Football League. The "Stags" had two points deducted from their total in 1981-82 for paying him when not registered. Colin Calderwood had to wait a long time for his international debut - this came on 29 March 1995 against Russia at the Central Luzhniki Stadium in Moscow, when he was in his 31st year. With Mansfield's share of his subsequent transfer fee to 'Spurs, this move became the Club's record sale.

1981-82   1(0) apps   0 gls
1982-83   28(0)   "   0   "
1983-84   27(3)   "   1   "
1984-85   41(0)   "   0   "

Honours: Division 4 Championship 1986, Division 3 Promotion 1987, Football League Division 2 XI 1992, Division 2 Play-Offs 1989

1990, Promotion 1993 (all Swindon). Scottish International (Tottenham).

CALDWELL David W
1979 - 85 Forward   5' 10"   11st 6lbs(1980)
b: Aberdeen, 31 July 1960
Career: Inverness Caledonian, TOWN (June 1979), Carlisle United (Dec 1984 - loan), Swindon Town (Feb 1985 - loan), Chesterfield (£12,000 - Aug 1985), Torquay United (£4,000 - Nov 1987), K V Overpelt, Belgium ((Aug 1988), Torquay United (Dec 1989 - loan), Chesterfield (Oct 1990 - released May 1992)

A fiery striker who knew the way to goal, Dave Caldwell unfortunately had a very short temper and this resulted in him being sent off on many occasions, ultimately resulting in an eight match suspension when he was with Torquay.

1979-80	1(2) apps	0 gls		
1980-81	23(5) "	8 "		
1981-82	31(2) "	9 "		
1982-83	34(1) "	10 "		
1983-84	37(1) "	21 "	Leading scorer
1984-85	19(1) "	9 "	"	"

CALVERLEY Alfred
1946 - 47 Outside Left   5' 7"   11st 2lbs
b: Huddersfield, 24 November 1917
Career: Huddersfield Town (1939 - am, Nov 1943 - pro), TOWN (June 1946), Arsenal (£2,500 - Mar 1947), Preston North End (£1,500 - July 1947), Doncaster Rovers (£4,000 - Dec 1947 to May 1953)   One of new manager Roy Goodall's first captures,

Alf Calverley had the start of his career delayed by the war, during which he "guested" for Bradford City, Darlington, Leeds United, Sheffield United, Sheffield Wednesday, Clapton Orient and Coventry City.

A clever winger who could centre accurately, he impressed at Mansfield, so much so that George Allison secured him for Arsenal for what was the "Stags" record fee at the time. After six successful years at Belle Vue, his career was terminated by injury in December 1952.

1946-47   30 apps   1 gl
Honours: Division 3 (North) Championship 1950 (Doncaster)

CAMPBELL Jamie
1994 - 95 Forward   6' 1"   11st 3lbs (1994)
b: Birmingham, 21 October 1972
Career: Luton Town (trainee, July 1991 - pro), TOWN (Nov 1994 - loan)

Came on loan to the "Stags" after making over 40 First Division appearances for Luton.

1994-95   3(0) apps   1 gl   (Loan)

CANN Ralph G
1957 - 58 Wing Half Back   5' 9"   10st 7lbs
b: Sheffield, 17 November 1934
Career: TOWN (c/s 1956 - am, May 1957 - pro)

1957-58   1 app   0 gls

CANNELL Paul A
1982 - 83 Forward   5' 10"   11st 0lbs (1982)
b: Newcastle on Tyne, 2 September 1953
Career: Juniors, Newcastle United (July 1972), Washington Diplomats, USA (£40,000 - Feb 1978), Memphis Rogues, USA (Nov 1979), Calgary, Canada (1980), Detroit Express, USA (Jan 1981), Washington Diplomats, USA (Apr 1981), North Shields (late 1981), TOWN (Jan 1982).

After nearly 50 appearances for the "Magpies", spent almost 4 years in the American League, followed by a season and a half with the "Stags".

1981-82	23 apps	4 gls	
1982-83	6(1)"	0 "	

CARR Andrew
1934 - 35 Centre Half Back   5' 10"   11st 7lbs (1934)
b: Burradon, Northumberland, 1909
Career: Percy Main Colliery, Middlesbrough (May 1930), TOWN (June 1934), Crewe Alexandra (c/s 1935), Rochdale (c/s 1936)

Andy Carr, who had First Division experience with Middlesbrough, joined Town in a blaze of publicity on 28 June 1934 as "the finest centre half the "Stags" have ever had, acquired at a substantial fee". It must have all gone wrong as he made a mere dozen appearances in the League team and languished in the reserves for most of the season before being given a free transfer in May 1935 whence he teamed up with Crewe. Perhaps he was a better player with both his future clubs as he played in 36 matches for Crewe and 32 for Rochdale before returning to the North East.

1934-35   12 apps   0 gls

CARR (Clifford) Paul
1991 - 92 Left Full Back   5' 5"   10st 4lbs
b: Hackney, London, 19 June 1964
Career: Fulham (1980 - appr, June 1982 - pro), Stoke City (£45,000 - July 1987), Shrewsbury Town (Aug 1991 - trial), Cardiff City (Sept 1991 - trial), Telford United (Sept 1991 - trial), TOWN (Sept 1991), Chesterfield (F.T. Aug 1972), Telford United (F.T. c/s 1994).

Rather small and lightly built for a full back, Cliff Carr nevertheless more than made the grade at Fulham and Stoke, gaining international recognition with the first named.

1991-92   20(0) apps 0 gls
Honours: England U/21 International (Fulham), Division 4 Promotion 1992 (Mansfield)

CARR (Leonard) William
1925 - 26 Full Back 5' 10"   11st 7lbs (1926)
·b: Sheffield, 19 September 1901
d: 1981
Career: St Bartholomews Sheffield, Norton Woodseats, Sheffield Wednesday (May 1925 - am), TOWN (Feb 1926 - am), Barnsley (Apr 1926 - pro), New Brighton (June 1927), South Liverpool (June 1935 - player/manager)

Stylish full back who gained amateur international honours, one of his caps being won only four days after he made his first appearance for the "Stags", the first player to receive a cap whilst with the club. Mansfield was his last club as an amateur as he turned pro on joining Barnsley. Subsequently astablished himself well with the "Rakers" for whom he played in over 300 games.

1925-26   11 apps   0 gls Midland League
Honours: England Amateur International (Norton Woodseats & Mansfield), Midland League runners up 1926 (Mansfield).

CARTER Michael
1979   Midfield 5' 9"   10st 7lbs (1987)
b: Warrington, 18 April 1960

Career: Bolton Wanderers (1976 - appr, July 1977 - pro), TOWN (Mar 1979 - loan), Swindon Town (Mar 1982 - loan), Plymouth Argyle (Aug 1982), Hereford United (Mar 1983 - loan) Wrexham (F.T. July 1987)

Taken on loan from Bolton until the end of the 1978-79 season.

1978-79   18(0) apps 4 gls (Loan)

CARTER (Sydney) Youles
1938 - 47 Centre Forward   5' 11"   12st 0lbs (1938)
b: Brimington, Chesterfield, 28 July 1916
d: Mansfield, 1978
Career: Chesterfield Boys, Bolsover Colliery (c/s 1933), Sheffield United (c/s 1935), Wolverhampton Wanderers (c/s 1936), Macclesfield Town (c/s 1937), TOWN (May 1938 - player, 1949 - trainer to 1970, qualified masseur from 1958)

Had a tremendous scoring record with Macclesfield, netting 55 goals in 1937-38 and many clubs were keen to secure his signature. Jack Poole, the Town manager outwitted the opposition by discovering that Syd was attending a film show at a cinema in Brimington, so he went there, had a message flashed on the screen and when Carter emerged from the gloom of the auditorium wondering what on earth he was wanted for, there was Poole, pen and contract in hand. Thus Sydney Carter signed for Mansfield Town in the foyer of the cinema on 17 May 1938. After his playing days were over, he served the club loyally for over 20 years as Trainer and Masseur. Guested for Notts County during WW II.

1938-39	27 apps	7 gls
WW II	10 "	5 "
1946-47	12 "	3 "

CARTWRIGHT Herbert
1936 - 37 Inside Right   5' 10"   11st 8lbs
b: Pleasley, Mansfield, c1915
Career: Brunts O B, Rotherham United (1934 - am), Brunts O B, TOWN (Sept 1936 - am), Brunts O B.

Amateur inside forward who made a handful of appearances in the League team during 1936-37 season, scoring one goal, although he did play fairly regularly with the reserves

1936-37   5 apps   1 gl

CASSELLS (Keith) Barrington
1985 - 89 Forward 5' 10"   11st 12lbs (1984)
b: Islington, London, 10 July 1957
Career: Wembley, Watford (£500 - Nov 1977), Peterborough United (Jan 1980 - loan), Oxford United (£5,000 - Nov 1980), Southampton (£115,000 - Mar 1982), Brentford (£25,000 - Feb 1983), TOWN (£17,000 - Aug 1985)

A great striker with all his clubs, Cassells, a former London postman had four very successful seasons at Field Mill in which he added further to the honours he had already won in the game. Was leading scorer in his last season at Brentford, a performance he repeated twice with Mansfield. Ian Greaves dearly wished him to continue for longer with the "Stags" but after delaying his departure for an extra season, he achieved his ambition to join the Hertfordshire Constabulary in 1990 - with as much success as on the football field apparently, for he won a "Golden Scroll" in his first year, the top honour for a trainee policeman.

1985-86	40(0) apps	13 gls	
1986-87	46(0) "	16 "	Leading Scorer
1987-88	40(0) "	9 "	
1988-89	36(1) "	14 "	Leading Scorer

Honours: Division 4 Championship 1978, Runners-Up Division 3 & F L Cup Semi-Finalists 1979 (all Watford), Fright Rover Trophy Finalist 1985 (Brentford), Division 4 Promotion 1986, Freight Rover Trophy Winners 1987, Notts F A County Cup Winners 1987, 1988 & 1989 (all Mansfield)

CASTLEDINE (Gary) John
1990 - 95 Midfield 5' 7" 10st 6lbs (1992)
b: Dumfries, 27 March 1970
Career: Shirebrook Colliery, TOWN (Oct 1990 - am, Feb 1991 - pro), Telford United (Mar 1995 - trial).

A skilful scheming player of the old inside forward type who never quite established himself in the hurly burly of the lower divisions, but his time may well come in the future and Town could rue the day they released him. Trained at St Andrews after leaving Mansfield.

1991-92	3(4) apps	0 gls	
1992-93	23(5) "	3 "	
1993-94	14(7) "	0 "	
1994-95	3(7) "	0 "	

CAWTHORNE Harold
1929 - 30 Full/Wing Half Back
b: Darnall, Sheffield, c1900
d: 1967
Career: Woodhouse, Huddersfield Town (Oct 1919), Sheffield United (Feb 1927), TOWN (Oct 1927), Manchester Central ((Oct 1929), Connah's Quay.

Harry Cawthorne was a full back turned wing half who enjoyed considerable success when with Huddersfield, but stayed with the "Stags" for less than four weeks before moving on to Manchester Central.

1929-30	2 apps	0 gls

Honours: Division 1 Championship 1924 and 1926, Division 1 Runners Up 1927 (all Huddersfield)

CHADBOURN William (Gordon)
1946 - 48 Inside Forward
b: Mansfield, 29 October 1922
Career: South Normanton, TOWN (Apr 1947), Sutton Town (c/s 1948)

Signed for the "Stags" from South Normanton after spending 4½ years in the H M Forces during the war.

1946-47	6 apps	2 gls	
1947-48	3 "	1 "	

CHAMBERLAIN Derek C
1956 - 58 Full Back 5' 10 ' 11st 0lbs
b: Nottingham, 6 January 1933
Career: Parliament Street Methodists, Nottingham Forest (am), Aston Villa (Nov 1953), TOWN (Nov 1956), York City (July 1958).

Strong full back whose father Stan had been a pro with Notts County, Torquay and Worksop Town between the wars.

1956-57	24 apps	0 gls
1957-58	19 "	0 "

CHAMBERLAIN Neville P
1985 - 87 Forward 5' 7" 11st 5lbs (1984)
b: Stoke on Trent, 22 January 1960
Career: Port Vale (1976 - appr, Feb 1978 - pro), Stoke City (£40,000 - Sept 1982), Newport County (Nov 1983 - loan), Plymouth Argyle (Mar 1984 - loan), Newport County (June

1984), TOWN (£7,000 - Aug 1985), Cambridge United (F.T. c/s 1987), Doncaster Rovers (F.T. Aug 1987), Stafford Rangers (F.T. 1988), Boston United.

After a fruitful six year spell at Port Vale, Neville Chamberlain became a much travelled player and was a vital cog in Mansfield's promotion team of 1985-86. He was leading scorer in successive seasons with Port Vale and achieved a similar distinction with both Newport and the "Stags".

| 1985-86 | 39(1) apps | 16 gls | Leading Scorer |
| 1986-87 | 17(4) " | 3 " | |

Honours: Division 4 Promotion 1986, Notts F A County Cup Winners 1987 (both Mansfield)

CHAMBERS Bernard
1928 - 33 Centre Half 6' 0"   12st 10lbs (1928)
b: Bramcote, Nottingham, c 1904
Career: Carter Lane School Shirebrook, Derbyshire Boys, Langwith Athletic (1922), Rotherham Town (1923 - trial), Warsop Colliery (1923), Nottingham Forest (c/s 1924), Shirebrook (c/s 1925), Rotherham United (c/s 1926), Boston (c/s 1927), TOWN (c/s 1928 to May 1933).

A tall commanding centre half who had experienced regular Third Division football with Rotherham. Was the hub of the defence during the famous giant killing F A Cup run of 1928-29. Although born in Nottingham was brought up in Shirebrook. Elder brother of Hector (below) who was a goalkeeper with the "Stags" and younger brother of Frank, a full back with Bolton Wanderers. Jack Baynes, that summer to take over the reins at Mansfield, gave him a trial at Clifton Lane in early 1923 - at ouside left! A very good servant to the "Stags" for five seasons through to the Football League.

1928-29	47 apps	2 gls	Midland League
1929-30	44 "	1 "	"	"
1930-31	40 "	0 "	"	"
1931-32	9 "	0 "	
1932-33	1 "	0 "	

Honours: Blackwell Schoolboys 1918, Derbyshire Schoolboys 1919, Notts Junior Cup Winners 1924 (Warsop Colliery), Midland League Championship 1929, Mansfield Hospital Charity Cup Winners 1929 & 1930, Byron Cup Winners & Bayley Cup Winners 1930, Notts Senior Cup Winners 1931 (all Mansfield).

CHAMBERS Hector
1929 - 31 Goalkeeper 5' 11½"   12st 0lbs (1929)
b: Bramcote, Nottingham, c1909
Career: Welbeck Athletic, Staveley Town (c/s 1928), TOWN (c/s 1929)

| 1929-30 | 6 apps | 0 gls | Midland League |
| 1930-31 | 7 " | 0 " | " | " |

Honours: Byron Cup Winners & Bayley Cup Winners 1930 (both Mansfield).

CHAMBERS J D
1924 - 25 Centre Forward
Career: Clifton Colliery, TOWN (Jan 1925 - am)

| 1924-25 | 3 apps | 2 gls | Midland League |

CHAMBERS Stephen
1986 - 90 Midfield   5' 10"   10st 10lbs (1988)
b: Worksop, 20 July 1968
Career: Sheffield Wednesday (1984 - appr, 1985 - pro), TOWN (Nov 1986), Boston United (c/s 1990)

Failed to gain a place in the "Owls" league XI and it was only in his last season at Field Mill that he became a regular.

1986-87	4(1) apps	0 gls
1987-88	1(7) "	0 "
1988-89	3(2) "	0 "
1989-90	4(3) "	0 "
1990-91	30(2) "	0 "

Honours: Notts F A County Cup Winners 1988 (Mansfield)

CHANDLER (Jeffrey) George
1986 Midfield/Winger   5' 7"   10st 11lbs (1987)
b: Hammersmith, London, 19 June 1959

Career: Blackpool (1975 - appr, Aug 1976 - pro), Leeds United (£100,000 - Sept 1979), Bolton Wanderers (£40,000 - Oct 1981), Derby County (July 1985), TOWN (Nov 1986 - loan), Bolton Wanderers (July 1987), Cardiff City (£15,000 - Nov 1989)

Effective left-sided midfield player who was loaned to the "Stags" during the same season that he assisted Derby to the Second Division title. Gained two caps for Eire through parental qualification when he was at Leeds

1986-87   6(0) apps   0 gls (Loan)
Honours: Eire under 21 and full international (Leeds).

CHAPMAN Gary A

1990 Forward   5' 10"   12st 0lbs (1991)
b: Leeds, 1 May 1964
Career: Ossett Town, Frickley Athletic, Bradford City (Aug 1988), Notts County (Sept 1989 - loan, £15,000 Feb 1990 - permanent), TOWN (Oct 1990 - loan), Exeter City (£10,000 - Sept 1991), Torquay United (F.T. Feb 1993), Darlington (F.T. Aug 1993)

Didn't quite make the grade at Meadow Lane and his ability to score goals did not take off until he joined the "Quakers".

1990-91   6(0) apps   0 gls (Loan)

CHAPMAN (Roy) Clifford

1961 - 65 Centre/Inside Forward   6' 1"   13st 3lbs (1960)
b: Kingstanding, Birmingham, 18 March 1934
d: March 1984
Career: Kingstanding Youths, Kynoch Works, Birmingham County F A, Aston Villa (Nov 1951 - am, Feb 1952 - pro), Lincoln City (£6,000 - Nov 1957), TOWN (£10,000 - Aug 1961), Lincoln City (£5,000 - Jan 1965), Port Vale (Aug 1967), Chester (June 1969), Stafford Rangers (Oct 1969 - player/manager), Stockport County (Sept 1975 - manager), Stafford Rangers (Aug 1977 - manager to Feb 1980), Walsall Sportsco - 1980 - manager)

Roy Chapman's playing career was during the period when football was undergoing many changes and it would probably be more correct to describe him as a striker. Nevertheless, his ability as a goalscorer was superb, netting over 200 in league matches. In three and a half seasons with Mansfield he scored many more goals than he obtained with any of his other clubs and that included two spells with Lincoln. His pairing with Wagstaff was one of the most lethal attacking forces in the Third and Fourth Divisions. His son Lee has also made a name for himself as a goalgetter and is currently with Ipswich. He was leading scorer six times with three clubs and interestingly enough, when he achieved his highest total in a season,(Town 1962-63, 30 goals - he was not the highest scorer -

that honour fell to Ken Wagstaff with 34 ! Chapman died from a heart attack whilst playing in a five a side game. He lies Fifth in Mansfield's list of League goalscorers and Eighth overall.

1961-62	37 apps	20 gls	Leading Scorer
1962-63	44 "	30 "	
1963-64	36 "	19 "	
1964-65	19 "	9 "	

Honours: Division 4 Promotion 1963, Division 3 - 3rd 1965 (both Mansfield)

CHAPMAN (Samuel) Edward Campbell

1956 - 58 and 1961 - 64 Wing Half Back/Inside Forward
5' 9"   11st 4lbs
b: Belfast, 16 February 1938

44

Career: Glenavon (c/s 1955 - am), Manchester United (1955 - am), Shamrock Rovers (Feb 1956), TOWN (Aug 1956), Portsmouth (Feb 1958), TOWN (Dec 1961 - suspended sine die May 1964), Stafford Rangers (c/s 1979 to May 1980), Crewe Alexandra (1983 - coach), Wolverhampton Wanderers (chief scout, Aug to Sept 1985 - caretaker manager, Nov 1985 to Aug 1986 - manager), Leicester City (1989 - chief scout).

Sammy Chapman was a wing half who could score goals, netting 40 during his two spells with the "Stags". Secured when playing for a League of Ireland side, he gained International "B" honours whilst with the club - the first player to do so. Sadly, he was deeply involved in the infamous "Fixed Odds" bribery and betting scandal which did not come into the open until the summer of 1964 and this resulted in him being suspended for life and also receiving a six months prison sentence at Nottingham Assizes in January 1965. Reinstated by the F A in 1972 under the recently introduced "Seven Year" rule, Chapman was eventually lured out his enforced obscurity, playing one season in the Alliance Premier League before moving into the administrative side of the game.

1956-57	21 apps	10 gls	
1957-58	29 "	15 "	
1961-62	20 "	8 "	
1962-63	40 "	5 "	
1963-64	45 "	2 "	

Honours: Northern Ireland Youth Inter-national (Glenavon). Northern Ireland 'B' International, Division 4 promotion 1963 (both Mansfield).

CHAPMAN Thomas
1930 - 31 Inside Forward
b: c1910
Career: TOWN (Jan 1931 - am)

1930-31	1 app	0 gls	Midland League

CHAPPELL Archibald
1930 - 31 Inside Right   5' 10"   11st 0
b: Hucknall, Notts., 14 April 1910
d: Hucknall, Notts., 23 June 1977
Career: Hucknall Boys (1924), Hucknall Church, Sunderland (Mar 1927 - am), Norwich City (Jun 1928), Charlton Athletic (Jun 1929), TOWN (May 1930), Guildford City (c/s 1931), Walsall (Aug 1932)

Talented as a schoolboy, but did not quite make the grade at a higher level. Norwich was the only side for which he appeared in the top flight playing in 10 games and scoring 2 goals.

1930-31	8 apps	2 gls	Midland League

CHARLES Stephen
1987 - 93 Midfield   5' 9"   11st 12lbs (1990)
b: Sheffield, 10 May 1960
Career: Sheffield Schoolboys, Sheffield Wednesday (am - c/d 1974), Sheffield University (c/s 1978), Sheffield United (Jan 1980), Wrexham (Nov 1984), TOWN (£15,000 - Aug 1987), Scunthorpe United (Nov 1992 - loan), Scarborough (Feb 1993).

An experienced player when he joined Mansfield, Steve Charles was a good servant to the club and always dependable. Enjoyed league football with the "Blades" whilst still at University where he ultimately gained two degrees - in mathematics and marketing. Became regular penalty taker at Field Mill - a tradition he has carried on at Scarborough and he rarely misses.

1987-88	46(0) apps	12 gls	Leading Scorer
1988-89	45(1) "	7 "	
1989-90	42(1) "	7 "	
1990-91	36(3) "	4 "	
1991-92	40(0) "	6 "	
1992-93	22(1) "	3 "	

Honours: England Schoolboy International (U/15), Division 4 Champions 1982 (Sheffield United). Welsh Cup Winners 1986 (Wrexham). Notts F A County Cup Winners 1988 & 89, Division 4 promotion 1992 (all Mansfield).

CHEESEBROUGH Albert
1965 - 67 Outside Left   5' 7"   11st 4lbs
b: Burnley, 17 January 1935
Career: Burnley (Jan 1952), Leicester City (£19,775 - June 1959), Port Vale (July 1963), TOWN (July 1965)

Possessor of a powerful left foot shot, "Cheesy" formed a strong left wing partnership with Irish International, Jimmy McIlroy at Burnley and gained an England U/23 cap in 1956. On the losing side in the F A Cup Final of 1961, his career was terminated by a broken leg at Mansfield in 1967.

1965-66	20(0) apps	0 gls
1966-67	4(0) "	0 "

Honours: England U/23 International (Burnley), F A Cup Finalists 1961 (Leicester).

CHESSELL Samuel

1942 - 54 Full Back 5' 9" 11st 6lbs
b: Shirebrook, Derbys., 9 July 1921
Career: Shirebrook Warren Terrace, Welbeck C W, TOWN (1941 - am, Sept 1945 - pro), Spalding United (Aug 1954).

A wonderful servant to Mansfield Town, Sammy Chessell first played for the "Stags" during the war years as a forward, subsequently forming excellent full back partnerships in turn with Ernie Bramley, Dai Jones and Don Bradley. He broke a leg in December 1951, but returned successfully to the side by the following April. After leaving the game Chessell worked at Shirebrook Colliery and is still living in retirement in the village.

WW II	68 apps	10 gls
1946-47	35 "	1 "
1947-48	22 "	1 "
1948-49	36 "	2 "
1949-50	32 "	0 "
1950-51	46 "	0 "
1951-52	24 "	0 "
1952-53	45 "	3 "
1953-54	16 "	0 "

Honours: Division 3 (North) Runners Up 1951 (Mansfield)

CHRISTIE Trevor

1989 - 91 Forward 6' 1½" 12st 0lbs (1991)
b: Cresswell, Northumberland, 28 February 1959
Career: Leicester City (Sept 1975 - appr, Dec 1976 - pro), Notts County (June 1979), Nottingham Forest (£175,000 - July 1984), Derby County (£100,000 - Feb 1985), Manchester City (Aug 1986), Walsall (£30,000 - Oct 1986), TOWN (£30,000 - Mar 1989), Kettering Town (F.T. July 1991), V S Rugby (Mar 1992), Hucknall Town (Nov 1992), Arnold Town (Mar 1995).

Whilst Christie was something of a disappointment with Forest and Manchester City, he was successful with his other clubs, scoring almost 150 goals in the Football League. He carried on playing in non-league football until Oct 1994, when his career ended due to an achilles tendon injury.

1988-89	12(0) apps	1 gl
1989-90	43(2) "	13 "
1990-91	33(2) "	10 "

Honours: Division 3 promotion 1986 (Derby), Division 3 promotion 1988 (Walsall)

CHRISTOPHER Paul A

1973 - 74 Forward 5' 9" 11st 3lbs (1974)
b: Poole, Dorset, 19 June 1954
Career: A F C Bournemouth (Jan 1971 - appr, Nov 1971 - pro), TOWN (July 1973 to May 1974)

1973-74	7(1) apps	1 gl

CLARK Jeremiah

1925 - 26 Inside Forward/Wing Half Back
b: Warsop, Notts.
Career: Newark Town, TOWN (Aug 1925)

1925-26	1 app	0 gls	Midland League

CLARK Joseph

1919 - 20 Inside Forward
Career: Blackpool, TOWN (Sept 1919)

1919-20	1 app	0 gls	Central Alliance

CLARK Martin J

1990 - 92 Midfield 5' 9" 10st 11lbs
b: Uddingston, Lothian, 13 October 1968
Career: Hamilton Accademicals (c/s 1986), Clyde (c/s 1987), Nottingham Forest (£125,000 - Feb 1989), Falkirk (Sept to Oct 1989 - loan), TOWN (Mar to May 1990 - loan, £40,000 + £10,000 after 35 appearances - Aug 1990 perm), Partick Thistle (£20,000 - July 1992), Falkirk, (1994), Clyde (c/s 1994).

An influential member of Clyde's team for two seasons prompted Brian Clough to pay a large fee for him, but he failed to make the first XI at the

City Ground and was loaned out in turn to Falkirk and the "Stags", culminating in George Foster buying him for £50,000. He did not, however, shine as expected at Field Mill and was transferred to Partick Thistle at a loss after two seasons. Son of John Clark, who was an influential member of Celtic's European Cup winning side of 1967.

1989-90	14(0) apps	1 gl	(Loan)
1990-91	24(0) "	0 "	
1991-92	7(2) "	0 "	

CLARK Peter J
1960 - 61 Half Back   5' 9½"   11st 0lbs
b: Doncaster, 22 January 1938
Career: Wolverhampton Wanderers (1954 - appr, Mar 1955 - pro), Doncaster Rovers (July 1959), TOWN (F.T. June 1960), Hednesford Town (c/s 1961), Stourbridge, Stockport County (Aug 1965), Crewe Alexandra (July 1966)

1960-61	2 apps	0 gls

CLARKE George B
1921 - 23 Outside Left
b: Bolsover, Derbys., 24 July 1900
d: 11 February 1977
Career: Welbeck Colliery, TOWN (c/s 1921), Aston Villa (£350 - Dec 1922), Crystal Palace (July 1925), Queens Park Rangers (July 1933), Folkestone (1934)

A lithe, speedy winger who attracted the interest of Villa mid way through his second season with Mansfield and they paid what was for a non-league club the not inconsiderable fee of £350 for his services. His career languished at Villa Park however and he only made the league team on one occasion. Moving on to Selhurst Park, his future really took off and he was a regular for eight seasons before moving on. A miner at Welbeck Colliery when the "Stags" signed him, he was the elder brother of inside left, Horace (below).

1921-22	42 apps	9 gls	Midland League
1922-23	17 "	3 "	

Honours: Mansfield Hospital Charity Cup Winners 1922 (Mansfield), Division 3 (South) Runners-up 1929 and 1931 (Crystal Palace)

CLARKE Horace
1922 - 23 Inside Left
b: Bolsover, Derbys., c 1902
Career: TOWN (Mar 1923 - am)

Partnered his elder brother (above) on the left wing towards the end of the 1922-23 season. Played cricket for Mansfield Colliery too.

1922-23	6 apps	3 gls	Midland League

CLARKE Nicholas J
1991 - 94 Defender   5' 11"   13st 7lbs (1991)
b: Willenhall, Staffs., 20 August 1967
Career: Wolverhampton Wanderers (1983 - appr, Feb 1985 - pro), TOWN (£25,000 - Dec 1991), Chesterfield (Feb 1993 - loan), Preston North End (Aug 1993 - trial), Doncaster Rovers (Dec 1993 - loan), Bromsgrove Rovers (Feb 1994), Preston North End (1994 - loan).

After being a regular in the Wolves first team between 1985 and 1987, Nicky Clarke fell out of favour and George Foster paid a fee for him part way through Town's promotion season as extra cover. He made only a handful of appearances and thereafter was out of favour, making several loan excursions and playing trials before he settled in with Conference side, Bromsgrove.

1991-92	16(0) apps	1 gls
1992-93	9(3) "	1 "
1993-94	14(1) "	3 "

Honours: Division 4 promotion 1992 (Mansfield). Bob Lord Trophy Winners 1995 (Bromsgrove).

CLARKE (Raymond) Charles
1974 -76 Forward   5' 11"   11st 0lbs (1975)
b: Hackney, London, 25 September 1952
Career: Islington Schools, Tottenham Hotspur (Oct 1969), Swindon Town (£8,000 - June 1973), TOWN (£8,000 - Aug 1974), Sparta Rotterdam, Holland (£90,000 - July 1976), Ajax Holland (£80,000 - c/s 1977), F C Bruges Belgium (c/s 1978), Brighton & Hove Albion (£200,000 - Oct 1979), Newcastle United (£180,000 - July 1980).

Ray Clarke cost quite a sizeable sum when he joined the "Stags" after playing in only 15 league matches with his previous clubs, but his scoring ability errupted at Mansfield where he averaged more than a goal every two games - sufficiently so for Sparta Rotterdam to be more than willing to pay what was Town's record transfer fee and the first sale of a player abroad too. After spending three years in the low countries, Clarke returned for another two years in England before an injury caused his retirement in 1981. Now a hotelier in the Isle of Man, having previously spent some time in East Anglia in the same trade.

1974-75	46(0) apps	28 gls	Leading Scorer
1975-76	45(0) "	24 "	" "

Honours: Islington Schoolboys, London Schoolboys, Middlesex Schoolboys, England Youth International. Division 4 Champions 1975 (Mansfield), Nederlands League Runners-Up 1978 (Ajax).

CLAYTON John (No.1)

1925 - 26 Right Half Back
b: Sheffield, 23 April 1904
Career: Anston Athletic, TOWN (c/s 1925 - am), Frickley Colliery (c/s 1926), Rotherham United (c/s 1927)

1925-26   3 apps   0 gls Midland League

CLAYTON John (No.2)

1933 - 34 Left Half Back
b: Mansfield, c1908
Career: Loughborough Corinthians (1927), Chesterfield (c/s 1929), Wrexham (c/s 1930), Carlisle United (c/s 1932), TOWN (c/s 1933), Grantham (c/s 1934)

Local born player that Mansfield missed as a youngster, the "Corries" snapping him up. Finished his career as he started it - in the Midland League.

1933-34 15 apps   1 gl
Honours: Welsh Cup Winners 1931 (Wrexham).

CLENSHAW (Leslie) James

1935 - 36 Outside Left   5' 6"   11st 5lbs (1935)
b: Southend on Sea, 1908
Career: Brewery Road School, Southend, Westcliff (am), Southend United (Aug 1924 - am, July 1925 - pro), Chelmsford (July 1925 - May 1926 - loan), Barrow (May 1934), TOWN (c/s 1935), Chelmsford (c/s 1936)

Experienced winger who had his best years at Southend - nine seasons of them !

1935-36   27 apps   6 gls

CLIFFORD George

1931 - 32 Full Back
b: New Sawley, Notts., 10 February, 1896
Career: Sutton Junction (c/s 1923), Portsmouth (May 1924), TOWN £250 - July 1931), Ilkeston United (c/s 1932)

"Ginger" Clifford was a mature 27 year old when he began his professional football career with Sutton Junction in the Central Alliance. Within a year he was snapped up by Portsmouth and moved almost immediately into their league team, where he carved out an illustrious career playing in 175 matches and assisting the club to promotion in 1927. He cost Town a sizeable fee for a 35 year old for their first season in the Football League, moving back to the Central Alliance with Ilkeston United after just one season.

1931-32   39 apps   0 gls
Honours: Division 3 (South) Championship & F A Charity Shield runners up 1927 - Professionals v Amateurs (both Portsmouth)

CLIFFORD Mark

1994 onwards Defender   5' 8"   10st 4lbs (1994)
b: Nottingham, 11 September 1977
Career: Nottingham Forest (1992 - assoc schoolboy), TOWN (Aug 1994 - appr).

Debut for "Stags" in the last match of the 1994-95 season, when still a 17 year old apprentice.

1994-95   1(0) app   0 gls

CLOUGH John H

1932 - 33 Goalkeeper 6' 1"   13st 0lbs (1932)
b: Murton, Co Durham, 13 May 1902
Career: Fatfield Albion (1921), Middlesbrough (Sept 1922), Bradford P A (July 1926), TOWN (£250 - Aug 1932), Brentford (£100 - June 1933 - £100), Rotherham United (F.T. c/s 1934), TOWN (Aug 1937 - asst trainer, May 1939 - trainer to June 1949).

Jack Clough came to Mansfield with vast experience in First and Second Division football with his former clubs. After one season at Field Mill, he was unsettled and asked to be put on the open to transfer list - successfully appealing to the F A in May 1933 to get his fee reduced. Brentford, who were in the middle of their run of promotions from the Third Division to the First in three seasons, signed him, but released him at the end of the season as he wished to leave the South. He finished his playing career by spending three good seasons with the "Millers" before returning to Field Mill as Assistant Trainer to Jack Poole in the summer of 1937. Appointed full trainer in May 1939, he served the "Stags" loyally in this capacity until 1949. His playing days were however, not quite over. He made one appearance during WW II, when Mansfield were the visitors at Fellows Park. The Walsall 'keeper failed to arrive, so at the last minute Jack volunteered to stand in for him against his own club. Town lost 4 - 2 with Gilbert Alsop netting all four for the home side - Clough was then within ten days of his 42nd birthday and presumably the Walsall trainer dealt with both team's injuries that day! Won the Military Medal and bar in WWI.

1932-33   30 apps   0 gls
Honours: Division 3 (North) Championship 1928 (Bradford). Midland League Championship 1932 (Bradford)

COATES David P

1960 - 64 Inside Forward   5' 10"   11st 7lbs
b: Shiney Row, Co Durham, 11 April, 1935
Career: Fatfield Juniors, Shiney Row, Hull City (Oct 1952), TOWN (£1,000 - Mar 1960), Notts County (£2,250 - July 1964 - player, youth coach - 1967), Aston Villa (Dec 1968 - asst coach), Luton Town (Jan 1978 - coach)

Struck up a wonderful partnership with Ken Wagstaff and was responsible for many of his goals. A fine constructive inside forward, he became involved in the coaching side of the game after he hung up his boots.

1959-60	5 apps	0 gls
1960-61	38 "	5 "
1961-62	40 "	3 "
1962-63	40 "	5 "
1963-64	36 "	4 "

Honours: Division 3 Runners-Up 1959 (Hull), Division 3 Promotion 1963 (Mansfield)

COCHRANE Colin
1947 - 48 Inside Left
b: Sutton in Ashfield, 16 August 1921
Career: TOWN (Sept 1947)

1947-48	1 app	0 gls

COFFEY Michael J J
1978 - 79 Midfield 5' 9" 9st 8lbs
b: Liverpool, 29 September 1958
Career: Everton (1974 - appr, July 1976 - pro), TOWN (July 1978)

1978-79	2(1) apps	0 gls

COLEMAN (John) Henry
1966 - 68 Half Back 5' 7" 10st 10lbs (1968)
b: Hucknall, Notts., 3 April 1946
Career: Juniors, Nottingham Forest (Mar 1963), TOWN (Aug 1966 - trial, F.T. - Sept 1966), York City (July 1968)

Rather light weight player who was with the "Stags" for just two terms.

1966-67	30(0) apps	0 gls
1967-68	13(0) "	1 "

COLEMAN Simon
1983 - 89 Defender 6' 0" 10st 8lbs (1987)
b: Worksop, 13 March 1968
Career: TOWN (1983 - appr, July 1985 - pro), Middlesbrough (Sept 1989 - £600,000), Manchester City (1991 - loan), Derby County (£300,000 - Aug 1991), Sheffield Wednesday (Nov 1983 - loan, £250,000 - perm Jan 1994), Bolton Wanderers (£350,000 - Oct 1994).

Simon Coleman was one of the many products from the youth policy introduced by Ian Greaves. Made his debut at 19 and sufficiently impressed 'Boro to pay what is still Mansfield's record transfer fee when he was only 21. Has not quite fulfilled his original promise but is nevertheless a workmanlike defender who may not yet have found his true niche. Was a regular member of the "Trotters" 1994-95 promotion team, but had the misfortune to miss the play-off final at Wembley due to injury.

1986-87	2(0) apps	0 gls
1987-88	44(0) "	2 "
1988-89	45(0) "	5 "
1989-90	5(0) "	0 "

Honours: Notts F A County Cup Winners 1988 & 1989 (both Mansfield), Football League Division 2 XI (Derby), Division 1 promotion - via play-offs 1995 (Bolton).

COLES David A

1983 Goalkeeper 6' 0"   12st 0lbs (1988)
b: Wandsworth, London, 15 June 1964
Career: Birmingham City (1980 - appr, Apr 1982 - pro), TOWN (Mar 1983), Aldershot (F.T. Aug 1983), Newport County (Jan 1988 - loan H J K Helsinki (1988). Colchester United (Aug 1988 - trial), Crystal Palace (Sept 1988 - trial), Brighton & Hove Albion (Feb 1989 - N/C), Aldershot (July 1989), Fulham (Aug 1991)

A much travelled player, Aldershot seemed to be the only place where he settled for any length of time. Dropped out of League football when the "Shots" gave him a free transfer in May 1992.

1982-83   3 apps   0 gls

COLLIER Austin

1938 - 39 Wing Half or Full Back   5' 7"   12st 0lbs (1938)
b: Dewsbury, South Yorks., 24 July 1914
Career: Upton Colliery (1935), Frickley Colliery (Aug 1937), TOWN (May 1938), York City (F.T. May 1939), Queen of the South (Oct 1946), Rochdale (Apr 1947), Halifax Town (Nov 1947), Goole Town (Aug 1948), Scarborough (July 1949), Halifax Town (asst trainer - 1950 to 1955)

"Ossie" Collier was signed by manager Poole from Midland League side Frickley Collery at the same time as Alf Somerfield. Rather stocky for a wing half he was somewhat lacking in speed and was given a free transfer at the end of his first season. Played for a time after the war, finishing back in the Midland League. During WW II "guested" for Clapton Orient, York City, Reading, Leeds United, Partick Thistle, Celtic, Third Lanark, East Fife, Aberdeen and Hibernian. When stationed in Italy with the H L I in 1944, played regularly for the British Army team with Matt Busby.

1938-39   21 apps   0 gls
Honours: Notts F A County Cup Winners 1939 (Mansfield)

COLLINS (Arthur) Henry

1929 - 30 Goalkeeper
b: Smethwick, Birmingham, c1902
Career: Clay Cross, Derby County (Nov 1924), Brentford (Aug 1926), Scarborough (Aug 1927), TOWN (Aug 1929)

Only league appearances were with Brentford where he made four.

1929-30   32 apps   0 gls   Midland League

COLLINS Roderick

1986 - 87 Forward   6' 1"   12st 8lbs (1987)
b: Dublin, 7 August 1961
Career: Bohemians, Athlone Town, Drogheda United, Dundalk, TOWN (£17,000 - Jan 1986), Cambridge United (Aug 1987 - trial), Newport County (Aug 1987), Cheltenham Town (F.T. Sept 1988), Shamrock Rovers (1989), Sligo Rovers (c/s 1991), Crusaders (Nov 1991), Bohemians (Nov 1993 to Dec 1993), Bangor (May 1994)

Ian Greaves signed Rod Collins with high hopes for his future, but sadly they did not materialise and he quickly moved on to a string of clubs, moving with great frequency.

1985-86   7(5) apps   0 gls
1986-87   4(0) "   1 "
Honours: Ulster Cup Winners 1994 (Crusaders).

CONGRIEVE Frederick

1914 - 20 Inside Right
b: c1893
Career: Newhall Swifts (1912), TOWN (c/s 1914), Newark Town (1920)

1914-15 N K apps 1 gl Notts & Derbys League
1915-16 N K   "   9 "   Central Alliance
1919-20 14   "   6 "   "   "
Honours: Central Alliancs - Subsidiary Competition Championship 1916 & Central Alliance Championship 1920 (both Mansfield).

COOK Ronald

1937 - 38 Inside Forward   5' 7"   10st 8lb (1937)
b: South Normanton, Derbys., 23 September 1917
Career: Brunts School, Ripley Town (1933 - am), Sutton Town (1935 - am), Heanor Town (Oct 1936 - am), TOWN (Jan 1937 - am, May 1937 - pro), Huthwaite C W S (c/s 1938 - permit player, reverting to amateur status)

Although Ron Cook only played in a couple of league matches for the "Stags" he can at least claim to have played alongside the renowned Teddy Harston! After spending 6½ years in the Army in WW II, during which he played in a number of Services matches both home and abroad, he retired from competitive football upon being demobbed in 1946. Joining the newly created British Rail, he rose to be Area Transport Manager before retirement. Cook now lives in retirement in Sutton in Ashfield.

1936-37   2 apps   1 gl

COOK Trevor

1973 - 74 Forward
Career: TOWN (1972 - appr, July 1974 - pro)

1973-74   1(0) app   0 gl

COOKE A

1927 - 28 and 1928 - 29 Inside Left
b: Sutton in Ashfield, Notts.
Career: TOWN (c/s 1927 - am), Sutton Town (c/s 1928 - am), TOWN Feb 1929 - am)

Had two brief spells with Mansfield, the second when he was called in from service with the "Snipes" to help out over an injury crisis.

| 1927-28 | 4 apps | | 1 gl | Midland League |
| 1928-29 | 2 " | | 1 " | " " |

COOKE Edwin (Richard)

1922 - 23 and 1929 - 31 Wing Half Back
b: Kirkby in Ashfield, Notts., c1905
Career: Kirkby Colliery, TOWN (Nov 1922 - am), Barnsley (July 1923), Brentford (July 1924), Grantham (c/s 1926), TOWN (June 1929)

The youngest of three brothers who all played league football - George (Mansfield - see below) and Bobby (Accrington) being the others.

1922-23	4 apps		0 gls	Midland League
1929-30	5 "	0 "	"	"
1930-31	1 "	0 "	"	"

Honours: Byron Cup Winners & Bayley Cup Winners 1930 (both Mansfield).

COOKE (George) Henry

1928 - 29 Outside Left 5' 6½" 11st 4lbs (1928)
b: Clowne, Derbys., 16 April 1902
d: Chesterfield, 6 March 1976
Career: Creswell White Star, Bolsover Town, Bolsover Colliery, Chesterfield (Feb 1921 - trial), Shirebrook (Aug 1921), Norwich City (May 1923), Portsmouth (July 1924), Southend United (May 1925), Wigan Borough (Aug 1926), TOWN (May 1928), Bradford P A (May 1929), Connah's Quay (Aug 1930), Grantham (Jan 1931).

The middle brother of the three footballing Cookes (see Richard above), George was something of a teenage progeny, playing for Bolsover Town when he was only 16! A vastly experienced player when he joined the "Stags", he was a member of the famous "egg and milk" Cup team that met Arsenal, having beaten Wolves at Molineux.

| 1928-29 | 46 apps | 14 gls |

Honours: Midland League Championship & Mansfield Hospital Charity Cup 1929 (both Mansfield)

COOKE Robert L

1975 - 78 Forward 5' 9" 10st 8lbs (1980)
b: Rotherham, 16 February 1957

Career: TOWN (1973 - appr, Feb 1975 - pro), Grantham (c/s 1978), Peterborough United (May 1980), Luton Town (loan), Cambridge United (Feb 1983), Brentford (Dec 1984 - loan, Jan 1985 - permanent), Millwall (Dec 1987), Kettering Town (1989).

A much travelled footballer who blossomed out after Mansfield released him.

| 1976-77 | 3(6) apps | 1 gl |
| 1977-78 | 4(2) " | 0 " |

Honours: England International - semi pro (Kettering).

COOKE Thomas V

1934 - 36 Centre Half Back 5' 11½" 12st 0lbs
b: Melton Mowbray, Leics., 1916
Career: Sheepbridge, TOWN (May 1934 - am, Mar 1935 - pro), Bournemouth & Boscombe Athletic (July 1936), Luton Town, Sutton Town (1950).

An ex pit boy who also played for Bradford City as a WW II guest.

| 1934-35 | 7 apps | 0 gls |
| 1935-36 | 6 " | 0 " |

Honours: Bass Charity Vase Winners 1935 (Mansfield).

COOLE William

1948 - 53 Outside Right 5' 7½" 10st 0lbs
b: Manchester, 27 January 1925
Career: Royal Navy, TOWN (Jan 1948), Notts County (£5,000 - Oct 1953), Barrow (July 1956).

Billy Coole was much loved by the "Stags" supporters and they were numbed when he moved to Meadow Lane, having appeared to be firmly established after 5½ years at Field Mill.

Originally an inside forward, Town converted him into an ouside right. Fleet of foot and able to beat his man, he was a very effective winger indeed. In 1950-51 season he was the club's leading scorer - as a winger - no mean performance. Signed by Mansfield when he was demobbed after four years in the Royal Navy.

1947-48	8 apps	1 gl	
1948-49	5 "	0 "	
1949-50	41 "	8 "	
1950-51	44 "	16 "	Leading Scorer
1951-52	37 "	6 "	
1952-53	35 "	3 "	
1953-54	12 "	1 "	

Honours: Division 3 North Runners Up 1951 (Mansfield)

COOLING Roy
1947 - 50 Inside Forward   5' 7½"   11st 6lbs
b: Barnsley, 9 December 1921
Career: Mitchells's M W, Barnsley (Mar 1942), TOWN (Sept 1947)

A rugged, hard grafting inside forward who had appeared in Barnsley's Second Division side. An ex miner, he had started his career at Oakwell during the war years when he also "guested" with Bradford City.

1947-48	33 apps	7 gls
1948-49	29 "	7 "
1949-50	3 "	0 "

COOPER James E
1964 - 65 Forward   5' 9½"   11st 7lbs
b: Chester, 19 January 1942
Career: Juniors, Chester (Sept 1959), Southport (June 1962), Blackpool (July 1963), TOWN (F.T. May 1964), Crewe Alexandra (July 1965)

1964-65	7 apps	4 gls

COOPER
1929 - 30 Goalkeeper
Career: TOWN (1929)

Young reserve 'keeper whose only senior appearance was in the Hospital Cup winning team during his only season with the club.

1929-30	0 apps	0 gls

Midland League Honours: Mansfield Hospital Charity Cup Winners 1930 (Mansfield)

COPESTAKE Oliver F P
1946 - 47 Inside Forward
b: Mansfield, 1 September 1921
Career: Church Warsop, TOWN (Jan 1946)

Played fairly consistently during the disastrous first post war season and was not retained at the close. Had played for Dukeries Schoolboys in 1935 and was still turning out for Heanor Town as late as 1957. Made his debut during the last wartime season.

WW II	16 apps	4 gls
1946-47	33 "	7 "

Honours: Dukeries Schoolboys 1935

COTTAM John B
1920 - 21 Outside Right
b: Langwith, Notts., c1900
Career: Notts County (c/s 1919), Shirebrook (Dec 1919), TOWN (c/s 1920).

Jackie Cottam was a rugged winger signed afer a season shared with both teams of "Magpies".

1920-21	19 apps	1 gl	Central Alliance

Honours: Central Alliance runners up 1921 (Mansfield)

COTTAM John E
1972 Defender   6' 0"   10st 12lbs (1971)
b: Warsop, Notts., 5 June 1950
Career: Nottingham Forest (1966 - appr, Apr 1968 - pro), TOWN (Nov to Dec 1972 - loan), Lincoln City (Nar 1973 - loan), Chesterfield (Aug 1976), Chester (July 1979), Scarborough (c/s 1982 - player manager to c/s 1984), Local N/L football (c/s 1984 to 1987)

John Cottam only played in a couple of matches during a month's loan spell at Field Mill, but did enjoy considerable success with Forest, Chesterfield and Chester. Was player-manager of Scarborough for two years in the early 1980s when they were still a non league side.

1972-73	2(0) apps	1 gl	(Loan)

COUPLAND Clifford A
1923 - 25 Right Half Back   5' 8½"   11st 10lbs (1924)
b: Grimsby, 29 May 1900
d: 30 January 1969
Career: Haycroft Rovers - Grimsby (1917), Grimsby Town (Jan 1920), TOWN (June 1923), Manchester City (£725 - March 1925), Grimsby Town (July 1927), Caernarvon Town (1928), Sittingbourne, Crystal Palace (Feb 1931)

A fine constructive wing half who was a key member of Town's successive Midland League championship teams. Snapped up by Manchester City in the Spring of 1925, he went straight into their First Division XI, but had drifted back into non league football by 1928.

1923-24	41 apps	2 gls	Midland League	
1924-25	23 "	6 "	"	"

Honours: Midland League Championship 1924 and 1925 (Mansfield)

COX Brian R
1988 - 90 Goalkeeper 6' 1"   13st 10lbs (1986)
b: Sheffield, 7 May 1961
Career: Sheffield Wednesday (1977 - appr, Feb 1979 - pro), Huddersfield Town (Mar 1982), TOWN (£25,000 - Aug 1988), Hartlepool United (Aug 1990 to c/s 1991).

Tall goalkeeper who gave his best performances when at Leeds Road. Fell out of favour part way into his second season at Mansfield and had to give way to Andy Beasley.

1988-89	39 apps	0 gls
1989-90	15 "	0 "

Honours: Notts F A County Cup Winners 1989 (Mansfield)

COX J
1923 - 24 Outside Right
Career: Aston Villa 1921), TOWN (c/s 1923), Frickley Colliery (c/s 1924)

1923-24   2 apps   0 gls Midland League

CRAWFORD Alan P
1973 Forward   5' 8"   9st 10lbs (1987)
b: Rotherham, 30 October 1953
Career: Rotherham United (Oct 1971 - appr, June 1972 - pro), TOWN (Jan 1973 - loan), Chesterfield (Aug 1979), Bristol City (F.T. Aug 1982), Exeter City (F.T. July 1985 to May 1987)

Played for a great number of clubs but never managed to command a regular place apart from three seasons at Rotherham , his best being 1976-77, when he was leading scorer with 23 goals.

1972-73   1(1) apps   0 gls   (Loan)

CRAWFORD P Graeme
1971 - 72 Goalkeeper 6' 2"   13st 0lbs (1978)
b: Falkirk, 7 August 1947
Career: East Stirlingshire), Sheffield United (Sept 1968), TOWN (July 1971 - loan), York City (Oct 1971 - loan, Nov 1971 - perm), Scunthorpe United (Aug 1977), York City (Jan 1980), Rochdale (Sept 1980), Scarborough (c/s 1983 to 1984 - rtd), Goole Town (Sept 1989).

Had a great run at York, where he played in 235 games and Scunthorpe - 104. Five years after retirement, at the age of 42, he was persuaded to play in one F A Cup tie for Goole when their regular 'keeper was injured.

1971-72   2 apps   0 gls   (Loan)

CRAWSHAW (Harold) William Stanley
1937 - 38 Centre Forward   5' 11½"   11st 0lbs (1938)
b: Prestwich, Manchester, 18 February 1912
Career: Newton Heath Loco, Ashington (c/s 1932), Portsmouth (Feb 1935), TOWN (£225 - Aug 1937), Nottingham Forest (£1,500 + Gardiner - July 1938)

Signed from Portsmouth as replacement for Harston, recently transferred to Liverpool, Crawshaw was an instant success and emulated his predecessor by scoring a hat trick in his first league game for the "Stags", the repeat of a similar performance in the pre-season practice match. He was transferred to Forest for a large fee, being their top scorer in the final pre-war season - also having netted a hat trick in the "Reds" pre-season practice match. Leading scorer in Division 3 South and for Mansfield in 1937-38, he played in a few games for Oldham during WW II. His elder brother Richard was an inside forward in the Manchester City team during the 1920s. Whilst working at Airspeeds on aircraft production in 1942, he recommended a works player, Peter Harris to his old club Portsmouth. In the immediate post-war years, Harris became an outstanding right winger with Pompey and won three England caps.

1937-38   41 apps   25 gls Leading Scorer
Honours: London Combination Championship 1936 and 3rd 1937 (both Portsmouth), Notts F A County Cup Winners 1938 (Mansfield)

CROFT Charles
1947 - 50 Outside Left/Left Half Back   5' 8"   11st 0lbs
b: Thornhill, Dewsbury, Yorks., 26 November 1918
Career: Huddersfield Town (Jun 1938 - am, May 1939 - pro), TOWN (May 1947), Boston (c/s 1950 to 1954).

A left winger with the "Terriers", Charlie Croft was soon converted into a wing half by Roy Goodall and this coincided with the emergence of Harry Oscroft on the flank. A determined and resourceful player he gave sterling service to Mansfield until he had to give way to Jack Lewis in 1949. Guest player for Brighton during WW II, when he was a Sergeant Instructor in the Army.

1947-48   40 apps   5 gls
1948-49   38   "   0 "
1949-50   7   "   0 "

CROMACK Victor
1946 - 47 Goalkeeper
b: Mansfield, 17 March 1920
Career: TOWN (Jan 1946), Sutton Town (c/s 1947)

Signed by Mansfield upon his demob from the forces, Vic Cromack held his place in the first post-war season until displaced by Dennis Wright.

WW II   17 apps   0 gls
1946-47   10   "   0 "

CROOKES George
1926 - 27 Goalkeeper
Career: TOWN (c/s 1926 - am), Staveley Town (c/s 1927)

1926-27   7 apps   0 gls
Honours: Notts Senior Cup Winners & Byron Cup Winners 1927 (both Mansfield).

CROPPER Reginald W
1932 - 33 Outside Right   5' 8"   11st 6lbs (1932)
b: Brimington, Chesterfield, 21 January 1902
d: Chesterfield, 25 May 1942
Career: Matlock Town, Staveley Town, Watford (trial), Notts County (Nov 1924), Norwich City (July 1926), Guildford City (Sept 1928), Tranmere Rovers (Aug 1929), Guildford City (July 1930), Crystal Palace (Sep 1931), TOWN (Aug 1932 to May 1933).

After breaking a leg when at Notts in 1924, Reg Cropper only managed double figures of appearances with two of his clubs, Norwich and Tranmere, being leading scorer with the former during his first season there. His younger brother Arthur played for Clapton Orient and Gillingham in the 1930s and indeed both brothers were at Norwich together 1927-28. When serving in the Army during WW II, he was drafted in to play in four games for Southport during the 1941-42 season.

1932-33   6 apps   1 gl

CROWE (Charles) Alfred
1957 - 58 Wing Half Back   5' 10"   12st 0lbs
b: Byker, Northumberland, 30 October 1924
Career: Wallsend St Lukes, Heaton & Byker Juniors, Newcastle United (£10 - Oct 1944), TOWN (Feb 1957), Whitley Bay (manager).

A very experienced defender who joined Mansfield in the twilight of his career and rendered excellent service for two seasons. F A Cup medalist with Newcastle and played in a League representative match whilst at Field Mill. Later took over licenced premises in Newcastle whilst working in the civil service.

1956-57   13 apps   0 gls
1957-58   24   "   0 "
Honours: F A Cup Winners 1951, F A XI 1955 (both Newcastle).   Division 3 North XI 1957 (Mansfield).

CUMMINGS Thomas S
1962 - 63 Centre Half Back   5' 10"   12st 10lbs
b: Castletown, Nr Sunderland, 12 September 1928
Career: Stanley United, Hilton C W, Burnley (Oct 1947), TOWN (Mar 1963 - player manager to July 1967), Aston Villa (July 1967 - manager to Nov 1968), Burnley (scout), Sunderland (scout)

Tommy Cummings had been long established as a First Division centre half, with Burnley, for whom he played in 434 games, when he joined the "Stags" as Player Manager. Unlucky not to gain full international recognition, but did win "B" caps for England and Football League XI selection. A former chairman of the P F A, he only played in 10 matches for Mansfield, before hanging up his boots and concentrating solely on management.

1962-63   6 apps   0 gls
1963-64   4   "   0 gls
Honours: Division 1 Championship 1960, runners-up 1962, F A Cup, League Cup semi finalists & F A Charity Shield - shared 1961, F A Cup runners up 1962 (all Burnley).

CUNNINGHAM John
1984 - 86 Forward   5' 7"   10st 6lbs
b: Londonderry, 30 November 1966
Career: Oxford B C Londonderry, TOWN (Aug 1984), Derry City (Apr 1986), Sunderland (trial), Derry City, Bangor (Jan 1989), Omagh Town (July 1991), Cliftonville (May 1992), Coleraine (Dec 1992)

Young player who was recruited from Northern Ireland junior football but did not impress sufficiently and was released after 18 months to play in the Irish League.

1984-85   3(1) apps   0 gls
1985-86   0(0) "   0 "
Honours: Northern Ireland Youth International

CUPIT William W
1932 - 33 Outside Right   5' 7"   11st 0lbs
b: 1912
Career: Sutton Junction (c/s 1930), Luton Town (c/s 1931), TOWN (c/s 1932), Sutton Town (c/s 1933)

1932-33   2 apps   0 gls

CURRY (William) Morton
1965-68 Centre Forward   5' 9"   11st 9lbs
b: Newcastle on Tyne, 12 October 1935
d: Mansfield, 20 August 1990
Career: Juniors, Newcastle United (Oct 1953), Brighton & Hove Albion (£13,000 - July 1959), Derby County (£10,000 - Oct 1960), TOWN (£10,000 - Feb 1965), Chesterfield (£2,000 - Jan 1968), Boston (Jan 1969 - loan), Worksop Town (Jun 1969 - trainer), Boston (Feb 1971 - manager to May 1976), Sutton Town (May 1977 - manager -to May 1980).

Bought as replacement for Ken Wagstaff who had recently been transferred to Hull City and an established goalscoreer, Bill Curry made an immediate impact with a flurry of goals and was

soon taken to heart by the "Stags" faithful. Leading scorer in the two full seasons he spent with the club, he stayed in the area when his playing days were over and passed away at the age of 54. Leading scorer for Derby in 1960-61, 1961-62 and 1962-63, he also holds the distinction of having played and scored, in the first League match played under floodlights in the United Kingdom - for Newcastle v Portsmouth at Fratton Park on 22 February 1956.

1964-65   16 apps   15 gls
1965-66   36   "   14 "   Leading Scorer
1966-67   45   "   22 "   "   "
1967-68   5   "   2 "
Honours: England U/23 International (Newcastle), Division 3 - 3rd 1965 (Mansfield).

CURTIN Douglas J
1965 - 66 Outside Left
b: Cardiff, 15 September 1947
Career: Cardiff City (TOWN (Nov 1965)

1965-66   3(0) apps   0 gls
Honours: Welsh Schoolboy International

CURTIS George
1921 - 22 Inside Left
Career: TOWN (Apr 1923 - am).

1921-22   1 app   0 gls Midland League

CURTIS Robert D
1978 - 80 Defender   5' 9½"   11st 0lbs (1979)
b: Langwith, Notts., 25 January 1950
Career: Charlton Athletic (Feb 1967), TOWN (Feb 1978)

A vastly experienced, locally born defender who had made his name with Charlton, Bob Curtis moved into the forward line late in his career and remarkably was leading scorer in his first full season, albeit with only six goals !

1977-78	5(0) apps	0 gls	
1978-79	33(1) "	6 "	Leading Scorer
1979-80	31(3) "	1 "	

CUTHBERTSON John
1953 -54 Inside Left
b: Glasgow, 10 March 1932
Career: Juniors, TOWN (Oct 1953)

1953-54	3 apps	0 gls

CUTTS George H
1919 - 20 Goalkeeper
b: Hucknall, Notts., c1898
Career: TOWN (c/s 1919), Watford (c/s 1920), Sutton Town.

A key member of Town's first Central Alliance championship winning side, Cutts was signed by Watford of Division 3 South at the end of the season, but made few appearances for them before being released. His son, also a goalkeeper, made a single appearance for Nottingham Forest during the first season of WW II.

1919-20	27 apps	0 gls

Honours: Central Alliance Championship 1920 (Mansfield)

DAINES (Barry) Raymond
1983 - 84 Goalkeeper 5' 11½"   11st 8lbs (1976)
b: Witham, Essex, 30 September 1951
Career: Tottenham Hotspur (July 1968 - appr, Sept 1969 - pro), Bulova Hong Kong (Sept 1981), TOWN (N/C Oct 1983 to Mar 1984)

Barry Daines had to wait a long time before he got his chance at White Hart Lane, but when it came he grabbed it with both hands and was Spurs regular 'keeper for three seasons. Finished his career with short spells in Hong Kong and at Mansfield.

1983-84   21(0) apps 0 gls
Honours: Chelmsford, Mid-Essex and Essex Schoolboys, England Youth International

---

DALEY (Alan) James
1946 - 47 and 1953 - 56 Outside Left   5' 9"
11st 7lbs (1947)
b: Mansfield, 11 October 1927
Career: Pleasley B C, TOWN (Sept 1946), Hull City (July 1947), Bangor City (1948), Worksop Town (1949), Doncaster Rovers (Mar 1950), Peterborough United (Oct 1950), Boston (Mar 1951),
Scunthorpe United (July 1952), Corby Town (1953), TOWN (Nov 1953), Stockport County (Feb 1956), Crewe Alexandra (June 1958), Coventry City (Nov 1958), Cambridge United (Jan 1961), Burton Albion (1961), Sutton Town (1963)

"Digger" Daley, as he had been known from his schooldays, was a very widely travelled player and rarely stayed anywhere more than a season, his career encompassing some 14 clubs and one of them twice!   A fast direct winger who possessed a strong shot and was never afraid to have a shot at goal. Now lives in retirement at Bedford.

1946-47	0 apps	0 gls
1953-54	29 "	12 "
1954-55	41 "	12 "
1955-56	27 "	2 "

DALEY
1919 - 20 Outside Right
Career: TOWN (1919)

1919-20	2 apps	0 gls	Central Alliance

DALLISON Arthur R
1922 - 23 and 1928 - 30 Full Back
b: Sutton in Ashfield, c1901
d: Skegness, c1978
Career: Rotherham County, TOWN (May 1922), Sutton Town (c/s 1923), Newark Town (c/s 1925 to 1928), TOWN (c/s 1928), Sutton Town (Mar 1931)

A full back who had played in two games for Rotherham County in Division 2 before joining Mansfield. Rejoined the "Stags" five years later before finishing his career with Sutton Town. After his playing days were over he was employed at Huthwaite C W S, rising to the position of supervisor before retirement in 1966, when he moved to Skegness.

1922-23	34 apps	0 gls	Midland League	
1928-29	3 "	0 "	"	"
1929-30	34 "	0 "	"	"

Honours: Notts Senior Cup Winners 1923, Mansfield Hospital Charity Cup Winners 1930 (both Mansfield)

DALLMAN William
1938 - 48 Centre Half Back
b: Mansfield, 8 August 1918
Career: Bestwood Colliery (1936), Notts County (c/s 1938 - am), Rufford Colliery (Dec 1937), TOWN (c/s 1938 - am, Mar 1947 - pro), Bentinck C W (c/s 1948)

1946-47	4 apps	0 gls	
1947-48	1 "	0 "	

DANGERFIELD Harold
1919 - 22 Wing Half Back
b: Warsop, Notts., c1897
Career: Welbeck Colliery, TOWN (c/s 1919), Sutton Town (c/s 1922), Welbeck Athletic (1928)

Harry Dangerfield was a dependable Mansfield player for three seasons immediately following the end of WW I. In 1930, he was captain of the Welbeck Athletic team which made history by playing in the first competitive floodlit match in Great Britain at Field Mill. After he finished playing, he became Secretary of Welbeck Colliery F C. He was also played cricket for the same colliery team for a number of years.

1919-20	29 apps	0 gls	Central Alliance
1920-21	33 "	0 "	" "
1921-22	9 "	0 "	Midland League

Honours: Central Alliance Championship 1920, runners up 1921 (both Mansfield)

DANSKIN Jason
1986 - 88 Forward   5' 8"   10st 8lbs (1987)
b: Winsford, Cheshire, 28 December 1967
Career: Everton (July 1984 - appr, July 1985 - pro), TOWN (Mar 1987 - loan, Apr 1987 - permanent), Hartlepool United (Jan 1988 - loan), Northwich Victoria (F.T. Feb 1988)

Young forward who came to Field Mill, signing permanently at the end of his one month loan period and a month later played on the winning side at Wembley in the Freight Rover Trophy Final. Forced to retire due to injury in 1990 when only 22 years of age, he joined his father's haulage business as a lorry driver.

1986-87	10(0) apps	0 gls
1987-88	0(0) "	0 "

Honours: Fright Rover Trophy 1987, Notts F A County Cup Winners 1988 (both Mansfield)

DARVILL (Gerald) Moffat
1935 - 36 Full Back 6' 0½"   12st 0lbs (1935)
b: High Wycombe, Bucks., 1916
Career: Wycombe Wanderers, Reading (Dec 1934), TOWN (May 1935), Wolverhampton Wanderers (£350 - Dec 1935)

Talented young full back who after only 13 appearances for the "Stags" was signed by Major Buckley of Wolves for a large fee. Played for Aldershot and Norwich City as a "guest" player in WW II.

1935-36	13 apps	0 gls

DARWIN (George) Hedworth
1953 - 57 Inside Forward   5' 10½"   11st 0lbs
b: Chester le Street, Co Durham, 16 May 1932
Career: Wimblesworth Juniors, Huddersfield Town (May 1950), TOWN (Nov 1953), Derby County (p/e Savin + £4,000 - May 1957), Rotherham United (£5,000 - Oct 1960), Barrow (July 1961), Boston (c/s 1964).

George Darwin netted a total of 125 goals for his clubs although he did not manage a game with the "Terriers". Leading scorer for Mansfield in his last season at Field Mill.

1953-54	26 apps	17 gls	
1954-55	28 "	8 "	
1955-56	37 "	19 "	
1956-57	35 "	19 "	Leading Scorer

Honours: Division 3 North XI 1955 (Mansfield).

DAVIES Reginald

1932 - 33 Wing Half Back
b: Stanton Hill, Notts., 29 September 1897
d: 1977
Career: Sutton Town, Portsmouth (July 1922), Brentford (£250 - May 1928), TOWN (F.T. - c/s 1932), Rufford Colliery.

A classy wing half who made his name with Portsmouth and played at all three levels of the Football League with them in a six year spell there. Appointed captain of Brentford when he joined them in 1928 and led their reserve side to the London Combination championship his last season there before joining Mansfield. Not a great success at Field Mill and soon drifted into non-league soccer. Played in 335 Football League matches.

1932-33   18 apps   0 gls
Honours: Division 3 South Championship 1924 & Division 2 Runners-Up 1927 (both Portsmouth)

DAVIS Bert

1925 - 26 Inside Right   5' 8"   10st 10lbs (1925)
b: Daybrook, Nottingham, 1902
Career: Boston, Reading (c/s 1923), TOWN (c/s 1925).

Although he played in 32 matches for Reading in the Third Division, he was not impressive at Mansfield and languished in the reserves for most of the season before being released in May 1926.

1925-26   6 apps   3 gls
Honours: Notts Senior Cup Winners 1926 (Mansfield)

DAVIS Charles F

1931 - 32 Centre Half Back   6' 0"   13st 7lbs (1930)
b: Bristol, 1905
Career: Bath City, Torquay United (June 1927), York City (July 1929), TOWN (F.T. July 1931), Glastonbury Town (F.T. 1932)

Charlie Davis seemed to make a habit of joining football clubs who had just been elected to the League as he did this with both York and Mansfield. One of three centre halves used by the "Stags" during their inaugural season in Division Three and from the number of appearances he made, the least successful.

1931-32   5 apps   1 gl

DAVISON John Edward

1926 - 27 Goalkeeper 5' 7"
b: Gateshead, 2 September 1887
d: Wortley, Sheffield, 1971
Career: St Chads, Gateshead Town, The Wednesday (Apr 1908), TOWN (c/s 1926 - player manager), Chesterfield (Dec 1927 - manager), Sheffield United (June 1932 - manager), Chesterfield (Aug 1952 - manager to May 1958, May 1958 - chief scout).

Long serving Wednesday goalkeeper who was rather on the short side for this position, Teddy Davison joined the "Stags" as player-manager at the end of an illustrious career of 18 years, where surprisingly the only honour he won was one England cap in 1922. When he left Mansfield he embarked on a long and very successful stint of managership, lasting until he was nearly 71 years old, winning the Division 3 (North) Championship, Division 2 runners-up spot and F A Cup runners-up place. He also found one one of the best goalkeepers of the post-war era in Gordon Banks. Davison remains the smallest goalkeeper to play for England.

1926-27   16 apps   0 gls
Honours: England International (The Wednesday). Midland Combination runners up & Midland Combination Cup Winners 1927 (both Mansfield)

DAWKINS (Derek) Anthony

1978 - 81 Defender   5' 10"   11st 0lbs (1977)
b: Edmonton, London, 29 November 1959
Career: Leicester City (1975 - appr, Nov 1977 - pro), TOWN (Dec 1978), A F C Bournemouth (Aug 1981), Weymouth, Torquay United (Feb 1984 to 1989)

Made over 70 appearances for the "Stags", but his most successful period was at Torquay where he played 153 times in five seasons.

1978-79	26(0) apps	0 gls	
1979-80	35(0) "	0 "	
1980-81	12(0) "	0 "	

DAWS James

1919 - 20 Centre Half Back
b: Mansfield Woodhouse, Notts., 27 May 1898
d: Nottingham, June 1985
Career: Notts County (May 1918 - am), Woodhouse Exchange, TOWN (Sept 1919), Birmingham (£100 - Jan 1920), Bristol Rovers (May 1924), Woodhouse Exchange (July 1925), Poole Town (Aug 1925 to May 1927).

After only making a handful of appearances for Mansfield, Jimmy Daws managed to be selected for 46 matches with First Division Birmingham during his spell there.

1919-20	5 apps	0 gls	Central Alliance

DAY Clive A
1982 b: Grays, Essex, 27 January 1961
Career: Fulham (1977 - appr, Aug 1978 - pro), TOWN (Aug 1982 - loan), Aldershot (Aug 1983).

1982-83	10(2) apps	1 gl	(Loan)

DAYKIN (Harold) Reginald
1929 - 30 Outside Left
b: Somercotes, Derbys., 1909
Career: Alfreton Town, Southend United (May 1927), Fulham (Aug 1928), TOWN (c/s 1929), Ilkeston Town (c/s 1931), Sutton Town (1934)

Did not impress overmuch in his one season at Field Mill.

1929-30	12 apps	1 gl

Honours: Byron Cup Winners & Bayley Cup Winners 1930 (both Mansfield).

DEAN Samuel
1926 - 27 Goalkeeper
Career: TOWN (Feb 1927 - am), Bradford P A (May 1927), Ollerton Colliery (c/s 1933).

1926-27	12 apps	0 gls

Honours: Midland Combination runners up & Midland Combination Cup Winners, Mansfield Hospital Charity Cup 1927 (all Mansfield).

DEATH (William) George
1923 - 24 and 1931 - 32 Outside Left 5' 9" 12st 0lbs (1931)
b: Rotherham, 13 November 1900
d: Nottingham, 3 July 1984
Career: Broome Athletic, Rotherham Town (1918), Notts County (£400 - c/s 1920), TOWN (c/s 1923), Sunderland (£500 - Mar 1924), Exeter City (Sept 1928), Gillingham (c/s 1930), TOWN (F.T. c/s 1931), Grantham (c/s 1932), Sutton Town (Feb 1933), Nottingham City Transport F C (Aug 1934).

A tricky winger with a powerful shot, Billy Death was a key player in Mansfield"s Midland League championship side of 1924, soon attracting the attention of the bigger clubs and it was First Division Sunderland who signed him. He returned to Field Mill for the club's first season in League football at the age of 32, moving down into non-league soccer at the season's end. He played on in minor football until the outbreak of WW II, when he was 40.

1923-24	31 apps	14 gls
1931-32	14 "	2 "

Honours: Division 2 Championship 1923 (Notts County), Midland League Championship 1924 (Mansfield)

DELAPENHA Lloyd Lindbergh
1958 - 61 Outside Right 5' 7" 11st 10lbs
b: Jamaica, 20 May 1927
Career: Arsenal (am), Portsmouth (Apr 1948), Middlesbrough (Apr 1950), TOWN (June 1958), Hereford United (July 1961), Burton Albion, Heanor Town.

Lindy Delapenha, born in the West Indies, was the first coloured player to turn out for the "Stags", who he joined for a "substantial" fee after a brilliant eight year career at Ayrsome Park, in which he netted 90 goals - extremely good for a winger. Three very productive seasons at Field Mill ended with a move to Hereford who were then a non-league club. At the conclusion of his playing career, he returned to Jamaica where he ultimately attained a senior position with the sports department of the Jamaican Broadcasting Corporation.

1958-59	39 apps	9 gls
1959-60	41 "	10 "
1960-61	35 "	8 "

DELLOW (Ronald) William

1934 - 35 Outside Right   5' 9"   10st 5lbs (1934)
b: Crosby, Liverpool, 13 July 1914
Career: Bootle St Marys, Blackburn Rovers (1932 - am, Aug 1933 - pro), TOWN (F.T. June 1934), Manchester City (£1,300 - Jan 1935), Tranmere Rovers (Mar 1936), Carlisle United (Aug 1939 to May 1947), Ards (Jun 1947 - player manager), Holland (Jun 1948 - coaching), Vollendam Holland (Nov 1963 - trainer/coach to May 1969).

Fast, tricky. goalscoring winger who made a nice profit for Mansfield when he was transferred to Manchester City, after only 24 games for what was then the "Stags" record transfer fee. Served in the Merchant Navy as a boy and scored 20 goals in 15 matches for his his first club in Bootle. Guested for Tranmere, New Brighton, Manchester City, Everton, Southport, Wrexham and Blackburn during WW II and returned to Carlisle for one season after the end of hostilities. Coached in the Netherlands for over 20 years, marrying a Dutch girl along the way.

1934-35   24 apps   10 gls
Honours: Division 3 North Championship 1938 (Tranmere)

DEPLEDGE Joseph

1925 - 26 Centre Half Back   5' 11"   11st 10lbs (1925)
b: Heeley, Sheffield, 15 April 1897

Career: Portsmouth (1919), Halifax Town (c/s 1922),Rotherham Town (Nov 1922), Stoke (£130 - Apr 1923), TOWN (May 1925).

Had the distinction of being signed twice by Jack Baynes - once for Rotherham and again by Mansfield where Baynes was by then Town's first secretary manager. A centre forward at Clifton Lane, the "Potters" played him at centre half and so did Mansfield, where he was reserve to Jack Bryan. Made more senior appearnces at Stoke than he managed at Field Mill.

1925-26   3 apps   0 gls Midland League

DERKO T Franco

1962 - 67 Full Back 5' 10"   11st 0lbs
b: Italy, 22 December 1946
Career: TOWN (Jan 1962 - appr, Jan 1965 - pro)

1966-67   1(0) apps   0 gls

DERRICK Jantzen S

1971 Outside Right   5' 11"   11st 10lbs (1969)
b: Bristol, 10 January 1943
Career: Bristol City (Jan 1960), TOWN (Mar 1971 - loan),

Joined the "Stags" on loan but not retained, following a long career at Ashton Gate, where he made over 250 appearances, scoring in excess of 30 goals.

1970-71   2(1) apps   0 gls   (Loan)
Honours: England Schoolboy International

DEVEY Raymond

1947 - 50 Wing Half back   5' 10"   12st 0lbs
b: Tysley, Birmingham, 19 December 1917
Career: Forman's Road School, Shirley Juniors, Shirley O B, Birmingham (May 1937 - am, Jun 1938 - pro), TOWN (Aug 1947).

Ray Devey had only played in one match for Brum in spite of 10 seasons there, although the war did intervene, but he did make a number of wartime appearances for them. A steady reliable half back, he later became Youth Team Trainer at St Andrews, a post he retained up to 1988 when he retired. Served as a C Q M S in the R.A.S.C. for 6½ years during the war.

1947-48	41 apps	1 gl
1948-49	34 "	3 "
1949-50	1 "	0 "

DEVLIN (William) Alexander

1930 - 31 Centre Forward   5' 9"   11st 11lbs
b: Bellshill, Lanarks., 30 July 1899
d: July 1972
Career: Scottish Juniors, Clyde (1921), Kings Park (1921-22 - loan), Cowdenbeath (1923), Huddersfield Town (£4,200 - Mar 1926), Liverpool (May 1927), Heart of Midlothian (Dec 1927), Macclesfield Town (Nov 1928), Cowdenbeath (June 1929), TOWN (June 1930), Cowdenbeath (Jan 1931), Burton Town (Mar 1931), Shelbourne (June 1931), Bangor City (Aug 1932), Boston (Aug 1933), Ashton National (Aug 1934), Olympique Marseilles, France (Aug 1935).

Willie Devlin certainly liked to try a new club at least once each season. He established a tremendous reputation with his scoring ability each side of the border. During his first spell with Cowdenbeath he knocked in 33, 37 and 40 goals in successive seasons - the first two, in 1995, were still Scottish Division One records and the last one stood as Cowdenbeath's club record. This scoring prowess prompted First Division Huddersfield Town to pay the very large sum of £4,200 for him, but he was not a great success at Leeds Road and soon passed on to Liverpool where he netted 14 goals in 18 games. Hearts was his next port of call where his tally was 12 goals in 15 matches. He reached Field Mill in Town's last season before being elected to the Football League and claimed 15 goals in 21 appearances, before he was released in January 1931 to return to Scotland as he claimed "homesickness". It was rather strange therefore when he resurfaced with Burton Town just two months later! When at Mansfield he was reputed to be the highest paid non-league player. Scored well over 250 goals during his career.

1930-31   21 apps   15 gls MIdland League

DICKINSON Sydney

1925 - 27 Left Half Back   5' 7½"   10st 6lbs (1925)
b: Nottingham, 17 August 1906
d: 2 February 1984
Career: Dale Rovers, Nottingham Forest (Jan 1924 - am, pro - c/s 1924), TOWN (c/s 1925), Bradford P A (Feb 1927), Port Vale (Nov 1933), Lincoln City (Aug 1934), Grantham (Aug 1935), Notts County (chief scout).

Youthful defender, who matured well at Park Avenue with whom he made 124 league appearances in five full seasons. Was chief scout to the "Magpies" for many years through to the 1960s.

1925-26   24 apps   0 gls
1926-27   17 "   1 "
Honours: Midland League runners up & Notts Senior Cup Winners 1926, Midland Combination runners up & Cup Winners 1927 (all Mansfield), Division 3 North Championship 1928 (Bradford).

DICKSON William

1956 - 58 Wing Half Back   5' 10"   12st 11lbs
b: Lurgan, N I, 15 April 1923
Career: Sunnyside F C, Glenavon (am), Notts County (Nov 1945), Chelsea (Nov 1947), Arsenal (£15,000 - Oct 1953), TOWN (F.T. July 1956), Glenavon (Jan 1958)

A fine constructive wing half, Bill Dickson won 12 caps for Northern Ireland when playing for Chelsea and Arsenal.

1956-57   19 apps   0 gls
1957-58   0 "   0 "
Honours: Northern Ireland International.

DONALDSON (O'Neill) Matthias

1994   Forward   6' 0"   11st 4lbs (1994)
b: Birmingham, 24 November 1969
Career: Manchester United (1987), Luton Town (trial), Derby County (trial), Hinckley Town, Shrewsbury Town (Nov 1991), Doncaster Rovers (F.T. Aug 1994), TOWN (Dec 1994 - loan), Sheffield Wednesday (£50,000 - Jan 1995)

Tall strong striker who made a tremendous impact at Field Mill by scoring two goals on his loan debut in the 7-1 rout of Hereford on Boxing Day 1994 and followed this up with two goals in each of the succeeding matches versus Scarborough and Barnet. He also netted a goal in the Third Round F A Cup tie v Wolves at Field Mill. As it had been made quite clear that there was no future for him with Rovers, Andy King had agreed a fee of £15,000 with Sammy Chung to buy him if his loan period proved satisfactory - which it did, but Trevor Francis stepped in for Wednesday with a higher offer which Doncaster accepted. Perhaps Doncaster got their just desserts the same evening when Mansfield beat them 2 - 0 at Belle Vue to pass them into a play-off position.

1994-95   4(0) apps   6 gls   (Loan)

DONALDSON William

1950 - 52 Outside Left   5' 6"   10st 0lbs
b: Wallaceton, Edinburgh, 20 January 1920
Career: Leith Athletic (1938), Bradford P A (May 1946), TOWN (Oct 1950)

Diminutive winger who was always likely to cut in and have a shot at goal. Had typical Scottish guile.

1950-51   22 apps   1 gl
1951-52   30   "   9   "
Honours: Division 3 Runners Up 1951 (Mansfield)

DONOVEN Alfred Ernest

1922-25 Centre/Inside Forward & Wing Half
5' 6" 10st 9lbs (1924)
b: Bulwell, Nottingham, 20 June 1900
Career: Bulwell Schoolboys, Nottingham Forest (c/s 1919), TOWN (F.T. - May 1922), Southend United (£500 - May 1925).

Legendary goalscorer in the successful "Stags" teams of the early 1920s. Diminutive, but skilful at all aspects of the game. Converted to wing half with great success when he joined Southend where he was a regular until retirement in May 1936. In spite of his first names, he was always known as "Dickie". A pit lad before becoming a professional footballer. Stands fifth in the list of "Stags" overall goalscorers.

1922-23 40 apps 14 gls Midland League.
1923-24 42   "   36   "   "   " Lead.Scorer
1924-25 37   "   37   "   "   "   "

Honours: Notts Senior Cup Winners 1923, Midland League Championship 1924 and 1925 (all Mansfield), North Notts League Tour (May 1923 - to Algeria), Division 3 South - 3rd 1932 (Southend)

DOOLAN John

1994 onwards Utility   5' 11"   10st 9lbs (1993)
b: Liverpool, 7 May 1973
Career: Everton (1991 - appr, June 1992 - pro), Witton Albion (c/s 1994 - N/C), TOWN (N/C Sept 1994).

Strong young player released by Everton. Originally a full back, but used by the "Stags" in a utility role.

1994-95   20(2) apps   1 gl

DOWNIE (John) David

1958 - 59 Inside Forward
b: Falkirk, 19 July 1925
Career: Lanark A T C, Bradford P A (1942 - groundstaff, Dec 1944 - pro), Manchester United (£18,000 - Mar 1949), Luton Town (£10,000 - Aug 1953), Hull City (July 1954), Kings Lynn (July 1955), Wisbech Town (c/s 1957), TOWN (Oct 1958), Darlington (May 1959 to May 1960, when retired)

Johnnie Downie joined Bradford's groundstaff as a 16 year old during the war and soon blossomed out into a fine, intelligent inside forward. Manchester United paid out their record transfer fee to secure his services. Well past his best when he joined the "Stags", he nevertheless, showed some of his old touches, but was released at the season's end. Guested for Hull City when he was unable to get leave during WW II

1958-59   18 apps   4 gls
Honours: Division 1 Championship 1952, Runners Up 1949 & 1951 (Manchester United)

DOWSON William H

1920 - 21 Centre Forward   5' 11½"   12st 0lbs (1921)
b: 1898
Career: Royal Navy, Bishop Auckland, Staveley Town (am), TOWN (Jan 1921)

1920-21   4 apps   2 gls   Central Alliance

DRANSFIELD Edward

1934 - 37 Right Full Back   5' 9"   11st 6lbs (1935)
b: High Green, Nr Sheffield, 28 November 1906
Career: High Green Swifts, Rotherham United (c/s 1927), Birmingham (c/s 1930), Swindon Town (c/s 1931), Southampton (c/s 1933), TOWN (c/s 1934 to May 1937)

A strong tackling full back, Ted Dransfield did not appear in either the Birmingham or Southampton league teams, but was a regular member of their reserve elevens, e.g. 34 appearances with the "Saints" in the season before he joined Mansfield. An ever present in 1935-36, he lost favour next term as he was displaced in favour of Frank Perfect, and when he was transferred to Wolves - Ted Vaux.

1934-35	34 apps	1 gl
1935-36	42 "	0 "
1936-37	2 "	0 "

Honours: Bass Charity Vase Winners 1935 (Mansfield).

DRING W Harry

1924 - 25 Inside Right
Career: TOWN (c/s 1924), Blackpool (£150 - May 1925).

Inside forward who regularly found the net during Town's Midland League championship squad in 1924-25. Did not make the first team at Blackpool.

1924-25   17 apps   11 gls Midland League
Honours: Midland League Championship 1925 (Mansfield)

DRURY D

1927 - 28 Goalkeeper
Career: TOWN (1927 - am)

1927-28   1 app   0 gls Midland League

DUNGWORTH John H

1982 - 84 Utility   6' 0"   12st 1lb (1983)
b: Rotherham, 30 March 1955
Career: Huddersfield Town (July 1970 - appr, July 1972 - pro), Barnsley (Oct 1974 - loan), Oldham Athletic (F.T. May 1975), Rochdale (Mar 1977 - loan), Aldershot (F.T. July 1977), Shrewsbury Town (£100,000 - Nov 1979), Hereford United (Oct 1981 - loan), TOWN (F.T. Aug 1982), Rotherham United (£5,000 - Feb 1984), Frickley Athletic (c/s 1988), Sheffield United (c/s 1991 - Youth Development Officer).

Play anywhere type player who had good stints at both Aldershot and Shrewsbury where he made 105 and 86 appearances respectively. Became Sheffield United's Youth Development Officer in 1991.

1982-83	36(3) apps	14 gls	Leading Scorer
1983-84	14(3) "	2 "	

Honours: Welsh Cup runners up 1980 (Shrewsbury).

DUTTON Thomas

1938 - 39 Inside/Outside Left   5' 8"   10st 7lbs (1935)
b: Southport, 11 November 1906
d: Rochdale, 1982
Career: Southport Schools, Southport Juniors, Chorley, Leicester City (c/s 1932), Queens Park Rangers (c/s 1934), Doncaster Rovers (June 1935), TOWN (c/s 1938), Rochdale (c/s 1939)

Experienced forward who played club cricket between seasons. During WW II "guested" for Southport and Watford.

1938-39   39 apps   12 gls Leading Scorer
Honours: Division 3 North runners up 1938 (Doncaster). Notts F A County Cup Winners 1939 (Mansfield).

DYE E Lewis

1926 - 27 Outside Right
b: Clay Cross, Derbys., 1886
d: Chesterfield, 10 March 1975
Career: Staveley Town, Chesterfield (c/s 1924), TOWN (c/s 1926), Loughborough Corinthians (c/s 1927), Sutton Town (c/s 1931).

Probably the oldest player to turn out for the "Stags", Lewis Dye was 41 years old when he made his only senior appearance in the Byron Cup Final and he was still playing at the Avenue Ground when he was 45! He had previously played in the Division 3 North with Chesterfield.

Honours: Byron Cup Winners 1927 (Mansfield).

DYSON William H

1925 - 28 Inside Forward 5' 6"   10st 0lbs (1926)
b: Gedling, Notts., c1904
Career: Gedling Colliery, TOWN (Sept 1925 - am, Jan 1926 - pro), Ilkeston United (c/s 1928), Grantham (Feb 1929), Sutton Town (c/s 1931), Heanor Town (c/s 1934), Ilkeston Town (c/s 1935).

Sharpshooting forward who joined the "Stags" as an amateur, becoming a pro four months later. Had descended into local non-league soccer within three seasons.

1925-26	13 apps	11 gls	Midland League		
1926-27	13 "	9 "	"	"	
1927-28	19 "	13 "			

Honours: Midland League runners up 1926. Midland Combination runners up & Cup Winners, Notts Senior Cup Winners, Notts Benevolent Bowl Winners & Mansfield Hospital Charity Cup Winners 1927 (all Mansfield). Derbyshire League Championship 1932 & 1933, Sutton Charity Cup 1933 (all Sutton Town).

EATON (Joseph) David
1947 - 54 Inside Forward   5' 11"   10st 0lbs (1947)
b: Cuckney, Notts., 16 May 1931
Career: Langwith B C, TOWN (Aug 1947 - am, Mar 1951 - pro, Jan 1955 - Assistant Secretary, July 1956 - Secretary to July 1993).

Promising career was cut short by injury in 1954. Appointed Town's Assistant Secretary the following year and full Secretary in July 1956 when long serving Honorary Secretary, Herbert N Mee retired from the post. Served the "Stags" faithfully in this position until his enforced retirement in July 1993. At the time of his departure, was the longest serving club secretary in the Football League, having served Mansfield for 37 years in that capacity. Born on the Duke of Portland's Welbeck Estate where his father was employed. Another of the "Stags" long serving and faithful servants - Stan Searl dubbed him "Mr Mansfield Town" - very apt!

1952-53	2 apps	0 gls	
1953-54	2 "	1 "	

ECCLES Terence S
1973 - 77 Forward   6' 0½"   13st 0lbs (1977)
b: Leeds, 2 March 1952
Career: Pudsey Juniors, Blackburn Rovers (1968 - appr, Aug 1969 - pro), TOWN (£6,000 - July 1973), Huddersfield Town (£110,000 - Jan 1977), Ethnikos, Greece (Apr 1978), York City (Sept 1979).

Danny Williams signed Terry Eccles for Mansfield three years after he made his debut at Ewood Park and what an excellent buy he turned out to be. He averaged almost a goal every two games during perhaps the most successful run in the "Stags" history, when they won the Division 3 and Division 4 championships and achieved the furthest in the League Cup the club has ever progressed - all in the space of three seasons. When transferred to the "Terriers" this was for the first six figure fee that Town received and was thus a club record too. Suffered a broken cheekbone and ankle during his spell with Blackburn. Later was "mine host" at the White Horse, Upper Poppleton, Nr. York. As a schoolboy Eccles also played under the Rugby Union code and was no mean performer either - playing for England Schoolboys versus Scotland at Twickenham.

1973-74	44(0) apps	20 gls	Leading Scorer	
1974-75	32(0) "	17 "		
1975-76	29(3) "	3 "		
1976-77	10(0) "	7 "		

Honours: Division 4 Championship 1975, Division 3 Championship 1977 (both Mansfield)

EDMONDS (Alfred) John
1934-35 Right Half Back   5' 9"   11st 10lbs (1934)
b: Brighton, 1908
Career: Brighton & Hove Albion (1926), Clapton Orient (c/s 1929), Bury (c/s 1932), TOWN (c/s 1934).

Stylish wing half, Alf Edmonds was a regular during his one season at Field Mill, but was released at the season's end.

1934-35	33 apps	4 gls

EDWARDS Joseph A

1933 - 34 Goalkeeper 5' 11" 12st 6lbs (1933)
b: Staveley, Derbys., 1907
Career: Staveley Town, Chesterfield, Derby County, Bolsover Colliery (c/s 1932), TOWN (May 1933), Ollerton Colliery (c/s 1934 to 1939)

Shared the goalkeeping duties with Williams during Town's third season in the Football League, before finishing his playing days with Ollerton Colliery.

1933-34   20 apps   0 gls

EDWARDS Richard T

1967 - 68 and 1973- 74 Centre Half Back 6' 1"   13st 6lbs
b: Kirkby in Ashfield, Notts., 20 November 1942
Career: East Kirkby Welfare Juniors, Nottingham Forest (trial), Notts County (1957 - am, Oct 1959 - pro), TOWN (£5,000 - Mar 1967), Aston Villa (£30,000 - Mar 1968), Torquay Uniyed (£8,000 - June 1970 to May 1972), TOWN (F.T. July 1973), Torquay United (F.T. May 1974), Bath City (late 1974 - player coach to 1976)

Had an outstanding career with the "Magpies" before he joined Mansfield. Tommy Cummings remembered him when he moved to Villa and he re-signed him for the "Villans" shortly afterwards at a big profit to the "Stags". Returned to Field Mill for one season at the end of his career. Started up as a country and western singer and club entertainer during the summer months at Torquay in 1972 - a career he has pursued ever since.

1966-67   13 apps   0 gls
1967-68   32   "   1   "
1973-74   31(2)"   1   "
Honours: England Youth International

EDWARDS Walter

1947 - 49 Outside Right   5' 9½"   11st 0lbs
b: Mansfield Woodhouse, Notts., 26 June 1924
Career: Woodhouse Amateurs, TOWN (July 1947 - am, Nov 1947 - pro), Leeds United (Mar 1949), Leicester City (Aug 1949), Rochdale (Sep 1950),

Speedy right winger who progressed well before being transferred to Leeds United, where he made but two appearances. Did not appear for either of his other clubs. Served in Palestine during WW II in R.E.M.E.

1947-48   20 apps   4 gls
1948-49   5   "   1   "

ELAD Efon

1995   Winger   5' 10"   12st 0lbs (1994)
b: Nigeria, 5 September 1970
Career: Hillingdon, Cologne, Northampton Town (Jan 1994 - N/C), Cambridge United (Dec 1994 - trial), TOWN (Feb 1995 - 1 week's trial).

After impressing and scoring in a reserve fixture against Bradford City Reserves on 30 January 1995, Elad was brought on as substitute for the last 10 minutes against Walsall at Bescot Stadium the following Saturday - February 4 when he replaced Stewart Hadley. After one more substitute appearance however, he was not retained.

1994-95   0(2) apps   0 gls

ELLIOTT Frank F G

1956 - 58 Goalkeeper 6' 1"   12st 4lbs
b: Merthyr Tydfil, 23 July 1929
Career: Thornton Athletic, Merthyr Tydfil, Swansea Town (Sep 1949), Stoke City (Dec 1952), Fulham (Mar 1954), TOWN (July 1956)

Had a hard act to follow when he took over the custodian's role from long serving Dennis Wright, but he held the position for almost two seasons before being superceded by Ray Kirkham. Nicknamed "Lightning" at the club.

1956-57   36 apps   0 gls
1957-58   27   "   0   "

ELLIS Samual

1972 - 73 Central Defender 5' 11"   12st 9lbs (1972)
b: Ashton under Lyne, 12 September 1946
Career: Audenshaw G S, Snipe Wanderers, W H Smith Manchester, Sheffield Wednesday (Sep 1964), TOWN (Jan 1972 - loan, £10,000 - Mar 1972 - permanent), Lincoln City (£7,000 - May 1973), Watford (£15,000 - Aug 1977 - player coach, May 1979 - coach), Blackpool (June 1982 - manager to Mar 1989), Bury (manager - May 1989), Manchester City (Dec 1990 - asst manager to Aug 1993), Lincoln City (Mar 1994 - asst coach, manager - May 1994)

Sam Ellis had a glittering career with Wednesday, playing at Wembley in the 1966 F A Cup Final as a last minute choice when only 18 and winning three Under 23 caps for England. Gave long and faithful service to the "Imps" before developing his coaching and managerial skills. Recently appointed manager of near neighbours, Lincoln City.

1971-72   20(0) apps   0 gls
1972-73   44(0)   "   7   "
Honours: England Under 23 International. F A Cup Runners Up 1966 (both Sheffield Wednesday). Notts F A County Cup Winners 1972 (Mansfield)

EMERY Anthony J
1959 - 61 Centre Half Back   6' 1"   12st 0lbs (1959)
b: Lincoln, 4 November 1927
Career: Juniors, Lincoln City (Aug 1945 - am, Aug 1947 - pro), TOWN (£2,500 - June 1959)

After a long and fruitful career at Sincil Bank, Tony Emery played out his last season of League football with Town. Holder of Lincoln's record number of appearances with 402, Emery's uncle - Fred, also a half back, holds Doncaster Rovers record of 420 appearances during the 1920s and 30s. Worked in the building trade after retirement from the game and still living in North Hykeham.

1959-60   16 apps   0 gls
1960-61   10   "   0   "
Honours: Division 3 North Championship 1952. F A West Indies Tour 1955 (both Lincoln)

ENGLAND Ernest E ("Mac")

1931 - 35 Left Full Back   5' 8"   12st 0lbs
b: Shirebrook, Derbys., 3 February 1901
d: Radcliffe on Trent, 22 February 1982
Career: Shirebrook Foresters (1918), Shirebrook (c/s 1919),

Sunderland (£100 - Dec 1919), West Ham United (£500 - Oct 1930), TOWN (£350 - Aug 1931), Sutton Town (c/s 1935). TOWN (Aug 1936 - asst trainer), Notts County (May 1937 - asst trainer, Jun 1938 - trainer to Aug 1944).

What a bargain was obtained by Sunderland when they bought the young "Mac" England (as he was always known,) from Central Alliance club, Shirebrook. Nine seasons and 335 matches later they sold him for five times his original cost ! He also served the "Stags" well for 4 seasons in the twilight of his career, before he went into the training side of the game. A very good full back, who was unlucky to be contemporary with the likes of Wadsworth and Blenkinsop or he would surely have won international recognition. Was out of action for a long spell due to a cartilage operation in the Spring of 1933 and had never scored a goal until he came to Field Mill. Played cricket for Langwith Loco during the Summer months.

1931-32   42 apps   2 gls
1932-33   29   "   0   "
1933-34   36   "   1   "
1934-35   23   "   0   "
Honours: Division 1 runners up 1923, Division 1 - 3rd 1924/26/27, F A XI 1926 (all Sunderland).

EVANS Paul
1975 - 77 Goalkeeper 5' 9"   10st 7lbs (1977)
b: Kiveton Park, Sheffield, 24 February 1949
Career: Juniors, Sheffield Wednesday (Feb 1966), Boston, TOWN (Oct 1975), Scarborough, Burton Albion (c/s 1984), Scarborough 1986 - asst manager to 1988).

Deputy to Rod Arnold but had few opportunities at Field Mill. When playing for Burton in a 3rd round F A Cup tie in 1984-85 against Leicester at the Baseball Ground, Derby, Evans was hit by a missile thrown by a spectator which knocked him out. The match was ordered to be replayed behind closed doors at Coventry.

1975-76   6(0) apps   0 gls
1976-77   0(0)   "   0   "

EVANS Raymond
1949 - 54 Centre Forward   5' 10½"   11st 8lbs (1951)
b: Mansfield, 27 November 1927
Career: Coventry City (May 1948), Stafford Rangers), TOWN (Nov 1949), Stockport County (July 1954)

1949-50	1 app	0 gls	
1950-51	0 "	0 "	
1951-52	23 "	8 "	
1952-53	15 "	4 "	
1953-54	0 "	0 "	

EVANS T
1922 -23 Outside Left
Career: TOWN (1922)

1922-23	1 app	0 gls	Midland League

EVERETT Harold
1945 - 47 Left Full Back
b: Worksop, 11 November 1920
Career: Warsop Vale School, Dukeries Boys (1934), Shirebrook Welfare, Warsop Main, TOWN (Sep 1946).

1946-47	15 apps	0 gls

EVERETT Harry P
1946 - 47 Left Half Back
b: Worksop, 9 June 1922
Career: Dukeries Boys (1935), Rufford Colliery (Sep 1938), Notts County (Apr 1943), TOWN (Aug 1945).

Younger and better known of the two Everett brothers, Harold played a number of games for the Meadow Lane outfit during WW II.

WW II	31 apps	1 gl
1946-47	3 "	0 "

EVES (Melvyn) John
1987 Forward   5' 11"   10st 8lbs (1988)
b: Wednesbury, Staffs., 10 September 1956
Career: Juniors, Wolverhampton Wanderers (July 1975), Huddersfield Town (Mar 1984 - loan), Sheffield United (Dec 1984), Gillingham (F.T. Aug 1986), TOWN (Oct 1987 - loan), Manchester City, West Bromwich Albion, Telford United (c/s 1989).

Mel Eves had a long and successful career with Wolves, but moved rapidly thereafter from club to club.

1987-88   3(0) apps   0 gls   (Loan)
Honours: England "B" International, Division 2 Championship 1977, Runners Up 1983, F L Cup Winners 1980 (all Wolverhampton).

FAIRBROTHER John
1971 - 73 Centre Forward   5' 10"   12st 0lbs (1972)
b; Cricklewood, London, 12 February 1941
Career: Bennett's End, Watford (Aug 1959), Worcester City, Peterborough United (May 1965), Northampton Town (Feb 1968), TOWN (Sep 1971), Torquay United (June 1973)

Quite a sharpshooter, London born Fairbrother was a proven goalscorer from his early days, but it was not until he arrived at Mansfield that he topped a scoring list - then he did it twice in two seasons, when really at the end of his career.

1971-72	41(0) apps	18 gls	Leading Scorer	
1972-73	42(2) "	20 "	"	"

Honours: Notts F A County Cup Winners 1972 (Mansfield)

FAIRCLOUGH Wayne R
1990 - 94 Midfield   5' 10"   12st 2lbs (1993)
b: Nottingham, 27 April 1968
Career: Notts County (1984 - appr, Apr 1986 - pro), TOWN (£80,000 -Mar 1990), Chesterfield (F.T. June 1994).

Joint most expensive player that Mansfield have recruited, (Steve Wilkinson was the other,) when signed from the "Magpies". After a promising start at Field Mill his performances tailed off and he was released to the "Spireites" in 1994. Plays in either midfield or defensive roles.

1989-90	13(0) apps	0 gls	
1990-91	41(0) "	6 "	
1991-92	18(7) "	3 "	
1992-93	32(1) "	1 "	
1993-94	27(2) "	2 "	

Honours: Division 4 promotion 1992 (Mansfield). Division 3 promotion - via play-offs 1995 (Chesterfield).

FARDY
1922 - 23 Right Full Back
Career: TOWN (1922)

1922-23	1 app	0 gls	Midland League

FAWCETT Desmond H
1934 - 36 Goalkeeper 5' 10"   11st 6lbs (1935)
b: Middlesbrough, 1907
Career: Loftus Albion, Darlington (1925), Nelson (1927), Preston North End (c/s 1929), York City (Sep 1932), TOWN (c/s 1934), Rochdale (c/s 1936 to 1939)

A former railway worker, Fawcett joined the "Quakers" as an 18 year old. He spent most of his career in the Third Division, but had tasted a higher level with both Darlington and Preston.

1934-35	40 apps	0 gls
1935-36	32 "	0 "

FEATHERBY (Leonard) Walter
1931 - 32 Inside Forward   5' 9½"   11st 7lbs (1935)
b: Kings Lynn, 28 July 1905
d: Kings Lynn, 22 February 1972
Career: Lynn Whitefriars (1921), South Lynn Wednesday (1022), Kings Lynn Town (1922 - am), Norfolk County Juniors (1923), Glasgow Rangers (Jan 1924 - trial), Norwich City (May 1924 - am, Jun 1924 - pro), Northfleet (Oct 1927), Millwall (Oct 1927 - trial), Peterborough & Fletton United (Mar 1928), Merthyr Town (Aug 1928), Wolverhampton Wanderers (Jan 1929), Reading (June 1930), Queens Park Rangers (May 1931), TOWN (Dec 1931), Crewe Alexandra (July 1932), Merthyr Town (July 1933), Plymouth Argyle (Mar 1934), Notts County (June 1935), Kings Lynn (1937 to Oct 1939)

One would look a long way to find a more travelled player than Len Featherby, although Town's Willie Devlin might possibly rival him as a nomad! Didn't stay long enough anywhere to make much impression. Oddly enough won his only honour when his career was ending.

1931-32	22 apps	5 gls

Honours: Norfolk Senior Cup Winners 1939 (Kings Lynn)

FEE Gregory P
1991 - 93 Defender 6' 0"   12st 0lbs (1991)
b: Halifax, 24 June 1964
Career: Bradford City (Sep 1980 - am, May 1983 - pro), Kettering Town (Aug 1984), Boston United (c/s 1986), Sheffield Wednesday (£20,000 - Aug 1987), Preston North End (Sep 1990 - loan), Northampton Town (Nov 1990 - loan), Preston North End (Jan 1991 - loan), Leyton Orient (Mar 1991 - loan), TOWN (£20,000 - Mar 1991), Chesterfield (Nov 1992 - loan), Grantham Town (loan), Stamford Town (loan), Boston United (F.T. Aug 1993).

Greg Fee was a dominant central defender who fell out of favour under George Foster's management and was loaned out repeatedly until he was released and teamed up with Boston again. He set up a quite remarkable record whilst at Mansfield by turning out for Chesterfield (where he was on loan,) at Edgeley Park in a semi-final of the Autoglass Trophy on Tuesday 23 February 1993 and three days later, played for Town (having been recalled from loan due to injury problems,) on the same ground in a league match. Two matches against the same opposition on the same ground for two teams in three days and in different competitions! Currently a schoolteacher playing as a part time professional with Boston, and running a coaching school during the Summer months.

1990-91	10(0) apps	0 gls
1991-92	33(1) "	4 "
1992-93	7(3) "	3 "

Honours: Division 4 promotion 1992 (Mansfield)

FEEBERY Harold
1915 - 22 Full Back
b: Hucknall, Notts., c1894
Career: Hucknall, Derby County (1914), TOWN (1915), Bolton Wanderers (1919), Rugby Town (1920), TOWN (1921).

One of four brothers who all became professional footballers.

1915-16	N K apps	0 gls	Central Alliance
1921-22	18 "	0 "	Midland League

Honours: Central Alliance - Subsidiary Competition Championship 1916 (Mansfield).

FERNS Philip
1966 - 68 Full/Half Back   5' 8"   11st 8lbs (1967)
b: Liverpool, 14 November 1937

Career: Juniors, Liverpool (Sep 1957), Bournemouth & Boscombe Athletic (Aug 1965), TOWN (F.T. Aug 1966), Rhyl (c/s 1968)

As his career was winding down he joined the "Stags' where his vast experience helped and was often a steadying factor.

| 1966-67 | 44(0) apps | 1 gl |
| 1967-68 | 11(1) " | 0 " |

FERRARI (Frederick) Joseph

1930 - 31 Centre Half Back   5' 10"   12st 0lbs (1930)
b: Stratford, London, 22 May 1901
d: Sheffield, 6 August 1970
Career: Barking Town(am), Leyton (am), Northampton Town (Oct 1925), The Wednesday (£800 - Jun 1926), Flint Town (1926), Norwich City (£150 - Dec 1927), Barrow (F.T. Aug 1928), Nelson (£85 - Jun 1929), Chesterfield (Feb 1930 - trial), Burton Town (Mar 1930), Bedouins (Aug 1930), TOWN (Nov 1930), Queens Park Rangers (Jan 1931), Hillsborough O B (Sep 1933 - permit player)

Tried out at centre forward by Barrow, he hit two hat tricks, one against Nelson - so they bought him! Signed after playing for Bedouins at Field Mill, he did not make his mark, was not retained retained and moved to Sheffield to work in a steelworks.

| 1930-31 | 2 apps | 0 gls Midland League |

FIELD (Frederick) Stanley

1935 - 36 Centre Forward
b: Mansfield, 12 June 1914
Career: Bradford P A (c/s 1933), TOWN (c/s 1935), Sutton Town (1936)

| 1935-36 | 2 apps | 0 gls |

FIELD Norman

1950 - 53 Half back 6' 0"   12st 6lbs
b: Durham, 27 August 1927
Career: Portsmouth (Aug 1945), TOWN (June 1950).

A reserve player at Fratton Park for five years, Field did not make the first team during his stay there.

| 1951-52 | 4 apps | 0 gls |
| 1952-53 | 16 " | 0 " |

FIELDING Howitt

1937-38 Outside Right   5' 9"   11st 4lbs (1937)
b: Selston, Notts., 1916
d: Peterborough, 1982
Career: Ilkeston Town, Reading (1935), TOWN (Aug 1937 - trial), Peterborough & Fletton United (1938)

Came to Field Mill on a two month trial at the start of the 1937-38 season, but was not retained and moved into the Midland League. Oddly enough there were two H Fieldings on Reading's books at the same time, the other being Horace who also played for Grimsby Town and Crystal Palace - they were not related. Known to his team mates as Howard.

1937-38   4 apps   0 gls
Honours: Midland League - First Wartime Competition runners up 1940, Midland League - Second Wartime Competition Championship 1940 (both Peterborough).

FINCH (Desmond) Richard

1969 - 73 Goalkeeper 6' 0"   11st 4lbs (1972)
b: Worksop, 26 February 1950
Career: TOWN (Mar 1969), Worksop Town (c/s 1973), Boston (c/s 1975).

| 1968-69 | 2 apps | 0 gls |
| 1970-71 | 2 " | 0 " |

FISHER Frederick

1931 - 33 Inside Right   5' 10"   11st 7lbs (1935)
b: Hucknall, Notts., 1910
Career: Staveley Town (c/s 1928), Notts County (c/s 1929), Torquay United (c/s 1930), TOWN (F.T. c/s 1931), Swindon Town (F.T. c/s 1933), Gillingham (c/s 1935), Clapton Orient (c/s 1936), Newport I O W (c/s 1937)

Fred Fisher also played on the extreme flank with some of his clubs, but always inside right with the "Stags". Only club where he was a regular was Swindon, in spite of the fact that he scored a goodly number of goals. Appeared as a "guest" player with Derby County, Southampton and Arsenal during WW II.

| 1931-32 | 1 app | 1 gl |
| 1932-33 | 9 " | 5 " |

FISHER John

1927 - 28 Outside/Inside Right 5' 7½"   11st 10lbs (1927)
b: Hodthorpe, Derbys., 4 August 1897

d: Castleford, 22 June 1954
Career: Brodsworth Colliery (1919), Chesterfield (1921), Burnley (£1,000 - Mar 1922), Chesterfield (Apr 1923 - exch G Beel), TOWN (June 1927), Staveley Town (June 1928), Lincoln City (Oct 1928), Denaby United (Aug 1930), Hurst (Sep 1931), Sutton Town.

Had a fine career with Chesterfield and when he moved on to Burnley, the fee of £1,000 in 1922, was very substantial for the period and easily the "Spireites" record transfer fee. A more than useful cricketer, he played in three matches for Derbyshire between 1921 and 1922.

1927-28   37 apps   11 gls Midland League
Honours: Mansfield Hospital Charity Cup Winners 1928 (Mansfield)

FITZSIMONS (Arthur) Gerard

1959 - 61 Inside Forward   5' 8"   10st 7lbs (1960)
b: Dublin, 16 December 1929
Career: Shelbourne (1947), Middlesbrough (£18,000 with P Desmond - May 1949), Lincoln City (£5,000 - Mar 1959), TOWN (£6,000 - Aug 1959), Wisbech Town (July 1961 to 1962), Drogheda United (1967 - player coach), Shamrock Rovers (1969 - coach), League of Ireland (coach), Libya (coach).

A very talented grafting inside forward, Fitzsimmons came to Mansfield after spending ten years on Teeside and five months at Sincil Bank. Winner of 26 Republic of Ireland caps, he spent two excellent seasons at Field Mill, before dropping out of the League.

1959-60 38 apps 15 gls   Leading Scorer (Joint)
1960-61 24   "   8 "
Honours: Eire International (Middlesbrough), League of Ireland XI, F A of Ireland Cup Runners Up 1949 (both Shelbourne)

FLANDERS Frederick

1920 - 21 Full Back 5' 8"   12st 0lbs
b: Derby, 1 January 1894
d: Birmingham, late 1967
Career: Gerard Street School Derby, Derby Boys (1908), Sheldon United, Derby County (1910), Ilkeston Town (c/s 1912), Newport County (c/s 1913), TOWN (Oct 1920), Newport County (c/s 1921), Hartlepools United (c/s 1922), Nuneaton Town (c/s 1923).

After captaining Derby Boys to victory in the English Schools Championship and winning a Schoolboy International cap, Fred Flanders made his league debut with Derby County in October

1910 at the age of 16 years 287 days and this remained Derby's youngest league appearance until beaten by Stephen Powell (16 years 30 days) in October 1971. He went 11 seasons between consecutive Football League appearances - 1910-11 (Derby County) to 1921-22 (Newport County). Had a brother George, who played centre forward for the "Stags" during the 1913-14 season - see 1902-16 section.

1920-21   1 app   0 gls
Honours: English Schoolboy International, English Schools Shield Winners 1908 (both Derby Boys).

FLEMING Paul

1991 - 94 Right Full Back   5' 7"   10st 0lbs (1991)
b: Halifax, 6 September 1967
Career: Halifax Town (1983 - appr, Sep 1985 - pro), TOWN (£10,000 - July 1991), Guisley (Sep 1994), Halifax Town (Nov 1994).

A speedy defender who had serious injury problems in his last full season at Field Mill and subsequently was unable to regain a permanent place in the senior team. Finalist in the Professional Footballers' Sprint Competition held at Wembley Stadium in May 1992. Selected by the P F A for the Division 4 Representative Side in 1991-92.

1991-92   38(0) apps 0 gls
1992-93   0(0)   "   0 "
1993-94   25(3)   "   0 "
1994-95   2(0)   "   0 "
Honours: Division 4 Promotion 1992 (Mansfield)

FLETCHER L

1924 - 25 Outside Left
Career: TOWN (1924 - am)

1924-25   1 app   0 gls Midland League

FLINT J

1923 - 29 Inside Left
b: Mansfield Woodhouse, Notts., c 1907
Career: Woodhouse Exchange, TOWN (1923 - am), Brunts O B.

1923-24   5 apps   6 gls Midland League
1924-25   1   "   0 "   "   "
1925-26   1   "   0 "   "   "
1928-29   1   "   0 "   "   "
Honours: Nottinghamshire Schoolboys 1922.

FLINT J William

1924 - 25 Right Full Back
b: Mapperley, Notts.
Career: Heanor Town, TOWN (Jan 1925), Barnsley (Mar 1925)

1924-25   9 apps   0 gls
Honours: Midland League Championship 1925 (Mansfield)

FLINT W

1923 - 24 Inside Left
b: 1908
Career: TOWN (c/s 1923 - am)

1923-24   1 app   0 gls
Honours: Nottinghamshire Schoolboys 1922

FLOWERS (Ivan) Joseph

1939 - 44 Inside Left
b: Lowestoft, Suffolk, 1919
d: K I A, Caen, Normandy, France, July 1944.
Career: Eastern Coach Works Lowestoft, Wolverhampton Wanderers (c/s 1937), TOWN (Mar 1939 - p/exch A Somerfield + £500)

Ivan Flowers joined the "Stags" in a part exchange deal just before the war, which took Alf Somerfield to Molineux in exchange for Flowers and £500. He was one of the first Mansfield players to join the forces in October 1939 having enlisted in the Territorials the previous year, eventually reaching the rank of Sergeant. Played for the club at quite frequent intervals during hostilities and also guested for Grimsby Town, Norwich City and Scunthorpe United. Sadly killed in action shortly after "D" Day when serving in France, when aged 24 and is the only ex "Stag" to have his name recorded on the town's new war memorial at the Civic Centre.

1938-39   7 apps   2 gls
1939-40   1   "   1 "
WW II   6   "   2 "

FLOWERS Malcolm

1956 - 57 Centre Half Back   5' 10"   10st 7lbs
b: Mansfield, 9 August 1938
Career: TOWN (c/s 1955 - am, Aug 1956 - pro),

1956-57   3 apps   0 gls

FORD Gary

1991 - 93 Outside Right   5' 8"   11st 10lbs (1991)
b: York, 8 February 1961
Career: York City (1977 - appr, Feb 1979 - pro), Leicester City (£25,000 - July 1987), Port Vale (Dec 1987 - loan, Jan 1988 - perm), Walsall (Mar 1990 - loan), TOWN (p/exch + £80,000 for   Kent - Mar 1991), Lillestrom Norway (F.T. Aug 1993), Telford United (F.T. Nov 1993)

A stocky winger who was a rising star in his York days, but never quite made the rise to a higher level. Very effective during Town's promotion season, but could not quite make the grade one division higher. Followed George Foster to Telford when the latter was appointed manager there.

1990-91   12(0) apps   1 gl
1991-92   39(0)   "   4 "
1992-93   37(0)   "   2 "
Honours: Division 4 Championship 1984 (York), Division 4 promotion 1992 (Mansfield)

FOSTER Barry

1970 - 82 Left Full Back   5' 9"   10st 4lbs (1979)
b: Langold, Worksop, Notts., 21 September 1951
Career: TOWN (1967 - am, July 1970 - pro), Boston United (F.T. May 1982)

A former mining electrician at Steetley Colliery, who completed his apprenticeship before signing professional forms, Barry Foster took over at left back from Clive Walker and quickly made the position his own, keeping it for 10 years until he was released when 31 to join non league Boston United. Still operates with the family market-trading business. One of the "Stags" best ever servants. In 287 games he never scored a goal for Mansfield.

Year	Apps		Gls	
1971-72	9(0) apps		0 gls	
1972-73	11(2)	"	0	"
1973-74	19(3)	"	0	"
1974-75	40(0)	"	0	"
1975-76	44(0)	"	0	"
1976-77	39(0)	"	0	"
1977-78	25(0)	"	0	"
1978-79	39(0)	"	0	"
1979-80	15(0)	"	0	"
1980-81	13(0)	"	0	"
1981-82	28(0)	"	0	"

Honours: England Youth International, Notts F A County Cup Winners 1972, Division 4 Championship 1975, Division 3 Championship 1977 (all Mansfield)

FOSTER Colin

1970 - 79 Centre Half Back 5' 9" 11st 0lbs (1979)
b: Nottingham, 26 December 1952
Career: Bulwell St Mary's Junior School, Highbury Secondary School, TOWN (1968 - appr, Dec 1970 - pro), Peterborough United (£13,000 - June 1979), Corby Town (1981 - player manager), Kings Lynn (player manager).

No relation to Barry even though they played together in the same team for eight years. A hard but fair tackler, Foster was no mean scorer of goals from set pieces and could deputise in goal when required, before the days of substitute 'keepers. Father of Steve Foster (see below).

Year	Apps		Gls	
1971-72	1(0) apps		0 gls	
1972-73	6(0)	"	0	"
1973-74	24(3)	"	1	"
1974-75	42(1)	"	3	"
1975-76	34(2)	"	1	"
1976-77	44(0)	"	9	"
1977-78	35(0)	"	3	"
1978-79	9(4)	"	0	"

Honours: Nottingham Schoolboys, Nottinghamshire Schoolboys, Midland Intermediate League (Youth) Championship 1970 as captain, Division 4 Championship 1975, Division 3 Championship 1977 (all Mansfield).

FOSTER (George) William

1983 - 93 Centre Half Back 5' 10" 11st 2lbs
b: Plymouth, 26 September 1956
Career: Plymouth Argyle (1972 - appr, Sep 1974 - pro), Torquay United (Oct 1976 - loan), Exeter City (Dec 1981 - loan), Derby County (£40,000 - June 1982), TOWN (F.T. Aug 1983, player manager from Feb 1989, manager only from May to Sep 1993), Burton Albion (N/C Sep 1993), Chesterfield (N/C Oct 1993), Telford United (Oct 1993 - player- manager to June 1995), Doncaster Rovers (July 1995 - first team coach).

A stopper centre half of the old school, George Foster was a good servant to Mansfield Town for ten years, as player and then manager. Joining the "Pilgrims" as a youngster, he reached the "Stags" in 1983 and by the end of his playing days had amassed a total of 649 League outings and captained the "Stags" to victory in the Freight Rover Trophy at Wembley. After Ian Greaves departure he took over as player-manager and ceased playing for the club in April 1993 after 373 appearances, without even one as a substitute! Took the club to promotion from Division 4 in 1992, but following relegation the following season, fell out of favour with both fans and the new management and was sacked early in the new term. Was soon back in management with Conference side Telford United after brief playing stints with Burton Albion and Chesterfield. Unhappily, he is the only Town manager to suffer relegation twice, but to be fair he gained promotion in between - all in the space of only two years! Won the Division 4 Manager of the Month Award in October 1991 - during the promotion season. Sacked at Telford, but moved to Doncaster within 1 month.

1983-84	42(0)	apps	0	gls	
1984-85	44(0)	"	0	"	
1985-86	46(0)	"	0	"	
1986-87	45(0)	"	0	"	
1987-88	44(0)	"	0	"	
1988-89	42(0)	"	0	"	
1989-90	42(0)	"	0	"	
1990-91	34(0)	"	0	"	
1991-92	24(0)	"	0	"	
1992-93	10(0)	"	0	"	

Honours: Division 4 promotion 1986 and 1992, Freight Rover Trophy Winners 1987, Notts F A County Cup Winners 1987&89 (all Mansfield)

FOSTER Nigel

1984 - 85 Defender
b: Sutton in Ashfield, Notts., 23 March 1968
Career: TOWN (1984 - appr, Aug 1985 - pro)

1984-85	1(0)	0 gls

FOSTER Stephen

1993 - 94 Defender
b: Mansfield, 3 December 1974
Career: TOWN (1989 - assoc sch, 1990 - appr, May 1993 - pro), Telford United (F.T. Jan 1994).

After failing to make his mark after only seven months as a pro at Field Mill, Steve Foster was released and teamed up again with George Foster at Telford. Son of former "Stags" favourite, Colin Foster (see above).

1993-94	2(3) apps	0 gls

FOSTER Samuel (Bernard)

1920 and 1921 - 22 Centre Forward 5' 9½" 11st 7lbs (1920)
b: Southwell, Notts., 12 November 1897
d: 31 March 1965
Career: Southwell Federation, Lincoln City (Jan 1920 - am), TOWN (c/s 1920), Coventry City (£300 - Oct 1920), TOWN (May 1921), Newark Town (1922)

Amateur attacker who made a single appearance for the "Imps" in the Second Division before joining Mansfield as a pro a few months later. His prowess at Mansfield with 11 goals in only 7 matches, prompted Coventry to pay a sizeable sum for him, but he did not shine quite so brightly at Highfield Road, managing four goals in the ten matches he played in and he returned to Field Mill the following Summer.

1920-21	7 apps	11 gls	Central Alliance
1921-22	13 "	6 "	Midland League

Honours: Central Alliance Championship 1921 (Mansfield)

FOSTER William H

1931 - 34 Outside Left 5' 9" 11st 6lbs (1933)
b: Hucknall, Notts., 1911
Career: Hucknall Boys (1924), Newstead Colliery, TOWN (June 1931 - am, June 1932 - pro), Bilsthorpe Colliery (Aug 1934 - permit player - reverted to amateur status)

Son of B B Foster who played for Town from 1913 to 1916, and was also a winger, scoring 14 goals.

1932-33	2 apps	0 gls
1933-34	8 "	2 "

FOX Oscar

1950 - 58 Inside Forward/Wing Half 5' 8½" 11st 0lbs
b: Clowne, Derbys., 1 January 1921
d: 15 January 1990
Career: Sheffield Wednesday (Oct 1943), TOWN (June 1950, asst manager - Jun 1958 to Jan 1960).

Son of Oscar Fox Sr who was a professional with Castleford Town and Bradford City both before and after WW I, young Oscar was a regular member of Wednesday's senior squad and it took what was inevitably described as a "substantial" fee to prise him away from Hillsborough. He was an excellent buy and served the "Stags" well in both inside forward and later wing half roles before retiring from playing in May 1958 at the age of 37.

Appointed assistant to manager Sam Weaver the following month, both were dismissed on the last day of January 1960.

1950-51	34 apps	5 gls
1951-52	43 "	10 "
1952-53	38 "	5 "
1953-54	38 "	2 "
1954-55	41 "	4 "
1955-56	37 "	2 "
1956-57	17 "	2 "
1957-58	0 "	0 "

Honours: Division 3 North Runners Up 1951.

FOX Walter

1946 - 50 Full Back 5' 8½"   11st 7lbs
b: Oxcroft, Bolsover, Derbys., 10 April 1921
d: December 1991
Career: Creswell Colliery, TOWN (Jan 1946 - am, May 1946 - pro), Goole Town.

A rugged, strong tackling, but scrupulously fair defender, this ex miner was not related to Oscar, though they came from the same area.

1946-47	19 apps	0 gls
1947-48	27 "	0 "
1948-49	8 "	0 "
1949-50	8 "	0 "

FRAIN David

1994 Midfield 55' 8"   10st 5lbs (1993)
b: Sheffield, 11 October 1962
Career: Rowlinson Y C, Dronfield United, Sheffield United (Sep 1985), Rochdale (F.T. July 1988), Stockport County (£50,000 - July 1989), TOWN (Sep 1994 - loan)

Brought in to help strengthen the midfield area, but failed to fit the bill and was allowed to return to County after a month.

1994-95   4(2) apps   0 gls (Loan)
Honours: Division 4 Runners Up 1991 (Stockport)

FRAIN Peter A

1984 Forward   5' 8½"   11st 2lbs (1983)
b: Birmingham, 18 March 1965
Career: West Bromwich Albion (1981 - appr, Mar 1982 - pro), TOWN (Jan 1984 - loan)

1983-84   1(1) apps   0 gls (Loan)

FRASER David M

1958 - 59 Outside Left   5' 7"   10st 5lbs (1957)
b: Newtongrange, Nr Edinburgh, 6 June 1937
Career: Arniston Juniors, Hull City (July 1954), TOWN (July 1958)

1958-59   6 apps   1 gl

FRECK H

1922 - 23 Outside Left
Career: TOWN (1922 - am)

1922-23   1 app   0 gls Midland League

FREEMAN James (Alfred)

1928 - 29 Right Half Back   5' 8½"   11st 7lbs (1927)
b: Sutton in Ashfield, Notts., 13 July 1904
d: Ilkeston, January 1986
Career: Sutton Town, Blackpool (c/s 1925), Lincoln City (June 1927), TOWN (Oct 1928), Frickley Colliery (June 1929), Sutton Town (c/s 1030 to 1936).

Although present on the 1928-29 team photographs, taken during the record breaking F A Cup run, Alf Freeman did not appear in any of the six ties played and made insufficient appearances in the Midland League Championship side to gain a medal.

1928-29   12 apps   0 gls Midland League
Honours: Midland League Championship 1929 (Mansfield), Derbyshire League Championship 1931, 1932 & 1933, Sutton Charity Cup Winners 1933 (all Sutton Town).

FRITH (Robert) William

1921 - 23 Centre Half Back
b: Hassop, Nr Bakewell, Derbys., c1890
Career: Sheffield United (Apr 1909), Derby County (Dec 1910), Luton Town (July 1913), South Shields - (July 1919), Rotherham County (Mar 1920), TOWN (c/s 1921), Mid Rhondda (c/s 1923), Rochdale (c/s 1924).

Father of Billy Frith who played for the "Stags" a few years later (see below), Bob Frith was a dominant centre half who could come forward and attack, as was not uncommon before the off-side rule was changed in 1925 and as a result he scored a few goals too. Joined Mansfield for their first season in the Midland League. His father was trainer at Middlesbrough before WW I.

1921-22	35 apps	1 gl		Midland League
1922-23	25 "	4 "		

Honours: Mansfield Hospital Charity Cup Winners 1922, Notts Senior Cup Winners 1923 (all Mansfield), Welsh League Representative XI 1924 (Mid Rhondda)

FRITH William

1930 - 31 Inside Forward/Wing Half 5' 8½" 11st 6lbs (1935)
b: Sheffield, 9 June 1912
Career: Worksop Town (c/s 1929), TOWN (Apr 1930), Chesterfield (£150 - May 1931), Coventry City (F.T. May 1932), Port Vale (Feb 1945 - player manager), Coventry City (Jan 1947 - player, Apr 1947 - manager to Nov 1948 and Sep 1957 to Dec 1961)

A constructive inside forward, later in his career switching to wing half, Billy Frith really made his mark at Coventry where he played in 177 matches before hanging up his boots. Joined Vale for a stormy managerial introduction leaving to return to City as a player again for eight games, then took the manager's chair for 18 months when former "Stag" Dickie Bayliss died suddenly, but was then sacked and returned to full time schoolteaching and part time managership of Rugby Town and Stafford Rangers. A new Chairman pursuaded back to the hot seat at Coventry in Sep 1957 and he soon gained promotion from Division Four at a time when things looked black. After the humiliation of a Cup defeat by Kings Lynn, he and his entire management team were sacked by chairman Derrick Robins in December 1961, whereupon Frith returned to his beloved teaching until retirement in 1977 to Kenilworth, where he still resides. Guested for Leicester during WW II, when not appearing for Coventry. Son of Bob Frith (see above), a "Stags" centre half of the early 1920s.

1929-30	4 apps	1 gl	Midland League
1930-31	35 "	10 " "	"

Honours: Byron Cup Winners & Bayley Cup Winners 1930, Notts Senior Cup Winners 1931 (all Mansfield). Division 3 South runners up 1934, 3rd 1935, Championship 1936, Division 3 South Cup Winners 1936 (all Coventry). War South Championship 1942 (Leicester - guest player).

FRUDE Roger G

1967 - 69 Inside Forward 5' 11" 11st 6lbs
b: Plymouth, 19 November 1946
Career: Bristol Rovers (1962 - appr, Dec 1964 - pro), TOWN (£7,000 - Sep 1967), Brentford (July 1969 - trial), Falmouth Town (Oct 1969), Tavistock Town (Dec 1969).

In two seasons at Field Mill, failed to make his mark and was released to Brentford in July 1969. Made his debut with Bristol Rovers when only 17½.

1967-68	12(0) apps	0 gls
1968-69	2(1) "	0 "

Honours: England Youth International (Bristol Rovers)

GABBITAS Henry

1935 - 36 Centre Forward   5' 11"   11st 10lbs (1936)
b: Arkwright Town, Bolsover, Derbys., 1903
d: Mansfield, June 1992
Career: Mansfield L M S, Army-India, TOWN (Feb 1936 - am),
Worksop Town.

Amateur centre forward who was almost at retiring age when he linked up with the "Stags" following a lengthy spell in the Army.

1935-36   1 app   0 gls

GALLAGHER Barry P

1983 Forward   5' 11"   12st 3lbs (1983)
b: Bradford, 7 April 1961
Career: Bradford City (1977 - appr, Apr 1979 - pro), TOWN (Jan 1983 - loan), Halifax Town (Mar 1983)

1982-83   2(1) apps   0 gls   (Loan)

GALLOWAY Michael

1983 - 86 Defender   5' 11"   11st 7lbs (1987)
b: Oswestry, Salop., 30 May 1965
Career: Elthistone Primrose, Holyrood Star Belfast, Tynecastle B C, Rangers (1981 - trial), Leicester City (1981 - trial), Berwick Rangers (1982), TOWN (July 1983), Halifax Town (Jan 1986 - loan, £25,000 + half sell on fee - Feb 1986 - permanent), Heart of Midlothian (£60,000 - Nov 1987), Celtic (£500,000 - June 1989), Leicester City (Feb 1995 - loan, £200,000 - May 1995 - permanent).

After leaving the "Stags", Mick Galloway was involved in two big money transfer deals and won Scottish Under 21 and full International caps. The "Shaymen" were so keen to sign him and so short of money, that their manager, ex Town boss Mick Jones, organised sponsored walks to raise the cash to buy him! Mansfield received half the fee when Halifax transferred him to Hearts. One of a number of players brought to Filbert Street by new manager Mark McGhee, in an effort to save the drop from the Premiership.

1983-84   12(5) apps   0 gls
1984-85   23(8) "   3 "
1985-86   4(2) "   0 "
Honours: Scotland Youth International (Mansfield), Scotland U/21 International (Hearts), Scotland Full International (Celtic)

GARDINER Charles

1938-39 Utility Forward   5' 9"   11st 0lbs
b: Perth, 1915
Career: Roselea, Nottingham Forest (1935), TOWN (p/exch Crawshaw + £1,500 to Town), Portsmouth (c/s 1939).

Clever inside forward who was a regular with Forest before coming to Field Mill as part of the deal plus cash that took Crawshaw in the opposite direction. Wartime "guest" with Forest, Leicester, Bournemouth, Derby and Greenock Morton.

1938-39   27 apps   4 gls

GARNER (Herbert) Arthur

1925 - 26 and 1930 - 31 Full Back 5' 8½" 10st 11lbs (1925)
b: Mexborough, South Yorks., c1899
Career: Mexborough Great Central Loco (1918), Denaby United (c/s 1919), Lincoln City (May 1921), Wombwell (c/s 1922), Rotherham Town (June 1924), TOWN (Mar 1925), Leicester City (£350 - Feb 1926), Stockport County (Aug 1930 - trial), TOWN (Oct 1930).

Bert Garner was a dependable full back, who played mainly on the left side. Signed by Leicester City after some impressive performances before their scouts, but in five seasons at Filber Street failed to make the senior side and was released to Stockport, where after a trial period, which gave him two games in the first team, he rejoined the "Stags".

1924-25   11 apps   0 gls   Midland League
1925-26   22 "   1 "   "   "
1930-31   9   "   0 "   "   "
Honours: Midland League Championship 1925 & runners up 1926 (both Mansfield)

GARNER Paul

1984 - 89 Defender   5' 8½"   10st 8lbs (1983)
b: Doncaster, 1 December 1955
Career: Huddersfield Town (1971 - appr, Dec 1972 - pro), Sheffield United (Nov 1975), Gillingham (Sep 1983 - loan), TOWN (Sep 1984)

In an 18 year career in first class football, Garner made in excess of 450 league appearances for his clubs, before injury caused his retirement in 1989 when he became an insurance agent in Sheffield. He later bought his own milk round in Renishaw.

1984-85	38(1) apps	2 gls
1985-86	28(0) "	4 "
1986-87	21(1) "	2 "
1987-88	14(5) "	0 "
1988-89	1(1) "	0 "

Honours: England Youth International (Huddersfield). Division 4 Promotion 1986, Freight Rover Trophy Winners 1987, Notts F A County Cup Winners 1989 (all Mansfield)

GARNHAM John ("Jack")
1928 - 29 Outside Left
b: Clipstone, Nr Mansfield, c1907
Career: Clipstone Colliery, TOWN (c/s 1928 - am), Sutton Junction (c/s 1929), Grantham (Mar 1930)

| 1928-29 | 4 apps | 0 gls | Midland League |

GASKELL Alexander
1954 - 57 Centre Forward   5' 10"   12st 7lbs
b: Leigh, Lancs., 30 July 1932
Career: Manchester Amateurs, Southport (Nov 1952), Newcastle United (£5,000 - Oct 1953), TOWN (£3,500 - June 1954), Tranmere Rovers (June 1957), Rhyl, Wigan Rovers, Winsford.

Created quite a reputation as a goalscorer with all his clubs - except Newcastle, where he only played in one match. Overall, he netted 41 times in a career spanning 93 appearances.

1954-55	29 apps	11 gls
1955-56	13 "	6 "
1956-57	0 "	0 "

GAULD James
1960 - 61 Inside Forward   5' 10½"   11st 7lbs
b: Aberdeen, 9 May 1931
Career: Waterford, Charlton Athletic ((May 1955), Everton (Oct 1956), Plymouth Argyle (Oct 1957), Swindon Town (Aug 1959), St Johnstone (c/s 1960), TOWN (£4,000 - Nov 1960)

With a record embracing good performances with all his clubs and having played at the highest level, Jimmy Gauld broke his leg after only four matches with the "Stags" and this effectively finished his career. Implicated in football's biggest ever betting and bribery scandal in which Mansfield matches were involved and named as the ringleader of the fraud, he received a four year prison sentence plus £5,000 in costs for his part in the affair - he was also banned for life by the F A from taking part in any matters concerning football - a lamentable end to what had been a fine career.

| 1960-61 | 4 apps | 3 gls |

Honours: League of Ireland XI (Waterford). Division 3 Championship 1959 ((Plymouth).

GEDDES Andrew
1951 - 52 Wing Half Back
b: Craigneuk, Motherwell, 6 September 1922
d: 12 February 1958
Career: Connelpark Rangers Cumnock, Kilmarnock (Apl 1945), St Cuthbert Wanderers (Aug 1948), Bradford City (Jun 1949), TOWN (Aug 1951), Halifax Town (July 1952), Glenafton Athletic (1955 - coach)

Gritty, hard working player, strong in the tackle and who defended well. Died at the relatively early age of 35. WW II guest with Burnley and Stockport.

| 1951-52 | 11 apps | 2 gls |

GIBSON G
1921 - 23 Centre Forward/Inside Right
Career: TOWN (Oct 1922), Sutton Town (Jan 1923)

| 1921-22 | 16 apps | 5 gls | Midland League |
| 1922-23 | 1 " | 0 " | " |

GIBSON James
1929 - 31 Goalkeeper
Career: TOWN (1929)

Reserve goalkeeper who had few first team opportunities.

| 1929-30 | 4 apps | 0 gls | Midland League |
| 1930-31 | 0 " 0 " | " | " |

GIBSON Harry (William)
1929 - 30 Centre Forward
b: Scotland, c1906
Career: Partick Thistle (1926), TOWN (Aug 1929)

Outstanding centre forward who had been a shining light in the Scottish First Division. Refusing the terms offered, Willie Gibson refused to re-sign for Partick in May 1929 and had thrown in his lot with Mansfield by mid August where he was a great success before breaking his arm late in the season and returning to his native Scotland. Scored 33 goals for Thistle in two seasons.

| 1929-30 | 34 apps | 29 gls | Leading Scorer |

GILHESPY Thomas William (Cyril)
1931 - 32 Outside Right
b: Fence Houses, Co Durham, 18 February 1898
Career: Fence Houses, Chester le Street, Sunderland (Aug 1920), Liverpool (Aug 1921), Bristol City (May 1925), Blackburn Rovers (June 1929), Reading (June 1930), TOWN (£150 - Aug 1931), Crewe Alexandra (Aug 1932).

Before he joined Mansfield at the start of their first Football League season, Cyril Gilhespy had played for over 10 years in either First or Second Division football, excepting part of 1926-27 when he was a member of Bristol City's Division Three South promotion team. A speedy winger in his younger days.

1931-32   19 apps   4 gls
Honours: Division 3 South Championship 1927 (Bristol City)

GILL John B A
1961 - 66 Centre Half Back   5' 11"   12st 0lbs
b: Wednesbury, Staffs., 3 February 1941
Career: Juniors, Nottingham Forest (Mar 1958), TOWN (F.T. July 1961), Hartlepool United (Feb 1966)

Another player who provided Mansfield with five years of fine service, Gill came to Field Mill when released on a free transfer by Forest without making a senior appearance. Played in almost 150 matches for the "Stags" before moving on to Hartlepools for whom he gave six years of reliable play.

1961-62   19 apps   0 gls
1962-53   14   "   0   "
1963-64   41   "   0   "
1964-65   46   "   0   "
1965-66   18(1)"   0   "

Honours: Division 4 promotion 1963, Division 3 - 3rd 1965 (both Mansfield)

GILLATT Kenneth
1923 - 25 Inside Right   5' 8"   11st 0lbs (1924)
b: Wensleydale, Derbys., c 1900
Career: Hartshay Colliery, Matlock Town, Clapton Orient (c/s 1920), Burnley (Sep 1923), TOWN (Nov 1923), Barnsley (£175 - Feb 1925),

Clever inside forward who made an important contribution to the "Stags" achievement in winning the Midland League title two years in succession. Despite being christened Kenneth, he was always known as "Ernie", to the despair of statisticians.

1923-24   14 apps   4 gls Midland League
1924-25   21   "   6   "   "   "
Honours: Midland League Championship 1924 & 1925 (Mansfield)

GILMORE Henry (Patrick)
1935 - 36 Right Half Back   5' 11"   12st 0lbs (1936)
b: West Hartlepool, 1913
Career: Shotton C W, Hull City (Dec 1934), TOWN (July 1935), Bournemouth & Boscombe Athletic (June 1936), Runcorn (Feb 1937), Queens Park Rangers (May 1937), Hull City (May 1939).

Just one season with Mansfield. War time "guest" player with Barnsley. At club known as "Mike".

1935-36   20 apps   0 gls

GLASSEY (Robert) John
1939 - 45 Inside Forward   5' 11"   11st 7lbs (1939)
b: Chester le Street, Co Durham, 13 August 1914
d: Durham, July 1984
Career: Horden Colliery, Liverpool (1933), Stoke City (Nov 1936), TOWN (May 1939), Stockton (1945).

Bob Glassey had experience of First Division football before joining Mansfield just before the start of the war and the three matches he played for the club before the season was aborted, showed that he was a very talented player who could have been part of one of Town's best teams up to that time. Played as a "guest" with Hartlepools, Newcastle and Third Lanark during WW II.

1939-40   3 apps   1 gl

GLAZEBROOK E
1930 - 31 Centre Half Back
Career: TOWN (1930 - am)

1930-31   1 app   0 gls

GLAZZARD James

1956 - 58 Centre Forward   5' 10"   11st 6lbs (1957)
b: Normanton, Leeds, 23 April 1923
Career: Altofts Colliery, Bolton Wanderers (1942 - am),
Huddersfield Town (July 1943 - am, Oct 1943 - pro), Everton
(£3,750 - Sep 1956), TOWN (Dec 1956).

A great goal scoring machine, particularly with the
"Terriers", where he scored 30 goals in 1952-53 -
making it his fifth consecutive season as their
leading scorer. He netted a total of 153 goals in his
career there and a further 10 for Town. It was rather
surprising that he did not receive International
recognition, the nearest being selection as reserve for
the "B" team versus Germany in March 1954.

1956-57	20 apps	10 gls	
1957-58	1 "	0 "	

GLOVER Gerald M

1967 - 68 Inside Forward
b: Liverpool, 27 September 1946
Career: Everton (1962 - appr, Aug 1964 - pro), TOWN (Sep
1967)

1967-68   18(1) apps   0 gls
Honours: England Schools & Youth International

GODDARD (Charles) Percy

1925, 1927 - 29 and 1930 - 31 Outside Right
b: Rauceby, Lincs., 6 April 1910
Career: Clipstone Colliery, Rotherham Town (1924 - trial - am),
TOWN (Aug 1925 - trial - am), Shirebrook (Sep 1925 to Nov
1925 - am), Clipstone Colliery, TOWN (c/s 1927 - am, 1928 -
pro), Sheffield Wednesday (£250 - Oct 1928), Worksop Town
(c/s 1929), TOWN (c/s 1930), Northfleet (c/s 1931), Crystal
Palace (c/s 1932), Fulham (Oct 1935)

A Lincolnshire born player, whose family moved to
Clipstone when he was a teenager in search of work
in the mines, Charlie Goddard played for the "Stags"
on three separate occasions before making his name
in the League with Crystal Palace. He was no mean
scorer of goals - for a winger! Oddly enough, he
was signed by the "Glaziers" as replacement for ex
Mansfield winger, George Clarke.

1927-28	7 apps	3 gls	Midland League	
1928-29	3 "	0 "	"	"
1930-31	43 "	18 "	"	"

Honours: Mansfield Hospital Charity Cup Winners
1928, Notts Senior Cup Winners 1931 (both
Mansfield)

GODDARD (Howard) Vincent

1928 - 29 b: Warsop Vale, Nr Mansfield, 24 January 1905
d: Shirebrook, 6 June 1966
Goalkeeper 6' 0"   12st 7lbs (1928)
b: Warsop Vale, 16 February 1905
Career: Shirebrook (c/s 1925), Aston Villa (c/s 1927), TOWN (c/s
1928)

Essentially a reserve player at Field Mill, Howard
Goddard was also an accomplished cricketer,
keeping wicket for both Warsop Main and
Shirebrook Colliery in the Bassetlaw League.

1928-29   11 apps   0 gls Midland League
Honours: Midland League Championship 1929
(Mansfield)

GODWIN Verdi

1950 - 51 Centre Forward   5' 8"   12st 2lbs (1951)
b: Blackburn, 11 February 1926
Career: Blackburn Rovers (Mar 1946), Manchester City (June
1948), Stoke City (£3,000 - June 1949), TOWN (part exch
Oscroft + £8,000 to "Stags" - Jan 1950), Middlesbrough (Nov
1951), Grimsby Town (Jan 1952), Brentford (Mar 1952),
Southport (July 1954), Barrow (Aug 1955), Tranmere Rovers
(Aug 1956), Kings Lynn (1957).

Was a regular First Division player when manager
Freddie Steele persuaded Stoke City to part with
Godwin (valued at £22,000) in part exchange for
Harry Oscroft and pay an additional £8,000 - such
was Bob McGrory's keenness to sign the Mansfield
winger. Not an outstanding success at Field Mill in
the hurly burly of the Third Division , he moved on
18 months later to Middlesbrough and back to the
First Division. Presumably his parents were
enthusiastic patrons of opera as they named their son
after the famous Italian composer, Guiseppe Verdi!

1949-50	17 apps	7 gls	
1950-51	14 "	2 "	

Honours: Division 3 North Runners Up 1951
(Mansfield)

GOODACRE Reginald

1933 - 34 Right Full Back
b: Billingborough, Lincs., c1908
Career: Sleaford G S, Billingborough, Lincoln City (am), Boston,
West Ham United (c/s 1930), TOWN (May 1933), Peterborough
& Fletton United (c/s 1934), Gainsborough Trinity (c/s 1935)

In three seasons with West Ham, Reg Goodacre
made 20 appearances in the senior team, mainly in
the First Division.

1933-34   18 apps   1 gl

GOODFELLOW (James) Boyd

1968 - 71 Centre Forward 5' 8" 10st 9lbs (1970)
b: Edinburgh, 30 July 1938
Career: Third Lanark (1957), Leicester City (May 1963), TOWN (Mar 1968), Weymouth (July 1971 to May 1973)

Jimmy Goodfellow was well established in the Scottish First Division when Leicester manager, Matt Gillies prised him south of the border where he spent almost five fruitful seasons at Filbert Street, being leading scorer in 1964-65. One of the architects of Mansfield's record breaking run to the quarter finals of the F A Cup in 1969, he went into the catering business on the South Coast in the early 1970s.

1967-68	12 apps	0 gls
1968-69	39 "	6 "
1969-70	30 "	6 "
1970-71	15(4)"	2 "

Honours: Scottish League XI (Third Lanark). Football League Cup Runners Up 1965 (Leicester). "Giant Killers" Cup Winners 1969 (Mansfield).

GOODWIN David

1977 - 80 Forward 5' 9½" 11st 6lbs (1979)
b: Nantwich, Cheshire, 15 October 1954
Career: Stoke City (1970 - appr, June 1972 - pro), Workington (Oct 1976 - loan), TOWN (Nov 1977), Bury (F.T. Sep 1980), Rochdale (F.T. Aug 1981), Crewe Alexandra (F.T. Aug 1982)

Always struggled to get a place in the senior team at Mansfield.

1977-78	12(3) apps	1 gl
1978-79	26(1) "	4 "
1979-80	4(0) "	0 "

GOODWIN Eric

1953 - 55 Centre Half Back 5' 11" 12st 7lbs
b: Chesterfield, 6 March 1929
Career: Coventry City (am), St Aidans Stags, TOWN (Aug 1953 - am, Sep 1953 - pro).

A reserve player at Field Mill, Eric Goodwin was employed as a billposter during the 1970s.

| 1953-54 | 1 app | 0 gls |
| 1954-55 | 8 " | 0 " |

GOVAN Charles P

1963 - 65 Forward 5' 7" 10st 4lbs
b: Belfast, 12 January 1943
Career: Irish Juniors, Burnley (Jan 1960), TOWN (June 1963)

| 1963-64 | 10 apps | 0 gls |
| 1964-65 | 1 " | 0 " |

Honours: Northern Ireland Schoolboy International.

GRAHAM Gerald W

1964 - 65 Wing Half Back 6' 0" 12st 0lbs
b: Aspatria, Cumbria, 31 january 1941
Career: Blackpool (Aug 1959), Peterborough United (July 1960), TOWN (June 1964), Hereford United (c/s 1965), Workington (July 1968)

| 1964-65 | 18 apps | 3 gls |

Honours: Division 3 - 3rd 1965 (Mansfield)

GRAHAM Michael A

1985 - 88 Defender 5' 9" 11st 7lbs (1988)
b: Lancaster, 24 February 1959
Career: Bolton Wanderers (1975 - appr, Mar 1977 - pro), Swindon Town (F.T. July 1981), TOWN (F.T. July 1985), Carlisle United (£10,000 - Sep 1988 to May 1992)

A solid dependable full back, Mike Graham made a total of 458 Football League appearances and served each of his clubs well.

1985-86	46(0) apps	0 gls
1986-87	40(1) "	0 "
1987-88	46(0) "	1 "
1988-89	1(0) "	0 "

Honours: Division 4 promotion 1986, Freight Rover Trophy Winners 1987, Notts F A County Cup Winners 1987, 88 & 89 (all Mansfield)

GRATTAN James

1978 Forward 5' 9" 10st 10lbs (1978)
b: Belfast, 30 November 1958
Career: Sunderland (1974 - appr, Oct 1976 - pro), TOWN (Nov 1978 - loan).

Young attacker whose only league game was on loan at Mansfield

| 1978-79 | 1(1) app | 0 gls | (Loan) |

GRAY Kevin J

1988 - 94 Defender   6' 0"   13st 0lbs (1991)
b: Sheffield, 7 January 1972
Career: TOWN (1988 - appr, Jan 1989 - pro), Huddersfield Town (£50,000 - p/exch Onuora + £25,000).

Outstanding young centre half who joined Mansfield as a Y T S trainee direct from Tuxford Comprehensive School, but he was sacrificed to obtain the signature of Iffy Onuora, who the "Terriers" valued at £25,000 more.

1988-89	1(0) apps	0 gls	
1989-90	16(0)	"	0 "
1990-91	28(3)	"	1 "
1991-92	11(7)	"	0 "
1992-93	31(2)	"	0 "
1993-94	42(0)	"	2 "

Honours: Division 4 Promotion 1992 (Mansfield)

GRAY (Robert) Alexander

1929 - 30 Inside Forward   5' 10"   11st 6lbs (1931)
b: Huddersfield, 7 October 1903
Career: Huddersfield Town (c/s 1923), Tranmere Rovers (c/s 1927), Northwich Victoria (c/s 1929) TOWN (Oct 1929), Rotherham United (c/s 1930), Chester (c/s 1932), Southport (Nov 1932), Carlisle United (Feb 1933), Gateshead (c/s 1934), York City (July 1935), Goole Town (July 1937)

Regular inside right for the "Stags" in the 1929-30 season, who appeared to change clubs almost annually.

1929-30   31 apps   15 gls Midland League

GREATOREX George Arthur

1922 - 23 Inside Right   5' 5"
b: Huthwaite, Notts., 1900
Career: Sutton Junction (c/s 1919), Leicester City (May 1921), TOWN (May 1922), Sutton Town (c/s 1923), Frickley Colliery (c/s 1925), Scarborough (c/s 1928), Shirebrook (c/s 1929 to May 1930)

Only league team was Leicester where he played in only 11 games and scored 2 goals in 1921-22. A prolific goalscorer with Mansfield, it was surprising they allowed him to join the "Snipes". Because of his size, was nicknamed "Baby".

1922-23 31 apps 21 gls Midland Lge. Lead. Scorer
Honours: Notts Senior Cup Winners 1923 (Mansfield)

GREEN Alan P C

1972 - 73 Forward   3' 8"   11st 2lbs (1973)
b: Fordingbridge, Hants., 19 April 1951
Career: Bournemouth & Boscombe Athletic (July 1969), TOWN (July 1972)

After three years with the "Cherries", Alan Green joined the "Stags" and in his first game had a heart attack just before half time and never played again.

1972-73   1(0) apps   0 gls

GREGSON John

1964 - 67 Winger   5' 9"   10st 6lbs (1966)
b: Skelmersdale, Yorks., 17 May 1939
Career: Skelmersdale United, Blackpool (May 1957), Chester (May 1962), Shrewsbury Town (Mar 1963), TOWN (£12,000 - Nov 1964), Lincoln City (June 1967), Cambridge United (F.T. July 1968 - N/C to 1972)

After understudying Stanley Matthews and only managing three games, Gregson started his moves around the soccer world and was a member of one of Town's great sides in the 1960s.

1964-65	24 apps	2 gls	
1965-66	30(0)"	3	"
1966-67	21(1)"	0	"

Honours: Division 3 - 3rd 1965 (Mansfield)

GRICE Benjamin

1928 - 32 Centre Forward   5' 8"   11st 7lbs (1928)
b: Kings Lynn, Norfolk, c1906
Career: Rainworth Church, Notts County (c/s 1926), Coventry City (Aug 1927 - trial), Frickley Colliery (Oct 1927), Worksop Town (1928), TOWN (Oct 1928), Sutton Town (c/s 1932)

Family moved from Norfolk to find industrial employment and settled in Sutton in Ashfield early in the century. Although with Mansfield through to the end of the first Football League season, Grice did not get an opportunity in the League team with Harry Johnson and John Jepson around. Always a reserve at Field Mill. Elder brother of Tom (below).

1928-29	13 apps	9 gls	Midland League	
1929-30	6 "	1 "	"	"
1930-31	8 "	6 "	"	"
1931-32	0 "	0 "		

Honours: Midland League Championship 1929 (Mansfield). Derbyshire League Championship & Sutton Charity Cup Winners 1933 (both Sutton Town).

GRICE (Thomas) William

1928 - 30 Centre Half Back   5' 11"   12st 7lbs (1935)
b: Sutton in Ashfield, Notts., c1908
Career: Rainworth Church, Coventry City (Aug 1927 - trial), Worksop Town (c/s 1928), TOWN (Oct 1928), Worksop Town (c/s 1930), Birmingham (c/s 1931), Torquay United (c/s 1933), Walsall (c/s 1934), Teversall Colliery (1937).

Younger brother of Ben (above), Tom at least experienced League football in his travels. During the summer months played cricket for New Hucknall Colliery.

1928-29 3 apps   0 gls Midland League
1929-30 3 "   0 "   "   "
Honours: Division 3 South Cup runners up 1934 (Torquay). Division 3 North Cup runners up 1935 (Walsall).

GRIFFIN Kevin R
1975 Inside Forward
b: Plymouth, 5 October 1953
Career: Bristol City (1969 - appr, Sep 1971 - pro), TOWN (Mar 1975 - loan), Cambridge United (Sep 1975 - loan)

1974-75 4(0) apps   2 gls

GRIFFITHS Kenneth J
1957 - 59 Inside Forward   5' 8"   11st 0lbs
b: Stoke on Trent, 2 April 1930
Career: Port Vale (Mar 1950), TOWN (Jan 1958)

Vastly experienced inside forward who had played for Port Vale for eight years when he joined Town for two seasons.

1957-58 14 apps   4 gls
1958-59 28 "   3 "
Honours: Divison 3 North Runners Up 1953, Division 3 North Championship 1954 (both Port Vale)

GRIMWADE
1922 - 23 Centre Forward
Career: TOWN (c/s 1922)

Made just one senior appearance, in the F A Cup.

1922-23 0 apps 0 gls Midland League

GROGAN John
1947 - 52 Centre Half Back   5' 10½"   11st 0lbs
b: Nitshill, Paisley, 30 October 1915
d: Thurcaston, Leicester, 1975
Career: Shawfield Juniors, Leicester City (Oct 1933), TOWN (Sep 1947), Bentley Engineering F C (1952 - player manager)

A good solid stopper centre half who went about his duties with the minumum of fuss, was almost unobtrusively efficient and never had a bad game. Returned to Leicester after his league days were over and was associated with a local works team in

the Leicestershire Senior League for many years. Died at his home on the outskirts of Leicester in 1975 and my wife's floristry business prepared the family tributes, many of which had a soccer theme. During WW II played as a "guest" for Northampton, Luton, Swansea, Crystal Palace, and Grimsby. A serious road accident in June 1936 seriously threatened his career, but he recovered satisfactorily. Served in the R.A.F. during WW II.

1947-48 34 apps   0 gls
1948-49 42 "   0 "
1949-50 37 "   0 "
1950-51 46 "   0 "
1951-52 42 "   0 "
Honours: Division 3 North Runners Up 1951 (Mansfield)

GROVES John William
1920 - 23 Goalkeeper 5' 9"   11st 12lbs
b: Bulwell, Nottingham, 29 April 1899
Career: Army 1914), Basford N O F, Norwich City (May 1919), Halifax Town (Jan 1920), TOWN (Mar 1921), Sutton Town (c/s 1923).

Jack Groves was Town's regular goalkeeper for over two seasons and never lost his place. Very efficient too according to contemporary reports.

1920-21 6 apps   0 gls Central Alliance
1921-22 40 "   0 "   Midland League
1922-23 38 "   0 "   "   "
Honours: Mansfield Hospital Charity Cup Winners 1922 (Mansfield)

GROZIER William
1972 - 75 Full Back
b: Cumnock, Ayrshire, 24 August 1956
Career: TOWN (1972 - appr, Aug 1974 - pro)

Young Scot whose only senior appearance came whilst he was still an apprentice and had not reached his 18th birthday.

1973-74   1(0) apps   0 gls

GRUNDY William
1935 - 36 Left Half Back
b: Kirkby in Ashfield, Notts., c1913
Career: Annesley C W, Coventry City (c/s 1933), TOWN (c/s 1935), Annesley C W (1936)

Fair haired defender who made but a single appearance for the "Light Blues" in the season before he joined the "Stags".

1935-36   5 apps   0 gls

GUNN Brynley C
1986 Defender   6' 2"   13st 7lbs (1987)
b: Kettering, Northants., 21 August 1958
Career: Nottingham Forest (1974 - appr, Aug 1975 - pro), Shrewsbury Town (Dec 1985 - loan), Walsall (Jan 1986 - loan), TOWN (Mar 1986 - loan), Peterborough United (F.T. Aug 1986), Chesterfield ((July 1989), Corby Town (c/s 1992), Oakham United (c/s 1993 to 1994)

Very experienced defender who was reaching the end of his effective league career with Forest and was loaned out to several clubs in 1985-86, subsequently signing for the "Posh" and eventually the "Spireites", with both of whom he extended his career considerably before decending into non league circles.

1985-86   5(0) apps   0 gls   (Loan)

HACKETT (Christopher) Edward
1921 - 22 Outside Right   5' 7½"   10st 7lbs (1925)
b: Mansfield, 9 February 1903
d: Leicester, Jan 1983
Career: Langwith Colliery, TOWN (1921 - am), Welbeck Colliery (c/s 1922), Newark Town (c/s 1923), Grantham (c/s 1924), Leicester City (£35 - Dec 1924), Caernarfon Town (1928), Bury (Nov 1928), Scunthorpe United (July 1929), Bristol Rovers (May 1930), Loughborough Corinthians (Sep 1931), Accrington Stanley (June 1932)

Local amateur who soon joined the professional ranks after he left Field Mill and moved about with great frequency.

1921-22   2 apps   0 gls Midland League

HADLEY Stewart
1994 onwards Striker   6' 0"   12st 2lbs (1993)
b: Dudley, Worcs., 30 December 1973
Career: Halesowen Town, Derby County (July 1992), Nuneaton Borough (1993 - loan), TOWN (£5,000 - Feb 1994)

Tall energetic striker who works non-stop and worries opposing defences with his persistence. After the emergence of Onuora, was used extremely effectively as a late goalscoring substitute. Nicknamed "Turbo" by the fans.

1993-94   14 (0) apps   4 gls
1994-95   28(11)   "   14 " (+1gl Play-offs)

HAILWOOD David J
1973 - 75 Forward   6' 0"   11st 2lbs (1973)
b: Nottingham, 17 October 1954
Career: TOWN (July 1973 to May 1975)

1974-75   1(0) app   0 gls

HALL Brian S
1959 - 65 Winger   5' 9"   11st 7lbs
b: Burbage, Leics., 9 March 1939
Career: Belper Town (1955 - am, May 1957 - pro), TOWN (Apr 1959), Colchester United (£5,000 - Mar 1965 to Jan 1973)

Had a most distinguished career, for after playing in 72 matches for Mansfield, he went on to amass a further 324 appearances for the Layer Road side. Was mainly a reserve at Field Mill, Although contemporary with his namesake Ian, whilst with the "Stags", they were not related.

1958-59	2 apps	1 gl	
1959-60	15 "	3 "	
1960-61	4 "	0 "	
1961-62	14 "	3 "	
1962-63	16 "	4 "	
1963-64	11 "	6 "	
1964-65	10 "	2 "	

Honours: Division 4 Promotion 1963 (Mansfield)

HALL (Ian) William

1962 - 68 Inside Forward   5' 7"   10st 10lbs (1965)
b: Sutton Scarsdale, Derbys., 27 December 1939
Career: Wolverhampton Wanderers (Aug 1958 - am), Derby County (May 1959 - am, Sep 1959 - pro), TOWN (Sep 1962), Tamworth (Aug 1968), Burton Albion (July 1971), Derbyshire Amateurs (1973 - permit player), Tamworth (1974)

This great clubman was an all round sportsman, combining League football and County cricket for his native Derbyshire and was equally successful at both. After his playing days were over, he took a degree at University, teaching diploma at Loughborough College and pursued a teaching career at grammar and public school level - and to add to his range of activities, he is a cricket commentator on Radio Derby and handles soccer phone-in lines too! He played in 270 matches for Deryshire C C C between 1959 and 1972.

1962-63	16 apps	1 gl	
1963-64	7 "	1 "	
1964-65	34 "	4 "	
1965-66	41(0)"	1 "	
1966-67	34(0)"	3 "	
1967-68	13(0)"	0 "	

Honours: England Scoolboy International, England Youth International (Derby), Division 4 promotion 1963 & Division 3 - 3rd 1965 (both Mansfield)

HAMBY W

1927   Full Back 5' 10"   11st 0lbs (1927)
b: Staveley, Derbys., c1904
Career: Newstead, Aston Villa (c/s 1925), Birmingham (c/s 1926), TOWN (May 1927), Staveley Town (Oct 1927), Newark Town (c/s 1928).

1927-28	10 apps	2 gls	Midland League

HAMILTON (Neville) Roy

1979 - 81 Midfield   5' 8"   10st 0lbs (1980)
b: Leicester, 19 April 1960
Caree: Leicester City (1976 - appr, Nov 1977 - pro), TOWN (£25,000 - Jan 1979), Rochdale (F.T. Aug 1981), Wolverhampton Wanderers (F.T. c/s 1984, C/C Mar 1985)

At the centre of the "Stags" midfield for two and a half seasons before being released. Shortly after he joined Wolves, Hamilton had a heart attack during pre-season training and retired from playing, but by August 1986 he had qualified as an F A Coach.

1978-79	16(2) apps	1 gl	
1979-80	32(1) "	1 "	
1980-81	36(2) "	2 "	

HARDSTAFF James

1923 - 25 Goalkeeper 5' 10½"   11st 7lbs (1924)
b: Nottingham, 1895
Career: Sutton Junction (1919), Loughborough Corinthians (1921), Rotherham County (c/s 1922), TOWN (c/s 1923)

Regular goalkeeper during the two championship seasons 1923-25

1923-24	29 apps	0 gls	Midland League
1924-25	30 "	0 "	

Honours: Midland League Championship 1923-24 & 1924-25 (Mansfield)

HARDY Edgar F

1927 - 28 Outside Left
b: Sunderland, 10 February 1899
d: Sunderland, January 1932
Career: Rotherham United (c/s 1925), TOWN (Sep 1927)

Edgar Hardy started quite late in league soccer, making his debut for Rotherham at the age of 27. He died at a very early age too - aged 32.

1927-28	14 apps	1 gl	Midland League

Honours: Mansfield Hospital Charity Cup Winners 1928 (Mansfield)

HARDY L
1928 - 30 Goalkeeper
Career: TOWN (c/s 1928), Shirebrook (Apr 1930), Welbeck Colliery.

1928-29	2 apps	0 gls	Midland League
1929-30	8 "	0 "	" "

Honours: Mansfield Hospital Charity Cup Winners 1929 (Mansfield)

HARFORD (Raymond) Thomas
1971 Centre Half Back   6' 1"   12st 12lbs (1970)
b: Halifax, 1 June 1945
Career: South London Schools, Charlton Athletic (May 1961 - pro May 1964), Exeter City (£750 - Jan 1966), Lincoln City (July 1967), TOWN (£6,000 - June 1971), Port Vale (Dec 1971 - loan, £10,000 - Jan 1972), Colchester United (Jan 1973 - loan, Feb 1973 - permanent), Romford (July 1975), Colchester (Sep 1975 - coach), Fulham (July 1981 - coach, Jun 1982 - asst manager, Apr 1984 - caretaker manager - Apr 1984, May 1984 - manager), Luton Town (July 1986 - coach, Jun 1987 - manager to Jan 1990), Wimbledon (Mar 1990 - asst manager, Jun 1990 - caretaker manager, Dec 1990 - manager), Blackburn Rovers (Oct 1991 - asst manager).

Only at Field Mill a few months before Port Vale signed him. Managed the England Under 21 squad during the 1995 Tournament in Toulon, during which Paul Holland received his first cap.

1971-72	7(0) apps	0 gls

HARGREAVES Harold
1930 - 31 Wing Half Back   5' 9"   11st 7lbs
b: Sheffield, c1903
Career: Blackpool (1924), Lincoln City (c/s 1927), Wath Athletic (c/s 1928), Merthyr Town (c/s 1929), TOWN (c/s 1930), Worksop Town (c/s 1931)

Previous League experience was limited to Second Division with Blackpool and Third Division South with Merthyr. Quoted as "good attacking wing half" with Mansfield.

1930-31	46 apps	7 gls	Midland League

Honours: Notts Senior Cup Winners 1931 (Mansfield)

HARKIN James
1939-47 Wing Half/Inside Forward 5' 7" 11st 0lbs (1935)
b: Brinsworth, South Yorks., 8 August 1913
Career: Rossington Main C W, Denaby United, Doncaster Rovers (Aug 1934), Shrewsbury Town (May 1936), TOWN £100 - Feb 1939), Gainsborough Trinity (F.T. c/s 1947), Peterborough & Fletton United (c/s 1948)

Sturdy little wing half who played inside forward on occasions. Member of Shrewsbury's Midland League Championship team, the war blunted his rising career, like many players and by the end of it, he was 32. A former miner, he returned to the pits during WW II and when not required by the "Stags" guested for Chesterfield and Doncaster.

1938-39	16 apps	2 gls	
1939-40	3 "	0 "	
WW II	179 "	23 "	
1946-47	7 "	3 "	

Honours: Welsh Cup Winners & Midland League Championship 1938 (Shrewsbury).

HARPER Donald
1946 - 47 Outside Right   5' 7"   10st 7lbs (1946)
b: Mansfield, 26 October 1921
Career: Chesterfield (Dec 1943), TOWN (July 1946)

Speedy winger developed by the "Spireites" during the war, when he also was a "guest" player with Lincoln, but his star faded in the more competitive post war scene.

1946-47	21 apps	1 gl

HARRINGTON Colin A
1971 - 72 Inside Forward   6' 1"   12st 7lbs (1971)
b: Bicester, Oxon., 3 April 1943
Career: Wolverhampton Wanderers (am), Oxford United (Oct 1962), TOWN (June 1971), Kettering Town (F.T. May 1972)

Played in over 230 matches for the "Us" in a career spanning nine seasons, but was past his best at Mansfield. Member of the Oxford team which reached the Sixth Round of the F A Cup in 1963-64 - a record for a Fourth Division club.

1971-72	7(6) apps	0 gls

Honours: Division 4 promotion 1965, Division 3 Championship 1968 (both Oxford)

HARRIS (George) Joseph
1925 - 26 Goalkeeper
b: Underwood, Notts., 22 January 1904
d: Swansea, 28 December 1988
Career: Netherfield Rangers, TOWN (Dec 1925), Swansea Town (c/s 1926)

Perhaps better known as a cricketer as he was on the Nottinghamshire ground staff for a time in 1925/26, but when he moved to Swansea, linked up with Glamorgan and played in one first class match for them in 1932. After leaving professional sport, he joined the police force in South Wales.

1925-26	5 apps	0 gls	Midland League

HARRISON Charles
1924 - 25 Outside Right
b: Mansfield, 15 April 1894
d: Mansfield, 1 August 1977
Career: Rufford Colliery,Clifton Colliery,TOWN (Apr 1925 - am)

Mainly a reserve at Field Mill, Harrison subsequently served as the Mayor in the town on three separate occasions. For a number of years he was a Midland League referee.

1924-25   3 apps   0 gls Midland League

HARSTON Edwin
1935 - 37 Centre Forward   5' 9"   11st 12lbs (1930)
b: Monk Bretton, Nr Barnsley, 27 February 1907
Career: Cudworth Village, Sheffield Wednesday (c/s 1928), Barnsley (May 1930), Reading (c/s 1931), Bristol City (c/s 1934), TOWN (£250 - Oct 1935), Liverpool (£3,000 - June 1937), Ramsgate Town (June 1939 - player manager)

Perhaps the best known centre forward that the "Stags" have ever had and certainly one that will stay in the record books for posterity. Holds in perpetuity the Division 3 North goalscoring record with 55 goals in season 1936-37. Oddly enough the Third Division South record of exactly the same number of goals by Joe Payne of Luton Town and ex Bolsover Colliery, was set up in the same term and the two players were neck and neck all season. Quite unskilled as a creator and no dribbler, Teddy Harston received excellent service by way of passes from the providers - Hart, Anderson, Atkinson and Horne, together with accurate centres from the two wingmen, Rattray and Roy. All Harston had to do was to put the ball in the net and possessing a strong and accurate shot in either foot and no mug with his head either, he could not help putting them away

regularly - just about the perfect centre forward! After he went to First Division Liverpool, he scored three goals in five games before a broken leg finished him for the season and the next season, confined to the reserves, he netted 27 times. Teddy Harston replaced another goalscoring legend at Mansfield - Harry Johnson. Seventh in the list of Town's all time goalscorers and Fourth in Football League matches - all in just a season and a half! He was never so prolific elsewhere, although the "Stags" had good cause to remember the time he put six past them for Barnsley in a Yorkshire Mid Week League game in April 1931!

1935-36   29 apps   26 gls   Leading Scorer
1936-37   41   "   55 "   "   "

HART (Ernest) Arthur
1936 - 37 Centre Half Back   5' 11"   12st 6lbs (1935)
b: Overseal, Staffs., 3 January 1902
d: Adwick le Street, Nr Doncaster, 21 July 1954
Career: Woodlands Wesleyans, Leeds City (1919), Leeds United (c/s 1920), TOWN (£350 - Aug 1936 to Mar 1937), Tunbridge Wells Rangers (July 1938 - manager)

Ernie Hart was the first player signed by new manager Arthur Fairclough for the newly formed Leeds United after the forced disbandment of the former Leeds City club by the Football League in October 1919. He went on to a glittering career of 16 years at Elland Road, winning England caps and Football League appearances along the way. In the twilight of his career he joined Mansfield, but did not play for the club after March 1937 due to a serious problem that arose and he left the club in disgrace. An attacking centre half of the old school, he would not compromise his ideas in this respect, even though the stopper centre half was now well established and this cost him further international recognition. His attacking role and excellent through passes, played no small part in Teddy Harston's record breaking goals tally.

1936-37   28 apps   0 gls
Honours: England International, Football League XI, Division 2 Championship 1924, Division 2 Runners Up 1928 & 1932, F A Charity Shield Winners - pros v amateurs 1929 (all Leeds)

HART John Leslie
1925 - 26 Centre Forward   6' 1"   12st 7lbs (1925)
b: Bolsover, Derbys., c1905
Career: New Hucknall Colliery (1920), Bolsover Colliery, Worksop Town (c/s 1924), Chesterfield (Mar 1925), TOWN (Sep 1925), Derby County (£550 - Jan 1926), Newark Town (c/s 1927), Ebbw Vale.

Although with Town barely half a season, Jack Hart was a veritable goalscoring whirlwind here, netting an incredible 24 goals in only 13 matches, including four hat tricks and a five - in his final match - then Derby County could wait no longer to sign him for what was a huge fee at that time! He had previously scored only one goal in four outings with Chesterfield's Third Division team. He subsequently netted three in four games for Derby in their Second Division promotion season.

1925-26   13 apps   24 gls   Midland League
Honours: Midland League runners up 1926 (Mansfield)

HASELDEN John J
1972 Half back
b: Doncaster, 3 August 1943
Career: Denaby United, Rotherham United (Feb 1962), Doncaster Rovers (Sep 1968), TOWN (Feb 1972 - loan, c/s 1974 - trainer coach to 1977), Reading (1987 - physio), Nottingham Forest (coach/physio - Oct 1994).

Well respected defender who had long spells at both Rotherham and Doncaster. Of recent times qualified as a physiotherapist and served Reading for seven years in this capacity before joining Forest in a similar sphere as recently as October 1994.

1971-72   4(0) apps   0 gls   (Loan)
Honours: Division 4 Championship 1969 (Doncaster).

HATHAWAY Ian A
1989 - 91 Forward   5' 8"   10st 6lbs
b: Worsley, Manchester, 22 August 1968
Career: West Bromwich Albion (1984 - appr, 1985 - pro), Bedworth United (c/s 1987), TOWN (£8,000 - Feb 1989), Rotherham United (exch Spooner - Mar 1991), Torquay United (F.T. July 1993)

Initial promise was not fulfilled after Mansfield paid out the receord fee that Bedworth have ever received for a player. Did not shine with the "Millers" either, but has blossomed out somewhat with Torqay and his future looks more assured.

1988-89   4 (8) apps   1 gl
1989-90   11(11)   "   1 "
1990-91   6 (4)   "   0 "

HAWKSFORD Edward
1952 - 53 Outside Right   5' 8"   10st 7lbs
b: Liverpool, 7 November 1931
Career: R A O C Chilwell, TOWN (c/s 1951-am, Mar 1952 - pro)

1952-53   1 app   0 gls

HAWLEY Sidney
1934 - 35 Inside Right   5' 10" (1934)
b: Langwith, Notts., 1912
Career: Bolsover Colliery, Sheffield Wednesday (c/s 1933), TOWN (c/s 1934), Sutton Town (c/s 1935).

1934-35   4 apps   1 gl

HEATHCOTE James
1925 - 26 Inside Left/Centre Forward 5' 9" 12st 0lbs (1925)
b: Bolton, 17 January 1894
Career: Juniors, Army (1914), Bolton Wanderers (c/s 1917), Blackpool (Mar 1919), Notts County (£1,500 - June 1922), Pontypridd (c/s 1923), Lincoln City (June 1924), TOWN (May 1925), Coventry City (£400 - July 1926), Accrington Stanley (Jan 1929 to Mar 1929).

Smart centre or inside forward who joined the "Trotters" during WW I whilst still in the Army and "guested" for Blackpool before being transferred to them, where his best season was 1920-21 with 18 goals. Notts County paid a lot of money for him, but he was a poor investment scoring only one goal for the "Magpies". Netted 13 goals for the "Imps" and 21 for the "Stags", followed by the same number for Coventry, but Herbert pipped him by two for the leading scorers spot there. He did however manage it the next season when he led the "Light Blues" list with 16, by which time he was 34 and becoming a spent force.

1925-26   35 apps   21 gls   Midland League
Honours: Midland League runners up, Notts Senior Cup Winners 1926 (both Mansfield)

HEATHER John L
1952 - 54 Inside Forward   5' 10"   11st 0lbs
b: Winchcombe, Glos., 25 April 1923
Career: Derby County (am), Belper Town, TOWN (Aug 1952 - 1 month trial, perm - Sep 1952), Ransome & Marles (c/s 1954).

1952-53   0 apps   0 gls
1953-54   1   "   0   "

HEMSTOCK S
1922 - 24 Wing Half Back/Inside Forward
b: Huthwaite, Notts., c1892
Career: Sutton Town, Shirebrook (c/s 1914), TOWN (c/s 1922)

Getting towards the end of his career when he joined the "Stags", but had enjoyed a good run at Shirebrook before WW I.

1922-23	1 app	0 gls	Midland League
1923-24	6 "	5 "	" "

HERRING Clifford

1932 - 33 Left Half Back
Career: TOWN (c/s 1932), Ollerton Colliery (c/s 1933).

1932-33	2 apps	0 gls

HERRIOT James

1970 Goalkeeper
b: Chapelhall, Nr Airdrie, 20 December 1939
Career: Douglasdale, Dunfermline Athletic (Aug 1957 - am, Jan 1958 - pro), Birmingham City (£17,000 - May 1965), Aston Villa (1969 - loan), TOWN (Nov 1970 - loan), Hibernian (Aug 1971), St Mirren (July 1973), Partick Thistle (Feb 1975), Morton (Oct 1975 - loan), Dunfermline Athletic (1976), Morton (late 1976).

After seven very successful seasons at East End Park, Jim Herriot spent six excellent seasons at Birmingham. Winner of many honours at both international and club level, he drifted around the Scottish clubs for a further five seasons before finally hanging up his boots at the age of 38. Interestingly enough, Alf Wight the well known Scottish author and T V vet. writing as James Herriot and who only died as recently as 23 February 1995, adopted this pseudonym because he was an avid supporter of Birmingham City and Jim Herriot in particular. Now works as a bricklayer in Larkhall.

1970-71 5(0) apps 0 gls (Loan)
Honours: Scottish U/23 & "B" International, Scottish League XI, Scottish Cup Final runners up 1965 (all Dunfermline). Scottish International (Birmingham). Scottish Cup Final Runners Up 1972 and Scottish League Cup Winners 1973 (both Hibernian).

HETHERINGTON John (Arthur)

1927 - 28 Outside Left/Centre Half 5' 10" 9st 0lbs (1925)
b: Rotherham, 7 August 1906
d: Rotherham, April 1977
Career: Dalton United, Shirebrook (Nov 1925), Mexborough (Mar 1926), Gainsborough Trinity (c/s 1926), Sheffield Wednesday (1927 - trial), Barnsley (1927 - trial), TOWN (Jan 1928), Wolverhampton Wanderers (c/s 1928), Preston North End (Jan 1935), Swindon Town (c/s 1936), Watford (Apr 1938).

Winger with Shirebrook, centre half with Mexborough and Mansfield, inside forward with Wolves and "play anywhere" with his other clubs, Arthur Hetherington was certainly a utility player in the full sense of the word! Retired during WW II after a long and fruitful career lasting almost 20 years.

1927-28 1 app 0 gls Midland League
Honours: Division 2 Championship 1932 (Wolves)

HEWITT Harry

1945 - 47 Outside Right
b: Chesterfield, 24 June 1919
Career: Chesterfield (1943 - am), TOWN (Nov 1945)

In the last wartime season Hewitt was an effective speedy right winger, but could not adjust to the more competitive rigours of peacetime soccer and was released in May 1947. During the war whilst on Chesterfield's books,"guested" for Notts County & Stags.

WW II	26 apps	8 gls
1946-47	1 "	0 "

HIBBARD

1920 - 21 Centre Forward
Career: TOWN (1920), Worksop Town (1921), Hucknall Byron (1923), Shirebrook (June 1925)

1920-21	1 app	1 gl	Central Alliance

HICKLING Cyril

1928 - 30 Centre Forward
Career: Bilsthorpe Colliery, TOWN (1928 am), Bilsthorpe Colliery.

Dashing centre forward called on by the "Stags" occasionally for reserve matches 1928-30, but he did get one senior appearance in 1930 and helped in winning the Charity Cup too.

Honours: Mansfield Hospital Charity Cup Winners 1930 (Mansfield)

HILL Amos

1936 - 37 Outside Left 5' 8½" 10st 7lbs (1936)
b: Wath on Dearne, Yorks., 21 June 1910
d: Doncaster, 1973
Career: Mexborough, Wath National O B, Howson Street Wombwell, Lincoln City (Aug 1935), TOWN (Oct 1936).

Signed as cover for Jack Roy, but failed to grasp his opportunity when Roy was transferred to Wednesday, only managing a single appearance.

1936-37	1 apps	0 gls

HILL Harold

1933 - 34 Inside Forward 5' 5½" 10st 0lbs (1933)
b: Newton, Blackwell, Derbys., 24 August 1899
d: Blackwell, Derbys., 14 February 1969
Career: New Hucknall Colliery, Notts County (1918), The Wednesday (Oct 1924), Scarborough (c/s 1929), Chesterfield (c/s 1932 - player coach), TOWN (c/s 1933), Sutton Town (c/s 1934).

Had a tremendous First Division career with both Notts County and The Wednesday, as they were officially known then, the prefix Sheffield not being added until 1929. Joined the "Stags" at the end of his playing days, but he still made an important contribution to the team with his undoubted skills, albeit a little slower. After retirement, worked at B Winning Colliery as a miner. Grandfather of Hedley Hill, the club's Commercial Manager for a short period - December 1994/January 1995.

1933-34   22 apps   5 gls
Honours: Division 2 Championship 1923 (Notts) & 1926 (Wednesday). Midland League Championship 1930 (Scarborough).

HILL Joseph
1930 - 31 Inside Forward
b: Sheffield, c1907
Career: Leeds United (1927), Torquay United (Jan 1929), TOWN (c/s 1930), Newark Town (c/s 1931), Barnsley (Feb 1932), Queens Park Rangers (c/s 1932), Stockport County (c/s 1933), Walsall (c/s 1938)

Town's regular inside right in the last season before their election to the Third Division. The "Hatters" leading scorer in both 1935-36 and 1936-37 (their championship season), with 19 goals in each. Retired in May 1939 to his native Yorkshire where he worked as a bookmaker's assistant.

1930-31   41 apps   23 gls Midland League.
Leading Scorer Honours: Notts Senior Cup Winners 1931 (Mansfield), Division 3 North Cup Winners 1935 & Division 3 North Championship 1937 (both Stockport).

HILL Matthew A
1936 - 37 Wing Half Back   5' 11'   10st 13lbs (1936)
b: Northumberland, c1914
Career: Carlisle United (am, Dec 1935 - pro), TOWN (Aug 1936 - 2 month's trial, Oct 1936 - permanent).

Young trialist who was retained and given a single league outing in the final match of the season before being released.

1936-37   1 app   0 gls

HILL William H
1947 - 48 Inside Forward
b: Skegby, Notts., 15 March 1920
Career: Skegby M W, Chesterfield (1943 - am), TOWN (Nov 1947), Teversall Colliery (1949)

1947-48   2 apps   0 gls

HITCHCOCK (Kevin) Joseph
1984 - 88 Goalkeeper 6' 1"   12st 2lbs
b: Custom House, London, 5 October 1962
Career: Barking, Nottingham Forest (Aug 1983), TOWN (Feb 1984 - loan, July 1984 - perm), Chelsea (£250,000 - half to Forest - Mar 1988), Northampton Town (Dec 1990 - loan - to Mar 1991), West Ham United (Apr 1993 - loan)

Impressed greatly during his initial loan spell at Field Mill and was signed permanently during the following close season. Gained a reputation of being something of a penalty saver, two being kept out when Town won the Freight Rover Trophy at Wembley. Chelsea took him to Stamford Bridge the following season for a large fee but his opportunities there have been somewhat limited, although he did have a good run between 1991 and 1993. Missed only 3 games in 1984-85 when the "Stags" conceded only 38 goals - a record for the club.

1983-84	14(0) apps	0 gls	(Loan)
1984-85	43(0) "	0 "	
1985-86	46(0) "	0 "	
1986-87	46(0) "	0 "	
1987-88	33(0) "	0 "	

Honours: Division 4 promotion 1986, Freight Rover Trophy Winners 1987, Notts F A County Cup Winners 1987 & 1988 (all Mansfield)

HODGES David
1986 - 91 Midfield   5' 9"   10st 2lbs
b: Hereford, 17 January 1970
Career: TOWN (1986 - appr, Aug 1987 - pro), Torquay United (Jan 1991 - loan, Feb 1991 - perm), Kettering Town (F.T. Dec 1991), Gloucester City (F.T. c/s 1993).

Youngster who did not bear out his initial promise.

1986-87	1 (2) apps	0 gls	
1987-88	21 (1) "	2 "	
1988-89	37 (2) "	4 "	
1989-90	8(11) "	1 "	
1990-91	0(2) "	0 "	

Honours: Notts F A County Cup Winners 1988 (Mansfield)

HODGETTS Joseph H

1938 - 39 Outside Left
b: Mansfield, c1916
Career: Mansfield Colliery, Forest Town St Albans, Brighton & Hove Albion (Jan 1938), TOWN (c/s 1938), Ollerton Colliery (c/s 1939), Mansfield Hosiery Mills (1946 to 1953).

After a short professional career with the "Seagulls", Dennis Hodgetts spent one season with Mansfield before being released. He did however, make a few "guest" appearances for the "Stags" during the war, whilst working as a miner.

1938-39	1 app	0 gls	
WW II	3 "	0 "	

HODGSON Gordon H

1974 - 78 Midfield 5' 11" 12st 9lbs (1974)
b: Newcastle on Tyne, 13 october 1952
Career: Juniors, Newcastle United (June 1971), TOWN (£8,000 - May 1974), Oxford United (£35,000 - Sep 1978), Peterborough United (£10,000 - Aug 1980)

Cultured midfielder who impressed chief scout Sam Weaver sufficiently to persuade manager Dave Smith to sign him - the new manager's first capture. Had an impressive spell at Field Mill before Oxford lured him away in return for a big fee and substantial profit to Mansfield. After retirement joined the police force.

1974-75	44(0) apps	10 gls	
1975-76	46(0) "	7 "	
1976-77	46(0) "	4 "	
1977-78	42(0) "	2 "	
1978-79	6(0) "	0 "	

Honours: England Schoolboy International, England N A B C International, England Youth International (Newcastle). Division 4 Championship 1975, Division 3 Championship 1977 (both Mansfield).

HODGSON Samuel

1948 - 49 Wing Half Back 5' 11½" 11st 10lbs
b: Seaham, Co Durham, 21 January 1919
Career: Seaham Colliery, Grimsby Town (Jan 1936), TOWN (July 1948)

Did not get a first team match with the "Mariners" until he had been on their books for over 10 years! War-time "guest" for Darlington, York, Bradford P A, Reading, Brighton, Swansea and Middlesbrough. Seved for six years in the Forces during the Second World War. Holds an F A Coaching Cerfificate.

1948-49	2 apps	0 gls

HODSON (Simeon) Paul

1993 Full Back 5' 9" 11st 8lbs (1993)
b: Lincoln, 5 March 1966
Career: Notts County (1982 - appr, Mar 1984 - pro), Charlton Athletic (Apr 1985), Lincoln United (Dec 1985), Lincoln City (Jan 1986), Newport County (F.T. Aug 1987), West Bromwich Albion (£5,000 - Mar 1988), Doncaster Rovers (Sep 1992 N/C), Kidderminster Harriers (Jan 1993 N/C), TOWN (Feb 1993), Shrewsbury Town (Aug 1993 - trial), Kidderminster Harriers (Sep 1993).

After a promising start with Notts County, Simeon Hodson moved around the League and non league scene, winning a semi pro England cap on the way. Captained the Harriers team that shook the football world by reaching the Fifth Round of the F A Cup in 1993-94, beating Birmingham at St Andrews and Preston at home, before succumbing to premiership West Ham United by the narrow margin of 0 - 1.

1992-93 17(0) apps 0 gls
Honours: England Semi Professional International (Kidderminster)

HOGG C George

1928 - 31 Right Full Back 5' 10" 12st 7lbs (1928)
b: Kiveton Park, Sheffield, 1900
Career: Anston F C, Lincoln City (Apr 1924), Southend United (June 1926), Peterborough & Fletton United (c/s 1927), TOWN (June 1928)   Described as "a bustling hefty player and a relentless tackler" by the "Post" Football Annual at the time, but was only in fact a reserve at Field Mill, although he had appeared in the Third Division for both Lincoln and Southend.

1928-29	8 apps	0 gls	Midland League
1929-30	11 "	1 "	" "
1930-31	3 "	0 "	" "

Honours: Byron Cup Winners & Bayley Cup Winners 1930 (both Mansfield).

HOGG (Frederick) William

1945 - 47 Inside Forward/Wing Half 5' 5" 10st 4lbs (1946)
b: Bishop Auckland, 24 April 1918
Career: Luton Town (Dec 1936), TOWN (£350 - Nov 1945), Halifax Town (£450 - Oct 1947)

Diminutive player who, however, was not lacking in guts and gave the "Stags" useful service until he moved on to The Shay. Had played as a "guest" for Darlington, York, Halifax, Chesterfield, Nottingham Forest, Notts County, Rotherham and Town during WW II, but he only managed four games for Luton pre-war.

WW II	47 apps	12 gls
1946-47	35 "	6 "
1947-48	10 "	2 "

HOGG Raymond A

1958 - 60 Wing Half Back   5' 10"   11st 7lbs
b: Lowick, Northumberland, 11 December 1929
Career: Berwick Rangers, Aston Villa (Mar 1955), TOWN (July 1958), Peterborough United (Aug 1960).

A player who did well with Villa before joining the "Stags".

| 1958-59 | 1 app | 0 gls |
| 1959-60 | 10 " | 0 " |

HOLBEACH Frederick

1929-30 Outside Right
b: Mansfield, 1911
Career: Newgate Lane School (1924), Welbeck Colliery, TOWN (c/s 1929 - am), Welbeck Athletic (1930), Luton Town (c/s 1933), Yeovil & Petters United.

| 1929-30 | 2 apps | 0 gls | Midland League |

HOLDEN Jack

1914 - 15 and 1923 - 24 Outside Left
b: Pleasley, Mansfield, c1893
Career: Pleasley Colliery, TOWN (c/s 1914), Mansfield United (1919), Sutton Town (c/s 1920), TOWN (c/s 1923), Alfreton Town (c/s 1924)

1914-15 N.K.apps 5 gls Notts & Derbys League
1923-24 13 "   2 "   Midland League Honours:
Midland League Championship 1924 (Mansfield)

HOLLAND Paul

1987 - 95 Midfield 5' 10" 12st 4lbs (1992)
b: Lincoln, 8 July 1973
Career: Carre's G S Sleaford, TOWN (Aug 1987 - assoc sch, July 1989 - appr, July 1991 - pro), Sheffield United (£250,000 + up to £350,000 after set number of league and international appearances).

Young midfielder who should have a glittering career ahead of him. Given his first taste of League football before he was 18 years old in the last match of the 1990-91 season. This rising star had been watched enviously by many clubs and indeed offers as high as £250,000 were rejected. It was inevitable that he would move to higher things in the future and in footballing terms, the world could be his oyster. Received a nasty medial ligament injury in early March 1995 which should have sidelined him for the remainder of the season, but such was his enthusiasm for recovery that he was back in action within a month. Selected by P F A for Division 3 Representative Side 1994-95 and his most successful season yet was completed by a call-up to the England Under 21 squad, making his debut versus Brazil in the Toulon Tournament and playing in all four matches up to the semi-finals - the only Third Division player to receive this honour. His expected departure came immediately after the end of this tournament when Dave Bassett flew out to Toulon to obtain his signature, at a fee which should eventually equal Mansfield's second highest (when Simon Coleman went to Middlesbrough in 1989).

1990-91	1(0) apps	0 gls
1991-92	38(0) "	6 "
1992-93	39(0) "	3 "
1993-94	38(0) "	7 "
1994-95	33(0) "	9 " (+1gl Play-offs)

Honours: Kesteven Schools, Lincolnshire Schools. England Schoolboy International, England Youth International 1990 & 1991, Division 4 promotion 1992, England Under 21 International 1995 (all Mansfield).

HOLLETT Ivan R
1958 - 64 Inside Forward   6' 1"   12st 0lbs
b: Pinxton, Derbys., 22 April 1940
Career: Derby County (am), Sutton Town, TOWN (Aug 1958), Chesterfield (Dec 1964), Crewe Alexandra (Nov 1968), Cambridge United (Nov 1970), Hereford United (Jan 1972).

A thrustful forward who had his most successful period with the "Spireites". Netted a total of 136 League goals during his career. Played for both Cambridge and Hereford in their first seasons in the Football League. Has helped out with the coaching at Field Mill since the 1980s and is currently still looking after the schoolboys. Sales mining engineer by profession.

Season	Apps		Gls	
1958-59	2 apps		0 gls	
1959-60	21	"	15	" Leading Scorer (Joint)
1960-61	26	"	10	"
1961-62	15	"	3	"
1962-63	19	"	9	"
1963-64	10	"	1	"
1964-65	5	"	2	"

Honours: Division 4 promotion 1963 (Mansfield)

HOLLINS David M
1967 - 70 Goalkeeper 5' 11½"   13st 0lbs
b: Bangor, N Wales, 4 February 1938
Career: Onslow School, Merrow Guildford, Brighton & Hove Albion (Nov 1965), Newcastle United (£12,500 - Mar 1961), TOWN (£2,500 - Feb 1967), Nottingham Forest (Mar 1970 - loan), Aldershot (July 1970), Portsmouth (Apr 1971 - loan), Romford (May 1971)

Outstanding custodian who gained both under 23 and full caps for Wales whilst with Newcastle. Replaced Alan Humphries.

Season	Apps	Gls
1966-67	13 apps	0 gls
1967-68	41 "	0 "
1968-69	44 "	0 "
1969-70	13 "	0 "

Honours: Wales Full and U/23 International (Newcastle).
"Giant Killers" Cup Winners 1969 (Mansfield)

HOLMES Martin Maxwell
1937 - 38 Centre/Inside Forward   5' 8"   11st 4lbs (1938)
b: Pinchbeck, Nr Spalding, 24 December 1908
Career: Spalding G S, London University, Spalding United (1928), Grimsby Town (May 1931), Hull City (May 1935), TOWN (July 1937), Lincoln City (Aug 1938)

Centre forward signed to replace Harston who had just left for Liverpool, but as Crawshaw was also signed that summer, he played mainly at inside forward to good effect. A schoolmaster by profession, he also played Rugby Football, quite well too it would seem as he represented Midland Counties at wing threequarter. Known as "Maxey", he "guested" for Grimsby during WW II.

Season	Apps	Gls
1937-38	17 apps	4 gls

Honours: Midland League Championship 1933 & 1934, Division 2 Championship 1934 (all Grimsby)

HOLT Arnold
1920 - 21 Outside Right
Career: Sutton Town, Chesterfield Municipal (c/s 1919), Gillingham (c/s 1920), TOWN (Nov 1920), Wath Athletic (c/s 1921)

Season	Apps	Gls
1920-21	21 apps	2 gls

Honours: Midland League Championship 1920 (Chesterfield Municipal). Central Alliance runners up 1921 (Mansfield)

HOPKINSON (Michael) Edward
1968 - 70 Wing Half Back   5' 9"   11st 1lb
b: Ambergate, Derbys., 24 February 1942
Career: West End Boys Club, Derby County (July 1959), TOWN (£5,500 - July 1968), Port Vale (July 1970), Boston (June 1971), Belper Town (Nov 1973 - coach, Dec 1974 - manager), Burton Albion (coach, Nov 1978 - asst manager).

A versatile player who had his best spell at Derby.

Season	Apps	Gls
1968-69	44(0) apps	1 gl
1969-70	2(0) "	0 "

Honours: "Giant Killers" Cup Winners 1969 (Mansfield)

HORNE Alfred
1936 - 38 Wing Half Back   5' 8½"   11st 0lbs (1936)
b: Stafford, 1903
d: April 1976
Career: Alvechurch, West Bromwich Albion (am), Stafford Rangers, Hull City (May 1925), Southend United (May 1927), Manchester City (Mar 1928), Preston North End (£2,000 - Sep 1929), Lincoln City (June 1932), TOWN (Dec 1936).

Well over 30 when he joined the "Stags", Alf Horne was still a quite effective force in football and was provider of many telling through balls to Harston from which the centre forward benefited greatly. Originally a winger, he played half back and inside forward later in his career which effectively ended in 1938.

| 1936-37 | 22 apps | 3 gls |
| 1937-38 | 22 " | 6 " |

Honours: Notts F A County Cup Winners 1938 (Mansfield)

HOUSLEY Bernard
1927 - 28 Inside Right
b: Warsop, Notts.
Career: Warsop Rovers, TOWN (Jan 1928 - am)

This younger brother of Herbert Housley was called in to play in a single match in 1928.

| 1927-28 | 1 app | 0 gls | Midland League |

HOUSLEY Herbert
1914 - 22 Inside Forward
b: Warsop, Notts., c1894
Career: Warsop Rovers, Bradford P A (Aug 1914 - trial), TOWN (c/s 1914), Norwich City (Aug 1920 - trial), TOWN (Aug 1920), Loughborough Corinthians (Nov 1922), Halifax Town (c/s 1923 - T/L May 1924), Loughborough Corinthians (c/s 1924), Shirebrook (c/s 1925), Halifax Town (c/s 1926 to May 1928).

Had a long career with Mansfield from both before and after the First World War. Talented goalscorer he ultimately had a League spell with Halifax Town.

1914-15	N.K.	2 gls	Notts & Derbys.Lge.
1915-16	N.K.	16 "	Central Alliance
1919-20	24 apps	18 "	" "
1920-21	31 "	22 "	" " Lead.Scorer
1921-22	12 "	3 "	Midland League

Honours: Central Alliance - Subsidiary Competition Championship 1916, Central Alliance Championship 1920, runners up 1921, Mansfield Hospital Charity Cup Winners 1922 (all Mansfield).

HOWARD Lee
1984 - 85 Winger
b: Worksop, 6 February 1967
Career: TOWN (1983 - appr, Aug 1984 - pro)

| 1984-85 | 0(1) apps | 0 gls |

Lee Howard captained the "Stags" Youth team which reached the quarter finals of the F A Youth Cup in 1985.

HOWARTH Lee
1994 onwards Centre Half   6' 1"   12st 6lbs (1993)
b: Bolton, 3 January 1968
Career: Chorley, Peterborough United (Aug 1991), TOWN (£15,000 - Aug 1994)

Big strong centre back who tended to waver under pressure in his early days at the club, but improved considerably as the season progressed.

| 1994-95 | 39(1) apps | 2 gls |

HOWELL Henry ("Harry")
1922 - 23 Centre Forward   5' 8"   11st 6lbs
b: Hockley, Birmingham, 29 November 1890
d: Selly Oak, Birmingham, 9 July 1932
Career: Burslem Swifts, Burslem Port Vale, Stoke, Wolverhampton Wanderers (Mar 1913), Southampton (c/s 1920), Northfleet, Accrington Stanley (Oct 1922 - month's trial), TOWN (Nov 1922).

Dashing centre forward, but somewhat erratic. Much less so his bowling however, for as a fast bowler for Warwickshire and England he excelled - 161 wickets at an average of under 18 in 1920 and 152 for under 20 in 1923. Took all ten wickets for 51 runs v Yorkshire at Edgbaston in 1923. Twice took 9 in an innings - 9/35 v Somerset at Taunton in 1924 and he bettered this with 9/32 v Hampshire at Edgbaston in 1925. But perhaps his most devastating performance was when he and Calthorpe routed Hampshire for 15 in 1924 - Calthorpe taking 4/4 and Howell an amazing 6/7 in just 4.5 overs. The Hampshire innings lasted for just 53 balls! He twice toured Australia with the England party and played in five tests between 1920-24. His Warwickshire career lasted from 1913-28. Another oustanding performance was 6/40 and 6/13 for Players v Gentlemen at Lords in 1920. "Guested" for Stoke during WW I.

| 1922-23 | 18 apps | 12 gls | Midland League |

Honours: Notts Senior Cup Winners 1923 (Mansfield).

HOWSON Charles
1922 - 23 Right Full Back
Career: Wombwell (c/s 1921), Nelson (Aug 1922 - trial), Port Vale (Oct 1922 - trial), TOWN (Dec 1922)

| 1922-23 | 2 apps | 0 gls |

HOYLAND Walter
1932 - 33 Inside Left 5' 10"   12st 0lbs
b: Sheffield, 14 August 1901

Career: Sheffield United (Jan 1920), Fulham (£500 - Mar 1927), Boston (c/s 1928), Loughborough Corinthians (c/s 1929), Peterborough & Fletton United (c/s 1930), TOWN (c/s 1932).

Eight seasons with the "Blades" as a reserve, he managed some improvement at Craven Cottage before dropping into the Midland League. Mansfield revived his League career for a season, before he dropped out of the soccer scene altogether.

1932-33   25 apps   9 gls

HOYLE (Colin) Roy
1994 Defender/Midfield   5' 11"   12st 3lbs (1993)
b: Wirksworth, Derbys., 15 January 1972
Career: Arsenal (1988 - appr, Jan 1990 - pro), Chesterfield (Feb 1990 - loan), Barnsley (F.T. Sep 1990), Bradford City (£25,000 - Aug 1992), Notts County (F.T. - Aug 1994), TOWN (Oct 1994 - loan).

Had a fiery baptism, as his first match for the "Stags" during his loan spell, was against Leeds United in the Coca Cola Cup - being sent off in the final minute!

1994-95   4(1) apps   0 gls (Loan)

HUDSON
1929 - 30 Full Back
Career: Brighton & Hove Albion, TOWN (c/s 1929)

1929-30   1 app   0 gls Midland League

HUDSON William A
1954 - 55 Outside Right   5' 9"   10st 9lbs (1954)
b: Swansea, 10 March 1928
Career: Pembroke Borough, Manchester City (trial), Leeds United (May 1951), Sheffield United (May 1952), TOWN (F.T. May 1954)

1954-55   8 apps   1 gl
Honours: Welsh Amateur International (Pembroke).

HUFTON Clarence
1934 - 36 Right Half Back   5' 10"   11st 6lbs (1935)
b: Sutton in Ashfield, Notts., 1913
Career: Sutton Junction, Langwith Waggon Works, TOWN (Mar 1934 - am, May 1934 - pro), Sutton Town.

1934-35   3 apps   0 gls
1935-36   1 "   0 "
Honours: Bass Charity Vase Winners 1935 (Mansfield).

HUGHES John Iowerth
1937 - 39 Goalkeeper 5' 9½"   12st 10lbs (1937)
b: Rhosllanerchrugog, Nr Wrexham, 29 January 1913
Career: Rhos National School, Plas Bennion, Llanerch Celts, Aberystwyth Town, Afongoch, Druids, Llanerch Celts, Rhos F C, Blackburn Rovers (Jan 1933 - am, Mar 1933 - pro), Dick Kerr's XI (Mar 1933 - loan to May 1933), TOWN (£200 - June 1937), Bacup Borough (1945), Rossendale United (1947), Darwen (1948), Third Lanark.

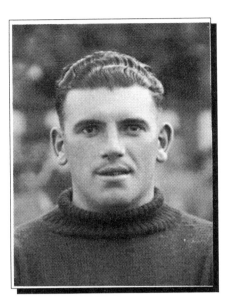

Jack Hughes was probably one of the best goalkeepers Mansfield have ever had. Gaining Welsh amateur international caps before joining Rovers, he quickly made the senior team and gained a full cap at the end of the 1934-35 season, against Ireland at Wrexham - Wales winning 3 - 1. A serious back injury then threatened his his career, but by playing in a special steel corset he was able to overcome this and joined the "Stags" in the Summer of 1937. He gave some superlative performances for two seasons until his back injury recurred and he was unable to start the 1939-40 campaign. Being unfit for military service, he spent the war years working in Lancashire and his Saturdays keeping goal for Nelson. After the war he revisited Field Mill in the hope of picking up his career, but complications regarding the compensation he had received from the P F A Benevolent Fund ruled that out and he played for a few non league clubs and had a brief flirtation with Scottish football before finally hanging up his boots at 37 years of age.

1937-38   39 apps   0 gls
1938-39   37 "   0 "
Honours: Welsh Amateur International (Llanerch Celts), Welsh Full International (Blackburn), Notts F A County Cup Winners 1938 & 1939 (Mansfield).

HUMBLE J Wilfred
1959 - 66 Full Back 5' 9"   11st 7lbs
b: Ashington, Co Durham, 10 May 1936
d: Mansfield, 1985
Career: Newcastle United (am), Ashington (c/s 1954), TOWN (May 1959).

A tremendous defender and tireless worker in the team, Wilf Humble served the "Stags" faithfully for seven seasons before he settled in the town after retirement and formed a successful clothing company until his untimely death at the age of 51. He played in almost 200 games for Mansfield and was part of the promotion campaigns of 1962-63 and 1964-65.

1959-60	37 apps	0 gls
1960-61	14 "	0 "
1961-62	21 "	1 "
1962-63	41 "	0 "
1963-64	46 "	0 "
1964-65	17 "	0 "
1965-66	22(0)"	0 "

Honours: Northumberland Youth XI. Midland League XI 1959 (Ashington), Division 4 promotion 1963, Division 3 - 3rd 1965 (both Mansfield).

HUMPHREYS Alan
1964 - 68 Goalkeeper 6' 0"   11st 5lbs (1960)
b: Chester, 18 October 1939
Career: Overleigh School - centre half, Lache Y C - goal, Shrewsbury Town (Oct 1956), Leeds United (Feb 1960), Gravesend & Northfleet (July 1962), TOWN (Jan 1964), Chesterfield (July 1968)

Came to Field Mill the holder of an England Under 23 Cap but had to await his opportunities as Colin Treharne was in the No. 1 slot. When Treharne retired from the scene, Dave Hollins arrived, so Humphreys was only ever really a stand-in, but he was reliable. Later became Commercial manager for Derbyshire C C C.

1963-64	0 apps	0 gls
1964-65	8 "	0 "
1965-66	17(0)"	0 "
1966-67	28(0)"	0 "
1967-68	5(0)"	0 "

Honours: England Under 23 International (Leeds). Division 4 Championship 1970 (Chesterfield).

HUNT David
1989 - 91 Midfield 5' 11"   11st 0lbs (1987)
b: Leicester. 17 April 1959
Career: Derby County (1975 - appr, May 1977 - pro), Notts County (£40,000 - Mar 1978), Aston Villa (F.T. June 1987), TOWN (F.T. June 1989), Burton Albion (F.T. Aug 1991), Leicester United (Sep 1991).

| 1989-90 | 21(1) apps | 0 gls |
| 1990-91 | 0(0) " | 0 " |

HUNT (John) Edward
1925 - 27 Goalkeeper 6' 1½"   11st 6lbs (1925)
b: Nottingham, 1905
Career: Lincoln City (1923), TOWN (c/s 1925), Shirebrook (c/s 1927).

| 1925-26 | 27 apps | 0 gls | Midland League |
| 1926-27 | 0 " | 0 " | " " |

Honours: Midland League runners up, Notts Senior Cup Winners 1926 (both Mansfield)

HUNT Samuel (Walter)
1934 - 35 Inside Left/Centre Forward 5' 11½"   11st 12lbs (1938)
b: Doe Lea, Derbys., 9 January 1909
d: Rochdale, 2 August 1963
Career: Welbeck Colliery Welfare, Lincoln City (May 1933), TOWN (July 1934), Torquay United (June 1935), Rochdale (Aug 1936), Stockport County (£400 - Dec 1937), Accrington Stanley (with Daniels exch for Bowles - July 1938), Carlisle United (Oct 1938), Southport (Sep 1939).

Quite a late starter in senior football, Wally Hunt had modest success as he moved around, until he moved to centre forward when he joined Carlisle and finished up the Division's leading scorer with 34 goals in 1938-39. A successful cricketer with Warsop Main Colliery, he played in five matches for Derbyshire during their County Championship season of 1936 and post-war played a few times for Northumberland in the Minor Counties League.

During WW II, Hunt "guested" for Rochdale where he served as a Special Constable and Auxilliary Fireman, as well as turning out for Southport when required.

1934-35   29 apps   14 gls
Honours: Bass Charity Vase Winners 1935 (Mansfield).

HUNTER (James) Boyd
1934 - 35 Outside Right   5' 7"   10st 12lbs (1935)
b: Dunfermline, 1913
Career: Wheeldon's United (1928), Stanton Ironworks (1929), Ilkeston United (1930), Fulham (1932 - trial), Ilkeston United (1933), Ripley Town (c/s 1934), TOWN (Nov 1934 - am, Feb 1935 - pro), Plymouth Argyle (£500 - Nov 1935), Preston North End (£5,500 with J E Wharton - July 1939)

Scottish born winger whose family moved down to work at Stanton Ironworks in the 1920s. After joining the "Stags" made rapid progress and was part of a big transfer deal just before the outbreak of war, from which Plymouth made a huge profit. During WW II "guested" for Mansfield, Forest, Newcastle, Blackburn, Plymouth, Notts County and Aldershot.

1934-35   16 apps   1 gl
1935-36   10   "   4   "
WW II   35   "   6   "
Honours: Bass Charity Vase Winners 1935 (Mansfield).

HUTCHINSON Robert
1982 - 84 Forward   5' 9"   11st 4lbs (1983)
b: Glasgow, 19 June 1953
Career: Aberdeen L Cu, Montrose (1972), Dundee (£20,000 - Aug 1974), Hibernian (Oct 1977), Wigan Athletic (July 1980), Tranmere Rovers (F.T. Aug 1981), TOWN (£15,000 - Oct 1982), Tranmere Rovers (Jan 1984), Bristol City (July 1984), Walsall (Feb 1987), Blackpool (Sep 1987 - loan), Carlisle United (Jan 1988 - loan)

Bobby Hutchinson was a much travelled Scot who was reasonably successful with all his clubs making nearly 450 appearances in first class football both sides of the border. Oddly enough, with goals, he only once achieved double figures in a season - 12 with Dundee in 1976-77.

1982-83   25(0) apps   3 gls
1983-84   10(0) "   0   "
Honours: Scottish Cup Finalists 1979 (Hibernian), Freight Rover Trophy Winners 1986 (Bristol City)

IBBOTSON Wilfred
1948 - 49 Inside Left 5' 11½"   11st 10lbs (1948)
b: Sheffield, 1 October 1926
Career: Juniors, Sheffield Wednesday (Apr 1944), TOWN Aug 1948), Goole Town (c/s 1949)

Part time professional who continued working as a draughtsman in Sheffield.

1948-49   2 apps   0 gls

IRELAND (Simon) Piers
1994 onwards Forward (Winger) 5' 11" 11st 12lbs (1993)
b: Barnstaple, Devon, 23 November 1971
Career: Huddersfield Town (July 1990), Wrexham (Mar 1992 - loan), Blackburn Rovers (£200,000 - Nov 1992), TOWN (Mar 1994 - loan,   £25,000 - Aug 1994 - permanent)

Speedy outside right who must have impressed Kenny Dalgleish sufficiently for him to pay a very large sum indeed to take him to Blackburn after only 10 full appearances for the "Terriers" and to understudy Stuart Ripley, but after a single senior appearance he suffered a broken ankle and was sidelined for a time. Following a loan spell at Field Mill, Andy King persuaded Ireland that his future lay away from Blackburn and bought him for a knock down price. Born in Devonshire, but brought up in Halifax where he still lives, he was the first Town player to adopt the modern trend towards the wearing of cycling shorts.

1993-94   8(1) apps   1 gl (Loan)
1994-95   38(2) "   5   "
Honours: England Schoolboy International.

JACKSON (Benjamin) Paul
1929 - 31 Wing Half Back
b: Creswell, Derbys., c1907
d: Creswell, Derbys., July 1972
Career: Shirebrook (Aug 1926 - am), Creswell Methodists, TOWN (Dec 1929 - am)

1929-30   1 app   0 gls   Midland League
1930-31   1   "   0   "   "   "

JACKSON Ernest
1927 - 28 Full Back 5' 8½"   11st 4lbs
b: Sheffield, 1903
Career: Boston (c/s 1922), Grimsby Town (May 1925), TOWN (Dec 1927), Wombwell (c/s 1928).

Full Back who had played in the "Mariners" league XI 20 times.

1927-28   27 apps   0 gls   Midland League
Honours: Division 3 North Championship 1926

(Grimsby). Mansfield Hospital Charity Cup Winners 1928 (Mansfield)

JACKSON James (Roy) Rowland
1927 - 28 Wing Half Back   5' 8"   11st 10lbs (1927)
b: Langwith, Notts., c1906
Career: Warsop Rovers, Halifax Town (c/s 1926), TOWN (July 1927)

1927-28   11 apps   5 gls   Midland League

JACKSON (William) Henry
1927 - 31 Left Full Back   5' 10"   12st 0lbs (1928)
b: Creswell, Derbys., c1903
d: Creswell, Derbys., 8 February 1977
Career: Whitwell St Lawrence (1921), Mansfield Colliery, Creswell Colliery, Shirebrook (c/s 1925), TOWN (c/s 1927), Creswell Colliery (c/s 1932), Sutton Town (1935), Wellington Town (1937)

Billy Jackson was a strong dependable full back who played his part in the club's very successful F A Cup run of 1928-29. Became a pro at Shirebrook and had two improving seasons with them in the the Midland League. Useful cricketer with Creswell Colliery during the football close season.

1927-28	22 apps	4 gls	Midland League
1928-29	46 "	2 "	" "
1929-30	43 "	0 "	" "
1930-31	17 "	3 "	" "

Honours: Midland League Championship 1929, Mansfield Hospital Charity Cup Winners 1928/9/30 (all Mansfield)

JARVIS (Alan) Leslie
1971 - 73 Wing Half Back   5' 9"   11st 0lbs (1972)
b: Wrexham, 4 August 1943
Career: Everton (1959 - appr, July 1961 - pro), Hull City (June 1964), TOWN (£11,000 - Mar 1971)

A Welsh international with three caps when he joined Town, Alan Jarvis was a classy wing half for whom Mansfield paid their record transfer fee at the time. An unfortunate injury sustained outside football ended his career prematurely when he lost the sight of an eye when playing squash in the summer of 1973 at the age of 29. lived in Shirebrook for a time after retirement, but later back to his roots in Wrexham where he is employed in the local council's Planning and Surveying Department.

1970-71	12(0) apps	0 gls
1971-72	40(2) "	0 "
1972-73	24(4) "	0 "

Honours: Welsh International & Division 3 Championship 1966 (both Hull). Notts F A County Cup Winners 1971 (Mansfield).

JAYES Brian
1956 - 60 Half back   5' 10"   11st 6lbs
b: Leicester, 13 December 1932
Career: Army, Leicester City (July 1954), TOWN (F.T. July 1956), Ramsgate (June 1960)

One of many City players who teamed up with the "Stags" in the first decade after the war. Suffered two long injury spells during his time at Field Mill, but still managed 115 games.

1956-57	42 apps	0 gls	
1957-58	34 "	1 "	
1958-59	19 "	0 "	
1959-60	20 "	0 "	

JEFFRIES William A

1946 - 47 Inside Forward
b: Acton, London, 11 March 1921
Career: Army, TOWN (Mar 1946), Hull City (Jan 1947), Colchester United (c/s 1947 to May 1949)

Young soldier, stationed locally, who was signed up by Town.

WW II	2 apps	1 gl	
1946-47	2 "	0 "	

JEPSON Arthur E

1934 - 35 Goalkeeper 5' 10"   11st 0lbs (1939)
b: Selston, Notts., 12 July 1915
Career: Newark Town, TOWN (Nov 1934 - am), Grantham (c/s 1935), Port Vale (June 1938), Stoke City (£3,750 - Sep 1946), Lincoln City (£250 - Dec 1948), Northwich Victoria (Aug 1950), Gloucester City (Oct 1951), Hinckley United (1953 - player manager), Coventry (scout), Middlesbrough (scout), Hinckley Athletic (July 1963 - manager).

Arthur Jepson was a young 19 year old amateur who was pitched into the action in January 1935 due to an injury to Fawcett and how well he rose to the occasion - receiving unstinted praise from Burnley's chairman for his display against them in the Third Round of the F A Cup at Turf Moor before nearly 21,000 spectators. Stoke paid out what was then the record fee for a 'keeper, when they were in dire straits in 1946, then let him go for a song to the "Imps" two years later. An accomplished cricketer, Jepson played for Notts as a medium pace bowler from 1938-59, taking over 1,000 wickets and then became an umpire, standing until 1984. He also officiated in four Test Matches between 1966-69. W W II guest player for York, Watford, Nottingham Forest, Notts County and Swansea. Now aged 80, he lives in retirement at Kirkby in Ashfield.

1934-35	2 apps	0 gls

Honours: Bass Charity Vase Winners 1935 (Mansfield).

JEPSON C Barry

1954 - 57 Centre Forward   5' 11"   11st 4lbs
b: Alfreton, Derbys., 29 December 1929
Career: Chesterfield (Nov 1948 - am), South Normanton, Bentinck C W, Ilkeston Town, TOWN (Mar 1954), Chester (Jan 1957), Southport (Nov 1959), Alfreton Town (Feb 1960)

Barry Jepson was a do or die type of player who would never give up and had a remarkably successful scoring record, averaging exactly a goal every two matches - more than acceptable in 1995! He was the season's top scorer with both Mansfield and Chester, netting 25 with the latter in 1957-58. A part time pro during his playing career. In his amateur days prior to joining the "Stags", he worked in the N C B area offices at Blackwell.

1953-54	2 apps	0 gls		
1954-55	8 "	1 "		
1955-56	26 "	22 "	Leading	Scorer
1956-57	19 "	13 "		

Honours: Welsh Cup runners up 1958 (Chester).

JEPSON (John) James

1931 - 32 Centre Forward   5' 10"   11st 2lbs
b: Heaton Norris, Stockport, July 1899
Career: New Mills, Atherton (1921), New Mills (1922), Notts County (May 1924), Accrington Stanley (F.T. Aug 1925), Carlisle United (June 1927), Accrington Stanley (June 1928), Wigan Borough (June 1930), TOWN (F.T. July 1931), Altrincham (Feb 1932), Nelson (Aug 1933), New Brighton (c/s 1934)

John Jepson was signed as cover for Harry Johnson during the "Stags" first season in the League, which meant that his chances were strictly limited - to one in fact! Wigan had released him on a free transfer, rather surprisingly really, as he had been their leading scorer the previous term with 28 goals - but strange things happen in football! In one season at New Mills, in the Cheshire League, he had netted a staggering 81 goals and the remainder of his career was filled with astounding performances - 47 goals in each of two separate spells with Accrington and in a mere 60 games too! He even managed to score 32 in the Lancashire League with Nelson in 1933-34 when he was 35 years old ! Over his entire League career he averaged a goal every 1.3 games - what a pity we had Harry Johnson at the same time - perhaps Jack Hickling should have played them both!

1931-32	1 app	0 gls

JOHNSON Harry

1931 - 36 Centre Forward   5' 8"   10st 0lbs (1931)
b: Ecclesfield, Sheffield, 4 January 1899
d: Sheffield, May 1981
Career: Barnsley G S, Ecclesfield, Sheffield United (1916), TOWN (£500 - July 1931 to May 1936).

Where does one start to describe a man who scored over 300 goals in his League career - 205 for the "Blades" and, starting a "new" career at 32 years of age with the "Stags", another 104? Signing up with United at 17 and then joining the Army during WW I Harry was in the Battle of Verdun in 1918 and leaving the forces after the armistice, rejoined the Bramall Lane club for the start of the first post-war season 1919-20. He immediately established himself as the no. 1 choice as leader and started rattling them in with great regularity, his best seasons being 1927-28 and the following term when he scored 33 in each. He won an F A Cup Medal in 1925 when the "Blades" beat Cardiff City by 1-0 at Wembley and how he never gained an England cap is difficult to imagine - but there was a lot of competition for the centre forward berth then. He did however earn a Football League call up and celebrated the occasion by scoring a hat trick in a 9 - 1 victory over the Irish League at St James's Park, Newcastle on 21 September 1927, all the League's goals being scored in a frantic first 45 minutes! He was, however outdone on this occasion as "Dixie" Dean scored four!

Son of Harry Sr, who also won a Cup medals with United in 1899 and 1902 and brother of Tom, a centre half who was on the losing side in 1936 against Arsenal, these footballing Johnsons were a truly remarkable family. Town's centre forward until he was 37 years old and replaced by Harston, Johnson was always a part-time footballer and carried on his job as an analytical chemist at Hadfields Steelworks in Sheffield until he retired in 1963 - he always maintained that if he became full time, he would lose his enthusiasm for the game - the old true amateur approach! He had a peaceful retirement for almost 20 years until he passed away aged 82 in May 1981. Aggregate League record of 476 games and 309 goals - a goal every 1.5 games for 17 seasons and 2/3 of them in the First Division. And how many players are there that possess the record of most League goals for their club - with two clubs ? Well Harry Johnson still does in 1995 - for Sheffield United and Mansfield Town! He also stands Second in Town's list of overall goalscorers, beaten only by Chris Staniforth.

1931-32	40 apps	32 gls	Leading Scorer	
1932-33	38 "	30 "	"	"
1933-34	32 "	18 "	"	"
1934-35	39 "	17 "	"	"
1935-36	14 "	7 "		

Honours: F A Cup Winner 1925, Football League XI 1930 (both Sheffield United). Bass Charity Vase Winners 1935 (Mansfield).

JOHNSON John
1923 - 24 Goalkeeper
b: Worksop, c1892
d: Shirebrook, Derbys., 10 January 1959
Career: Shirebrook (c/s 1919), Wombwell (c/s 1921), Worksop Town (c/s 1922), TOWN (c/s 1923), Gainsborough Trinity (c/s 1924), Shirebrook (c/s 1925), Warsop Main Colliery.

Did not play serious football before the Great War where he served in the R A M C from 1914-18. Jack shared the custodian's duties with Hardstaff during Town's championship season of 1923-24.

1923-24   13 apps   0 gls   Midland League
Honours: Midland League Championship 1924 (Mansfield)

JOHNSON Steven
1979 - 81 Defender   5' 9"   10st 10lbs (1980)
b: Netherfield, Notts., 23 March 1961
Career: TOWN (1977 - appr, Aug 1979 - pro),

1980-81   1(0) apps   0 gls

JOHNSTON Charles
1937 - 38 Outside Left   5' 6½"   10st 6lbs
b: Glasgow, 26 November 1912
Career: Motherwell (Dec 1932), Doncaster Rovers (May 1935), TOWN (£500 - May 1937), Dunfermline Athletic (£250 - June 1938), Rangers (£500 - 1940), Queen of the South (Aug 1946 to May 1954)

Charlie Johnston had played Scottish First Division football with Motherwell before joining Rovers and cost Mansfield a hefty fee when Harry Parkes signed him. He was a tricky winger who could centre accurately and provided Crawshaw with many telling crosses. When listed by Mansfield in May 1938, he appealed successfully to the F A about the fee placed on him and had it reduced sufficiently for the "Pars" to sign him. His career really blossomed during the war however, when he was transferred to Rangers and was a regular for them throughout the war when he won many honours including a wartime cap against England at Wembley in 1942 and he played for Rangers in the match against the touring Moscow Dynamo team in 1945 at Ibrox. In 1946 his Rangers career was considered over at 34, but after moving to Queen of the South he played on for a further eight seasons before finally retiring at the grand old age of 42!

1937-38   36 apps   4 gls
Honours: Scottish Youth International. Scottish Division 1 runners up 1933 & 1934 (Motherwell). Notts F A County Cup 1938 (Mansfield), Scottish WW II International, Scottish Southern League War Championship 1941, 1942, 1943, 1944, 1945. Scottish War Cup Winners 1941, 1942, 1943, 1945. Scottish War Cup Runners Up 1944. Scottish Division A Championship 1946 (all Rangers). Scottish Division B Championship 1952 (Queen of the South).

JONES Colin M
1984 - 85 Winger   5' 8"   11st 0lbs (1985)
b: Birmingham, 30 October 1963
Career: West Bromwich Albion (1979 - appr, Oct 1981 - pro), TOWN (Jan 1985 - N/C to Mar 1985 - C/C)

1984-85   5(0) apps   0 gls

JONES David Albert Brynmawr ("Dai")
1967 - 71 Forward   5' 10"   12st 0lbs (1970)
b: Ton Pentre, Rhondda, 31 March 1941
Career: Ton Pentre, Millwall (Mar 1964), Newport County (July 1965), TOWN (£1,500 - Oct 1967), Newport County (£500 - Nov 1971), Bath City (Nov 1973 - loan), Spencer Works.

One of the first signings by new "Stags" manager, Tommy Egglestone, "Dai" Jones made an immediate impact, when in concord with fellow striker Bob Ledger he netted six goals in his first five matches.

Only used as a substitute during the record breaking F A Cup run of 1968-69, he eventually returned to South Wales at his own request having scored 32 goals for Mansfield in 130 appearances. Currently employed as a foreman at the British Steel plant at Llenwern, Nr. Newport, he is also chairman of the works team which plays in Division 1 of the Welsh League.

1967-68	22(0) apps	8 gls	Leading Scorer
1968-69	19(4) "	4 "	
1969-70	31(3) "	10 "	
1970-71	39(2) "	9 "	
1971-72	5(5) "	1 "	

Honours: Welsh Youth International (Ton Pentre). "Giant Killers" Cup Winners 1969, Notts F A County Cup Winners 1971 (both Mansfield)

JONES David Owen ("Dai")
1947 - 49 Left Full Back   5' 11"   12st 0lbs
b: Cardiff, 28 October 1910
d: Oadby, Leicester, 20 May 1971
Career: Ely United, Ebbw Vale (1929), Millwall (1929 - trial), Charlton Athletic - (1929 - trial), Millwall 1929 - trial), Cardiff City (c/s 1930), Clapton Orient (Aug 1931), Leicester City (£200 - June 1933), TOWN (Oct 1947), Hinckley Athletic (c/s 1949 - player manager)

Having given Leicester very good service over 14 years and 226 games, "Dai" Jones must have thought his career was over at the age of almost 37, but Roy Goodall, himself a long serving full back too in his playing days, persuaded him otherwise and he served Mansfield well for two seasons, captaining the side. The oldest player to ever turn out in a League match for the "Stags" - v Wrexham (a) on 4 May 1949 -

aged 38 years 207 days. During WW II, whilst serving as a P T Instructor in the R.A.F., turned out as a "guest" for Notts County, Mansfield, West Ham and Wolves, when not in the Leicester team. His recorded hobbies in the 1930s were golf, swimming and squash.

WW II	4 apps	0 gls
1947-48	33 "	0 "
1948-49	41 "	0 "

Honours: Welsh International, Division 2 Championship 1937 (both Leicester)

JONES Dennis
1925 - 26 Right Half Back   5' 8½"   11st 6lbs (1925)
b: Bolsover, Derbys.,14 May 1894
d: Bolsover, Derbys., 7 September 1961
Career: Shirebrook (c/s 1913), Leicester City (June 1921), Southampton (£200 - May 1924), TOWN (June 1925), Shirebrook (c/s 1926), Sutton Town (Aug 1927), Wombwell (Aug 1928 to 1931).

Regular in Leicester's Second Division team for two seasons, but did not shine at The Dell. After playing days were over, he scouted for Leicester and Mansfield and from 1949-53 was acting as Assistant Trainer to the "Stags". During WW I, Jones was an P T instructor based at Roker Park, which had been commandeered by the army for the duration of the war.

1925-26	37 apps	1 gl	Midland League

Honours: Mansfield Hospital Charity Cup 1921 (Shirebrook). Midland League runners up & Notts Senior Cup Winners 1926 (both Mansfield)

JONES (George) William
1921 - 22 Centre Half Back
b: Carlton, Nottingham, 30 November 1896
Career: Nottingham Forest (1919), TOWN (c/s 1921).

This commanding centre half had played eight First Division games for Forest the season prior to joining the "Stags" for their first campaign in the Midland League.

1921-22	33 apps	1 gl	Midland League

JONES Glyn
1959 - 61 Centre/Inside Forward   5' 9"   12st 0lbs
b: Dalton, Rotherham, 8 April 1936
Career: School Football, Rotherham United (1951 - am), Sheffield United (June 1954), Rotherham United (Dec 1957), TOWN (July 1959), various Midland League teams.

Mansfield was the only spot where he found a regular place.

1959-60   31 apps   13 gls
1960-61   14   "   5   "
Honours: English Schoolboy International. English Youth International (Sheffield United)

JONES H
1926 - 27 Wing Half Back
Career: TOWN (1926 - am)

Young amateur wing half whose only senior appearance was in the 1927 Byron Cup Final.

Honours: Byron Cup Winners 1927 (Mansfield).

JONES James W
1923 - 25 Outside Left
b: Warsop, Notts., c1897
Career: Welbeck Colliery (1914), Notts County (c/s 1919), TOWN (May 1921 - trial), Alfreton (Sep 1921), Brighton & Hove Albion (c/s 1922), TOWN (Mar 1924), Worksop Town (c/s 1926), Welbeck Colliery.

Town missed him first time round after failing to impress in a trial, so he moved to Alfreton from where Brighton snapped him up and he played in 17 matches for them. Had earlier made 11 First Division appearances for Notts County between 1919 and 1921.

1923-24   7 apps   0 gls   Midland League
1924-25   16   "   3 "   "   "
Honours: Midland League Championship 1925 (Mansfield)

JONES Michael A
1960 - 66 Full Back 5' 10"   10st 7lbs (1961)
b: Sutton in Ashfield, Notts., 4 December 1942
Career: Mansfield Co-op Pathfinders, TOWN (Oct 1960)

Into his third season with the club before he got his chance and he took it with both feet eventually notching up 91 matches, before losing his place to Colin Nelson. Still lives in Sutton in Ashfield.

1962-63   7 apps   0 gls
1963-64   30   "   0 "
1964-65   35   "   0 "
1965-66   19(0)"   0 "

JONES Ormond (Henry)
1936-37 Goalkeeper 6' 0"   11st 8lbs (1931)
b: Towyn, Nr Abergele, 24 August 1910
d: Bilston, Staffs., 10 April 1972
Career: St Saviours School, Bilston Schoolboys, Hickmans, Towyn Town (1928), Bilston United (1929), Wednesbury Town (1930), Stoke City (Mar 1931), Blackpool (Aug 1931), Yeovil & Petters United   (1932), Port Vale (May 1933), Norwich City (June 1934), Watford (Feb 1935), TOWN (July 1936), Norwich City (Sep 1937), Queen of the South (July 1938), Yarmouth Town (Oct 1038).

Another player who moved annually, like many did pre war. Played in a single game for Mansfield as a "guest" during WW II.

1936-37   14 apps   0 gls
WW II   1   "   0 "
Honours: Bilston Schoolboys, Welsh Schoolboy International.

JONES Paul S
1973 - 74 Half Back 5' 9"   10st 8lbs (1973)
b: Stockport, 10 September 1953
Career: Manchester United (1969 - appr, Dec 1970 - pro), TOWN (June 1973), Rochdale (Nov 1973 - loan), Chesterfield (F.T. Aug 1974).

1973-74   15(5) apps 1 gl

JONES W A
1921 - 22 Left Half Back
Career: TOWN (1922)

Amateur whose only senior appearances were in the Charity Cup Final plus two in the league.

1921-22   2 apps   0 gls   Midland League
Honours: Mansfield Hospital Charity Cup Winners 1922 (Mansfield).

JURYEFF Ian M
1984 Forward   5' 11"   12st 0lbs (1982)
b: Gosport, Hants., 24 November 1962
Career: Southampton (1978 - appr, Nov 1980 - pro), Munkfurs Sweden (Mar to May 1983), TOWN (Mar 1984 - loan), Reading (Nov 1984 - loan), Leyton Orient (£5,000 - Feb 1985), Ipswich Town (Feb 1989 - loan), Halifax Town (£40,000 - Aug 1989), Hereford United (£50,000 - Dec 1989), Halifax Town (£50,000 - Sep 1990), Darlington (F.T. Aug 1992), Scunthorpe United (£5,000 - Aug 1993).

An opportunist who can often conjur up a goal out of nothing. Widely travelled and can worry opposing defences.

1983-84   12(0) apps 5 gls   (Loan)

KAY Harold
1928 - 30 Right Half Back 5' 9" 12st 0lbs (1928)
b: Chapeltown, Leeds, c1901
Career: Barnsley (1919), Southend United (c/s 1923), Barrow (c/s 1924), Crewe Alexandra (c/s 1925), TOWN (c/s 1928), Wombwell (c/s 1930).

Harold Kay started his career as a centre forward with his home town club, but was converted to wing half by the time he joined Southend. Prominent member of the "Stags" F A Cup run and championship team of 1928-29.

1928-29	46 apps	5 gls	Midland League	
1929-30	36 "	11 "	"	"

Honours: Midland League Championship & Mansfield Hospital Charity Cup Winners 1929 (both Mansfield)

KAY Kenneth
1947 - 48 Outside Left
b: Newark on Trent, Notts., 9 March 1920
Career: Ransome & Marles, TOWN (June 1947), Ransome & Marles (c/s 1948), Peterborough & Fletton United (c/s 1951)

1947-48 1 app 0 gls

KEARNEY Mark J
1983 - 91 Defender 5' 10" 11st 0lbs (1983)
b: Ormskirk, Lancs., 12 June 1962
Career: Marine (1979), Everton (£23,000 - Oct 1981), TOWN (F.T. Mar 1983), Bury (Jan 1991 - loan, exch Withe, permanent Mar 1991), Telford United (c/s 1994)

A great servant to the "Stags", Everton paid what was at the time one of the highest fees received by a non league club, but 18 months later, Mansfield got him for nothing.

When released by Bury, Andy King offered him the job of coaching the youngsters at Field Mill, but Mark preferred to carry on playing a little longer joining up with George Foster at Telford. Still lives in the town.

1982-83	11(0) apps		1 gl	
1983-84	17(0)	"	2	"
1984-85	37(1)	"	4	"
1985-86	31(0)	"	7	"
1986-87	43(0)	"	10	"
1987-88	4(0)	"	0	"
1988-89	44(1)	"	2	"
1989-90	41(0)	"	3	"
1990-91	20(0)	"	0	"

Honours: Division 4 promotion 1986, Freight Rover Trophy Winners 1987, Notts F A County Cup Winners 1987, 88 & 89 (all Mansfield)

KEE (Paul) James
1983 - 84 Forward
b: Londonderry, N I, 21 February 1967
Career: Faughen Valley Secondary School, Juniors, TOWN (Aug 1983 - appr), Nottingham Forest (Jan 1985 to May 1986), Coleraine (Aug 1987 to Aug 1989), Omagh Town (June 1991 - asst manager, June 1992 - manager to May 1994), Institute Derry (June 1994).

One of a number of youngsters brought over from Ireland by Ian Greaves in the early 1980s, but was released before his apprenticeship was completed.

1983-84 0(1) apps 0 gls
Honours: Northern Ireland U/15 International. Northern Ireland U/17 and U/18 International (both Mansfield)

KEEGAN Gerard Anthony ("Ged")
1983 - 84 Midfield 5' 6½" 10st 9lbs (1980)
b: Little Horton, Manchester, 3 October 1955
Career: Manchester City (Aug 1971 - appr, Mar 1973 - pro), Oldham Athletic (£25,000 - Feb 1979), TOWN (F.T. Aug 1983), Rochdale (July 1984)

Gained England Under 21 honours whilst at Maine Road, but his best days were probably at Oldham where he made 144 appearances.

1983-84 18(0) apps 1 gl
Honours: England U/21 International (Manchester City)

KEELEY Raymond B
1968 - 70 Forward 5' 10" 11st 7lbs
b: Battersea, London, 25 December 1946

Career: Charlton Athletic (1962 - appr, Dec 1964 - pro), Mar 1966 - Exeter City), Crawley Town (c/s 1967), TOWN (June 1968), Poole Town.

Signed to bolster the attack during the summer of 1968, Ray Keeley played an important part in the F A Cup triumphs of 1968-69.

| 1968-69 | 37(3) apps | 4 gls |
| 1969-70 | 11(1) " | 1 " |

Honours: "Giant Killers" Cup Winners 1969 (Mansfield)

KEELING Harold

1925 - 26 and 1933 - 34 Inside Right   5' 9"   11st 8lbs
b: Huthwaite, Notts., 10 February 1906.
Career: Huthwaite C W S, Grantham (1925), TOWN (Feb 1926), Wolverhampton Wanderers (July 1927), Notts County (Aug 1928), Luton Town (Apr 1929), Torquay United (Sep 1929), Swindon Town (Jun 1931), Norwich City (May 1932), TOWN (July 1933), Bath City (Oct 1934), Sutton Town (c/s 1935), Hereford United (c/s 1936), Tamworth Town (c/s 1937), Brierley Hill Alliance c/s 1938), Hereford United (c/s 1939).

The elder and better known of two brothers (see below) who both played for Mansfield and Sutton Town at different times. Harry is one of a select band who played for the "Stags" both both before and after Football League status was secured. Only a reserve during his first spell at Field Mill and making no first team appearances during his second season - the opposition was too great with the likes of Joe Beresford and Fred Laycock around - but he did manage to win a place in the team that won the Notts. Benevolent Bowl in May 1927 - albeit at outside right! Harry is now living quietly in retirement at Weston-Super-Mare and is believed to be the "Stags" oldest living player at the age of 89.

| 1925-26 | 2 apps | 0 gls | Midland League |
| 1933-34 | 8 apps | 0 gls | |

Honours: Notts Benevolent Bowl Winners 1927 (Mansfield)

KEELING Herbert

1928 - 29 Outside Right
b: Huthwaite, Notts., c1909
Career: Sutton Town, TOWN (C/S 1928 - am), Sutton Town, Gresley Rovers.

Amateur younger brother of Harry (see above), who failed to make an impact during his short stay at Mansfield.

| 1928-29 | 2 apps | 0 gls | Midland League |

KEERY Stanley

1957 - 58 Inside Forward/Wing Half   5' 7"   9st 12lbs
b: Derby, 9 September 1931
Career: Blackburn Rovers (am), Shrewsbury Town (Aug 1952), Newcastle United (£8,250 - Nov 1952), TOWN (£2,500 - May 1957), Crewe Alexandra (Oct 1958).

Lightly built player who had his best period at Crewe where he played in 254 matches for the "Railwaymen" and scored 23 goals.

| 1957-58 | 42 apps | 13 gls |
| 1958-59 | 11 " | 4 " |

KEETLEY (Harold) Baden

1927 - 28 Utility Forward   5' 8"   11st 12lbs (1927)
b: Derby, 17 April 1900
d: 14 October 1982
Career: St Dunstans Derby, Burton all Saints (1921), Victoria Ironworks Derby, Accrington Stanley (Nov 1923 - trial), Matlock Town (1923), Doncaster Rovers (c/s 1924), TOWN (c/s 1927), Blackburn Rovers (Dec 1927), Newark Town (c/s 1928).

Member of the amazing Keetley family of 11 boys and one girl, of which 9 boys became professional footballers - Albert, Arthur, Charles, Frank, Harry, Jack, Joe, Tom and Billy. It seems that George and Jim did not have the same enthusiasm! Most of them were successful at the sport and four of them were on Doncaster's books at the same time, with three apearing in the same match on more than one occasion! The "Stags" playing member of the clan, Harry, was signed by Blackburn from Mansfield, but he failed to make the senior team and was released at the end of the season, returning to Midland League football at Muskham Road.

| 1927-28 | 17 apps | 11 gls Midland League |

KEMP Samuel P

1958 Outside Right   5' 11"   12st 7lbs (1958)
b: Stockton on Tees, Co Durham, 29 August 1932
Career: Whitby Town, Sunderland (Mar 1952), Sheffield United (Feb 1957), TOWN (£2,000 - May 1958), Gateshead (Oct 1958).

| 1958-59 | 3 apps | 1 gl |

KENNEDY (Keith) Vernon

1982 - 83 Defender   5' 7"   10st 8lbs (1977)
b: Sunderland, 5 March 1952
Career: Newcastle United (1968 - appr, July 1970 - pro), Bury (£3,000 - Oct 1972), TOWN (F.T. Aug 1982).

Had slowed down too much when signed by Mansfield, but he had enjoyed a great spell at Bury where he appeared in 405 games.

| 1982-83 | 32(2) apps | 0 gls |

KENNIE George

1924 - 25 Outside Left   5' 8"   11st 0lbs (1924)
b: Bradford, 17 May 1904
Career: Bradford P A (c/s 1921), TOWN (June 1924), Halifax Town (£250 - c/s 1925).

1924-25   12 apps   2 gls   Midland League
Honours: Midland League Championship 1925 (Mansfield)

KENT Kevin J

1985 - 91 Forward/Defender/Midfield 5' 10" 11st 0lbs (1985)
b: Stoke on Trent, 19 March 1965
Career: West Bromwich Albion (1981 - appr, Dec 1982 - pro), Newport County (F.T. June 1984), TOWN (F.T. July 1985), Port Vale (p/exch Ford + £80,000 - Mar 1991)

Gave his all for Town in 229 League matches until he was transferred to his home town club in exchange for Gary Ford plus £80,000. has played in a variety of roles in more recent times and was the scorer of Town's goal at Wembley in 1987.

1985-86	31(3) apps	8 gls		
1986-87	46(0)	"	6	"
1987-88	45(0)	"	10	"
1988-89	36(3)	"	5	"
1989-90	38(0)	"	2	"
1990-91	27(0)	"	4	"

Honours: Division 4 Promotion 1986, Freight Rover Trophy Winners 1987, Notts F A County Cup Winners 1987, 88 & 89 (all Mansfield), Autoglass Trophy Winners 1993 (Port Vale)

KENWORTHY Anthony D

1986 - 89 Defender   5' 10"   10st 10lbs (1982)
b: Leeds, 31 October 1958

Career: Sheffield United (1974 - appr, July 1976 - pro), TOWN (Mar 1986 - loan, May 1986 - permanent to May 1989), Huddersfield Town (Aug 1990 - trial), Chesterfield (Mar 1991 - trial), Ashfield United (Dec 1993), Oakham United (c/s 1994).

Tony Kenworthy was a redoubtable player for the "Blades' making a total of 286 appearances for them in the League in twelve seasons and was signed by Mansfield, initially on loan, for the final promotion run to the end of the season in 1985-86 and the transfer was made permanent the same summer. A year after leaving Field Mill, whilst playing a trial at Huddersfield, he was convicted of a motoring offence and sentenced to six months imprisonment. He returned to football however, when he was released in March 1991.

1985-86	13(0) apps	0 gls	(Loan)	
1986-87	36(0)	"	0	"
1987-88	29(1)	"	0	"
1988-89	19(1)	"	0	"
1989-90	1(0)	"	0	"

Honours: Division 4 Championship 1982, Division 3 promotion 1984 (both Sheffield United). Division 4 promotion 1986, Freight Rover Trophy Winners 1987, Notts F A County Cup Winners 1987, 88 & 89 (all Mansfield). Wakefield Cup Winners 1995 (Oakham).

KERRY (Christopher) Brian

1994 onwards Forward   5' 8"   10st 4lbs (1994)
b: Chesterfield, 15 April 1976
Career: TOWN (1991 - appr, Apr 1994 - pro)

1993-94   1(1) apps   0 gls

KERRY Edward ("Ned")

1928 - 29 Inside Left 5' 10"   10st 6lbs (1928)
b: Creswell, Derbys., c1905
d: July 1978
Career: Creswell United Methodists (c/s 1922), Creswell Colliery (c/s 1925), Long Eaton (c/s 1926), Shirebrook (Jan 1927), Matlock Town (Mar 1927), Liverpool (Aug 1927 - trial and retained to May 1928), Notts County (July - 1928 - 2 months trial), TOWN (Oct 1928), Barnsley (Aug 1929 - trial, £250 - retained), TOWN (Feb 1934).

After touting his services around a number of League clubs, Ned Kerry only found regular senior play at Field Mill and Oakwell. Valuable member of F A Cup and Midland League Championship team in 1928-29. As a cricketer was a useful wicketkeeper for Creswell Colliery in the Bassetlaw League, once taking six catches in an innings v Kiveton Park.

Returned to Field Mill towards the end of his career, but was unable to gain a place in the senior team and was released at the end of the season.

1928-29   33 apps   16 gls   Midland League
1933-34   0   "   0   "
Honours: Midland League Championship & Mansfield Hospital Charity Cup Winners 1929 (both Mansfield).

KILCAR (Stephen) Peter
1933 - 34 Inside Left 5' 10"   11st 7lbs (1933)
b: Bo'ness, 22 December 1907
Career: Linlithgow Rose, East Stirlingshire (Apr 1927), Bradford P A (May 1929), Coventry City (May 1932), TOWN (£100 - Dec 1933), Chester (F.T. Nov 1934), Burnley (May 1935), Bournemouth & Boscombe Athletic (Sep 1936), Watford (c/s 1937).

Quite successful player at Mansfield until a breach of club rules caused his contract to be cancelled on 17 November 1934, but he soon fixed himself up with Chester. A knee injury sustained in pre season training during August 1937 prompted Steve Kilcar's retirement.

1933-34   21 apps   12 gls
1934-35   10   "   2   "
Honours: Midland League Championship 1932 (Bradford P A)

KIRK (William) Henry
1933 - 34 Outside Right   5' 10"   12st 0lbs (1933)
b Grantham, Lincs., 1914
Career: Grantham, TOWN (May 1933), Gainsborough Trinity (Aug - 1934), Yeovil & Petters United (c/s 1937).

1933-34   7 apps   1 gl

KIRKHAM Raymond N
1957 - 60 Goalkeeper 5' 11"   12st 0lbs
b: Thorne, South Yorks., 16 December 1934
Career: Thorne Town, TOWN (Dec 1957)

Able reserve who almost established himself in 1958, but then Rob Wyllie came along.

1957-58   18 apps   0 gls
1958-59   16   "   0   "
1959-60   8   "   0   "

KITE (Philip) David
1991 - 92 Goalkeeper 6' 1"   14st 7lbs (1984)
b: Bristol, 26 October 1962
Career: Bristol Rovers (1978 - appr, Oct 1980 - pro), Tottenham Hotspur (Jan 1984 - loan), Southampton (Aug 1984), Middlesbrough (Mar 1986 - loan), Gillingham (F.T. Feb 1987), A F C Bournemouth (£55,000 - Aug 1989), Sheffield United (£25,000 - Aug 1990), TOWN (Nov 1991 - loan), Plymouth Argyle (Sep 1992 - loan), Rotherham United (Oct 1992 - loan), Crewe Alexandra (Nov 1992 - loan), Stockport County (Mar 1993 - loan), Cardiff City (F.T. July 1993)

A goalkeeper who has spent a great deal of time on loan to various clubs. Made a dreadful start to his spell at Mansfield with some terrible mistakes, which proved to be costly.

1991-92   11(0) apps 0 gls   (Loan)
Honours: England Schoolboy and Youth International.

KNOX Thomas
1967 Outside left   5' 7½"   10st 4lbs
b: Glasgow, 5 September 1939
Career: East Stirlingshire (1958), Chelsea (£5,000 - June 1962), Newcastle United (£10,000 - Feb 1965), TOWN (£7,000 - Mar 1967), Northampton Town (£5,000 - Dec 1967), St Mirren c/s 1969),
Tonbridge (June 1972)

A player who had sampled football at a higher level before he came to Field Mill, where he failed to settle satisfactorily and soon moved on to Northampton.

1966-67   13(0) apps   2 gls
1967-68   21(0) "   3   "

KRUSE (Patrick) Karl
1974 Defender 5' 11"   12st 4lbs (1979)
b: Arlesey, Nr Biggleswade, Beds., 30 November 1953
Career: Arlesey Town, Leicester City (June 1970 - appr, Feb 1972 - pro), TOWN (Sep 1974 - loan), Torquay United (Mar 1975 - loan, May 1975 - permanent), Brentford (Mar 1977), Northampton Town (Feb 1982 - loan), Barnet (F.T. May 1982)

Pat Kruse's best period was at Brentford where he amassed 186 appearances for the "Bees".

1974-75   6(0) apps   1 gl   (Loan)

LAIDLAW Joseph D
1982 - 83 Midfield 5' 8½"   11st 12lbs (1977)
b: Whickham, Nr Wallsend, Northumberland, 12 July 1950

Career: Middlesbrough (1966 - appr, Aug 1967 - pro), Carlisle United (July 1972), Doncaster Rovers (June 1976), Portsmouth (June 1979), Hereford United (Dec 1980), TOWN (July 1982)

Another player whose star had shone in the past, but had lost his edge by the time he arrived at Field Mill. Was leading scorer twice at Carlisle and once at Doncaster.

1982-83   4(0) apps   0 gls
Honours: Division 2 promotion 1974 (Carlisle).
Division 4 promotion 1980 (Portsmouth)

Came to Mansfield as makeweight in the deal that took Dennis Longhorn to Roker Park, the "Stags" receiving £20,000 cash too. Figured prominently in the club's Championship campaign of 1974-75. Returned to the club in 1979 but was released 18 months later.

1973-74	17(0) apps	5 gls
1974-75	45(0) "	9 "
1975-76	10(2) "	0 "
1979-80	29(0) "	1 "

Honours: Division 4 Championship 1975 (Mansfield)

LAMBERT Brian
1954 - 60 Full Back 5' 10"   11st 7lbs
b: Sutton in Ashfield, Notts., 10 July 1936
Career: New Hucknall Colliery B C, Sutton Town, Derby County (am), TOWN (Oct 1954), Sutton Town 1960.

Reserve player who had the odd outing, sometimes at half back. Spent his National Service in the Sherwood Foresters. Currently a window cleaner in the Ashfield district.

1954-55	1 app	0 gls	
1955-56	6 "	0 "	
1956-57	12 "	0 "	
1957-58	0 "	0 "	
1958-59	2 "	0 "	
1959-60	3 "	0 "	

LAMPKIN Kevin
1994 to date Midfield/Defence   5' 10"   11st 8lbs (1992)
b: Liverpool, 20 December 1972
Career: Liverpool (1989 - appr, May 1991 - pro), Huddersfield Town (F.T. July 1992), TOWN (F.T. Feb 1994)

Came to Mansfield late in the 1993-94 season after being released by the "Terriers". Suffered from a niggling injury sustained pre season, which kept him out of action for several months, but he returned to first team duty on Boxing Day 1994, when Hereford were thrashed 7-1 at Field Mill.

1993-94	11(2) apps	1 gl
1994-95	22(1) "	2 "

LATHAN John G
1974 - 76 and 1979 - 81 Midfield   5' 7" 11st 0lbs (1974)
b: Sunderland, 12 April 1952
Career: Sunderland Boys, Manchester City (1968 - trial), Sunderland (1968 - appr, Apr 1969 - pro), TOWN (£11,000 - Feb 1974 - p/exch Longhorn who was valued at £31,000 - £20,000 to Mansfield), Carlisle United (£11,000 - Feb 1976), Barnsley (Feb 1977 - loan), abroad (c/s 1977), Portsmouth (Mar 1978), TOWN (Aug 1979 - C/C Jan 1981), abroad (1981-82).

LAVERICK Michael G
1970 - 76 Midfield   5' 8"   10st 0lbs (1975)
b: Trimdon, Co Durham, 13 March 1954
Career: Dukeries Comprehensive School, Ollerton Youth Club, TOWN (1970 - appr, Jan 1972 - pro), Southend United (Oct 1976), Huddersfield Town (July 1979), York City (£10,000 - Jan 1982), Huddersfield Town (Jan 1983 - loan), Boston United (Mar 1983), Ollerton (1985).

A product of the Town's youth policy, Mick Laverick joined Mansfield as a trainee, his family having moved Ollerton in 1962. Always a steady and consistent player, he followed Dave Smith to the "Shrimpers" when the ex Mansfield boss took over there.

1972-73	12(5) apps	2 gls
1973-74	30(6) "	5 "
1974-75	9(2) "	3 "
1975-76	22(3) "	3 "
1976-77	0(0) "	0 "

Honours: Notts F A County Cup Winners 1972 (Mansfield)

LAWRIE Thomas

1923 - 24 and 1925 Inside Forward   6' 0"   12st 3lbs (1923)
b: c1899
Career: Worksop Town (c/s 1919), TOWN (c/s 1923), Gainsborough Trinity (c/s 1924), TOWN (Apr 1925), Scunthorpe & Lindsey United (c/s 1925), Gainsborough Trinity (c/s 1926 to 1930)

A clever inside forward who could beat his man and deliver telling through passes. Holds the unique experience, which is believed to be a record, of having won three Midland League Championship medals with three different clubs.

1923-24   27 apps   7 gls   Midland League
1924-25   1   "   0   "   "   "
Honours: Midland League Championships 1922 (Worksop), 1924 (Mansfield) and 1928 Gainsborough)

LAWS Jonathan

1982 - 83 Midfield   5' 9"   10st 7lbs (1983)
b: Peterborough, 1 September 1964
Career: Wolverhampton Wanderers (1980 - appr, Sep 1982 - pro), TOWN (F.T. Mar 1983)

1982-83   0(1) apps   0 gls

LAYCOCK (Frederick) Walter

1926 - 27 Inside Forward   5' 7½"   11st 2lbs
b: Sheffield, 31 March 1897
Career: St Marys Sheffield, Shirebrook (c/s 1921), Rotherham Town (c/s 1922), The Wednesday (Mar 1923), Barrow (July 1924), Nelson (Mar 1925), TOWN (Aug 1926), New Brighton (July 1927), Peterborough & Fletton United (Sep 1928), Darlington (Sep 1929), York City (June 1930), Swindon Town (May 1931), Derry City (July 1933), Witton Albion (Oct 1934), Nuneaton Town (Oct 1935).

This nomadic player played his part in Town achieving runners up spot in the club's only season in the Midland Combination. His transfer to Nelson must be unique in football history - he was playing for Barrow v Rotherham County in March 1925 and left the field with an alleged injury, but in actual fact to sign for Nelson! For this grave misdemeanour, Laycock was severely censured by the F A and Nelson fined 5 guineas.

1926-27   19 apps 14 gls Midland Combination
Honours: Midland Combination runners up & Cup Winners 1927 (Mansfield).

LEAFE

1920 - 21 Outside left
Career: TOWN (1921)

1920-21   11 apps   1 gl   Central Alliance

LEDGER Robert H

1967 - 69 Outside Right   5' 11"   12st 4lbs
b: Craghead, Stanley, Co Durham, 5 October 1937
Career: Juniors, Huddersfield Town (Oct 1954), Oldham Athletic (£6,000 - May 1962), TOWN Dec 1967), Barrow (Oct 1969)

Bob Ledger, with his balding head, was a popular figure at Field Mill. A member of the famous 1968-69 F A Cup team, his skill was undoubted and he is still fondly remembered by "Stags" fans.

1967-68   15(2) apps   4 gls
1968-69   34(1) "   9 "
1969-70   2(3)   "   5 "
Honours: "Giant Killers" Cup Winners 1969 (Mansfield)

LEE Harry

1955 - 56 Inside Forward
b: Mexborough, South Yorks., 13 January 1933
Career: Thomas Hill Y C, Derby County (Oct 1950), Doncaster Rovers (July 1955), TOWN (Aug 1955)

1955-56   3 apps   2 gls

LEE Richard

1965 - 66 Centre Half Back
b: Sheffield, 11 September 1944
Career: Juniors, Rotherham United (May 1963), Notts County (June 1964), TOWN (Aug 1965), Halifax Town (July 1966)

1965-66   3(1) apps   1 gl

LEISHMAN Graham

1988 - 91 Forward   5' 9"   10st 7lbs
b: Salford, Manchester, 6 April 1968
Career: Irlam Town, TOWN (Dec 1988), Burton Albion (loan), Gainsborough Trinity (Feb 1991), Gateshead (Dec 1991)

Young player signed from non league who failed to develop on to League standard.

1988-89   6(6) apps   1 gl
1989-90   1(3)   "   1 "
1990-91   1(10) "   1 "

LENNON Alexander V

1949 Inside Forward
b: Glasgow, 23 October 1925
Career: Rotherham United (Nov 1944), Queens Park Rangers (Jan 1947), TOWN (Feb 1949)

1948-49   3 apps   0 gls

LEWIS John

1948 - 53 Wing Half Back   6' 0"   12st 0lbs
b: Aldridge, Staffs., 6 October 1923
Career: West Bromwich Albion (1939 - groundstaff, Oct 1945 - pro), TOWN (F.T. Aug 1948)

A good reliable half back from the Freddie Steele era who always gave of his best in his five years with the club. Jack Lewis was a keen golfer and won the Professional Footballers Golf Championship at Royal Lytham in 1952.

1948-49	4 apps	0 gls	
1949-50	39 "	1 "	
1950-51	46 "	5 "	
1951-52	46 "	4 "	
1952-53	28 "	1 "	

Honours: Division 3 North runners up 1951 (Mansfield).

LIDDLE (Daniel) Hamilton Seddon

1946 - 47 Outside Left   5' 7¼"   10st 6lbs
b: Bo'ness, 19 February 1912
d: Wigston, Leicester, 9 June 1982
Career: Scottish Juniors, East Fife (1930), Leicester City (May 1932), TOWN (July 1946).

After starring for East Fife and winning three Scottish international caps whilst at Bayview Park, Danny Liddle was Peter Hodges' first signing since his appointment as Leicester manager a month earlier. After being converted into an inside forward, he had a meteoric career at Filbert Street and was leading scorer for two seasons. Played for Leicester from 1932 to the end of the war - 13 consecutive seasons, apart from a little "guesting" with Notts County, Northampton and Mansfield

when Leicester did not have a game. Made 255 peacetime appearances for the "Filberts", scoring 64 goals.

WW II	21 apps	1 gl	
1946-47	1 "	0 "	

Honours: Scottish Junior International. Scottish Full International (East Fife). Division 2 Championship 1937, War South Championship 1942 (both Leicester).

LILL James A

1953 - 56 Outside Left   5' 8"   10st 7lbs
b: Wentworth, Sheffield, 4 June 1933
Career: Wentworth, TOWN (Oct 1953 - am, Mar 1954 - pro)

1953-54	2 apps	0 gls	
1954-55	0 "	0 "	
1955-56	1 "	0 "	

LINACRE William

1955 - 56 Outside Right   5' 10½"   11st 0lbs
b: Chesterfield, 10 August 1924
Career: Chesterfield (1942 - am, Feb 1944 - pro), Manchester City (Oct 1947), Middlesbrough (Sep 1949), Goole Town (c/s 1952), Hartlepools United (Aug 1953), TOWN (Oct 1955)

What a pity that Mansfield did not have this talented player until he was past his best. During the war years, the writer well remembers him tantalising "Stags" full backs with his jinking runs. WW II "guest" with Forest and Southport.

1955-56	13 apps	0 gls

LING Martin

1991 Forward   5' 7"   9st 12lbs
b: West Ham, London, 15 July 1966
Career: Exeter City (1982 - appr, Jan 1984 - pro), Swindon Town (£25,000 - July 1986), Southend United (£15,000 - Oct 1986), TOWN (Jan 1991 - loan), Swindon Town (Mar 1991 - loan, £15,000 - July 1991 permanent)

Scheming footballer who was involved in Swindon's promotion to the Premiership in 1991-92.

1990-91   3(0) apps   0 gls   (Loan)
Honours: Division 2 promotion 1992 (Swindon)

LINLEY Edward A

1927 - 28 Outside Left
b: Worksop, 26 September 1901
Career: Worksop Town (c/s 1919), Birmingham (Dec 1920), Nottingham Forest (c/s 1926), Sutton Town (c/s 1927), TOWN (Feb 1928).

This promising Worksop born player was a success at Central Avenue, St Andrews and the City Ground before suddenly losing his momentum and dropping down from Division 1 to the Central Alliance in one foul swoop.

1927-28   6 apps   1 gl Midland League

LITTLEDYKE Robert
1936 - 37 Inside Left 5' 8½"   11st 6lbs (1936)
b: Chester le Street, Co Durham, 5 July 1913
Career: Durham City, Lincoln City (Nov 1935), TOWN (June 1936), Grantham (F.T. May 1937)

Young reserve player from the North east who "guested" for Northampton Town during WW II.

1936-37   9 apps   1 gl

LIVIE Gordon
1952 - 54 Left Full Back   6' 0"   12st 5lbs
b: Billingham, Co Durham, 10 June 1932
Career: South Bank (1946), Leicester City (1948 groundstaff - am, Dec 1949 - pro), TOWN (July 1952), Bourne Town.

In six years at Filbert Street, did not get one senior game.

1952-53   5 apps   0 gls
1953-54   16   "   0   "

LIVINGSTONE (Allan) McKenzie
1933 - 34 Half Back/Inside Forward 5' 8" 11st 7lbs (1933)
b: Alexandria, Dunbartonshire, 2 December 1899
d: 1970
Career: Vale United, Everton (trial), Dumbarton Harp, Hull City (May 1922), Scunthorpe & Lindsey United (May 1923), Hartlepools United (Oct 1924 - trial), Crewe Alexandra (Oct 1925 - trial), New Brighton (Nov 1925), Clapton Orient (Dec 1926), Merthyr Town (June 1927), Swansea Town (£95 - June 1928), Ayr United (Sep 1929), East Fife (1930), Walsall (Sep 1931 - trial), Oswestry Town (Nov 1931 - trial), Colwyn Bay (Dec 1931), Chester (Apr 1932 - trial), Colwyn Bay (July 1932), Dumbarton (Nov 1932 - trial), Colwyn Bay (Jan 1933, Ayr United (Mar 1933 - trial), TOWN (Aug 1933), Stockport County (F.T. Nov 1934).

To say that Allan Livingstone was a much travelled player, would be rather an understatement! He certainly played a great number of trial periods, so he could not have impressed overmuch. However, both Jack Hickling and Harry Martin must have seen something in him, for between them they used him in 44 games at Mansfield and when he was 34 years old too! The only other club where he had reached even double figures of appearances was at Penydarren Park, where he managed 25. Younger

brother of Dugald Livingstone (1898-1981), who ultimately managed Newcastle, Fulham and Chesterfield.

1933-34   33 apps   1 gl
1934-35   10   "   0   "

LLEWELLYN David J
1974 - 75 Forward
b: Cardiff, 9 August 1949
Career: West Ham United (1965 - appr, Aug 1966 - pro), Peterborough United (Aug 1973), TOWN (Aug 1974 - loan)

1974-75   6(2) apps   0 gls
Honours: Welsh Under 23 International (West Ham)

LLOYD (Charles) Frederick
1931 - 33 Left Full Back   5' 8½"   12st 8lbs (1927)
b: North Shields, Northumberland, 27 September 1906
d: 1979
Career: Percy Main Colliery, Hull City (Aug 1926), Southend United (May 1928), Loughborough Corinthians (Aug 1929), TOWN (F.T. c/s 1931), Ripley Town (Aug 1934).

1931-32   1 app   0 gls
1932-33   4   "   0   "

LOCKIE Thomas
1935 - 36 Centre Half Back   6' 0"   12st 6lbs (1935)
b: Duns, 13 January 1906
d: New Earswick, Nr York, July 1977
Career: Duns, Rangers (1927), Leith Athletic (1931), Barnsley (Aug 1932), York City (May 1933), Accrington Stanley (July 1934), TOWN (May 1935), York City (Aug 1936 - asst trainer, 1937 - trainer, 1952 - coach, July 1960 - manager to Oct 1967)

Strong defensive pivot for Mansfield before being replaced by Wright. Returned to York in a training capacity in 1936 and stayed with the club for over 30 years, successfully taking them to promotion from the Fourth Division in 1964-65 when he was manager there. Worked in Rowntree's wages office until retirement in 1971.

1935-36   14 apps   1 gl

LOGAN David
1984 - 87 Midfield   5' 9"   10st 11lbs (1987)
b: Middlesbrough, 5 December 1963
Career: Marske United Redcar, Whitby Town (c/s 1981), TOWN (June 1984), Northampton Town (£20,000 - Feb 1987), Halifax Town (Aug 1988), Stockport County (Nov 1988), Scarborough (£10,000 - Aug 1990), Chesterfield (F.T. Mar 1992 - N/C), Billingham Synthonia (c/s 1992), Gainsborough Trinity (c/s 1993), Bishop Auckland (c/s 1994)

A midfielder pulled out of the non league ranks by Ian Greaves in 1984 and he made good at Field Mill before tranferring to Northampton two and a half years later.

1984-85	17(0) apps	0 gls
1985-86	24(0) "	1 "
1986-87	26(0) "	0 "

Honours: Division 4 promotion 1986, Notts F A County Cup Winners 1987 (both Mansfield)

LONGHORN Dennis
1971 - 74 Midfield   6' 0"   11st 1lb (1972)
b: Southampton, 12 September 1950
Career: Bournemouth & Boscombe Athletic (1966 - appr, Aug 1968 - pro), TOWN (£5,000 - Dec 1971), Sunderland (£31,000 - exch for Lathan + £20,000 - Feb 1974), Sheffield United (Oct 1976 - loan, £25,000 - Nov 1976 permanent), Aldershot (£20,000 - Feb 1978), Colchester United (May 1980), Halstead Essex (1989 - manager)

First signing made by Danny Williams after his appointment as Mansfield manager. Longhorn developed well and attracted the attention of Bob Stokoe at Sunderland, who paid out a hefty fee plus the up and coming Lathan to secure his services.

1971-72	26(1) apps	1 gl
1972-73	39(1) "	2 "
1973-74	28(1) "	2 "

Honours: Notts F A County Cup Winners 1972 (Mansfield)

LOWDE Ernest
1922 - 23 and 1929 - 30 Inside/Centre Forward
b: Mansfield Woodhouse, Notts., c1901
Career: Whitwell, TOWN (Apr 1923 - am), Whitwell (c/s 1924), TOWN (Apr 1930 - am), Whitwell.

Amateur forward called up twice for first team duty by the "Stags" in seven seasons!

| 1922-23 | 1 app | 1 gl | Midland League |
| 1929-30 | 1 " | 0 " | " " |

LOWE Henry Charles ("Harry")
1923 - 24 Centre Half Back   5' 8½"   11st 2lbs (1924)
b: Whitwell, Derbys., 20 March 1886
d: Worksop, 25 October 1958
Career: Whitwell, Gainsborough Trinity (1907), Liverpool (Apr 1911), Nottingham Forest (Mar 1920), TOWN (c/s 1923), Newark Town (1929)

Harry Lowe had a long and consistent career in League football with both Gainsborough and Liverpool and was unfortunate to miss the 1914 F A Cup Final due to injury.

Rather small for a centre half, but this was before the off-side law was changed and attacking centre halves were the vogue. Well past his best when he joined Forest, he only made one appearance for them. Turned out for Newark when he was well into his 40s.

| 1923-24 | 1 app | 0 gls | Midland League |

LOWERY Anthony W
1983 - 91 Midfield   5' 9"   10st 6lbs (1983)
b: Wallsend, Northumberland, 6 July 1961
Career: Ashington, West Bromwich Albion (£3,500 - Mar 1981), Walsall (Feb 1982 - loan), TOWN (Apr - 1983 - loan, F.T. May 1983 permanent), Walsall (Sep 1990 - loan), Carlisle United (F.T. July 1991), Gateshead (F.T. c/s 1992)

Nearly 250 senior appearances for the "Stags" - that is Tony Lowery's record and what a fine player he turned out to be - he cost nothing too! Still playing in his native North East, after giving Mansfield magnificent service for eight years.

1982-83	1(0) apps	0 gls	(Loan)
1983-84	45(0) "	6 "	
1984-85	45(0) "	3 "	
1985-86	40(0) "	5 "	
1986-87	44(0) "	5 "	
1987-88	44(0) "	0 "	
1988-89	11(1) "	0 "	
1989-90	14(0) "	0 "	
1990-91	5(2) "	0 "	

Honours: Division 4 promotion 1986, Freight Rover Trophy Winners 1987, Notts F A County Cup Winners 1987 & 1989 (all Mansfield)

LUKE Noel E

1984 - 86 Midfield   5' 11"   10st 11lbs (1987)
b: Birmingham, 28 December 1964
Career: West Bromwich Albion (1980 - appr, Apr 1982 - pro), TOWN (F.T. July 1984), Peterborough United (F.T. Aug 1986), Rochdale (F.T. Mar 1993), Boston United (F.T. May 1993)

This Birmingham born player had his best period with the "Posh" where he played in almost 300 games before drifting out of the League scene.

1984-85   33(3) apps   6 gls
1985-86   8(6)   "   3 "
Honours: Division 4 promotion 1986 (Mansfield), 1991 (Peterborough), Division 3 promotion 1992 (Peterborough).

LUMBY James A

1981 - 82 Forward   5' 9"   11st 7lbs (1978)
b: Grimsby, 2 October 1954
Career: Grimsby Town (Oct 1972 - appr, Mar 1974 - pro), Boston Gainsborough Trinity, Brigg Town, Scunthorpe United (Mar 1977), Carlisle United (£35,000 - Apr 1978), Tranmere Rovers (£40,000 - July 1979), TOWN (£50,000 - Jan 1981), Boston United (F.T. May 1982).

An opportunist in front of goal, Jim Lumby was the son of a pre war Grimsby and Stockport centre forward. Leading scorer with Tranmere in his last full season before joining the "Stags" with 18 goals, he also managed this feat with Mansfield, netting 14 in his first full season here. After he hung up his boots, Lumby took over the licence of a public house in Cleethorpes, near Blundell Park.

1980-81   11(1) apps   4 gls
1981-82   38(1)   "   14 "   Leading Scorer

LYON David G

1973 Defender   6' 3½"   14st 7lbs (1977)
b: Northwich, Cheshire, 18 January 1951
Career: Bury (1967 - appr, Jan 1969 - pro), Huddersfield Town (Sep 1971), TOWN (Nov 1973 - loan), Cambridge United (July 1974), Northampton Town (Oct 1977)

Giant of a defender who played in just two matches on loan.

1973-74   2(0) apps   0 gls   (Loan)

McBRIDE Vincent

1958 - 59 Goalkeeper
b: Manchester, 21 January 1934
Career: Ashton United, Walsall (May 1954), Aston Villa (Mar 1956), TOWN (July 1958)

1958-59   10 apps   0 gls

McCAFFREY James

1972 - 77 Outside Left   5' 7"   9st 10lbs (1971)
b: Luton, 12 October 1951
Career: St Albans B C, Leeds United (trial), Nottingham Forest (1967 - appr, Mar 1969 - pro), TOWN (F.T. July 1972), Huddersfield Town (Jan 1977), Portsmouth (Feb 1978), Northampton Town (Dec 1978)

Tricky diminutive winger who was a great favourite with the Field Mill faithful, Jimmy McCaffrey had shone as a Youth International, but failed to secure a regular senior place at the City Ground. Fell out of favour in the Peter Morris managerial era and moved on, Johnny Miller being preferred by the new "Stags" boss. After retiring, in 1979, he became a newsagent in the Lake District, later taking up a similar position in Leicestershire.

1972-73   45(0) apps   7 gls
1973-74   37(3)   "   3 "
1974-75   37(2)   "   6 "
1975-76   35(1)   "   2 "
1976-77   16(2)   "   3 "
Honours: England Youth International (Nottingham Forest), Division 4 Championship 1975 & Division 3 Championship 1977 (both Mansfield)

McCARTER (James) John

1948 - 50 Outside Left   5' 8"   10st 12lbs
b: Glasgow, 19 March 1923
Career: Vale of Clyde, Sheffield Wednesday (1944 - am, Jan 1946 - pro), TOWN (Aug 1948)

Direct Scottish winger who liked to cut in on goal, but very one footed and this restricted him on occasions, particularly as his inside partner at the time was left footed too.

| 1948-49 | 26 apps | 4 gls |
| 1949-50 | 41 " | 6 " |

McCLELLAND John

1978 - 81 Centre Half   6' 1½"   11st 4lbs (1978)
b: Belfast, 7 December 1955
Career: Portadown, Cardiff City (Feb 1974), Bangor City (F.T. c/s 1975), TOWN (£10,000 - May 1978), Rangers (£90,000 - May 1981), Watford (£220,000 - Nov 1984), Leeds United (£110,000 - June 1989), Watford (Jan 1990 - loan), Notts County (Mar 1992 - loan), St Johnstone (c/s 1992 - player manager to Nov 1993), Carrick Rangers (Nov 1993), Arbroath (Nov 1994), Wycombe Wanderers (Feb 1994), Woking (Mar 1994)

After being discarded by Cardiff, who failed to see his potential, John McClelland had a spell with non league Bangor from where Town recruited him for a modest fee early in 1978 as one of manager Billy Bingham's early captures. He developed so well at Field Mill, that not only did mighty Rangers pay out a big fee to sign him, but in his three years here, collected six full Northern Ireland caps, the first and so far only, Mansfield player to gain full international recognition whilst with the club. In a long career culminating with the player-managership of Scottish Premier side St Johnstone, he eventually won 53 caps for his country.

1978-79	33(3) apps	1 gl
1979-80	43(0) "	1 "
1980-81	46(0) "	6 "

Honours: Northern Ireland International (Mansfield, Rangers, Watford & Leeds). Hennessy Gold Cup 1973 (Portadown). Welsh Cup runners up 1975 (Cardiff). Welsh League play offs & City Cup Winners 1976, Welsh Cup runners up 1978 (all Bangor). Scottish League Cup 1982 & 1984 (both Rangers). Division 1 Championship 1992 (Leeds).

McCORD (Brian) John

1992 Midfield   5' 10"   11st 6lbs
b: Derby, 24 August 1968
Career: Derby County (1984 - appr, June 1987 - pro), Barnsley (Nov 1989 - loan, £100,000 - Mar 1990 - permanent), TOWN (Aug 1992 - loan), Stockport County (F.T. Dec 1992),

| 1992-93 | 11(0) apps | 1 gl | (Loan) |

MACREADY Brian L

1964 - 66 Winger   5' 8½"   10st 10lbs
b: Leicester, 25 March 1942
Career: Willerby B C, Hull City (1959), West Bromwich Albion (Feb 1960), TOWN (July 1964),

Although this winger was a part of the promotion challenging team of 1964-65, he disappeared from the league scene when released by Town. Holds the distinction of being the first player to be used as a substitute when the new ruling was introduced in 1965.

| 1964-65 | 31 apps | 7 gls |
| 1965-66 | 18(1) " | 4 " |

Honours: Division 3 - 3rd 1965 (Mansfield)

McDONALD Gary

1989 - 90 Forward   5' 9"   11st 12lbs (1989)
b: Sunderland, 20 November 1969
Career: Ipswich Town (1985 - appr, 1987 - pro), TOWN (F.T. Aug 1989).

| 1989-90 | 1(1) apps | 0 gls |

McDONALD (Ian) Clifford

1975 - 77 Midfield   5' 9"   11st 9lbs (1987)
b: Barrow in Furness, 10 May 1953
Career: Barrow (1969 - appr, May 1971 - pro), Workington (£3,000 - Feb 1973), Liverpool (£33,000 - Jan 1974), Colchester United (Feb 1975 - loan), TOWN (£10,000 - July 1975), York City (£7,000 - Nov 1977), Aldershot (Exch M Crosby - Nov 1981), Farnborough Town (1989), Aldershot (1990, Nov 1991 to Mar 1992 - player manager), Millwall (c.s 1992 - reserve team coach)

| 1975-76 | 32(2) apps | 4 gls |
| 1976-77 | 15(7) " | 0 " |

Honours: Division 3 Championship 1977 (Mansfield)

McDONALD Roger

1955 - 56 Full Back   5' 10"   11st 2lbs
b: Glasgow, 2 February 1933
Career: St Mirren (1951), TOWN (Mar 1955), Cheltenham Athletic (c/s 1956), Crystal Palace (Jan 1958)

| 1954-55 | 6 apps | 0 gls |
| 1955-56 | 7 " | 0 " |

McEWAN William J M

1977 Midfield   5' 10"   11st 2lbs (1977)
b: Cleland, Wishaw, 20 June 1951
Career: Hibernian (1969), Blackpool (June 1973), Brighton &
Hove Albion (Feb 1974), Chesterfield (£15,000 - Nov 1974),
TOWN (£18,000 - Jan 1977), Peterborough United (Nov 1977),
Rotherham United (July 1979), Sheffield United (Mar 1986 -
manager to Jan 1988), Rotherham United (Apr 1988 - manager to
Jan 1991), Darlington (July 1992 - manager to Oct 1993), Derby
County (Oct 1993 - coach).

Influential player in "Stags" promotion to Division
2, but was allowed to join the "Posh" ten months
later. Has now been involved in soccer management
for almost ten years.

1976-77   23(0) apps   3 gls
1977-78   9(0)   "   0   "
Honours: Division 3 Championship 1977 (Mansfield)

McGEORGE James L

1966 - 67 Forward
b: Sunderland, 8 June 1945
Career: Spennymoor, Leyton Orient (Mar 1964), TOWN (July
1966)

1966-67   5(4) apps   0 gls

McGOWAN James

1961 - 62 Outside Right   5' 6"   10st 0lbs
b: Glasgow, 31 July 1939
Career: St Johnstone (Dec 1959), TOWN (June 1961), Margate
(Mar 1962), Rainworth M W

1961-62   3 apps   0 gls

McGREGOR William

1953 - 56 Full Back 5' 9"   11st 3lbs
b: Paisley, 1 December 1923
Career: Mossdale Y M C A, Leicester City (£2,500 - Apr 1947),
TOWN (Sep 1953).

Virtually an ever present during his time with
Mansfield, he missed few matches in his three
seasons at Field Mill. Bill McGregor was a dour
Scot who was strong but scrupulously fair in his
tackling.

1953-54   42 apps   0 gls
1954-55   39   "   0   "
1955-56   38   "   0   "

McJANNET William (Leslie)

1979 - 82 Full Back 5' 10"   10st 4lbs (1980)
b: Cumnock, Ayrshire, 2 August 1961

Career: Scottish Juniors, TOWN (Aug 1979), Kings Lynn (F.T.
c/s 1982), Matlock Town (c/s 1983), Burton Albion (c/s 1984),
Scarborough (Aug 1987), Darlington (Dec 1988 - loan, Feb 1989
- permanent), Boston United (c/s 1992), Matlock Town (c/s
1993), Eastwood Town (c/s 1994)

A youngster recruited from Scottish Junior football,
Les McJannet was rather on the light side for a
defender, but nevertheless did quite respectably for
the "Stags" for three seasons. Still lives in the
district and continues playing at the age of 34 for
the "Gladiators" in the Northern Premier League.

1979-80   2(0) apps   0 gls
1980-81   34(0)   "   0   "
1981-82   37(1)   "   0   "

McKENNA John

1927 - 30 Left Half Back   6' 0"   12st 0lbs (1928)
b: Belfast, c1900
d: Belfast, April 1933
Career: St Malchays College (c/s 1920), Barrow (c/s 1921),   St
Pauls Swifts (c/s 1922), St Marys Barrow, Ards United (c/s
1924), Bohemians (c/s 1926), Ards United (Jan 1927), New
Brighton (Aug 1927), TOWN (Sep 1927), Northern Ireland Junior
teams.

Had three good seasons with Mansfield during which
time he was a member of the 1929 F A Cup giant
killing team. Released by the "Stags" in May 1930,
he returned to Ulster and played in minor football
before being stricken down by a mysterious virus
from which he died aged only 32.

1927-28	33 apps	1 gl	Midland	League
1928-29	40 "	3 "	"	"
1929-30	27 "	0 "	"	"

Honours: Irish Intermediate League Championship 1925, Irish League Cup and Irish Intermediate League Championship 1927 (all Ards). Mansfield Hospital Charity Cup Winners 1928 & 1929, Midland League Championship 1929 (all Mansfield)

McKENZIE Duncan
1970 and 1973 Forward   5' 10"   11st 2lbs (1973)
b: Grimsby, 10 June 1950
Career: Nottingham Forest (1967 - appr, July 1968 - pro), TOWN (Mar 1970 & Feb 1973 - both loans), Leeds United (£240,000 - Aug 1974), Anderlecht Belgium (£200,000 - c/s 1976), Everton (£200,000 - Dec 1976), Chelsea (£165,000 - Sep 1978), Blackburn Rovers (£80,000 - Mar 1979), Tulsa Roughnecks U S A (c/s 1981), Chicago Sting U S A (c/s 1982), Hong Kong (c/s 1983).

His second loan spell at Field Mill was with a view to a permanent transfer and Tommy Eggleston had agreed a fee of £15,000 with Forest - but Town could not raise the money to buy him, more's the pity! He was at that time only in the Forest first team spasmodically, but by netting seven goals in six games, he was recalled by Dave Mackay, soon won a regular place in the "Reds" senior squad and went on to glory!

| 1969-70 | 7(3) apps | 3 gls | (Loan) |
| 1972-73 | 6(0) " | 7 " | (Loan) |

MACKENZIE Ian S
1975 - 78 Defender   6' 0"   10st 10lbs (1976)
b: Rotherham, 27 September 1950
Career: Juniors, Sheffield United (June 1968 - appr, Sep 1968 - pro), Southend United (Mar 1975 - loan), TOWN (F.T. July 1975)

Reliable defender signed from the "Blades" where he was mainly a reserve.

1975-76	36(1) apps	1 gls
1976-77	28(0) "	0 "
1977-78	5(0) "	0 "

Honours: Division 3 Championship 1977 (Mansfield)

McKERNON Craig A
1984 - 89 Defender   5' 9"   11st 0lbs (1988)
b: Gloucester, 23 February 1968
Career: TOWN (1984 - appr, Feb 1986 - pro), Arsenal (£250,000 - Dec 1989), Kettering Town (1992), Hinckley Town (Apr 1993), Oakham United (Jan 1994)

Outstanding player who first played in the senior XI when he was still a trainee. Brought along steadily by Bill Dearden until he really blossomed out in 1988-89 season. Having seen his potential, Arsenal paid a sizable fee to get him early in the following term, but he suffered a nasty knee injury which failed to respond to treatment and he retired from the first class game at only 22. Happily he made sufficient recovery to take up soccer again, albeit at a lower level and married to a Mansfield girl and living locally, he is currently turning out for Oakham United.

1984-85	1(1) apps	0 gls
1985-86	7(4) "	0 "
1986-87	13(5) "	0 "
1987-88	9(5) "	0 "
1988-89	42(0) "	0 "
1989-90	7(0) "	0 "

Honours: Notts F A County Cup Winners 1987 (Mansfield)

McKINNEY William E
1966 - 68 Full Back   5' 11½"   12st 11lbs
b: Newcastle on Tyne, 20 July 1936
Career: Wallsend Rising Sun, Wallsend St Leonards, Wallsend St Lukes, Newcastle United (£50 - May 1956), Bournemouth & Boscombe Athletic (£2,750 - Aug 1965), TOWN (F.T. July 1966), Wellington Town (c/s 1968).

Long kicking full back signed by Tommy Cummings, but fell out of favour when Tommy Egglestone took over the manager's chair.

| 1966-67 | 40(0) apps | 2 gls |
| 1967-68 | 11(1) " | 0 " |

McLACHLAN Edwin Rowland

1928 - 30 & 1931 - 32 Outside Right 5'10" 11st 0lbs (1928)
b: Glasgow, 24 September 1903
d: Leicester, 16 March 1970
Career: Glasgow B B, Queens Park (c/s 1921), Clyde (c/s 1922 - am) Third Lanark (c/s 1924 - am), Vale of Leven (c/s 1925 - am), Leicester City (Jan 1927 - am), Nottingham Forest (May 1927), TOWN (c/s 1928), Northampton Town (July 1930), TOWN (F.T. c/s 1931)

A renowned amateur winger in Scotland who was a trialist for Amateur International honours, Teddy McLachlan's job brought him down to Leicester where he signed amateur forms for City. Forest offered him a pro contract the following summer and he played in eight Second Division games for them before joining Mansfield in the close season of 1928. Member of the famous "Egg & Milk" F A Cup team of 1928-29, he served a term with the "Cobblers" before returning to Field Mill to end his career, but only played in the reserves. Became Secretary to the Leicestershire Senior League in the mid 1930s and served as Chairman of the Leicestershire County F A from 1963 until his death in 1970. Reputedly the fastest winger in the Midland League in 1929.

1928-29	41 apps		16 gls	Midland League
1929-30	32 "		23 "	"	"
1931-32	0 "		0 "	"	"

Honours: Midland League Championship, Mansfield Hospital Charity Cup Winners 1929 (both Mansfield)

McLOUGHLIN Paul B

1992 - 94 Forward 5' 10" 10st 7lbs
b: Bristol, 23 December 1963
Career: Bristol Schools, Bristol Rovers (trial), Bristol City (1980 - am), Yeovil Town (1980), Gisborne City N Z (1981), Cardiff City (Jan 1985), Oster Vaxjo Sweden (c/s 1986), Bristol City (Jan 1987 - N/C), Hereford United (July 1987), Wolverhampton Wanderers (£45,000 - July 1989), Walsall (Sep 1991 - loan), York City (Jan 1992 - loan), TOWN (£35,000 - Jan 1992), Bath City (c/s 1994), Weston (Nov 1994 - loan)

Not only widely travelled as far as number of clubs are concerned, but has played in New Zealand and Sweden too. Not a great success at Mansfield although he did score on his debut at Rotherham (a) and played a small part in the promotion run in of 1992 during which he had been signed as cover.

1991-92	10(2) apps	3 gls
1992-93	20(6) "	4 "
1993-94	19(4) "	2 "

Honours: Bristol Schoolboys.

McNULTY James

1920 - 21 Outside Left
b: Scotland, c1899
Career: Stanton Ironworks, Ilkeston Town, TOWN (c/s 1920)

1920-21	2 apps	0 gls	Central Alliance

MADDEN Lawrence D

1975 Defender 5' 11" 13st 1lb (1897)
b: Hackney, London, 28 September 1955
Career: Arsenal (am), TOWN (Apr 1975 - N/C), Manchester University, Charlton Athletic (Mar 1978), Boston United (c/s 1981), Millwall (£10,000 - Mar 1982), Sheffield Wednesday (F.T. Aug 1983), Leicester City (Jan 1991 - loan), Wolverhampton Wanderers (F.T. Aug 1991), Darlington (c/s 1993), Chesterfield (Oct 1993)

A prospective university student, Lawrie Madden joined the "Stags" from April to November 1975 before going on to university. He was a talented constructive defender who went on to long and successful careers with both Charlton and Wednesday in a track record spanning 20 years - to date! This remarkable player is still giving sterling performances at the ripe old age of 40, but he still has a little way to go to become the "Spireites" oldest player - that distinction still belongs to Billy Kidd who turned out for them when aged 40 years 322 days in September 1947. Oddly enough he is currently playing alongside Kevin Davies who is the second youngest player to appear for Chesterfield at 16½ - Madden is more than double his age!

1974-75   6(1) apps   0 gls
1975-76   3(0)   "   0 "
Honours: Football League Cup Winners 1991 (Sheffield Wednesday), Division 3 promotion - via play-offs 1995 (Chesterfield).

MADDISON John (Arden) Brown

1933 - 34 Centre Half Back   5' 8"   11st 3lbs
b: Chester le Street, Co Durham, 1900
Career: Usworth Colliery, Stoke City (Nov 1923), Port Vale (Oct 1924), Oldham Athletic (May 1927), Non League (1929-32), TOWN (Aug 1933), Nimes France (Dec 1934), Gresley Rovers (Feb 1934), Sutton Town (1935).

Over the hill by the time he came to Mansfield after an extended period of non league football, Arden Maddison had his best years during the mid 1920s with Port Vale in the Second Division. Did not play for the "Stags" in a League match but did turn out in two cup ties.

1933-34   0 apps   0 gls

MALLINSON David J

1964 - 67 Half Back 6' 0"   11st 7lbs (1965)
b: Sheffield, 7 July 1946
Career: Juniors, TOWN (1964 - am, Apr 1965 - pro)

1965-66   10(1) apps   1 gl
1966-67   0(0)   "   0 "

MANN Arthur F

1979 - 82 Midfield   5' 9"   10st 8lbs (1980)
b: Burntisland, Fifeshire, 23 January 1948
Career: Heart of Midlothian (1965), Manchester City (£85,000 - Nov 1968), Blackpool (Nov 1971 - loan), Notts County (£15,000 - July 1972), Shrewsbury Town (June 1979), TOWN (Oct 1979), Boston United (F.T. c/s 1982), Grimsby Town (1989 - asst manager), West Bromwich Albion (Oct 1994 - assistant manager).

His best era was with Notts County where in seven years he made over 240 appearances. Joining Mansfield after the briefest of spells at Gay Meadow, Arthur Mann was a great success at Field Mill where this classy midfielder fitted extremely well into the Mansfield side. In 1989 became assistant to Alan Buckley at Grimsby, the pair of them moving to the Hawthorns in October 1994.

1979-80   35(0) apps   0 gls
1980-81   44(0)   "   2 "
1981-82   35(2)   "   1 "

MARKS Michael D

1988 Forward
b: Lambeth, London, 23 March 1968
Career: Millwall (1984 - appr, July 1986 - pro), TOWN (Jan 1988 - loan), Leyton Orient (Feb 1988)

1987-88   0(1) apps   0 gls   (Loan)

MARLOW Owen

1927 - 28 Goalkeeper 5' 11½"   12st 0lbs (1927)
b: Swansea, c1905
Career: Swansea Town (c/s 1925 - am, c/s 1926 - pro), TOWN (June 1927)

Young 'keeper who had appeared in Swansea's Second Division side the previous term, Marlow was a part time pro whose job took him to Nottingham in the Summer of 1927 and he was allowed to team up with the "Stags", appearing in almost every match for a season before his job became more important than soccer.

1927-28   43 apps   0 gls
Honours: Mansfield Hospital Charity Cup Winners 1928 (Mansfield)

MARRON Christopher

1952 - 54 Centre Forward   5' 9½"   11st 7lbs
b: Jarrow, Co Durham, 7 February 1925
d: Mansfield, 1986
Career: Sunderland, South Shields, Chesterfield (Oct 1947), TOWN (July 1952), Bradford P A (July 1954), Heanor Town (1960 - player manager)

From the North East's hot bed of football, Chris Marron had a good career at both Saltergate and Field Mill. Settled in the town after his playing days were over and until his death in 1986.

1952-53   39 apps   16 gls   Leading Scorer
1953-54   14   "   9   "

MARROWS Dean

1990 onwards Defender 5' 8"   11st 10lb (1994)
b: Sutton in Ashfield, Notts., 30 September 1975
Career: TOWN (1990 - assoc schoolboy, 1991 - appr, Apr 1994 - pro), Glapwell (Nov 1994 - loan).

Young full back whose only appearance in the senior team was in the Autowindscreens Shield match against Wrexham, when he came on as substitute. Released in May 1995.

1994-95   0 apps   0 gls

MARSH W
1942 - 43 and 1945 - 46 Left Full Back
Career: TOWN (c1942)

A local wartime recruit who played in 4 of the F A Cup ties during the 1945-46 season and also 5 War League games too. He had earlier made 6 appearances during 1942-43, scoring one goal.

WW II   15 apps   1 gl

MARTIN (Dennis) William
1978 - 79 Winger   5' 11"   10st 12lbs (1978)
b: Edinburgh, 27 October 1947
Career: Kettering Town, West Bromwich Albion (July 1967), Carlisle United (July 1970), Newcastle United (£40,000 - Oct 1977), TOWN (£30,000 - Mar 1978), Kettering Town (c/s 1979).

Experienced and clever winger who was signed by Mansfield in their struggle to avoid relegation from the Second Division - to no avail. Had his best years at Brunton Park where he played in 275 matches in a seven year period and assisted them in their run through to the First Division.

1977-78   13(0) apps   0 gls
1978-79   33(0)   "   3   "
Honours: Division 2 promotion 1974 (Carlisle)

MARTIN George
1919 - 22 Full Back
b: Annesley, Notts., c1896
Career: Annesley Colliery, TOWN (c/s 1919), Annesley Colliery (c/s 1922).

1919-20   15 apps   0 gls   Central Alliance
Honours: Central Alliance Championship 1920 (Mansfield)

MATTHEWS (John) Melvin
1982 - 84 Midfield   6' 0"   12st 6lbs (1987)
b: Camden, London, 1 November 1955
Career: Arsenal (July 1971 - appr, Aug 1973 - pro), Sheffield United (£90,000 - Aug 1978), TOWN (F.T. Aug 1982), Chesterfield (F.T. Aug 1984), Plymouth Argyle (Aug 1985), Torquay United (F.T. July 1989)

Tall midfielder who started his career with the "Gunners", John Matthews had long terms with both Sheffield United and the "Pilgrims" before finally retiring at the age of 35.

1982-83   39(1) apps   3 gls
1983-84   31(1)   "   3   "
Honours: Division 4 Championship 1985 (Chesterfield), Division 3 runners up 1986 (Plymouth)

MATTHEWS (Paul) William
1972 - 77 Midfield   5' 9"   10st 3lbs (1973)
b: Leicester, 30 September 1946
Career: Leicester City (Aug 1963 - appr, Aug 1964 - pro), Southend United (Sep 1972 - loan), TOWN (£5,000 - Dec 1972), Rotherham United (Oct 1977), Northampton Town (Mar 1979 - loan), Heanor Town, Oadby Town.

A former winger, converted by the club into a midfield player, Paul Matthews did not kick a football until he left school, as during his years of education rugby was the chosen sport and he excelled at this sufficiently to represent Leicestershire at schools level. Lost his place at Field Mill when Peter Morris bacame player manager. Won Championship medals in Divisions 2, 3 and 4 in the space of six years.

1972-73	16(0) apps	1 gl
1973-74	12(1) "	0 "
1974-75	44(0) "	2 "
1975-76	28(1) "	1 "
1976-77	17(1) "	2 "
1977-78	4(0) "	0 "

Honours: Division 2 Championship 1971 (Leicester). Division 4 Championship 1975 & Division 3 Championship 1977 (both Mansfield).

MAXWELL Neil
1927 - 28 Inside Forward
Career: Dulwich Hamlet, TOWN (Dec 1927 - am)

Noted player from the famous South East London amateur club who played a short time for the "Stags", mainly in the reserves, whilst working temporarily in the town.

1927-28   1 app   0 gls Midland League

MAYFIELD George
1921 - 22 Inside Forward
Career: Ilkeston, TOWN (c/s 1921), Newark Town (c/s 1923).

1921-22   3 apps   0 gls Midland League

MAYFIELD Leslie
1948 - 53 Full Back 5' 9"   11st 5lbs
b: Mansfield, 19 January 1926
Career: Clipstone Welfare, Ferryhill Athletic, TOWN (Mar 1948 - am, Sep 1948 - pro), Sutton Town.

One of a number of ex High Oakham schoolboys who gained contracts with Mansfield in the 40s and 50s. His grandson was on Town's books for a time in the 1980s.

1949-50	1 app	0 gls	
1950-51	4 "	0 "	
1951-52	23 "	0 "	
1952-53	6 "	0 "	

MEADS James
1927 - 28 Inside Right 5' 8½"   10st 7lbs (1925)
b: Warsop, Notts., c1906
Career: Tupton, Grassmore Comrades, Chesterfield (1925), TOWN (Sep 1927), Staveley Town (Nov 1927), Shirebrook (Feb 1929), Frickley Colliery (c/s 1930)

Jimmy Meads was the twin brother to the much better known Tommy Meads who played in nearly 400 Football League games between 1924 and 1936 - 117 Stockport, 40 Huddersfield, 31 Reading, 184 Spurs and 18 for Notts County. A younger brother, Johnny, also played League football - for Chesterfield.

1927-28   5 apps   1 gl Midland League

MEAKIN Arthur
1938 - 39 Wing Half back
b: Heanor, Derbys., c1917
Career: Heanor Town, TOWN (c/s 1938).

Young wing half who made a single appearance for the senior XI v Walsall in the Jubilee Fund match in August 1938.

1938-39   0 apps   0 gls

MEE Bertram O B E
1939 Outside Left   5' 7"   10st 0lbs (1939)
b: Bulwell, Nottingham, 25 December 1920
Career: Bulwell, Derby County (c/s 1937 - am, Jan 1939 - pro), TOWN (Feb 1939), Arsenal (Aug 1960 - physiotherapist & trainer, Jun 1966 - manager to July 1976), Watford (1978 - assistant manager, 1982 - director & general manager to retirement Sep 1991).

Younger brother of Georgie Mee (see below), Bertie joined the "Rams" as a 17 year old but did not get a senior appearance at the Baseball Ground as was allowed to join the "Stags" towards the end of the last pre war season. An injury towards the end of that term ultimately finished his playing career for good when he was only 18. Served in the Army during WW II as a physiotherapist in the R A M C after demob became Rehabilitation Officer to disabled ex servicemen. An appointment as Arsenal's physio came in 1960 followed by the managership in 1967, a job he did with great success until he retired in 1976 - having taken the club to the "double" (Division 1 Championship and F A Cup win) in 1971. He had also secured the European Fairs Cup the previous season. Took the post of Watford assistant manager in 1978, later becoming General Manager to 1986 when he was appointed to the board - a position he fulfilled until finally going into full retirement in 1992. His life, seemingly shattered by a teenage injury, came to fruition by becoming one of the game's leading administrators in the post war era. Perhaps their was some significance in that he played only 13 League matches! Awarded the O B E in the New Year Honours List of 1972.

1938-39   13 apps   1 gl

MEE (George) Wilfred
1933 - 34 Outside Left   5' 4"   11st 2lbs
b: Bulwell, Nottingham, 12 April 1900
d: Poulton le Fylde, 9 July 1978
Career: Highbury Vale Athletic, Notts County (Aug 1918), Blackpool (July 1920), Derby County (£3,750 - Feb 1926 joint transfer with Gill), Burnley (Sep 1932), TOWN (July 1933), Great Harwood (Nov 1934), Accrington Stanley (Oct 1935), Rochdale (July 1938 - trainer coach), Accrington Stanley (Jan 1939 - player coach)

A clever winger who was very small - he only measured 5' 4" and was known as "Shortie". Elder brother of Bertie Mee (see above), he was also well known as a fine vocalist and banjo player - an occupation he pursued each Summer in Blackpool. He had very good years at both Blackpool and Derby where he amassed totals of 230 and 155 appearances respectively. His playing career lasted for 20 years and he settled in Lancashire, close to his beloved Blackpool, after he hung up his boots and until his death aged 78.

1933-34	11 apps	0 gls	
1934-35	0 "	0 "	

Honours: Division 2 runners up 1926 (Derby), Division 3 North Cup runners up 1939 (Accrington).

MEEHAN Tobias
1921 - 22 Wing Half Back
b: Manchester, c1899
Career: Rochdale (c/s 1919), Manchester United (c/s 1920), TOWN (Aug 1921)

Younger brother of the better known Tommy Meehan of Chelsea, Manchester United and England fame, Toby Meehan joined the "Stags" for their inaugural season in the Midland League. He is a nightmare to statisticians, having the same initial as his brother and his career was entirely in parallel with Tommy, moving to the same clubs together until they left Old Trafford.

1921-22   13 apps   0 gls Midland League

MELLING Terence
1967 - 68 Inside Forward   6' 0"   12st 4lbs (1967)
b: Haverton Hill, Billingham, Co Durham, 24 January 1940
Career: Town Law Town (am), Newcastle United (Dec 1965), Watford (May 1966), Newport County (£2,500 - Feb 1967), TOWN (£3,000 - Nov 1967), Rochdale (Sep 1968), Darlington (Mar 1969), Scarborough (c/s 1969), Tow Law Town.

Terry Melling's career took off rather late for he was almost 26 when he signed as a professional with the "Geordies". He went full circle too, starting and finishing his career with the same club. During this tour he managed to fit in eight clubs in five years!

1967-68	27(0) apps	5 gls	
1968-69	6(0) "	2 "	

MELLOR Kenneth E
1957 - 59 Centre Half back   6' 0"   12st 7lbs
b: Leicester, 22 August 1934
Career: Leicester City (July 1955), TOWN (F.T. July 1957), Swindon Town (July 1959).

Another of the players who trod the well worn trail from Filbert Street to Field Mill in the post war decades.

1957-58	34 apps	0 gls	
1958-59	32 "	0 "	

MELLORS Richard Dugdale ("Dick")
1921 - 22 Goalkeeper 6' 3"   13st 4lbs (1935)
b: Mansfield Woodhouse, Notts., 17 March 1902
Career: Mansfield Woodhouse Exchange (1918), Chesterfield (c/s 1920 - am), TOWN (c/s 1921 - am), The Wednsday (Dec 1925), Reading (c/s 1931), Bournemouth & Boscombe Athletic (c/s 1934), Queen of the South (Jan 1938).

This giant of a custodian played for the "Stags" as a teenage amateur and moved on to Hillsborough where he unsderstudied the great John Brown for six years. His chance came with Reading in 1931 and he went on to be his clubs' regular goalkeeper up to the outbreak of WW II. Made a single "guest" appearance for Lincoln City in 1940 at the age of 38. This appears to have been his final game.

1921-22   2 apps   0 gls   Midland League
Honours: Division 3 South runners up 1932 (Reading)

MERCER Stanley
1948 - 49 Centre Forward   5' 8"   11st 12lbs
b: Birkenhead, Cheshire, 11 September 1919
Career: Blackpool (Jan 1944 - am), Leicester City (July 1944 - am, Nov 1944 - pro), Accrington Stanley (£750 - Jan 1947), TOWN (£1,500 - Oct 1948, 1950 - asst trainer, Jun 1952 - sec/asst manager, Aug 1953 - manager to Jan 1956).

Another late starter, but in this case the war and Army service were resposible. It is difficult to see why Leicester parted with him as he was knocking in goals with great regularity in their reserves, but they had got Arthur Rowley at the time and what a goal machine he turned out to be! Outstanding with Accrington, which prompted Roy Goodall to pay Town's record fee to secure him as Banks' successor, but after only 12 games he suffered a knee injury which ended his playing career. Could so easily have become one of the "Stags" most free scoring centre forwards but for his career being so tragically terminated. Joined the club's training staff and in 1953 accepted the manager's chair only to resign in January 1956 when he refused to take on the secretarial duties as well without extra remuneration. He went to live in Blackpool and became an administrator in the Premium Bond Office there, a position he fulfilled until his retirement in 1989

1948-49   12 apps   6 gls

METHVEN A Harold

1933 34 Centre Forward
b: Loughborough, Leics., c1908
Career: Gresley Rovers, Portsmouth (May 1930), TOWN (May 1933), Tunbridge Wells Rangers (June 1934)

Brought in to understudy Harry Johnson and in spite of doing this well - he scored 9 goals in his 10 appearances, he was given a free transfer at the season's end.

Season	apps	gls
1933-34	10 apps	9 gls

MIDDLETON Alfred

1908 - 12 and 1913 - 21 Inside Left
b: c1890
Career: WESLEY (c/s 1909), TOWN (c/s 1910), Mansfield Mechanics (c/s 1912), Stockport County (£65 - Dec 1912), TOWN (c/s 1913), Sutton Junction (Oct 1921), Grantham (c/s 1923).

Alf Middleton is the only Mansfield player to have been with the club from the Wesley days through to post WW I. Apart from one season shared between Mansfield Mechanics and Stockport County, he was with the club for 14 years and played under both titles and in three different leagues for them. A prolific goal-scorer, he netted 104 League goals in his career with Wesley/Town and a further 9 for the Mechanics. He must have been a truly great clubman. Stands Fourth in the list of Mansfield's overall goalscorers. Retired from playing in May 1925. First player to net 100 goals for the "Stags".

Season	apps	gls	League
1909-10‡	N K apps	*15 gls	Notts & Derbys.Lge.
1910-11	N K	9 "	" " "
1911-12	N K	11 "	Cent.Allian. Lead.Scorer
1913-14	N K	10 " "	" " "
1914-15	N K	7 "	Notts & Derbys.Lge.
1915-16	N K	15 "	Cent.Allian. Lead.Scorer
1919-20	28 "	23 " "	" " "
1920-21	33 "	12 " "	" "
1921-21	2 "	2 "	Midland League

‡ Wesley, all other seasons, Town. * Approx.total

Honours: Central Alliance - Subsidiary Competition Championship 1916, Central Alliance Championship 1920, runners up 1921 (all Mansfield).

MIDDLETON Harry

1964 - 66 Centre Forward   5' 10½"   11st 10lbs (1965)
b: Birmingham, 18 March 1937
Career: Juniors, Wolverhampton Wanderers (Aug 1954), Scunthorpe United (Sep 1959), Portsmouth (June 1961), Shrewsbury Town (Feb 1962), TOWN (Nov 1964), Walsall (Mar 1966), Worcester City (c/s 1968)

Tommy Cummings made a joint signing when he brought Middleton and John Gregson to Field Mill to assist in Town's Division Three promotion push in 1964-65. His scoring record was very good at a little over one goal every two games.

Season	apps	gls	
1964-65	24 apps	16 gls	Leading Scorer
1965-66	21(1) "	8 "	

Honours: England Youth International 1955 (Wolves), Division 3 - 3rd 1965 (Mansfield)

MILLER Ernest

1927 - 28 Outside Left   5' 8½"   10st 10lbs (1927)
b: Sheffield, c1903
Career: Rotherham Town, Rotherham County (c/s 1924), TOWN (c/s 1927), Shirebrook (Oct 1927).

Season	apps	gls	
1927-28	2 apps	0 gls	Midland League

MILLER (John) Tony

1976 - 80 Outside Left   5' 8"   10st 9lbs (1978)
b: Ipswich, 21 September 1950
Career: Thurleston Sec Mod School, Ipswich Schoolboys, Suffolk Schoolboys, Ipswich Town (1966 - appr, July 1968 - pro), Norwich City (£47,000 - Oct 1974), TOWN (£10,000 - July 1976), Port Vale (F.T. Oct 1980 N/C), Oakham United (1983), Selston, Blidworth Welfare (Mar 1993 - asst manager)

Fast winger with a powerful shot, Johnny Miller was brought in as manager Peter Morris's first signing, for Mansfield's successful attempt at winning promotion to the Second Division.

Settled in the area after his first class career was ended and is currently on the staff at Ashfield District Council's Huthwaite leisure centre. Was still turning out occasionally for Blidworth as recently as March 1995, when he won the man of the match award - not bad for a 44 year old!

1976-77	40(0) apps	5 gls
1977-78	32(0) "	5 "
1978-79	28(3) "	4 "
1979-80	9(1) "	0 "

Honours: Ipswich Schoolboys, Suffolk County Schoolboys. League Cup finalists & Division 2 promotion 1975 (both Norwich). Division 3 Championship 1977 (Mansfield).

MILNER Harold
1927 - 28 Outside Left   5' 8"   11st 0lbs (1927)
b: Whitwell, Derbys., c1901
Career: Whitwell Colliery, Chesterfield (c/s 1923), Loughborough Corinthians (c/s 1924), Gainsborough Trinity (c/s 1925), Newark Town (c/s 1926), TOWN (c/s 1927), Staveley Town (c/s 1928)

Winger who had enjoyed Third Division football with Chesterfield, but then dropped into the Midland League.

| 1927-28 | 15 apps | 2 gls |

MITCHINSON Thomas W
1966 - 67 Inside Forward   5' 7½"   10st 11lbs
b: Sunderland, 24 February 1943
Career: Sunderland & District Schools (1958), Sunderland (June 1960 - am, Dec 1960 - pro), TOWN (£10,000 - Jan 1966), Aston Villa (£18,000 - Sep 1967), Torquay United (£8,000 - May 1969), A F C Bournemouth (£2,000 - Dec 1973)

The first player to be signed by manager Tommy Cummings when he took over the reins at Field Mill, Tommy Mitchinson was also the first player to be taken to Villa Park when Mitchinson became manager there, much to the chagrin of the Town faithful. His career finally ended due to injury in 1973 after he had made a total of almost 300 appearances in the Football League.

1965-66	28(0) apps	5 gls
1966-67	46(0) "	10 "
1967-68	2(0) "	0 "

MITE Robert
1921 - 23 Wing Half Back/Inside Forward
b: Rotherham, c1897
Career: Rotherham County, Coventry City (Sep 1919), Rotherham Town (c/s 1920), TOWN (Dec 1921)

Honours: Mansfield Hospital Charity Cup 1922 (Mansfield)

MITTEN Charles
1956 - 58 Outside Left   5' 8"   11st 0lbs
b: Rangoon, Burma, 17 January 1921
Career: Manchester United (1936 - am, Jan 1938 - pro), Bogota Colombia (Jun 1950), Fulham (Jan 1952), TOWN (Feb 1956 - player manager), Newcastle United (June 1958 - manager to Oct 1961), Altrincham (manager)

Mitten's father was serving in the Army in Burma at the time of Charlie's birth, but by the time he left school, the family was resident in Manchester. Charlie signed amateur forms for United when he was only 15 and his career really took off during WW II when he "guested" for Tranmere, Cardiff, Southampton, Chelsea & Wolves, playing in two wartime Cup Finals for the "Pensioners" and gaining a wartime cap for England. Very successful with United after the end of hostilities, winning an F A Cup Final medal in 1948, he was one of a number of top players who absconded to South America for the big money being offered there in 1950. He only stayed six months before returning to this country where the F A suspended him from the game for 18 months. Player manager of Town for nearly two and a half years, he moved on to Newcastle where he was sacked after they were relegated, later managing the White City greyhound stadium in Manchester for a time and organis- ing football world tours. All three of his sons became footballers, one becoming a County Cricketer too.

1955-56	17 apps	3 gls
1956-57	45 "	11 "
1957-58	38 "	11 "

Honours: Football League South Cup runners up 1944 & Winners 1945 (both Chelsea as "guest"). England WW II International, F A Cup Winners 1948 & F A Charity Shield runners up 1949 (all Manchester United).

MITTEN John E
1957 - 58 Winger
b: Davyhulme, Manchester, 30 March 1941
Career: Juniors, TOWN (1957 - am), Newcastle United (June 1958 - am, Sep 1960 - pro), Leicester City (F.T. Sep 1961), Manchester United (Apr 1963 - trial), Coventry City (F.T. Aug 1963), Plymouth Argyle (£5,000 - Jan 1967), Exeter City (July 1968), Bath City (Aug 1971), Tiverton Town.

Son of a famous father, (see above,) John Mitten had a few games for the "Stags" as an amateur at only 16 years of age, when his father was manager - but they never played in the same team as John was his father's understudy at outside left. Followed Dad to Newcastle but his career did not take off until he reached the South West where he was reasonably successful. After being on Notts C C C groundstaff in the late 50s, he teamed up with Leicestershire in 1961 and played in 14 County Championship matches between 1961 and 1963.

1957-58   3 apps   0 gls
Honours: England Schoolboy International. England Youth International (Newcastle).

MOORE Brian
1960 - 61 Outside Left   5' 9"   11st 0lbs (1962)
b: Handsworth, Birmingham, 24 December 1938
Career: Loughborough College, TOWN (Sep 1960 - am), Notts County (Dec 1961), Doncaster Rovers (July 1963)

Talented amateur left winger who turned out on both flanks for the "Stags" before signing professional forms with the "Magpies".

1960-61   4 apps   0 gls

MOORE Charles
1925 - 26 Inside Left
Career: TOWN (Sep 1925)

1925-26   5 apps   3 gls Midland League

MOORE Harry
1924 - 26 Left Half Back   5' 7½"   11st 7lbs (1924)
b: 1898
Career: Worksop Town (c/s 1918), Notts County (Aug 1921), Worksop Town (c/s 1923), TOWN (c/s 1924), Worksop Town (1928).

Lightly built wing half who had a couple of seasons at Mansfield with some success. Had 16 First Division games with Notts County during 1921-22.

1924-25   34 apps   1 gl   Midland League
1925-26   22 "   0 "   "   "
Honours: Midland League Championship 1925 & runners up 1926 (both Mansfield)

MOORE James
1927 - 28 Inside Forward   5' 6"   10st 6lbs
b: Handsworth, Birmingham, 11 May 1889
Career: Quebec Albion, Glossop North End (May 1911), Derby County £1,500 - Oct 1913), Chesterfield (Mar 1926), TOWN (Nov 1927), Worcester City (May 1928).

A veteran of 38 when he came to Field Mill, "Gentleman Jim" Moore had been a star player both before and after WW I, assisting the "Rams" to two promotions and winning England Caps. Still useful at Mansfield where he scored a creditable 16 goals in 22 matches. Was leading scorer three times at Derby - 1914-15, 1921-22 & 1922-23. On one occasion he netted five goals in a match and also recorded one hat trick at the Baseball Ground. WWI "guest" at Saltergate.

1927-28   22 apps   16 gls Midland League
Honours: England International, Football League XI, Division 2 Championship 1915 & runners up 1926 (all Derby). Birmingham League Championship 1929 (Worcester City).

MOORE John
1987 Forward   6' 0"   11st 11lbs (1985)
b: Consett, Co Durham, 1 October 1966
Career: Sunderland (1982 - appr, Oct 1984 - pro), St Patricks Athletic (Jan 1985 - loan), Newport County (Nov 1985 - loan), Darlington (Nov 1986 - loan), TOWN (Mar 1987 - loan), Rochdale (Jan 1988 - loan), Hull City (June 1988), Sheffield United (Mar 1989 - loan), Utrecht Holland (1989), Shrewsbury Town (Aug 1990), Crewe Alexandra (F.T. Jan 1991 - N/C), Utrecht Holland (Mar 1991), Scarborough (Aug 1991)

1986-87   5(0) apps   1 gl (Loan)

MOORE William
1939 - 40 Left half Back   5' 10"   11st 7lbs (1939)
b: Washington, Co Durham, March 1916.
d: 1982
Career: Walker Celtic, Stoke City (Aug 1935), TOWN (F.T May 1939) Notts County (1949 - trainer), Aston Villa (1953 - asst manager & trainer, 1955 - trainer), Walsall (Dec 1957 - manager to 1964), Fulham (1965 - scout), Walsall (Feb 1969 - manager to Mar 1972)

Strong tackling half back, known as "The Iron Man", Bill Moore only played in two matches for Town, one in the League and the other , the Jubilee Fund game versus Walsall in August 1939. He joined the administration side of the game after retiring from playing, following Eric Houghton fron Notts to Villa. Had very good managerial spell at Fellows Park, taking the "Saddlers" from the Fourth to the Second Division in successive seasons. After his second spell in the Walsall hot seat, he became landlord of the Fox Hotel, Stafford, only relinquishing this position shortly before his death in 1982. "Guested" during WW II with Stockport.

1939-40   1 app   0 gl

MORAN John
1936 - 37 Left Full Back   5' 10¼'   11st 7lbs (1936)
b: Wigan, 9 February 1906
d: Newton le Willows, 12 October 1959
Career: Earlstown, Wigan Juniors, Wigan Borough (1925), Tottenham Hotspur (May 1931), Watford (Sep 1932), TOWN (Mar 1936).

A full back with plenty of previous League experience, Jack Moran joined the "Stags" at the end of a long career as successor to Gerry Darvill, recently transferred to Wolves, as Charlie Bisby had not proved an adequate replacement.

1935-36   11 apps   0 gls
1936-37   19   "   0   "
Honours: Division 3 South Cup runners up 1935 (Watford).

MORFITT John William
1927 - 28 Centre Forward   5' 9½"   10st 12lbs (1928)
b: Sheffield, 29 September 1908
d: 1973
Career: Great Central Railway Sports, Anston Athletic, Sheffield Heeley, Sheffield United (trial), TOWN (Oct 1927), Birmingham (£250 - May 1928), Blackpool (May 1931), Bradford P A (Mar 1932), Southend United (June 1932)

The rate at which Jack Morfitt was rattling in goals for Town attracted the attention of First Division Birmingham and they signed him at the end of the season, but he failed to make the first team there and moved on. Reasonably successful at Southend where he played regularly for four seasons until injury forced his retirement in the Summer of 1936.

1927-28   30 apps   22 gls Midland League.
Leading Scorer Honours: Mansfield Hospital Charity Cup Winners 1928 (Mansfield)

MORGAN Trevor J
1981 - 82 Forward   6' 1"   13st 1lb (1987)
b: Forest Gate, London, 30 September 1956
Career: Leytonstone, Ilford, A F C Bournemouth (£3,000 - Sep 1980), TOWN (£10,000 - Nov 1981), A F C Bournemouth (£4,000 - Mar 1982), Bristol City (Mar 1984), Exeter City (Nov 1984), Bristol Rovers (Sep 1985), Bristol City (Jan 1987), Bolton Wanderers (June 1987), Colchester United (Oct 1989), Happy Valley H K (1990), Exeter City (Oct 1990)

Trevor Morgan's short stay with Mansfield made the club a big loss, as he moved back to the "Cherries" for £6,000 less than the "Stags" had paid for him four months earlier. Obviously had a liking for the West Country as he spent his best years there.

1981-82   12(0) apps   6 gls

MORRIS Austin
1937 - 39 Right Half Back   5' 11"   11st 0lbs (1938)
Career: Thurcroft Main, TOWN (Nov 1937), Gainsborough Trinity (Aug 1939)

Reserve who "guested" for Doncaster and Rotherham in WW II.

1937-38   1 app   0 gls

MORRIS (Frederick) William
1957 - 58 Outside Right   5' 10"   12st 2lbs
b: Pant, Nr Oswestry, Salop, 15 June 1929
Career: Oswestry Town, Walsall (£500 - May 1950), TOWN (£1,500 - Mar 1957), Liverpool (£7,000 - May 1958), Crewe Alexandra (£4,000 - Jun 1960) Gillingham (£1,500 - Jan 1961), Chester (July 1961), Altrincham (c/s 1962), Oswestry Town (player manager).

Had made over 200 appearances for Walsall before he joined the "Stags" and his clever and speedy wing play brought out the cheque book from Phil Taylor of Liverpool. He went into their first team straight away and held his place for over a season, before being deposed by Morrissey and Lewis.

1956-57   10 apps   2 gls
1957-58   46   "   15   "

MORRIS Harold
1928 - 29 Centre Forward   5' 9"   11st 7lbs (1928)
b: Bolsover, Derbys., c1904
Career: Bolsover Town (goalkeeper), Bolsover Colliery (c/s 1924), Watford (c/s 1925), TOWN (c/s 1928), Barnsley (£350 - May 1929), Shirebrook (Aug 1930)

Star goalscorer during in the record breaking side of 1928-29 when the club were league champions and reached the Fourth Round of the F A Cup for the first time, beating Wolves, but finally succumbing to the mighty Arsenal at Highbury. Started his career as a goalkeeper and finished it at Shirebrook as a wing half.

1928-29 41 apps 38 gls Midland Lge. Lead.Scorer
Honours: Midland League Championship & Mansfield Hospital Charity Cup Winners 1929 (both Mansfield)

MORRIS (Peter) John

1960 - 68 and 1976 - 78 Midfield 5' 8" 11st 3lbs (1978)
b: New Houghton, Derbys., 8 November 1943
Career: Langwith B C, New Houghton Baptists, Ladybrook Colts, TOWN (Jan 1959 - appr, Nov 1960), Ipswich Town (£15,000 - Mar 1968), Norwich City (£60,000 - June 1974), TOWN (£10,000 - July 1976 player manager to Feb 1978), Newcastle United (Feb 1978 - asst manager to Feb 1979), Peterborough United (Feb 1979 - manager to May 1982), Crewe (Nov 1982 - manager to June 1983), Southend (July 1983 - manager to Feb 1984), Nuneaton Borough (June 1985 - manager), Aajar Sporting Saudi Arabia (coach), Leicester City (Jan 1987 - coach), Kettering (June 1988 - manager to May 1992), Boston United (Jun 1992 - manager), Northampton Town (Sep 1993 - asst manager, Dec 1994 - acting manager to Jan 1995).

One of Mansfield's greatest post war discoveries. Peter Morris was becoming a legend with the Field Mill faithful after making his debut under Raich Carter at 17 and becoming one of the youngest captains the "Stags" have ever had. Then after 8 years as the bedrock of the team and apparently a fixture for the remainder of his career, he was suddenly sold to First Division Ipswich for the give away price of £15,000!

The fans were shell shocked, not only by him leaving - although none could expect him to turn down the offer of higher grade football - but by the ridiculously low fee the directors accepted. He was, as expected, a great success at Portman Road and later at Norwich and Town had to pay out nearly the same fee to bring him back here as player -manager when his career was drawing to its close and he was 17lb heavier! He took Town to Division 2 for the first time in their history, but when he couldn't prevent relegation the following term, he was sacked. Morris has subsequently had a rather varied career in management with a number of clubs and is currently assistant manager of Northampton Town. He made over 300 appearances for Mansfield and over 200 for Ipswich.

1960-61	13 apps	0 gls
1961-62	40 "	10 "
1962-63	33 "	6 "
1963-64	45 "	3 "
1964-65	46 "	7 "
1965-66	39(1) "	4 "
1966-67	41(0) "	13 "
1967-68	29(0) "	7 "
1976-77	32(0) "	3 "
1977-78	9(0) "	0 "

Honours: Division 4 promotion 1963, Division 3 - 3rd 1965 (both Mansfield). Division 2 Championship 1968 (Ipswich), Division 2 promotion & League Cup finalists 1975 (both Norwich). Division 3 Championship 1977 (Mansfield - as player manager).

MOSS Ernest

1976 - 79 Forward   6' 1"   12st 11lbs (1978)
b: Chesterfield, 19 October 1949
Career: Chesterfield Tube, Chesterfield (Oct 1968), Peterborough United (£16,000 - Jan 1976), TOWN (£18,000 - Dec 1976), Chesterfield (£15,000 - Jan 1979), Port Vale (£16,000 - Jun 1981), Lincoln City (Mar 1983), Doncaster Rovers (June 1983), Chester- field (£30,000 - July 1984), Stockport County (Dec 1986), Scarborough (Aug 1987), Rochdale (Mar 1988 - loan), Kettering Town (F.T. Jun 1988, May 1990 - player coach), Boston United (May 1992 - player asst manager), Gainsborough Trinity (Jun 1994 - asst manager, May 1995 - manager).

Known to followers as "Big Ern", Moss was working in local government in Matlock and playing for a minor club, when the "Spireites" invited him for a trial when he was 18 and he played in over 270 matches for them. Has played for many clubs during his career and this evergreen player was still turning out in the Vauxhall Conference when he was well over 40 years of age and the goals were still coming! Peter Morris has signed him three times, for Mansfield in December 1976, Kettering June 1988 and for Boston in May 1992.

1976-77	29(0) apps	13 gls
1977-78	15(0) "	6 "
1978-79	12(1) "	2 "

Honours: Division 4 Championship 1970 & 1985, Anglo Scottish Cup Winners 1981 (all Chesterfield), Division 3 Championship 1977 (Mansfield).

MUNNINGS Charles Edward

1933 - 34 Outside Right   5' 9½"   11st 0lbs (1930)
b: Boston, Lincs., c1906
d: Washingborough, Lincoln, 10 March 1995
Career: Boston (c/s 1926), Grimsby Town (Sep 1927), Swindon Town (c/s 1930), Hull City (Aug 1931), Swindon Town (July 1932), TOWN (July 1933), Boston (1934).

Winger who had a liking for Wiltshire as he signed for the "Robins" on two separate occasions. Started his career with Midland Leage side Boston and rejoined them eight years later. A more than useful cricketer, he played in 23 games for Lincolnshire in the Minor Counties between 1928 and 1938.

1933-34   29 apps   7 gls

MURPHY Lionel ("Spud")

1929 - 31 Outside Left   5' 7"   10st 10lbs (1932)
b: Hovingham Spa, North Yorks., 15 September 1895
d: Derby, 27 October 1968

Career: Melton Mowbray, Army, Derby County (Feb 1922), Bolton Wanderers (£2,500 - Jan 1928), TOWN (Sep 1929), Norwich City (May 1931), Luton Town (Oct 1934), Southport (Feb 1935)

Tricky, elusive left winger who cost big money when Bolton signed him only 18 months before he joined Town. "Spud" Murphy was a favourite with the supporters and they were downcast when he threw in his lot with the "Canaries" only weeks before Mansfield were elected to the Third Division and he played against his old club at Field Mill in their first season of League football.

| 1929-30 | 42 apps | 14 gls | Midland League |
| 1930-31 | 42 " | 10 " " | " |

Honours: Division 2 - 3rd 1924 & 1925, promotion 1926 (Derby), Mansfield Hospital Charity Cup Winners 1930, Notts Senior Cup Winners 1931 (both Mansfield), Division 3 South 3rd - 1933, Championship 1934 (both Norwich).

MURRAY Kenneth

1953 - 57
Inside Forward   6' 0"   12st 3lbs
b: Darlington 2 April 1928
d: Newcastle on Tyne, 8 January 1993
Career: Bishop Auckland (am), Darlington (July 1950), TOWN (July 1953), Oldham Athletic (£1,500 - Mar 1957), Wrexham (Feb 1958), Yeovil & Petters United (July 1959), Gateshead (Aug 1959)

After a successful spell with Bishop Auckland, who were the North's leading amateur club at the time, Ken Murray had the chance to turn professional with his local club Darlington and he jumped at the opportunity. After scoring 19 goals with the "Quakers", he added a further 60 for the "Stags" and by the time his career was over he had made nearly 300 Football League appearances and scored over 110 goals. Retired from football when his then club

Gateshead were voted out of the Football League after finishing in the bottom three of the Fourth Division.

Season	Apps	Gls	
1953-54	40 apps	21 gls	Leading Scorer
1954-55	37 "	13 "	" "
1955-56	38 "	17 "	
1956-57	25 "	9 "	

Honours: Welsh Cup Winners 1958 (Wrexham)

MURRAY Malcolm

1989 - 91 Defender 5' 11" 11st 12lbs
b: Buckie, Banffshire, Scotland, 26 July 1964
Career: Buckie Thistle, Heart of Midlothian (c/s 1983), Hull City (Mar 1989 - loan, Apr 1989 - permanent), TOWN (£30,000 - Dec 1989), Meadowbank Thistle (Nov 1991 - loan), Partick Thistle (£25,000 - Dec 1991), Clydebank (Sep 1992), Meadowbank Thistle (Sep 1992)

Full back who developed with Hearts after leaving Junior football north of the border. Signed for Town from Hull by George Foster early in his managership at Field Mill, but fell out of favour and returned to Scotland where he is still playing with Edinburgh based Meadowbank Thistle in the Scottish League.

1989-90	28(0) apps	0 gls	
1990-91	28(2) "	0 "	
1991-92	0(1) "	0 "	

NELSON F W

1939 - 40 Full Back 5' 11' 11st 7lbs (1939)
b: Bamber Bridge, Lancs., c1917
Career: Preston North End (1937), TOWN (May 1939)

One of a number of new signings made by Jack Poole before the start of the ill fated 1939-40 season. "Guested" for Clapton Orient during WW II.

1939-40	2 apps	0 gls

NELSON Colin A (M P S)

1965 - 66 Full Back 5' 10" 12st 0lbs
b: Boldon, Co Durham, 13 March 1938
Career: Usworth Colliery, Sunderland Technical College, Sunderland (Mar 1958), TOWN (£3,500 - Mar 1965)

Colin Nelson, a qualified pharmacist, was signed by Mansfield for the promotion seeking run in during the 1964-65 season when the "Stags" lost out narrowly to Bristol City on goal average.

1964-65	6 apps	0 gls
1965-66	32(0) "	0 "

NETTLESHIP Reginald

1946 - 47 Inside Forward
b: Warsop, Notts., 23 February 1925
Career: Welbeck Colliery, Sheffield United (May 1943), TOWN (F.T. July 1946)

Reg Nettleship's League career consisted of one single game for the "Stags" in the first post war season against Clapton Orient although he had turned out for the "Blades" and Mansfield during the war.

WW II	1 app	0 gls
1946-47	1 "	0 "

NEW Martin P

1978 - 80 Goalkeeper 5' 11" 12st 2lbs (1979)
b: Swindon, 11 May 1959
Career: Arsenal (1975 - appr, Mar 1977 - pro), TOWN (June 1978), Barnsley (June 1980)

Signed as cover for Rod Arnold and had a decent run in the senior side when Arnold was sidelined with a long term injury in 1979.

1978-79	18(0) apps	0 gls
1979-80	3(0) "	0 "

Honours: England Schoolboy International

NICHOLSON Gary A

1981 - 84 Forward 5' 7" 9st 11lbs (1982)
b: Newcastle on Tyne, 4 November 1960
Career: Newcastle United (1976 - appr, Nov 1978 - pro), TOWN (£10,000 - Aug 1981), York City (July 1984), Halifax Town (July 1985)

Nicholson had a good run at Field Mill, making 118 appearances in three seasons and scoring 21 goals.

1981-82	37(1) apps	5 gls
1982-83	37(2) "	8 "
1983-84	38(3) "	8 "

NOTEMAN (Kevin) Simon

1992 - 95 Winger 5' 10" 11st 10lbs (1993)
b: Preston, 15 October 1969
Career: Leeds United (1986 - appr, June 1988 - pro), Doncaster Rovers (£10,000 - Nov 1989), TOWN (£25,000 - Mar 1992).

One of several players brought in by George Foster to bolster Mansfield's promotion winning squad of 1991-92. Had rather mixed success with the club subsequently and was given a free transfer in May 1995.

1991-92	6(0) apps	0 gls
1992-93	15(9) "	4 "
1993-94	29(4) "	5 "
1994-95	27(5) "	6 "

NUGENT W Clifford
1958 - 60 Outside Left   5' 7"   11st 0lbs
b: Bicester, Oxon., 3 March 1929
Career: Headington United (c/s 1949), Cardiff City (Feb 1951), TOWN (Nov 1958)

Experienced First Division winger who joined Mansfield towards the end of his career to replace Charlie Mitten and gave nearly two seasons of good service to the club.

1958-59	27 apps	2 gls
1959-60	25 "	5 "

Honours: Division 2 runners up 1952 (Cardiff)

OAKLEY John C
1938 - 46 Goalkeeper
b: Mansfield, c1919
Career: Rufford Colliery, TOWN (c/s 1938 - am), Chesterfield (Mar 1942 - am), Nottingham Forest (1942 - am), TOWN (c/s 1943 - am)

Jack Oakley made no League appearances for the "Stags" although he was associated with the club on and off from 1938-1946. Played at various times for Chesterfield, Lincoln City, Nottingham Forest, Notts County and Mansfield during WW II. Played in 4 of the F A Cup ties during 1945-46.

WW II   42 apps   0 gls

O'BRIEN Noel W
1975 - 76 Half Back   5' 8"   10st 11lbs (1976)
b: Islington, London, 18 December 1956
Career: Arsenal (1972 - appr, Jan 1974 - pro), TOWN (June 1975), Halifax Town (F.T. July 1976)

1975-76   7(0) apps   0 gls

O'CONNOR Douglas
1974 - 75 Midfield   5' 10"   10st 5lbs (1975)
b: Barnsley, 29 April 1954
Career: Barnsley (Aug 1969 - appr, Apr 1972 - pro), TOWN (F.T. June 1974), Scunthorpe United (F.T. July 1975)

1974-75   11(6) apps   2 gls
Honours: Barnsley Schoolboys, England Schoolboys - trialist.

O'CONNOR (Francis) Raymond
1937 - 38 Right Half Back   5' 8½"   11st 0lbs (1937)
b: Newcastle on Tyne, c1912
Career: Jarrow, Portsmouth (c/s 1935), TOWN (F.T. c/s 1937), Darlington (c/s 1938), Gillingham c/s 1939

Joining the "Stags" from Portsmouth at the same time as Harold Crawshaw, Frank O'Connor was playing with Gillingham, who had been voted out of the League the previous season, by the outbreak of war.

1937-38   18 apps   0 gls
Honours: Notts F A County Cup 1938 (Mansfield)

OGDEN Christopher J
1970 Goalkeeper 5' 10½"   12st 5lbs
b: Oldham, 3 February 1953
Career: TOWN (1969 - am), Oldham Athletic (1970 - am, July 1971 - pro), Swindon Town (Aug 1978), Rotherham United (Nov 1979)

On Town's books as a 16 year old amateur but was not secured. Played in Semi-Final of County Cup Competition on 3 May 1969 when aged only 16 years 90 days - his only senior game.

OGILVIE (John) Forrest
1960 - 61 Full Back
b: Motherwell, 28 October 1928
Career: Thorniewood United, Hibernian (1947), Sheffield United (Aug 1955 - trial), Leicester City (Sep 1955), TOWN (Jan 1960)

Yet another ex "Fossil" who journeyed North to Mansfield.

1959-60	17 apps	0 gls
1960-61	7 "	1 "

Honours: Scottish Division 1 Championship 1951 & 1952 (Hibernian). Division 2 Championship 1957 (Leicester).

O'HARA Daniel
1961 - 62 Inside Forward   5' 10"   11st 7lbs
b: Airdrie, 28 September 1937
Career: Fauldhouse United, Celtic (Apr 1959), Cork Hibernian (Oct 1960 - loan), TOWN (June 1961), Albion Rovers (F.T. Aug 1962), Coltness United (c/s 1963 - trial), Armadale Thistle (July 1963).

Essentially a reserve with Glasgow Celtic, Dan O'Hara did make seven league appearances for the "Bhoys" and two in the Scottish League Cup. He also played for them in friendlies against Everton and Sunderland in January 1960.

1961-62   3 apps   1 gl
Honours: Scottish Division "A" Reserve League Championship 1960 (Celtic).

OLDHAM Arthur (John)
1967 - 68 Centre Forward   5' 8"   11st 7lbs
b: Nottingham, 24 October 1949
Career: Nuthall Boys, TOWN (Feb 1967), Arnold (c/s 1968), Sutton Town.

1966-67   0(1) app   0 gls

O'NEILL James
1938 - 39 Wing Half Back
b: Dumfries
Career: Gateshead (c/s 1936), Gillingham (c/s 1937), Notts County (Jan 1938), TOWN (c/s 1938)

Young Scot who had made 8 appearances for Gillingham, but failed to gain a League place at any of his other clubs. He made a single appearance for Mansfield in the County Cup in October 1938 at Meadow Lane, oddly enough against his former club.

ONUORA Ifem
1994 onwards Forward   6' 0"   11st 10lbs (1993)
b: Glasgow, 28 July 1967
Career: Bradford University, Huddersfield Town (July 1989), TOWN (£75,000 - exchange for Gray (valued at £50,000) + £25,000 - July 1994).

After almost breaking the bank to secure the services of this proven striker, who Andy King had been tailing for some time, Iffy Onuora had the misfortune to break a toe in a pre-season warm up match at Worksop and was disappointingly sidelined for six months, before making his senior debut in February 1995. Came back with a bang however, scoring a hat trick against Lincoln in his first full match - and in the space of only seven minutes!

1994-95   10(4) apps   7 gls

O'RIORDAN (Donal) Joseph
1989 Defender/Midfield   6' 0"   11st 12lbs
b: Dublin, 14 May 1957

Career: Derby County (1973 - appr, May 1975 - pro), Doncaster Rovers (Jan 1978 - loan), Tulsa Roughnecks U S A (£30,000 - Feb 1978), Preston North End (£30,000 - Oct 1978), Tulsa Roughnecks U S A (May 1979), Carlisle United (£30,000 - Aug 1983), Middlesbrough (£55,000 - Aug 1985), Grimsby Town (F.T. Aug 1986 - player coach, July 1987 - player assistant manager), Notts County (£16,000 - July 1988), TOWN (Sep 1989 - loan), Torquay United (F.T. Feb 1993, June 1993 - player manager)

1989-90   6(0) apps   0 gls   (Loan)
Honours: Eire Youth International, Eire U/21 International (Derby)

OSCROFT Harry
1947 - 50 Outside left   5' 7½"   10st 7lbs
b: Warsop, Notts., 10 March 1926
Career: Mansfield Colliery, Sheffield United (am), TOWN (Feb 1947 - am, Apr 1947 - pro), Stoke City (£30,000 - exchange for Godwin [valued at £22,000] + £8,000 - Jan 1950), Port Vale (exchange with Ford for Cunliffe - Sep 1959), Brantham United Suffolk (1961 - player manager), Stutton United Suffolk.

A great discovery by Roy Goodall, when Harry Oscroft was transferred to Stoke, by Freddie Steele, the supporters nearly revolted particularly when it was realised that £20,000 of his fee was covered by the signing of Verdi Godwin who was a virtual failure at Field Mill. He had a glorious period of over ten seasons at the Victoria Ground where he made well over 300 appearances for the "Potters", netting exactly 100 goals. Originally an inside left, converted by Mansfield into a speedy goalscoring left winger, Harry was recruited by manager Goodall upon demob. from the Royal Navy - a service for which he volunteered when only 17. Now living quietly in retirement near Ipswich.

1946-47	12 apps	3 gls	
1947-48	40 "	12 "	
1948-49	38 "	14 "	Leading Scorer
1949-50	23 "	12 "	

OSTLE David
1929 - 30 Wing Half back
Career: TOWN (Feb 1930), Victoria Terrace, Mansfield Invicta.

1929-30   8 apps   0 gls   Midland League
Honours: Mansfield Hospital Charity Cup Winners
1930 (Mansfield)

OTTEWELL K
1924 - 25 Inside Left
Career: TOWN (1924 - am).

1924-25   1 app   0 gl Midland League

OTTEWELL Sidney
1950 - 52 Inside Left   5' 7"   10st 12lbs (1950)
b: Horsley, Derbys., 23 October 1919
Career: Holbrook C W, Chesterfield (Nov 1936), Birmingham
(June 1947), Luton Town (Dec 1947), Nottingham Forest (July
1948), TOWN (Jan 1950), Scunthorpe United (Mar 1952),
Spalding United (1954 - manager), Lockheed Leamington (1960
- manager)

Recommended to Chesterfield by a Detective
Sergeant, Sid Ottewell made his debut for the
"Spireites" when he was only 17 and only managed
two more appearances before war broke out and
League football was abandoned for the duration of
hostilities. His footballing skills improved
considerably during the war years and whilst he was
in the R A F he regularly "guested" for Fulham,
Spurs, Blackpool, Bradford City, Birmingham &
Chester. Had a very powerful left foot shot.

1949-50	13 apps	3 gls
1950-51	38 "	15 "
1951-52	16 "	3 "

Honours: Division 3 North runners up 1951
(Mansfield)

OWEN Gordon
1988 - 89 Winger   5' 8"   10st 9lbs (1987)
b: Barnsley, 14 June 1959
Career: Sheffield Wednesday (1975 - appr, Nov 1976 - pro),
Rotherham United (Mar 1980 - loan), Doncaster Rovers (Nov
1982 - loan), Chesterfield (Mar 1983 - loan), Cardiff City

(F.T. Aug 1983), Barnsley (£27,000 - c/s 1984), Bristol City
(£30,000 - Aug 1986), Hull City (Dec 1987 - loan), TOWN
(£35,000 - Jan 1988) Blackpool (£15,000 - Aug 1989), Carlisle
United (Oct 1990 - loan), Exeter City (Dec 1990 - loan)

An Ian Greaves signing, Gordon Owen had played
for the defeated Bristol City side in the Freight
Rover Trophy Final against the "Stags" at Wembley
the previous May, missing a penalty in the shoot out
which secured the trophy for Mansfield.

1987-88	15(2) apps	3 gls
1988-89	39(2) "	5 "

Honours: Notts F A County Cup Winners 1989
(Mansfield)

PAGE S
1934 - 35   Outside Left
b: c1911
Career: Bilsthorpe Colliery, TOWN (c/s 1930 - am), Bilsthorpe
Colliery, Chelsea (1933 - trial), Bilsthorpe Colliery, TOWN (1934
- am), Bilsthorpe Colliery.

Amateur reserve winger whose only senior
appearance was v Chesterfield at Saltergate in the
Division 3 North Cup - January 1935. In his first
spell at Field Mill, some four years earlier, he only
played in the reserves and some Yorkshire Midweek
League fixtures.

1934-35   0 apps   0 gls

PARKER (Ernest) Simmonds Henry
1934 - 36 Outside Left   5' 9½"   11st 0lbs (1934)
b: Anerley, London, 18 December 1913
d: Brighton, February 1983
Career: Anerley Argyle, Croydon, Crystal Palace (Nov 1932 - am,
Jan 1933 - pro), TOWN (Jun 1934), Bournemouth & Boscombe
Athletic (F.T Aug 1936), Bristol Rovers (F.T July 1937)

This young winger did not make his mark with any
of the clubs he served and had drifted out of the
senior game by 1938.

1934-35	11 apps	1 gl
1935-36	4 "	3 "

Honours: Bass Charity Vase Winners 1935
(Mansfield).

PARKIN (Stephen) John
1992 onwards Full Back/Midfield   5' 7"   11st 4lbs (1992)
b: Mansfield, 7 November 1965
Career: Portland School Worksop, Stoke City (1981 - appr, Nov
1983 - pro), West Bromwich Albion (£190,000 - June 1989),
TOWN (F.T. July 1992)

Signed by George Foster as a full back, but Andy King has played him out of position in midfield. Appointed team captain for 1993-94, he suffered a couple of troublesome injuries during the early part of both the last two seasons.

1992-93	16(0) apps	0 gls	
1993-94	21(2) "	1 "	
1994-95	22(0) "	1 "	

Honours: Bassetlaw Schoolboys, Nottinghamshire Schoolboys, England Schoolboys. England Youth International, England U/21 International (Stoke City).

PARKINSON Noel D

1980 - 81 Midfield 5' 8" 10st 7lbs (1981)
b: Hull, 16 November 1959
Career: Ipswich Town (1975 - appr, Dec 1976 - pro), Bristol Rovers (Nov 1979 - loan), Brentford (Feb 1980 - loan), TOWN (£35,000 - July 1980), Peterborough United (Sep 1981 - loan), Scunthorpe United (F.T. Aug 1982), Colchester United (Aug 1984)

A popular player with the fans, Noel Parkinson was a very industrious type of player. He was released when he refused terms during the close season of 1982 and nowadays commentates on local radio at Scunthorpe.

1980-81	35(0) apps	4 gls	
1981-82	31(4) "	9 "	

Honours: England Youth International.

PARRY (Anthony) John

1974 Wing Half Back 5' 8½" 11st 0lbs (1973)
b: Burton on Trent, Staffs., 8 September 1945
Career: Burton Albion (1963 - am, c/s 1964 - pro), Hartlepool (Nov 1965), Derby County (£3,000 - Jan 1972), TOWN (Jan 1974 - loan), Gresley Rovers (1976 to 1981)

1973-74	0(1) apps	0 gls	

PARSONS Jacob

1932 Inside Right 5' 10" 12st 4lbs
b: Barrow in Furness, 27 February 1903
Career: Whitehaven Athletic, Southport (July 1927), Barrow (Feb 1928), Accrington Stanley (May 1929), Exeter City (May 1930), Thames (June 1931), TOWN (Oct 1932 - trial), Rotherham United (Jan 1933)

1932-33	2 apps	0 gls	

PARTRIDGE John T

1983 - 84 Defender 5' 11" 11st 8lbs (1983)
b: Chesterfield, 14 September 1962 -
Career: Chesterfield (1978 - appr, Sep 1980 - pro), TOWN (Sep 1983 - loan)

1983-84	1(0) apps	0 gls	

PARTRIDGE Malcolm

1968 - 70 Forward 6' 0½" 11st 9lbs (1968)
b: Calow, Nr Chesterfield, 28 August 1950
Career: TOWN (Sep 1967 - appr, Aug 1968 - pro), Leicester City (£50,000 - Sep 1970), Charlton Athletic (Jan 1972 - loan), Grimsby Town (Mar 1975), Scunthorpe United (July 1979), Skegness Town (Mar 1982)

This youngster made his League debut aged only 17 years, 196 days when he turned out for the "Stags" on 11 March 1968 and within two years he had progressed sufficiently to impress Leicester to pay £50,000 for him, but he was not a great success there, although he did assist them to the Second Division title in 1971. After his showings with the "Stags" his best spells were with Grimsby and Scunthorpe where he was a consistent performer. His son Scott is currently on the books of Bristol City.

1967-68	5(0) apps	1 gl	
1968-69	16(2) "	3 "	
1969-70	39(0) "	13 "	
1970-71	5(0) "	3 "	

Honours: Division 2 Championship 1971 (Leicester)

PASS George

1920 - 22 Full Back
b: c1900
Career: Long Eaton, TOWN (c/s 1920), Alfreton (Oct 1921), Coalville Swifts (c/s 1922).

Regular full back in the runners up side of 1920-21 and was in the Coalville side which was beaten by the "Stags" in an F A Cup tie the following season.

1920-21	29 apps	0 gls	Central Alliance
1921-22	2 "	0 "	Midland League

Honours: Central Alliance runners up 1921 (Mansfield

PATE Alexander Montgomery ("Sandy")

1967 - 79 Full Back 5' 8" 10st 10lbs (1972)
b: Lennoxtown, Glasgow, 15 August 1943
Career: Anniesland Waverley, Renfrew Juniors, Watford (Mar 1965), TOWN (Oct 1967)

Sandy Pate is perhaps the greatest of the post WW II Town full backs. He held the record for the greatest number of appearances for the club at 471, (later beaten by goalkeeper Rod Arnold with 515,) and amazingly 366 of them were consecutive - he did not miss a game between 21 September 1968 and 9 August 1975!

The previous record was also by a full back, Don Bradley's 413 made between 1949 and 1962. But Pate was much more than a very good footballer, he was a great clubman and captained the side for many years. His first class career lasted until he was 36 years old and he spent 12 years of it with the "Stags" - no one has exceeded that since the club joined the Football League in 1931 and he served under six managers here! When he hung up his boots, Sandy stayed in the town and took over the licence of a local hostelry, the "Portand Arms" where sportsmen congregated, later moving to the "Travellers Rest" in Sutton in Ashfield. Of more recent times he has taken over the "Copper Beech" at Bilsthorpe. His sporting ability was further enhanced by his prowess at golf, badminton and bowls.

1967-68	34(0) apps	0 gls
1968-69	39(0) "	0 "
1969-70	46(0) "	0 "
1970-71	46(0) "	0 "
1971-72	46(0) "	0 "
1972-73	46(0) "	0 "
1973-74	46(0) "	0 "
1974-75	46(0) "	0 "
1975-76	40(1) "	1 "
1976-77	14(0) "	0 "
1977-78	9(0) "	1 "

Honours: Scottish Amateur International (Renfrew), "Giant Killers" Cup Winners 1969, Notts F A County Cup Winners 1971 & 1972, Division 4 Championship 1975, Division 3 Championship 1977 (all Mansfield).

PATERSON (John) William

1928 - 29 Centre Forward   5' 11"   12st 0lbs (1928)
b: Dundee, 14 December 1896
Career: Fort Hill, Dundee North End, Army, Dundee (c/s 1919), Leicester City (Dec 1919), Sunderland (£3,750 - Mar 1922), Preston North End (£3,500 - Oct 1924), Mid Rhondda (Sep 1925), Queens Park Rangers (Jan 1926), TOWN (c/s 1928), Airdrieonians (1929), Cowdenbeath (1930).

Famous Scottish International centre forward who signed for Mansfield towards the end of his career, but was released early the following year when a troublesome injury received in September looked like ending his playing days, but his career survived a few more years North of the border.

1928-29   5 apps   1 gl Midland League
Honours: Scottish International (Leicester), Welsh League XI (Mid Rhondda), Division 1 runners up 1923 (Sunderland)

PATERSON William

1937 - 40 Centre Half Back   5' 11"   12st 10lbs (1937)
b: Hamilton, c1912
Career: Greenock Morton (1930), Ballymena United (c/s 1932), Distillery (c/s 1933), Arbroath (c/s 1934), Stenhousemuir (c/s 1935), Lincoln City (Sep 1936), TOWN (May 1937)

Another big favourite with the schoolboys at Field Mill, Bill Paterson had only played in the Scottish Second Division and Northern Irish League before reaching the "Imps", where he was essentially a reserve player, although he had played a couple of games in the Scottish First Division when he was with Morton. Established himself straight away with the "Stags" but in 1938-39 lost favour to Lloyd Barke for a time, but was at the heart of defence again at the outbreak of war. A good stopper but lacked distributive ability.

1937-38	40 apps	0 gls
1939-39	21 "	0 "
1939-40	2 "	0 "

Honours: Notts F A County Cup Winners 1938 (Mansfield)

PATTISON

1920 - 21 Outside Left
b: c1902
Career: Whitwell, TOWN (Aug 1920)

1920-21   1 app   0 gls Central Alliance

PEACH S

1921 - 22 Right Full Back
Career: Sheffield United (c/s 1919), Darlington (c/s 1920), TOWN (Aug 1921)

A full back who had won his spurs the previous season when he was an ever present in the "Quakers" team which lifted the North Eastern League Championship in their last season before becoming founder members of the new Division 3 Northern Section.

1921-22   27 apps   0 gls   Midland League
Honours: North Eastern League Championship 1921 (Darlington), Mansfield Hospital Charity Cup Winners 1922 (Mansfield)

PEARCEY (Jason) Kevin
1987 - 94 Goalkeeper 6' 1"   13st 5lbs (1991)
b: Leamington Spa, Warwicks., 23 July 1971
Career: TOWN (Aug 1987 - appr, July 1989 - pro), Grimsby Town (Nov 1994 - loan, £10,000 - Dec 1994 - permanent).

Jason Pearcey's career looked rosy when he made his debut for the "Stags" before he had reached his 18th birthday for he seemed to be progressing nicely and by 1992 looked like establishing himself as first choice keeper. Then an even younger player, Darren Ward emerged from the apprentices' school and grabbed the senior slot for himself. Pearcey lost confidence and by the autumn of 1994 when he was given a few outings, the "bully boys" on the terraces killed his credence completely and he asked for a move. Mike Walker agreed to take him on trial at Goodison and appeared likely to sign him, but then he was sacked and his successor, Joe Royle failed to pursue the matter. Grimsby Town then showed an interest and, after a trial period at Blundell Park, he moved permanently.

1988-89	1 apps	0 gls	
1989-90	5 "	0 "	
1990-91	4 "	0 "	
1991-92	22 "	0 "	
1992-93	33 "	0 "	
1993-94	9 "	0 "	
1994-95	3 "	0 "	

Honours: Division 4 promotion 1992 (Mansfield)

PEARSON (John) Stewart
1994 - 95 Forward   6' 2"   13st 2lbs (1994)
b: Sheffield, 1 September 1963
Career: Sheffield Wednesday (1979 - appr, May 1981 - pro), Charlton Athletic (£100,000 - May 1985), Leeds United (£70,000 - Jan 1987), Barnsley (£135,000 - July 1991), Hull City (Jan 1992 - loan), Rotherham United (Mar 1992 - loan), Carlisle United (Aug 1993), TOWN (Nov 1994 - N/C), Cardiff City (Jan 1995).

Very experienced striker who was taken on a non-contract basis by Mansfield to help out during an injury crisis. Improved rapidly as he became match fit after prolonged injury problems, but elected to join Cardiff where his opportunities were greater.

1994-95   0(2) apps   0 gls
Honours: England Youth International (Sheffield Wednesday), Division 2 Championship 1990 (Leeds), Division 2 runners up 1984 (Sheffield Wednesday) & 1986 (Charlton).

PEARSON J
1926 - 27 Outside Right
b: Autumn 1910
Career: TOWN (c/s 1926 - am), Shaftesbury B C, Bournemouth and Boscombe Athletic.

One of the youngest players ever to turn out for Mansfield, being just about 16, give or take a day or two, when he played against Rochdale at Spotland on 30 October 1926 - probably the second youngest - that distinction goes to Cyril Poole who was under 16 when he made his debut in 1937.

1926-27   5 apps 0 gls Midland Combination
Honours: Byron Cup Winners 1927 (Mansfield).

PEARSON Richard
1923 - 24 Right Full Back   5' 8"   11st 6lbs (1923)
b: c1900
Career: Hathersage, Nottingham Forest (Jan 1923), TOWN (July 1923), Nelson, Newark Town (c/s 1929).

1923-24   1 app   0 gl   Midland League

PEEBLES Ian Peter
1937 - 38 Goalkeeper
b: Scotland.
Career: TOWN (1937)

Young Scottish trialist who made a single appearance in the semi final of the County Cup during October 1937.

1937-38   0 apps   0 gls

PEER Dean
1992 - 93 Defence/Midfield   6' 2"   11st 5lbs
b: Stourbridge, Worcs., 8 August 1969
Career: Ashwood Park School, Buckpool School, Lye Town, Stourbridge Falcons, Birmingham City (July 1985 - appr, July 1987 - pro), TOWN (Dec 1992 - loan), Walsall (Nov 1993)

Tall defender who has been played in midfield by Walsall - to good effect since he moved there.

1992-93   10(0) apps   0 gls   (Loan)
Honours: Leyland D A F Cup Winners 1991 & Division 3 runners up 1992 (both Birmingham).

PEPLOW (Stephen) Thomas
1973 - 74 Winger   5' 9"   11st 12lbs (1973)
b: Liverpool, 8 January 1949
Career: Liverpool Schools, Liverpool (1965 - appr, Jan 1966 - pro), Swindon Town (Mar 1970 - loan, May 1970 - permanent), Nottingham Forest (F.T. July 1973), TOWN (Dec 1973 - loan), Tranmere Rovers (£6,000 - Jan 1974).

1973-74   4(0) apps   3 gls   (Loan)

PERFECT (Frank) Thomas
1936 Full Back 5' 8½"   12st 0lbs (1936)
b: Gorleston, Norfolk, 9 March 1915
d: Guisley, W Yorks., 17 July 1977
Career: Stradbroke Road School, Yarmouth Town Boys, Gorleston (am), Norfolk County (1932), Norwich City (Mar 1933), TOWN (F.T. June 1936), Wolverhampton Wanderers (£1,500 - Dec 1936), Tranmere Rovers (Feb 1938), Southampton (Jan 1939).

Frank Perfect was picked up on a free transfer by new manager Harry Parkes and five months and 16 games later club made a handsome profit of £1,500 when Major Buckley bought him for Wolves at what was a new transfer record for the "Stags".

1936-37   13 apps   0 gls
Honours: Yarmouth Schoolboys

PERKINS Christopher P
1990 - 94 Full Back 5' 11"   10st 9lbs (1993)
b: Kimberley, Notts., 9 January 1974
Career: Notts County (assoc schoolboy - 1988), TOWN (1990 - appr, Nov 1992 - pro), Chesterfield (July 1994).

Mansfield did not want to lose Chris Perkins, but a technical error allowed Chesterfield to sign him for nothing.

1992-93   1(4) apps   0 gls
1993-94   2(1)   "   0   "
Honours: Division 3 promotion - via play-offs 1995 (Chesterfield).

PETERS Mark
1994 onwards Defender   6' 0"   11st 3lbs (1994)
b: St Asaph, Cornwall, 6 July 1972

Career: Manchester City (1989 - appr, July 1990 - pro), Norwich City (F.T. Sep 1992), Peterborough United (F.T. Aug 1993), TOWN (F. T. Sep 1994)

Talented defender who gained Under 21 international honours for Wales five times whilst with both Manchester City and Norwich.

1994-95   26(1) apps   4 gls
Honours: Welsh U/21 International (Manchester City & Norwich).

PETERS Thomas J
1949 Inside Left   5' 7"   11st 6lbs (1949)
b: Droylsden, Manchester, 22 October 1920
Career: Doncaster Rovers (1943 - am, May 1944 - pro), Bury (Dec 1944), Leeds United (Aug 1948), TOWN (Mar 1949), Droylsden (c/s 1949), Accrington Stanley (Oct 1949 - trial), Brighton & Hove Albion (Jan 1950 - trial).

A latecomer to the professional ranks due to the war and did not really make his mark anywhere. Wartime "guest" with Everton and Southend when on Doncaster's books.

1948-49   6 apps   2 gls

PHILLIPS (Brendan) Ulysees
1980 - 81 Midfield
b: West Indies. 16 July 1954
Career: Leicester City (1970 - appr, July 1972 - pro), Peterborough United (Oct 1973), Kettering Town, Boston United, TOWN (£15,000 - Aug 1980), Aylesbury United (1981), Bedworth United (manager), Stafford Rangers (Mar 1993 - manager to Nov 1994)

1980-81   17(0) apps   0 gls
Honours: England Semi-Pro International (Boston United)

PHILLIPS (Brian) John
1960 - 63 Centre Half Back   5' 11"   13st 0lbs
b: Manchester, 9 November 1931
Career: Bury (June 1953), Altrincham, Middlesbrough (June 1954), TOWN (June 1960), Nottinghamshire F A Representative Side (1975 - manager to 1978), Rainworth M W (team manager, general manager).

Experienced defender who joined the "Stags" from the "Boro" where he played in 121 matches. Made a substantial impact at Field Mill where he appeared in over 100 games before he was given a life suspension for his part in the illegal betting and bribery scandal of the mid 1960s. Sentenced to 15 months imprisonment at Nottingham Assizes in 1965 for his part in the affair and banned from taking any further part in the game, he longed to return to the game he loved so much. The first player to appeal under the newly introduced "Seven Year" rule, which allowed suspended players to appeal against their banishment, he was reinstated in 1971 and having settled locally, managed Rainworth M W to its F A Vase appearance at Wembley in 1982. Brian Phillips is currently General Manager of that club.

1960-61	36 apps	2 gls
1961-62	40 "	0 "
1962-63	28 "	1 "

Honours: Division 4 promotion 1963 (Mansfield).

PHILLIPS Ian A
1977 - 79 Defender   5' 8"   11st 3lbs (1978)
b: Kilwinning, Edinburgh, 23 April 1959
Career: Ipswich Town (1975 - appr), TOWN (Aug 1977 - pro), Peterborough United (F.T. Aug 1979), Northampton Town (Aug 1982), Colchester United (Sep 1983), Aldershot (Aug 1987)

| 1977-78 | 15(3) apps | 0 gls |
| 1978-79 | 3(2) " | 0 " |

PHOENIX (Arthur) Frederick
1931 - 32 Wing Half Back
b: Manchester, March 1902
Career: Urmston & District Schools, Hadfield, Glossop (1922), Birmingham (May 1923), Aston Villa (May 1924), Barnsley (May 1925), Exeter City (July 1926), Wigan Borough (July 1929), Bath City (June 1930), Torquay United (Nov 1930), TOWN (F.T. July 1931), R C de Paris France (Aug 1932), Sandbach Ramblers (Oct 1933), Shelbourne (Jan 1934), Colwyn Bay United (Aug 1934), Brierley Hill (Jan 1935).

Much travelled wing half - indeed the only club where he stayed for more than one season was Exeter where he survived for three! He did however play in the First Division with both Aston Villa and Birmingham.

| 1931-32 | 3 apps | 0 gls |

PLACE Arthur
1929 - 31 Right Half back   5' 11"   12st 10lbs (1929)
b: Mansfield, c1904
Career: TOWN (c/s 1923 - am), Birmingham (c/s 1924), Bradford P A (c/s 1925), Halifax Town (c/s 1926), Shirebrook (Nov 1928), TOWN (Nov 1929).

| 1929-30 | 9 apps | 0 gls Midland League |
| 1930-31 | 1 " | 0 " " " |

Honours: Byron Cup Winners & Bayley Cup Winners 1930 (both Mansfield).

PLACE Mark G
1988 - 90 Defender   5' 11"   10st 8lbs (1989)
b: Mansfield, 16 November 1969
Career: TOWN (1986 - appr, July 1988 - pro), Doncaster Rovers (F.T. Aug 1990), Ipswich Town (trial), Eastwood Town (1993)

Fair haired defender who failed to make the grade in senior football. He is currently playing for Eastwood Town in the Unibond League.

| 1988-89 | 11(3) apps | 0 gls |
| 1989-90 | 1(0) " | 0 " |

PLATNAUER Nicholas R
1993 - 94 Left Full Back   5' 11"   12st 10lbs (1993)
b: Leicester, 10 June 1961
Career: Northampton Town (am), Bedford Town, Bristol Rovers (Aug 1982), Coventry City (£50,000 - Aug 1983), Birmingham City (£55,000 - Dec 1984), Reading (Jan 1986 - loan), Cardiff City (F.T. Sep 1986), Notts County (£50,000 - Aug 1989), Port Vale (Jan 1991 - loan), Leicester City (F.T. July 1991), Scunthorpe United (Mar 1993 - N/C), TOWN (July 1993 - N/C), Lincoln City (F.T. Feb 1994, reserve team coach - Jan 1995), F.T. May 1995).

Established full back brought in by George Foster to replace Chris Withe, but discarded before the end of the season by the new management as he was considered too old to fit into Mansfield's future plans.

| 1993-94 | 25(0) apps | 0 gls |

Honours: Division 2 runners up 1985 (Birmingham). Welsh Cup Winners 1988 (Cardiff). Division 3 promotion 1990 (Notts County), Division 2 promotion 1991 (Notts County). Division 2 promotion 1992 (Leicester).

PLUMMER (Norman) Leonard

1952 - 56 Centre Half Back   5' 11"   12st 4lbs (1954)
b: Leicester, 12 January 1924
Career: Leicester A T C, Leicester City (July 1942 - am, Nov 1942 - pro), TOWN (July 1952), Kettering Town (Aug 1956)

A stopper centre half of the old school, Norman Plummer was one of the first signings made by new boss George Jobey, who immediately appointed him captain. Virtually an ever present at Mansfield, he gave the club excellent service for four seasons, then moved in to non league soccer with Kettering.

1952-53	45 apps	0 gls	
1953-54	45 "	5 "	
1954-55	38 "	0 "	
1955-56	38 "	0 "	

Honours: F A Cup Final losers 1949 (Leicester), Southern League Championship 1957 (Kettering).

POLLARD Brian E
1980 - 81 Forward   5' 5"   9st 6lbs (1978)
b: York, 22 May 1954
Career: Tang Hall J S York, Burnholme School York, York City (1971 - am, Mar 1972 - pro), Watford (£33,000 - Nov 1977), TOWN (£45,000 - Jan 1980), Blackpool (F.T. Aug 1981), York City (F.T. Sep 1981), Chesterfield (Sep 1984 - N/C), Scarborough (Nov 1984 - N/C), Hartlepool United (Jan 1985 - N/C), North Ferriby (1985), Sherburn Scarborough.

Brian Pollard was on the small side, but what he lacked in size he made up for in courage. Helped secure two promotions for York in ten years. A former fitter at Vickers in York, after retiring from playing, he kept a public house in Sherburn, between York and Scarborough.

1979-80	20(0) apps	4 gls	
1980-81	25(9) "	1 "	

Honours: England Youth International, Division 3 - 3rd 1974 and Division 4 Championship 1984 (all York).

POLLARD Gary
1984 - 87 Defender   6' 1"   11st 10lbs
b: Staveley, Derbys., 30 December 1959
Career: Chesterfield (am, pro - July 1977), Port Vale (June 1983), TOWN (July 1984), Peterborough United (Aug 1987), Eastwood Town (Dec 1987), Goole Town (Feb 1988), Rotherham United (Aug 1988 - trial).

A defender who did sterling work for the "Stags" for three seasons, Gary Pollard was not related to Brian and he drifted into non league soccer, with a brief return to the League with the "Millers" in 1988. Was an insurance agent in Chesterfield by 1989

1984-85	17(1) apps	0 gls	
1985-86	35(0) "	1 "	
1986-87	14(0) "	0 "	

Honours: Division 4 promotion 1986, Freight Rover Trophy Winners 1987 (both Mansfield)

POOLE (Cyril) John
1936-44 & 1949-51 Outside Left/Left Back 5'9" 10st 7lbs (1950)
b: Forest Town, Mansfield, 13 March 1921
Career: Annesley C W (c/s 1935), TOWN (c/s 1936 - am), Wolverhampton Wanderers (Dec 1937 - groundstaff), TOWN (c/s 1938 - am, Feb 1944 - pro), Gillingham (June 1946), TOWN (June 1949), Clipstone M W.

A schoolboy protege, Cyril Poole starred with the adults in the Annesley Colliery team and was signed on amateur forms by the "Stags" when he was only just turned 15. More was to follow when he became the youngest player ever to turn out for Mansfield, on 27 February 1937 aged 15 years 351 days! He is one of the youngest players to appear in a Football League match, perhaps the only younger ones being Derek Forster the Sunderland goalkeeper (15 years 185 days) and the joint record holders, Albert Geldard the Bradford P A outside right and Ken Roberts the Wrexham right winger (both 15 years 158 days) - it is reputed that Geldard actually wins the race by a few hours! Another distinction which Poole holds is that from his debut in 1937, his next appearance in the League was on 5 September 1949 - a gap of 12 years 190 days between consecutive appearances for the same club - this is believed to be a record too. He had of course played for Gillingham in between, but they were a non league club at the time. Cyril was also a redoubtable cricketer, playing firstly for Mansfield Colliery in the Bassetlaw League then graduating to Notts C C C as a left handed batsman. He appeared in 366 First Class matches for the County and in three Test Matches against India on the 1951-52 Winter Tour. He is a cousin of Billy Wheatley who also played for Town and during the war years, apart from turning out for Mansfield, he also assisted Chesterfield, Nottingham Forest and Sheffield United as a "guest".

1936-37	1 app	0 gls	
WW II	71 "	1 "	
1949-50	9 "	1 "	
1950-51	7 "	0 "	

Honours: Southern League Championship 1947 & 49, Southern League runners up 1948 (all Gillingham).

POYNTON William
1964 - 66 Full Back   5' 9"   11st 7lbs
b: Shiremoor, Newcastle on Tyne, 30 June 1944
Career: Burnley (1960 - appr, July 1961 - pro), TOWN (June 1964), Lockheed Leamington (Jun 1966), Oldham Athletic (Sep 1966 - trial), Lincoln City (Oct 1966 - two month's trial)

Bill Poynton spent his entire career as a reserve team player and indeed, other than at Mansfield and one match when he was a substitute with Lincoln, he made no League appearances for any of his other clubs.

1964-65   13 apps   0 gls
1965-66   7(0)"   0 "
Honours: Division 3 - 3rd 1965 (Mansfield).

POYSER (George) Henry
1930 - 31 Left Full Back   5' 11½"   12st 7lbs (1936)
b: Stanton Hill, Notts., 6 February 1910
d: Skegby, Notts., 30 January 1995
Career: Sutton & District Schools & Nottinghamshire Schools-as outside left, Teversal Colliery, TOWN (Aug 1927 - trial), Stanton Hill, Wolverhampton Wanderers (May 1928), Stourbridge Town (c/a 1929), TOWN (c/s 1930), Port Vale (May 1931), Brentford (June 1934) Plymouth Argyle (Apr 1946), Dover Town (c/s 1947 - player manager) Wolverhampton Wanderers (1949 - chief coach), Notts County (Oct 1953 - manager to Jan 1957), Manchester City (1957 - asst manager, May 1963 - manager to Apr 1965)

A stylish local born full back who was not signed after an initial trial when he was 17½. After a short flirtation with Wolves and Stourbridge, he returned to Field Mill a much more experienced player and enjoyed an excellent season, the clubs last before election to the Football League, before moving up to Second Division Port Vale. His transfer to newly promoted Brentford, saw him become an ever present in their Division 2 Championship season and apart from a spell out when injured during 1937-38, he was a regular and highly respected member of their team until the start of WW II. At the end of hostilities, Poyser was 36 and after a brief spell with the "Pilgrims" as a player. he turned to management and enjoyed spells as manager with Notts County and Manchester City. During the war he made a

single "Guest" appearance for the "Stags" during the 1940-41 campaign. In his earlier days, was well known as a pigeon fancier and bowls player. Unhappily he passed away early in 1995 at his home in Skegby.

1930-31   45 apps   0 gls
WW II   1 "   0 "
Honours: Sutton & District Schoolboys, Nottinghamshire Schoolboys, Notts Senior Cup Winners 1931 (Mansfield), Division 2 Championship 1935, London War Cup runners up 1941, Winners 1942, Cup Winners Challenge - tied 1942 (all Brentford).

PRENTICE David
1933 - 34 Inside Right   5' 8"   11st 0lbs
b: Alloa, 29 July 1908
Career: Alva Albion Rovers (May 1927), Celtic (Feb 1928), Stranraer (1928 - loan), Ayr United (Aug 1929 - loan), Nithsdale Wanderers (Oct 1929 - loan), Plymouth Argyle (June 1930), Walsall (July 1931), Bournemouth & Boscombe Athletic (1931), Raith Rovers (June 1932), TOWN (July 1933), Bath City (c/s 1934)

Tricky, typically traditionally Scottish style inside forward who had experienced a wide variety of clubs both sides of the border before he reached Field Mill, including two and a half years with Celtic where he scored 3 goals in 6 appearances.

1933-34   19 apps   1 gl

PRESGRAVE Gordon E
1936 - 37 Outside Right   5' 5"   10st 11lbs (1935)
b: Worksop, 1913
Career: Worksop Town, Halifax Town (c/s 1933), Carlisle United (c/s 1936), TOWN (Dec 1936)

North Nottinghamshire born player who was quite effective in the Midland League with Worksop Town, but never quite made the step up to senior football, spending most of his time in the reserves. Summer time cricketer for Ollerton Colliery.

1936-37   5 apps   1 gl

PRICE Llewellyn (Percy)
1920 - 21 Utility Forward   5' 9½"   11st 6lbs (1925)
b: Caersws, Nr Newtown, Mon., 12 August 1896
d: 1969
Career: Barmouth, Hampstead Town, TOWN (c/s 1920), Aston Villa (Mar 1921), Notts County (Jun 1922 to May 1928).

Played at inside right and centre forward at Field Mill, but became an outside left with both the "Villans" and "Magpies".

1920-21   5 apps   1 gl   Central Alliance
Honours: Division 2 Championship 1923 (Notts
County).

PRINDIVILLE (Steven) Alan
1989 - 91 Full Back 5' 8"   10st 11lbs
b: Harlow, Essex, 26 December 1968
Career: Leicester City (1984 - appr, Dec 1986 - pro), Chesterfield
(F.T. Jun 1988), TOWN (exch Ryan + fee - Jun 1989), Greece
(F.T. c/s 1991), Doncaster Rovers (Feb 1992 - N/C), Wycombe
Wanderers (Jan 1994), Halifax Town (July 1994).

Did not impress sufficiently at Field Mill and moved
on.

1989-90   22(0) apps   0 gls
1990-91   4(2) "   0 "

PRIOR John
1932 - 33 Outside Right   5' 9"   11st 5lbs
b: Choppington, Northumberland, 2 July 1904
d: 1982
Career: Blyth Spartans, Sunderland (£250 - Mar 1922), Grimsby
Town (Feb 1927), Ashington (Sep 1932 - loan), TOWN (£350 -
Oct 1932), Stalybridge Celtic (c/s 1933).

Jack Prior was a direct winger who became a first
team regular at both Sunderland, where he played
with "Mac" England and at Grimsby where he
helped them to reach the First Division.

1932-33   32 apps   7 gls
Honours: Division 1 - 3rd 1924 & 26 (Sunderland),
Division 2 runners up 1929 (Grimsby).

PRITCHARD (Thomas) Francis
1935 - 36 Centre Half Back   6' 1"   12st 12lbs (1926)
b: Wellington, Salop, 18 June 1904
Career: Wolverhampton Schools, G W R Wolverhampton,
Sunbeam Motors, Stockport County (June 1925 - am), Newport
County (P/exch - July 1926), Wolverhampton Wanderers (£1,100
- Sep 1927), Charlton Athletic (£700 - May 1929), Thames (Nov
1931), Marseilles France (Aug 1932), Preston North End (Aug
1933), Lancaster Town (July 1934), TOWN (June 1935 - trainer),
Lancaster Town (c/s 1936)

Another of the older experienced players that the
club signed with great regularity in the pre WW II
period, Tom Pritchard came ostensibly as trainer, but
he was pressed into playing service on one occasion.
He left the club when his 12 months contract
expired.   A keen cycle racer when he was a
teenager.

1935-36   1 app   0 gls
Honours: Wolverhampton Schoolboys, Lancashire
Combination Championship 1935 (Lancaster).

QUIGLEY John
1968 - 72 Inside Forward   5' 8"   11st 0lbs (1971)
b: Glasgow, 28 June 1935
Career: Ashfield Juniors, Nottingham Forest (July 1957),
Huddersfield Town (Feb 1965), Bristol City (Oct 1966), TOWN
(£3,000 - July 1968, c/s 1971 - trainer coach to Nov 1971),
Middle East coaching for several years.

An outstanding player for Forest for nearly eight
years, during which he made over 230 appearances
for them, John Quigley was a master of ball control
with that touch of guile for which Scottish inside
forwards were renowned.   He was captain of the
great 1968-69 F A Cup giant killing team and
became involved with the training side of the club
for a time after his playing days had ended.

1968-69   46(0) apps   2 gls
1969-70   43(0) "   0 "
1970-71   16(0) "   0 "
Honours: F A Cup Winners 1959 & F A Charity
Shield runners up 1960 (both Nottingham Forest).
"Giant Killers" Cup Winners 1969 (Mansfield).

RANDALL Kevin
1975 - 77 Forward   5' 10½"   12st 9lbs (1977)
b: Ashton under Lyne, Lancs.,20 August 1945
Career: Droylsden, Bury (Oct 1965), Chesterfield (F.T. July
1966), Notts County (£20,000 - Aug 1972), TOWN (Nov 1975),
York City (£8,000 - Oct 1977, c/s 1980 - youth coach, Aug 1981
- asst manager, Dec 1981 - caretaker manager to Mar 1982),
Alfreton Town (1982 - manager), Goole Town (June 1983 -
player coach), Chesterfield (1984 - coach, June 1987 - manager
to Nov 1988), TOWN (Feb 1989 - youth development officer),
Chesterfield (Feb 1993 - asst manager)

During a very fruitful six year spell with the
"Spireites", Kevin Randall struck up a very
successful scoring duo with Ernie Moss, later to be

renewed when they both were at Field Mill 1976-79 and they both played a crucial part in Mansfield achieving promotion to the Second Division. Largely and surprisingly ignored by Peter Morris the following season, he was allowed to go to York City. Subsequently developed a career in management and was four years as Town's Youth Decelopment Officer before going back to his old love, Chesterfield as Assistant Manager to John Duncan.

1975-76	18(0) apps	3 gls	
1976-77	44(0) "	17 "	Leading Scorer
1977-78	0(4) "	0 "	

Honours: Division 4 Championship 1970 (Chesterfield). Division 3 Championship 1977 (Mansfield).

RATTRAY (Charles) Robert

1936 - 37 Outside Right   5' 6"   10st 7lbs (1936)
b: Fleetwood, Lancs., 10 May 1911
Career: Fleetwood Windsor Villa, Blackpool (Nov 1929), Watford (July 1934), TOWN (Jun 1936), Port Vale (F.T. May 1937), Accrington Stanley (F.T. Jun 1938)

Speedy winger who had tasted both Second and First Division football at Blackpool before moving into the Third Division, where he performed well for all his clubs maintaining his place easily.

1936-37   36 apps   5 gls
Honours: Division 2 Championship 1930 (Blackpool)

RAYNER Frank W

1933 - 34 Inside Right 5' 9"   11st 6lbs (1933)

b: Goldthorpe, Nr Barnsley, 1913
Career: Rotherham United, Frickley Colliery (c/s 1932), TOWN (May 1933), Mexborough (c/s 1934), Burnley (Mar 1935), Notts County (£1,250 - June 1939).

Joined the "Stags" and went back to the same league when he left Field Mill. Established a fine reputation at Burnley and Notts County had to pay a large fee to secure his services just before the outbreak of war - to no avail as his career was over when the war ended and he hardly kicked a ball for them. "Guest" player with Doncaster, Grimsby, Rotherham and Hull during WW II.

1933-34   17 apps   8 gls

RAYNOR George S

1932 - 33 Outside Right   5' 7"   11st 0lbs
b: Wombwell, South Yorks., 13 January 1907
Career: Elsecar Bible Class, Mexborough Athletic (trial), Wombwell (c/s 1929), Sheffield United (1930), TOWN (F.T. July 1932), Rotherham United (F.T. Aug 1933), Bury (Feb 1935), Aldershot (c/s 1939. 1945 - asst trainer), A I K Sweden (1946 - coach), Sweden national coach (1947), Roma Italy (1951 - coach), Lazio Italy (1953 - coach), Coventry City (June 1955 - coach, Jan 1956 - manager to Jun 1956, Jun 1956 - coach), Lincolnshire Schools (Aug 1956 - coach), Sweden national coach (Dec 1956).

Although a more than useful player, George Raynor made a reputation for himself as a coach of international renown, leading the Swedish national team on two separate occasions and creating the roots of the great post-war Italian teams. In 89 matches under his leadership, Sweden won 51, drew 16 and lost only 22 - a fine record - if only England team managers could do so well! During his spell there, when the Swedish players were amateurs, he twice lost his entire international team to Italian professionalism too. As a player he was speedy and direct, but it was coaching that made him him a household name in football. In the army during WW II, he was a "guest"player for Charlton, Bury, Bournemouth, Hull and Crystal Palace, apart from turning out for his own club Aldershot, where he was often partnered by England International Jimmy Hagan.

1932-33   9 apps   1 gl
Honours: (as coach) Olympic Games Gold Medals 1948, Bronze Medals 1952, F I F A World Cup 3rd 1950, finalists 1958 (all Sweden).

READ Charles William ("Chuck")

1937 - 38 (sometimes referred to as REED)
Inside Forward   5' 7"   12st 0lbs (1938)
b: Holbeck, Nr Spalding, Lincs., 21 March 1912
d: Spalding, Lincs., 28 July 1964

Career: Spalding Institute, Spalding United (c/s 1929), Sheffield United (£50 - Nov 1930), Lincoln City (£125 - Aug 1932), Southport (Mar 1935), Chesterfield (Feb 1936), Spalding United (May 1937 - loan), TOWN (Dec 1937 - loan), Notts County (May 1938), Spalding United (1946).

"Chuck" Read netted over 50 goals for his various clubs in the League and when transfer listed by Chesterfield in May 1937, he was allowed out on loan to Spalding and then Mansfield, before going permanently to the "Magpies" in May 1938. The system of loan players, so common nowadays, was quite rare pre-war, except in Scotland, where it was not unusual. Served on Spalding United's committee in the 1950s.

1937-38   22 apps   9 gls   (Loan)
Honours: Division 3 North Championship 1936 (Chesterfield)

READMAN Joseph A
1931 - 33 Inside Right/Right Half Back   6' 0"   12st 10lbs
b: West Hartlepool, 1905
Career: Bolton Wanderers, Bournemouth & Boscombe Athletic (Jun 1924), Brighton & Hove Albion (Jun 1927), Millwall (c/s 1928), TOWN (July 1931).

To Joe Readman goes the distinction of being the first "Stag" to score a League goal for the club during the inaugural match at Field Mill on 29 August 1931, when Swindon Town were beaten 3-2. Perhaps his best period was with Millwall, when he was signed after they gained promotion to Division Two in 1928, netting 22 goals in 63 appearances for them over three years.

1931-32   39 apps   5 gls
1932-33   34   "   7   "

REED Arthur
1922 - 23 Inside Forward/Wing Half Back   5' 6"   10st 0lbs
b: c1901
Career: Mexborough (c/s 1921), TOWN (July 1922), York City (c/s 1923)

Grafting inside forward who had successful seasons both before and after his stint with Mansfield.

1922-23   29 apps   10 gls   Midland League

REED Charles William - see
READ Charles William

REED John P
1993 Right Winger   5' 10"   10st 11lbs (1993)

b: Rotherham, 27 August 1972
Career: Sheffield United (1988 - appr, July 1990 - pro), Scarborough (Jan 1991 - loan & Sep 1991 - loan), Darlington (Mar 1993 - loan), TOWN (Sep 1993 - loan)

Speedy winger who had not made a senior appearance for the "Blades" until he returned from his loan spell at Field Mill and is now established in the first team squad at Bramall Lane.

1993-94   12(1) apps   2 gls

REES Jason M
1993 - 94 Midfield   5' 5"   9st 8lbs (1991)
b: Aberdare, South Wales, 22 December 1969
Career: Luton Town (1986 - appr, July 1988 - pro), TOWN (Dec 1993 - loan), Portsmouth (F.T. July 1994)

One of the first signings, albeit on loan, made by new manager Andy King and brought in from the club of his departure. Almost came here when Luton gave him a free transfer in May 1994, but with Simon Ireland joining the club permanently, there was not scope for this bubbly and exhuberant Welsh International - more's the pity.

1993-94   15(0) apps   1 gl   (Loan)
Honours: Welsh Youth, U/21, B & Full International (Luton)

REEVE Kenneth E
1949 - 54 Centre Forward   5' 8½"   11st 7lbs (1950)
b: Grimsby, 13 January 1921
Career: Humber United, Grimsby Town (Feb 1938), Doncaster Rovers (July 1948), TOWN (July 1949), Gainsborough Trinity (July 1954)

Top scorer at Belle Vue before Freddie Steele signed him for the "Stags" as his eventual replacement, Ken Reeve was a youngster with the "Mariners" just before the war and perhaps was at his best when at Field Mill where he rattled in over 60 goals in his five seasons there. During WW II was a "guest" player with Darlington and Clapton Orient.

1949-50	27 apps	8 gls	
1950-51	24 "	12 "	
1951-52	37 "	21 "	Leading Scorer
1952-53	32 "	10 "	
1953-54	19 "	11 "	

Honours: Division 3 North runners up 1951 (Mansfield)

REVEL Gordon H
1948 - 52 Centre Half Back   5' 11½"   11st 10lbs
b: Mansfield, 19 September, 1927
Career: Westfield Folk House, TOWN (May 1948 - am, Aug 1950 - pro), Worksop Town (1955)

1952-53	1 app	0 gls

REYNOLDS Mark D
1982 - 83 Defender   5' 9"   11st 0lbs (1983)
b: Glapwell, Derbys., 1 January 1966
Career: TOWN (July 1982 - appr)

Only 16 years 306 days old when he made his debut for the "Stags" v Hartlepool (a) on 3 November 1982.

1982-83	4(0) apps	0 gls

RHODES Mark N
1983 Midfield   5' 8"   11st 7lbs (1987)
b: Sheffield, 26 August 1957
Career: Rotherham United (1973 - appr, Aug 1975 - pro), Darlington (Oct 1982 - loan), TOWN (Mar 1983 - loan), Burnley (Mar 1985 - loan, May 1985 - permanent)

1982-83	4(0) apps	0 gls	(Loan)

RICHARDS Anthony
1961 - 64 Half Back   5' 11"   12st 0lbs (1963)
b: New Houghton, Derbys., 9 June 1944
Career: TOWN (1959 - appr, June 1962 - pro).

Played his first game during season 1961-62 as an amateur.

1961-62	1 app	0 gls
1962-63	1 "	0 "
1963-64	1 "	0 "

RICHARDSON Frederick
1919 - 22 Utility
b: Mansfield, c1893
Career: Mansfield Mechanics (1912), TOWN (c/s 1919), Loughborough Corinthians (c/s 1922), Worksop Town (c/s 1923).

Played either at full back, on the wing, or centre forward - but also played in other positions as circumstances dictated.

1919-20	24 apps	2 gls	Central Alliance
1920-21	19 "	5 "	" "
1921-22	1 "	0 "	Midland League

Honours: Central Alliance Championship 1920, runners up 1921 (both Mansfield)

RICHARDSON William
1965 - 68 Full Back   5' 8"   11st 9lbs
b: Bedlington, Co Durham, 25 October 1943
Career: Juniors, Sunderland (Oct 1960), TOWN (Oct 1965), York City (Jun 1968)

Smallish full back who held his position for just over a season before being displaced by Tom Stanton.

1965-66	12(1) apps	0 gls
1966-67	41(0) "	0 "
1967-68	8(1) "	0 "

RINGSTEAD Alfred
1959 - 60 Outside Right   5' 6"   10st 6lbs
b: Dublin, 14 October 1927
Career: Stoke City (am), Northwich Victoria, Sheffield United (£2,850 - Nov 1950), TOWN (July 1959), Frickley Colliery (Aug 1960)

Alf Ringstead was born in Ireland, but brought up in the Potteries, first playing professionally for Northwich Victoria and they collected a sizeable fee for this talented youngster when he was signed by the "Blades". His career at Bramall Lane was distinguished and he was rewarded by appearing nearly 250 times in the senior team, scoring over 100 goals and winning international caps for Eire. Ringstead was no mean goal scorer either, leading United's scoring list for three successive seasons, which is superb for a winger. Had just one season at Mansfield before dropping down into the Midland League.

1959-60	27 apps	3 gls

Honours: Eire International, Division 2 Championship 1953 (both Sheffield United)

RIPLEY Stanley (Keith)

1958 - 60 Wing Half Back   6' 1"   11st 2lbs (1957)
b: Normanton, Leeds, 29 March 1935
Career: Normanton Sec School, Altofts Y M C A, Leeds United (juniors, pro - Apr 1952), Norwich City (Aug 1958), TOWN (Nov 1958), Peterborough United (July 1960), Doncaster Rovers (Aug 1962).

This tall, but lightly built, left sided wing half, had two seasons at Field Mill, having been being signed by Sam Weaver from Norwich in mid season, but he was not a great success here and was released to Peterborough and Doncaster, where his achievements were greater. Was a centre forward at Leeds, scoring 15 goals. Member of the "Posh" team which won the Division 4 Championship in their first season in the Football League.

1958-59	12 apps	1 gl	
1959-60	19 "	4 "	

Honours: Division 4 Championship & Nothamptonshire Senior Cup Winners 1961 (both Peterborough).

ROBERTS Dudley E

1968 - 73 Inside Forward   6' 0"   12st 2lbs (1971)
b: Derby, 16 October 1945
Career: Juniors, Coventry City (Nov 1963), TOWN (Mar 1968), Doncaster Rovers (Feb 1973 - loan), Scunthorpe United (Feb 1974)

One of players who played such an important part in one of the best periods in the "Stags" League history, Dudley was the son of the pre war Coventry centre forward, Ted Roberts. Powerful in the air, many of his goals being scored with his head, he netted over 70 during his stay at Field Mill. After hanging up his boots in 1976, Roberts stayed in the town and still works locally for East Midlands Electricity as a storekeeper at their Huthwaite depot.

1967-68	6(2) apps	0 gls		
1968-69	42(0) "	10 "		
1969-70	43(0) "	18 "	Leading	Scorer
1970-71	45(0) "	22 "	"	"
1971-72	15(1) "	1 "		
1972-73	16(2) "	8 "		
1973-74	27(1) "	7 "		

Honours: "Giant Killers" Cup Winners 1969, Notts F A County Cup Winners 1971 (both Mansfield)

ROBERTS Robert

1970 - 72 Wing Half Back   5' 9"   11st 4lbs (1971)
b: Edinburgh, 2 September 1940
Career: Motherwell (c/s 1958), Leicester City (£41,000 - Sep 1963), TOWN (F.T. Sep 1970), Coventry City (July 1972 - coach), Colchester United (Mar 1972 - player coach, Jun 1975 - manager to Apr 1982), Wrexham (Jun 1982 - manager to Mar 1985), El Shabar Kuwait (1985 - coach to 1987), Grimsby Town (July 1987 - manager to May 1988), Leicester City (Jun 1988 - coach)

A Scotsman, Bobby Roberts began his career with Motherwell, winning Under 23 caps before his move to Filbert Street. He made well over 200 appearances for Leicester before making the short trip up the road to Mansfield where he made his prescence felt in the two seasons he spent here.

1970-71	39(0) apps	2 gls	
1971-72	37(4) "	2 "	

Honours: Scottish U/23 International, Scottish League XI (both Motherwell). F A Cup Finalists 1969 (Leicester). Notts F A County Cup Winners 1971 (Mansfield).

ROBINSON Albert

1930 - 33 Right Full Back   5' 10'   11st 7lbs (1931)
b: South Normanton, Derbys., 1913
Career: South Normanton, TOWN (Mar 1931 - am, May 1932 - pro), Derby County (Aug 1933), Sutton Town (c/s 1938).

After an impressive performance for The Rest v Town Reserves in the end of season test match against the Derbyshire Senior League Champions, Jack Hickling signed the 17 year old. Slowly brought along through the 'A' and Reserve teams and developing into a stylish defender, Robinson was snapped up by the "Rams" just before the 1933-34 season opened.

1930-31	2 apps	0 gls	Midland League
1931-32	1 "	0 "	
1932-33	11 "	0 "	

ROBINSON E
1920 - 21 Inside Left
Career: TOWN (1920)

| 1920-21 | 1 app | 0 gls | Central Alliance |

ROBINSON Leslie
1984 - 86 Midfield   5' 8"   11st 1lb
b: Shirebrook, Derbys., 1 March 1967
Career: Chesterfield (1983 - appr), TOWN (Oct 1984 - pro), Stockport County (Nov 1986 - loan, £10,000 - Feb 1987 - permanent), Doncaster Rovers (£20,000 - Mar 1988), Oxford United (£150,000 - Mar 1990)

One could say that Robinson is one who slipped through the net, as both Chesterfield and Mansfield missed his potential and he made a name for himself at Stockport and Doncaster, increasing his value along the way. He is still very much part of the "U's" scene.

1984-85	4(2) apps	0 gls
1985-86	6(1) "	0 "
1986-87	1(1) "	0 "

Honours: Notts F A County Cup Winners 1987 (Mansfield)

ROBINSON (Samuel) Henry
1931 - 34 Centre Half Back   5' 10"   11st 7lbs
b: Hucknall, Notts., 1910
Career: Luton Town, Bournemouth & Boscombe Athletic (1928), Derby County (May 1931), TOWN (Oct 1931), Clapton Orient (Feb 1934).

Joined the "Cherries" from local football in Hucknall and made 10 appearances for them as an inside right. Only had a few months at the Baseball Ground, where he did not make the first team, before joining the "Stags" where he was converted into an effective centre half, soon displacing Bernard Chambers. He gave Mansfield good service until superceded by Les Butler in August 1933 and moved on to the "O's" towards the end of 1933-34 after failing to make a single League appearance that term, although he did appear in the F A Cup replay v New Brighton.

1931-32	28 apps	0 gls
1932-33	33 "	1 "
1933-34	0 "	0 "

ROBSON William
1924 - 25 Inside Right   5' 7"   11st 7lbs (1924)
b: Shildon, Co Durham, c1900
Career: Shildon Colliery (am), Leeds United (Dec 1921), TOWN (c/s 1924), Frickley Colliery (Jan 1925), Gainsborough Trinity (Dec 1925), Ashington (c/s 1926)

Bill Robson had made 10 Second Division appearances for Leeds before he joined the "Stags", but he did not impress at Field Mill during the club's second successive championship campaign and was allowed to link up with fellow Midland Leaguers, Frickley Colliery in mid season.

| 1924-25 | 2 apps | 1 gl | Midland League |

Honours: Yorkshire Mid Week League XI 1923 (Leeds)

ROE Arthur
1927 - 28 Half Back   5' 8½"   11st 7lbs (1923)
b: South Normanton, Derbys., 1892
Career: South Normanton, Luton Town (c/s 1914), Arsenal (Apr 1925), Bournemouth & Boscombe Athletic (c/s 1925), TOWN (c/s 1927)

This experienced half back was 35 years old when he joined Mansfield, having first tasted higher grade competitive football with Luton before WW I and indeed, had played in the First Division with Arsenal in 1924-25 and subsequently for Bournemouth in the Third. He played at both wing and centre half for the "Stags" in what was a fairly mediocre season for them.

| 1927-28 | 25 apps | 1 gl | Midland League |

Honours: Southern League (East) XI 1921 (Luton)

ROEBUCK Frederick
1926 - 27 Right Full Back   5' 8½"   12st 0lbs (1926)
b: Silverhill, Nr Rotherham, 6 November 1902
Career: Huddersfield Town (c1924), TOWN (c/s 1926), Barrow (c/s 1927), Peterborough & Fletton United (c/s 1928).

Reserve team player from the "Terriers" who had a good season with Mansfield in their only season in the Midland Combination, when they finished runners up and also won the Cup competition. Fred Roebuck's father Larrett, had also been a full back with Huddersfield pre war and was killed in action on the Somme in 1916.

| 1926-27 | 33 apps | 0 gls | Midland Comb. |

Honours: Midland Combination runners up, Midland Combination Cup Winners, Notts F A Senior Cup Winners & Mansfield Hospital Charity Cup Winners all 1927 (all Mansfield)

ROSE Michael J
1970 Goalkeeper 6' 2"   13st 7lbs (1971)
b: New Barnet, Herts., 22 July 1943
Career: St Albans City, Charlton Athletic (July 1963), Notts County (£3,000 - Mar 1967), TOWN (Aug 1970 - loan)

Brought in on loan from neighbours, Notts County when Graham Brown was injured at the start of the 1970-71 season.

1970 - 71   3 apps   0 gls   (Loan)

ROSEBOOM Edward

1929 - 30 Inside Forward   5' 8"   11st 8lbs (1929)
b: Glasgow, 24 November 1899
Career: Cardiff City (1920), Blackpool (Dec 1921), Nelson (c/s 1923), Clapton Orient (Mar 1924), Rochdale (c/s 1924), Chesterfield (c/s 1925), TOWN (Jun 1929), Newark Town (c/s 1930).

By the time he joined Mansfield, Teddy Roseboom had enjoyed a fair amount of Second and Third Division football, was 30 years old and very experienced. He had also slowed down a lot, a fact which was stated quite firmly in a contemporary report. However he performed quite satisfactorily in one of the "Amber & Blues" less impressive seasons and gave useful service to Newark Town subsequently.

1929-30   32 apps   5 gls

ROWBOTHAM Darren

1992 - 93 Forward   5' 10"   11st 5lbs
b: Cardiff, 22 October 1966
Career: Plymouth Argyle (1982 - appr, Nov 1984 - pro), Exeter City (Oct 1987 - loan, p/exch R T Marker - Nov 1987 - permanently), Torquay United (£25,000 - Sep 1991), Birmingham City (£20,000 - Jan 1992), TOWN (Dec 1992 - loan), Hereford United (Mar 1993 - loan), Crewe Alexandra (F.T. July 1993)

1992-93   4(0) apps   0 gls   (Loan)
Honours: Welsh Youth International (Plymouth), Division 4 Championship 1990 (Exeter), Division 3 runners up 1992 (Birmingham), Division 4 promotion 1994 (Crewe)

ROWLAND John D

1966 - 68 Winger   5' 10"   10st 4lbs
b: Riddings, Derbys., 7 April 1941
Career: Ironville Amateurs, Nottingham Forest (Apr 1961), Port Vale (Aug 1962), TOWN (Sep 1966), Tranmere Rovers (July 1968), South Shields (1972)

Smart winger who had his best spell at Vale Park, making nearly 150 appearances for the "Valiants"

1966-67   19(0) apps   9 gls
1967-68   30(0)   "   7   "
Honours: England Youth International

ROWLANDS John H

1967 - 68 Forward
b: Liverpool, 7 February 1945
Career: TOWN (Oct 1967), Torquay United (Jun 1968), Exeter City (Jan 1969 - loan), Stockport County (Aug 1969), Barrow (Jan 1971), Workington (July 1972), Crewe Alexandra (Nov 1973), Seattle U S A (1974), Hartlepool (Sep 1975)

"Scouser" signed by Town from local football on Merseyside, but was released at the end of his first season here. Assisted the two doomed North East clubs in their final seasons in the League.

1967-68   12(1) apps   3 gls

ROY John Robin

1936 - 37 Outside Left   5' 9"   11st 0lbs (1936)
b: Woolston, Southampton, 23 March 1914
d: Bournemouth, 24 November 1980
Career: Sholing Southampton (am), Norwich City (July 1933 - am, Aug 1933 - pro), TOWN (F.T. Apr 1936), Sheffield Wednesday (£1,750 - Feb 1937), Notts County (Mar 1938), Tranmere Rovers (Dec 1938), Yeovil & Petters United (May 1939), Southampton (Dec 1939), Ipswich Town (Feb 1946), Gravesend (Oct 1947).

Jack Roy was a speedy winger who could centre accurately and admirably contributed to Harston's record goal tally, before the ailing Sheffield Wednesday signed him in their struggle to avoid relegation from the First Division. The fee was a new record for Mansfield and a nice profit too, as he was signed on a free transfer only 9 months previously. During WW II assisted Ipswich, Southampton and Yeovil - also Aberaman Athletic in the Regional Welsh League. One of the few footballers who were transferred during the war, signing for the "Saints" on Christmas Day 1939!

1936-37   25 apps   2 gls

RUDKIN (George) William

1937 - 38 Outside Left
b: Horncastle, Lincs., c1916
Career: Grantham, TOWN (Sep 1937), Carlisle United (c/s 1938)

1937-38   1 app   0 gls

RUSHBY Alan

1957 Centre Half Back   6' 0"   12st 0lbs
b: Doncaster, 27 December 1933
Career: Doncaster Rovers (Jan 1952), TOWN (Mar 1957), Bradford P A (Nov 1957)

Very briefly at Field Mill before he moved on to Park Avenue.

1956-57	12 apps	0 gls
1957-58	8 "	0 "

RYAN Eric W

1950 - 57 Full Back/Half Back   5' 9"   10st 4lbs
b: Oswestry, Salop., 6 January 1933
Career: Oswestry Town (am), TOWN (c/s 1950 - am, May 1951 - pro)

Eric Ryan joined the club full of promise as a 17 year old, but in seven years at Field Mill only managed to play in 20 games.

1954-55	2 apps	0 gls
1955-56	17 "	0 "
1956-57	1 "	0 "

RYAN John B

1987 - 89 Defender/Midfield   5' 10"   11st 7lbs
b: Ashton under Lyne, Lancs., 18 February 1962
Career: Oldham Athletic (Jun 1979 - appr, Feb 1980 - pro), Newcastle United (£235,000 - Aug 1983), Sheffield Wednesday (exch Heard + £40,000 - Sep 1984), Oldham Athletic (£25,000 - Aug 1985), TOWN (Oct 1987 - loan, £25,000 - Oct 1987 - permanent), Chesterfield (exch Prindiville + cash to Town - Jun 1989), Rochdale (F.T. July 1991).

Signed by Ian Greaves after a month's loan period, John Ryan was a lynch pin in the middle of the park at a time when the "Stags" were languishing in the lower reaches of Division Three.

1987-88	30(2) apps	1 gls
1988-89	23(7) "	0 "

Honours: England U/21 International (Oldham), Notts F A County Cup Winners 1989 (Mansfield).

SAINTY John A

1972 Centre Forward   5' 10"   13st 4lbs (1970)
b: Poplar, London, 24 March 1946
Career: Tottenham Hotspur (1962 - appr, July 1963 - pro), Reading (Aug 1967), Bournemouth & Boscombe Athletic (£5,000 - Feb 1970), TOWN (Nov 1972 - loan), Aldershot (F.T. Aug 1974), A F C Bournemouth (coach), Norwich City (coach), Manchester City (1980 - coach), Chester (Aug 1982 - coach, Nov 1982 - manager to Dec 1983), Burnley (Jan 1984 - coach), Armthorpe C W (1986 - manager), Mossley (1987 - manager), Stockport County (1989 - asst manager)

1972-73	3(0) apps	0 gls	(Loan)

Honours: England Schoolboy International

SAMS Alfred

1937 - 38 Inside Left 5' 6½"   11st 0lbs (1937)
b: c1913
d: Adelaide, Australia, 1990.
Career: Shildon Colliery, Grantham (c/s 1935), TOWN (May 1937), Reading (c/s 1938), Accrington Stanley (c/s 1939), Grantham (1941)

Stocky inside forward from the North East, Alf Sams stayed just one season with each of his League clubs, returning to Grantham during the war years where he teamed up again with the "Gingerbreads" until he retired from playing in 1948.

1937-38	11 apps	2 gls

Honours: Notts F A County Cup Winners 1938 (Mansfield)

SAUNDERS (John) George

1966 - 72 Centre Half Back   6' 1"   12st 1lb (1970)
b: Worksop, 1 December 1950
Career: TOWN (1966 - appr, Dec 1968 - pro), Huddersfield Town (£30,000 - Oct 1972), Barnsley (Dec 1975 - trial, £5,000 - Mar 1976 permanent), Lincoln City (Jun 1979), Doncaster Rovers (Aug 1980), Worksop Town (c/s 1981, later manager, then ultimately, chairman).

This North Nottinghamshire youngster joined the "Stags" as a 16 year old apprentice, making his full debut before he was 19. Soon established himself as the first choice pivot and after nearly 90 senior appearances, made the move to Huddersfield, then Barnsley, playing in well over 100 matches for both. Ended his career with his home town club, later becoming manager and ultimately their chairman.

1969-70	2(0) apps	0 gls
1970-71	20(0) "	0 "
1971-72	44(0) "	2 "
1972-73	14(0) "	0 "

Honours: Notts F A County Cup Winners 1971 & 1972 (both Mansfield)

SAVIN (Keith) Anthony

1957 - 59 Full Back   5' 9"   11st 7lbs
b: Oxford, 5 June 1929
d: 18 December 1992
Career: Oxford City, Derby County (May 1950), TOWN (p/exch Darwin + £4,000 - May 1957), Nuneaton Borough (July 1959), Bourne Town (Mar 1960), Nuneaton Borough.

During a spell of seven years at the Baseball Ground, Keith Savin was in and out of the senior XI and never quite established himself as a first team regular. He did this however, for a couple of seasons at Field Mill, when he joined the club as makeweight when George Darwin was transferred to the "Rams".

1957-58	37 apps	0 gls
1958-59	31 "	0 "

Honours: Central Alliance Championship 1960 (Bourne).

SAXBY Gary P
1977 - 80 Defender   5' 8"   10st 3lbs (1980)
b: Mansfield, 11 December 1959
Career: Garibaldi School, TOWN (1975 - appr, Dec 1977 - pro),
Northampton Town (F.T. Aug 1980), Stafford Rangers, Ashfield
United (c/s 1992 - manager to Jun 1994).

Unlike his brother, Mick (below), Gary Saxby did not manage to establish himself in the first XI with Mansfield, although he did when he moved on to the "Cobblers'. Ended his career by becoming a security guard. Managed Ashfield United from the Summer of 1992 until June 1994.

| 1978-79 | 14(2) apps | 1 gls |
| 1979-80 | 0(0) " | 0 " |

SAXBY (Michael) William
1975 - 79 Defender   6' 0"   10st 0lbs (1978)
b: Mansfield, 12 August 1957
Career: Sherwood Hall School, Mansfield Boys, TOWN (1973 - appr, Jan 1975 - pro), Luton Town (Taylor + £150,000 - July 1979), Grimsby Town (Mar 1983 - loan), Lincoln City (Nov 1983 - loan), Newport County (July 1984 - trial), Middlesbrough (Sep 1984), Oakham United (c/s 1986), Nuneaton Borough (Nov 1986), Alfreton Town (Nov 1988 - asst manager), Sutton Town (joint manager).

Elder brother to Gary (above), Mick Saxby was far more successful in his League career, making his debut at 18 and three years later attracting the then, enormous transfer fee of £225,000 - Taylor was valued at £75,000 - easily Town's record transfer fee received at the time. Played in 10 games during Mansfield's promotion season of 1976-77, but his weight had increased to 13st 10lb by 1983 when he was on loan at Lincoln. Co-managed Sutton Town, now Ashfield United, for a time a couple of years ago. Went into the licenced trade at the end of his league career, later becoming Field Sales Manager of "Chad" and was appointed the "Stags" Commercial Manager towards the end of May 1995.

1975-76	1(1) app	1 gl
1976-77	10(0) "	0 "
1977-78	19(2) "	0 "
1978-79	46(0) "	4 "

Honours: F A County Youth Trophy Winners 1974 (Mansfield)

SCANLON (Albert) Joseph
1963 - 66 Outside Left   5' 9"   11st 7lbs
b: Manchester, 10 October 1935
Career: Manchester United (1950 - am, Dec 1952 - pro), Newcastle United (£18,000 - Nov 1960), Lincoln City (£2,000 - Feb 1962), TOWN (Apr 1963), Belper Town (Aug 1966)

One of the early "Busby Babes", Albert Scanlon survived the tragic Munich air disaster of February 1958. He was a nephew of Charlie Mitten, the ex Mansfield player manager, who signed him for Newcastle, when he was manager there. Scanlon was the first signing made by new manager Tommy Cummings when he joined the club and he showed his class during the three full seasons he spent here. After leaving the game, he suffered some hard times, being unemployed for much of the time when he eeked out a living on and off as a dock labourer in Manchester, but of recent times he has settled in Salford and is working as a warehouseman for Colgate - Palmolive.

1962-63	15 apps	3 gls
1963-64	36 "	5 "
1964-65	37 "	7 "
1965-66	20(0)"	6 "

Honours: England U/23 International, Football League XI. F A Youth Cup Winners 1953 & 1954, Division 1 runners up 1959(all Manchester United). Division 4 promotion 1963, Division 3 - 3rd 1965 (both Mansfield)

SCOTT Kenneth
1952 - 53 Outside Right   5' 8"   11st 4lbs (1952)
b: Maltby, South Yorks., 13 August 1931
Career: Denaby United, Derby County (Aug 1950), Denaby United (c/s 1951), TOWN (Aug 1952)

| 1952-53 | 5 apps | 2 gls |

SCOTT
1930 - 31 Wing Half Back
b: Birmingham, c1908
Career: Birmingham, Bedouins, TOWN (Dec 1930 - am)

| 1930-31 | 3 apps | 0 gls | Midland League |

SCRIMSHAW Harold W
1912 - 13 and 1919 - 21 Outside Right   5' 6"
b: Mansfield, c1891
Career: Mansfield Mechanics (1910), TOWN (c/s 1911), Shirebrook (c/s 1913), Woodhouse Exchange (c/s 1919), TOWN (c/s 1919)

Diminutive winger who played for both of the town's senior teams during his career. Broke his leg during a match in April 1921 and upon his return to the team in a reserve match the following October, he broke it again and this finished his career.

1912-13	N.K. apps	0 gls	Central Alliance	
1919-20	26 "	3 "	"	"
1920-21	22 "	6 "	"	"

Honours: Central Alliance Championship 1920, runners up 1921 (both Mansfield)

SCRIMSHIRE F
1927 - 28 Centre Forward
Career: TOWN (c/s 1928 - am)

| 1927-28 | 1 app | 0 gls |

SEARSON (Harold) Vincent
1947 - 49 Goalkeeper 6' 1"   12st 7lbs (1949)
b: Mansfield, 3 June 1924
Career: High Oakham School, Mansfield Schoolboys, Nottinghamshire County Schoolboys, Bilsthorpe Colliery (1941), Sheffield Wednesday (1942 - am, Aug 1946 - pro), TOWN (Jun 1947), Leeds United (£2,000 - Jan 1949), York City (Nov 1952), Corby Town (c/s 1954).

"Polly" Searson was another of the ex High Oakham schoolboys who played for his home town club. Played his first senior game as an 18 year old amateur with the "Owls" during the war in 1942-43 season. Served in India with the Forces during WW II and appeared with the Fleet Air Arm side whilst there. Mansfield got a large fee, for the time, particularly for a goalkeeper, when he was transferred to Leeds in 1949 and he made over 100 appearances for the Elland Road club. A former electrician.

| 1947-48 | 27 apps | 0 gls |
| 1948-49 | 15 " | 0 " |

Honours: Mansfield Schoolboys, Nottinghamshire County Schoolboys.

SHARKEY Dominic
1968 - 70 Centre Forward   5' 6"   10st 4lbs
b: Helensburgh, Dunbartonshire, 4 May 1943
Career: Sunderland (May 1958 - juniors, May 1960 - pro), Leicester City (£15,000 - Oct 1966), TOWN (£10,000 - Mar 1968), Hartlepool United (F.T. July 1970), South Shields (c/s 1972)

Another member of the "Stags" fine F A Cup campaign of 1968-69, Nick Sharkey was on the small side, but what he lacked in inches he made up in style and goalscoring ability. He scored five in a match for Sunderland on one occasion and this is still a jointly shared individual scoring record for the Wearside club.

1967-68	13(0) apps	2 gls	
1968-69	40(1) "	13 "	Leading Scorer
1969-70	14(1) "	2 "	

Honours: Scottish Schoolboy International. Scottish U/23 International & Division 2 runners up 1964 (both Sunderland). "Giant Killers" Cup Winners 1969 (Mansfield)

SHARKEY Patrick G
1977 - 78 Midfield   5' 8"   10st 7lbs (1978)
b: Omagh, N.I., 26 August 1953
Career: Portadown, Ipswich Town (Sep 1973), Millwall (Nov 1976 - loan), TOWN (£10,000 - Aug 1977), Colchester United £10,000 - Jun 1978), Peterborough United (£10,000 - Mar 1979), Whitby Town (1982).

When Mansfield signed Pat Sharkey, he had played for Northern Ireland the previous season and was clearly a skilful player, but falling out of favour with new boss, Billy Bingham, he moved back to East Anglia after just one term.

| 1977-78 | 31(1) apps | 5 gls |

Honours: Northern Ireland International (Ipswich).

SHARP (Arthur) Allen
1925 - 27 Outside Left   5' 9"   11st 8lbs
b: Nottingham, 1908
Career: St Mark's Nottingham, TOWN (Feb 1926), Blackpool (July 1927), Reading (May 1928), West Ham United (Mar 1929), Newark Town (1929), Carlisle United (May 1930), Bristol City (Jun 1932), Aldershot (May 1933), Oldham Athletic (Aug 1934), Shrewsbury Town (Aug 1935), Darlington (Jun 1936), Shrewsbury Town (Feb 1937).

Arthur Sharp had to try four League clubs before he got a game and then he managed 68 in two seasons with Carlisle! His best spell then followed with 28 for Bristol City and 34 for Aldershot before he dropped into the Birmingham League with the "Shrews" - amply compensated though, as they finished third.

| 1925-26 | 15 apps | 4 gls | Midland League |
| 1926-27 | 23 " | 5 " | Midland Comb. |

Honours: Midland League runners up & Notts F A Senior Cup Winners 1926, Midland Combination runners up, Midland Combination Cup Winners, Notts F A Senior Cup Winners, Mansfield Hospital Charity Cup Winners & Byron Cup Winners 1927 (all Mansfield).

SHARPE
1921 - 22 Centre Forward
Career: Ilkeston Town, TOWN (1921)

1921-22   3 apps   2 gls   Midland League

SHAW Thomas
1924 - 25 Goalkeeper 5' 10"   11st 6lbs (1924)
b: c1900
Career: Nottingham Forest, Newark Town (Feb 1923), TOWN (May 1924)

Reserve goalkeeper to Hardstaff during the club's second successive championship season, but he was four short of the required 14 appearances to qualify for a medal.

1924-25   10 apps   0 gls   Midland League

SHAW Thomas (Frederick)
1937 - 38 Inside Forward   5' 9½"   10st 7lbs (1936)
b: Hucknall, Notts., 1909
Career: Annesley Colliery, Darlaston, Birmingham (Sep 1932 - am. Oct 1932 - pro), Notts County (Dec 1934 - loan), Birmingham (May 1935), Notts County (Jan 1936), TOWN (July 1937), Bournemouth & Boscombe Athletic (Jun 1938), Ollerton Colliery (c/s 1939)

Fred Shaw was the subject of one of the early loan agreements eventually joining the "Magpies" on a permanent basis, reaching the "Stags" in July 1937 in time for their return to the Southern Section. He retired from active play in 1943.

1937-38   22 apps   1 gl
Honours: Division 3 South Cup Joint Winners 1937 (Notts County).

SHAW William
1930 Centre/Inside Forward   5' 11"   13st 0lbs (1929)
b: Kilnhurst, South Yorks., 3 October 1898
Career: Frickley Colliery (c/s 1919), Bradford City (c/s 1921), Chesterfield (c/s 1923), Scunthorpe & Lindsey United (c/s 1924), Southend United (May 1925), Gainsborough Trinity (Jun 1926), Cardiff City (£500 - c/s 1928), Gainsborough Trinity (1929), TOWN (Feb 1930).

Experienced forward who had tasted League football with Bradford City (First & Second Division) - Chesterfield and Southend (Third). He also had a short flirtation with Cardiff as they fought unsuccessfully to avoid relegation from the First Division and had the briefest of spells with Town - but was not a success, being released at the end of the season. Was a member of the quite outstanding Gainsborough team of the mid to late 1930s.

1929-30   8 apps   4 gls   Midland League
Honours: Midland League - 3rd 1927, Championship 1928, runners up 1929 (all Gainsborough). Bayley Cup Winners 1930 (Mansfield).

SHEFFIELD Alexander
1926 - 28 Right Half Back
b: Nottingham, early 1908
Career: Shirebrook (Sep 1925), TOWN (May 1926), Exeter City (c/s 1928), Bristol City (c/s 1930)

Alex Sheffield played in all half back positions at Mansfield as well as centre forward. He once scored four goals in a match in which he was playing centre half with none of the goals being penalties or free kicks and the new off-side law was operative! He made his professional debut with Shirebrook on 18 April 1926 when he was just 18.

1926-27   12 apps   0 gls   Midland Comb.
1927-28   23 "   0 "   Midland League
Honours: England Schoolboy International. Midland Combination runners up, Midland Combination Cup Winners, Notts Benevolent Bowl Winners, Mansfield Hospital Charity Cup Winners & Bayley Cup Winners 1927 (all Mansfield).

SHELDON Lancelot
1921 - 27 Outside Right   5' 9"   11st 0lbs (1925)
b: Underwood, Notts., c1896
Career: Selston Town (1914), Notts County (c1916), Coventry City (Dec 1918), Heanor Town (1920), TOWN (c/s 1921).

Mansfield's outstanding right winger of the 1920s and vital contributor to the success of the championship teams. Lance Sheldon was with Notts County during WW I, joining Coventry for their last season in the Southern League before becoming a "Stag" for their initiation into the Midland League in 1921. Regular outside right until retirement in May 1927, when he was 31.

1921-22	36 apps	3 gls	Midland League	
1922-23	38 "	5 "	"	"
1923-24	39 "	3 "	"	"
1924-25	34 "	8 "	"	"
1925-26	28 "	5 "	"	"
1926-27	21 "	2 "	Midland Comb.	

Honours: North Notts League Tour, Algeria 1923. Mansfield Hospital Charity Cup Winners 1922, Notts F A Senior Cup 1923 & 1926, Midland League Championship 1924 & 1925, runners up 1926, Midland Combination runners up 1927, Midland Combination Cup Winners 1927 (all Mansfield).

SHELDON Wilfred
1927 - 28 Outside Right
b: Mansfield, c1906
Career: TOWN (c/s 1927 - am), Luton Town, Shirebrook (Sep 1930)

Oddly enough it was this player who replaced his namesake in Lance's old position on the right wing when he retired. They were not related.

1927-28   9 apps   4 gls   Midland League

SHELL Francis H
1947 - 48 Centre Forward   5' 9" 11st 12lbs
b: Hackney, London, 2 December 1912
d: Axminster, Devon, July 1988
Career: Ilford Schools, Barking (Apr 1930 - am), Ford Sports Dagenham (Aug 1936), Aston Villa (May 1937 - pro), Birmingham City (Sep 1946), Hereford United (May 1947), TOWN (June 1947)

A noted amateur centre forward with Barking and Ford Sports in the 1930s, Frank Shell was a late starter in the professional ranks when he signed for Villa. He was nearly 25 and he played a vital part in their Division Two championship season in 1937-38. Played as a "guest" for Leicester, Northampton, Walsall and Notts County during WW II.

1947-48   22 apps   1 gl
Honours: Ilford Schoolboys. Division 2 Championship 1938 (Aston Villa).

SHEPHERD J
1920 - 21 Right Half Back
Career: TOWN (c/s 1920)

1920-21   3 apps   0 gls Central Alliance

SHEPPARD W H
1923   Right Full Back
b: Creswell, Derbys.
Career: Creswell Colliery, TOWN (Apr 1923 - am)

1922-23   3 apps   0 gls Midland League

SHERLOCK (Paul) Graeme
1995 onwards Defender/Midfield   5' 11" 11st 9lbs (1994)
b: Wigan, 17 November 1973
Career: Notts County (1990 - appr, July 1992 - pro), TOWN (£15,000 - Mar 1995).

Young player signed just before the transfer deadline to give extra defensive cover during the promotion seeking run in of 1994-5.

1994-95   1(1) apps   0 gls
Honours: Newark & Sherwood Schoolboys, Nottinghamshire Schoolboys.

SHORE Andrew (William)
1974 - 75 Defender
b: Kirkby in Ashfield, Notts., 29 December 1955
Career: TOWN (1972 - appr, July 1974 - pro),

1974-75   1(0) apps   0 gls

SHUTTLEWORTH J F
1919 - 20 Outside Left
b: Doncaster, c1898
Career: Denaby United (1918), TOWN (c/s 1919), Bolton Wanderers (£130 - c/s 1920), TOWN (c/s 1921), Denaby United (Oct 1921)

First choice outside left during the championship season of 1919-20. Transferred to Bolton the following Summer, but was released and returned to Mansfield. Failed to secure a first team spot due to the brilliance of George Clarke and moved back to Denaby where he had started his career.

1919-20   29 apps   10 gls Central Alliance
Honours: Central Alliance Championship 1920 (Mansfield)

SIDNEY Hilton
1922 - 23 Outside Left
b: Wearside

Career: Luton Town (c/s 1921), TOWN (Feb 1923)

Joined Mansfield towards the end of 1922-23 in time to win a place in the Notts Senior Cup winning side.

1922-23   18 apps   1 gl
Honours: Notts F A Senior Cup Winners 1923 (Mansfield)

SIMPSON George L
1951 - 54 Wing Half Back/Inside Forward 5' 8" 10st 7lbs (1952)
b: Shirebrook, Derbys., 3 December 1933
Career: TOWN (1949 - juniors, Aug 1951 - pro), Cheltenham Town (Aug 1954), Hereford United (1955), Gillingham (Aug 1956).

1952-53   5 apps   0 gls
1953-54   3 "   0 "

SINCLAIR Dennis
1953 - 54 Outside Right
b: Middlesbrough, 20 November 1931
Career: Derby County (May 1952), TOWN (July 1953), Brush Sports Loughborough (Aug 1954).

1953-54   1 app   0 gls

SINDALL Mark
1983 - 84 Midfield   5' 8"   10st 8lbs (1983)
b: Shirebrook, Derbys., 3 September 1964
Career: Notts County (1980 - appr), Luton Town (Aug 1981 - appr), TOWN (F.T. July 1982 - N/C)

1982-83   9(2) apps   0 gls
1983-84   9(1) "   0 "

SIVITER Eli
1932 - 34 Wing Half Back   5' 11"   11st 7lbs (1933)
b: Clowne, Derbys., 1911
d: Mansfield, March 1993
Career: Shirebrook (c/s 1929), TOWN (May 1932), Ollerton Colliery (May 1934), Ripley Town (Aug 1934), Ilkeston Town (Nov 1934)

His two matches for Town were consecutive - the last match of one season and the first of the next - both v Hartlepools and both at Field Mill! Made a "come back" during the war by turning out for the "Stags", in two consecutive matches - the last game of 1941-42 and the first of 1942-43 - but this time against different opponents! Played cricket for Langwith Colliery during the Summer months.

1932-33   1 app   0 gls
1933-34   1 "   0 "
WW II   2 "   0

SLACK Samuel
1929 - 30 Full Back
b: Skegby, Notts., c1907
Career: Shirebrook (c/s 1926), Sutton Town (c/s 1928), Charlton Athletic (Dec 1928), TOWN (c/s 1929), Sutton Town (c/s 1930).

Made three appearances for Charlton during their Division 3 South Championship season of 1928-29.

1929-30   8 apps   0 gls

SLACK William Bomford ("Wilf")
1932 - 36 Outside Left/Left Half Back 5' 7" 11st 0lbs (1933)
b: Skegby, Notts., 21 January 1906
Career: Sutton Junction (c/s 1924), Shirebrook (c/s 1926), Sutton Junction (Mar 1927), Blackpool (£125 - May 1927), Nelson (Mar 1928), Portsmouth (Aug 1928), Merthyr Town (Jun 1929), Norwich City (May 1930), TOWN (Aug 1932), Sutton Town (c/s 1936).

"Wilf" Slack, as he was known, was a left winger until Town converted him into an attacking wing half part way through his first season at Field Mill. He did not taste senior football until he reached Penydarren Park, where he was an ever present during 1929-30, followed by a couple of seasons at Rosary Road. Contemporary reports quoted him as "a keen tackler and good wing feeder" and after four good campaigns with the "Stags", he finished his career with Sutton Town. Still playing football during the war years when he served in the Army, he appeared in the Western Command team v the R A F at Molineux as late as February 1944. A cricketer during the Summer months for New Hucknall Colliery, Slack played his first and last matches for Mansfield at outside left.

1932-33	25 apps	0 gls	
1933-34	42 "	1 "	
1934-35	31 "	0 "	
1935-36	22 "	0 "	

SMALL Thomas

1931 - 32 Outside Right
Career: Aston Villa, TOWN (c/s 1931), Scarborough

1931-32	2 apps	0 gls

SMALLEY (Mark) Anthony

1989 - 91 Defender   5' 11"   11st 6lb
b: Newark on Trent, Notts., 2 January 1965
Career: Nottingham Forest (Jun 1981 - appr, Jan 1983 - pro), Birmingham (Mar 1986 - loan), Bristol Rovers (Aug 1986 - loan), Leyton Orient (Feb 1987 - loan, Mar 1987 - permanent), TOWN (Nov 1989 - loan, £15,000 Jan 1990 - permanent), Maidstone United (F.T. May 1991), Kettering Town (Aug 1992), Erith & Belvedere (Jan 1993), Sutton Town (c/s 1993 - player coach), Shepshed Dynamos (c/s 1994 - player coach), Hucknall Town (Feb 1995 - player coach).

East Nottinghashire born player who started as an apprentice with Forest and after a number of loan spells, reached Town via Leyton Orient. Was on the books of Maidstone at the time of that club's demise and is still playing and coaching in minor football in the East Midlands.   Holds the unique record of being the first Bristol Rovers player to score a goal at the club's newly adopted ground of Twerton Park in Aug 1986 - in a friendly against their hosts, Bath City.   His parents were obviously devotees of the Bard from their choice of names for their son.

1989-90	28(0) apps	1 gl	
1990-91	21(0) "	1 "	

Honours: England Youth International (Nottingham Forest)

SMALLEY R M

1926 - 27 Wing Half Back
Career: TOWN (1926 - am)

1926-27   19 apps   0 gls   Midland Combination
Honours: Midland Combination Cup Winners, Notts F A Senior Cup Winners, Notts Benevolent Bowl Winners, Mansfield Hospital Charity Cup Winners 1927 (all Mansfield)

SMALLEY Walter

1927 - 29 Wing Half Back   5' 9"   11st 0lbs (1928)
b: Spring 1911
Career: TOWN (c/s 1927 - am)

Wally Smalley was a mere 16 years old when he made his first senior appearance for the "Stags" on 3 September 1927 at home to Scarborough, but he didn't last the pace and faded from the scene the following season.

1927-28	7 apps	0 gls	Midland League	
1928-29	1 "	0 "	"	"

SMART J W

1920 - 23 Goalkeeper
Career: Welbeck Colliery, TOWN (c/s 1920)

1922-23   4 apps   0 gls   Midland League
Honours: Notts F A Senior Cup Winners 1923 (Mansfield)

SMEDLEY C

1924 - 25 Outside Left
Career: Newthorpe, TOWN (Feb 1925 - am)

1924-25   4 apps   0 gls   Midland League

SMITH Abraham

1928 - 30 Inside Forward
b: Mansfield, 17 December 1910
Career: Carter Lane School (1925), TOWN (c/s 1927 - am, May 1929 - pro), Portsmouth (May 1930)

Another schoolboy "wonder", Abe Smith's career really took off when he was signed by Portsmouth and he served them faithfully not only up to, but during the war too, playing mainly as a wing half for them.   Served in the Royal Navy during hostilities and made a few "guest" appearances for Everton when he was stationed in the Liverpool area for a time.   Had retired by the war's end. Unfortunately for him, was only 12th man when Portsmouth beat Wolves in the Cup Final at Wembley in 1939.

1928-29	4 apps	0 gls	Midland League	
1929-30	6 "	3 "	"	"

Honours: Mansfield Hospital Charity Cup Winners 1930 (Mansfield)

SMITH Frank (David)

1955 - 57 Outside Right   5' 7"   10st 8lbs
b: Holymoorside, Derbys., 27 July 1936
Career: Chesterfield (1951 - juniors, Sep 1953 - pro), Boston (c/s 1954), TOWN (Aug 1955), Derby County (July 1957), Coventry City (Nov 1957), Kidderminster Harriers (Aug 1959).

Only 19 when he joined Mansfield, Dave Smith had already been with two professional clubs. A reserve in his first season, he shared the right wing berth with Bobby Anderson and Fred Morris in his second.

1955-56	8 apps	0 gls
1956-57	23 "	4 "

SMITH G
1919 - 21 Goalkeeper
Career: TOWN (c/s 1919 - am)

1920-21	1 app	0 gls	Central Alliance

SMITH J
1936 - 38 Right Full/Half Back   5' 8"   11st 8lbs
Career: Warsop Vale, TOWN (c/s 1936 - am, May 1937 - pro)

Local player who made one appearance in the County Cup for the club in October 1937.

SMITH James S
1920 - 21 Centre/Wing Half Back
Career: Hucknall Byron, Ilkeston United, TOWN (c/s 1920)

1920-21	11 apps	2 gls	Central Alliance

SMITH John H
1921 - 22 Inside Right
Career: Clifton Colliery, TOWN (c/s 1921), Welbeck Colliery (c/s 1922), Sutton Junction

Jack Smith started off the season as first choice, but lost his place when Bob Mite was signed from Rotherham Town.

1921-22	9 apps	3 gls	Midland League

SMITH Leslie
1945 - 48 Wing Half Back   5' 10"   11st 0lbs
b: Tamworth, Staffs., 16 November 1921
d: January 1993
Career: Nottingham Forest (am), Bilsthorpe Colliery, TOWN (Aug 1945), Ilkeston Town (c/s 1948)

"Snowy" Smith, so named because of his fair hair, was a vigorous hard working half back who never gave up trying - he had what would be termed today, commitment. First played for Town during the last war.

WW II	43 apps	0 gls	
1946-47	28 "	0 "	
1947-48	10 "	0 "	

SMITH (Mark) Alexander
1991 Right Winger   5' 9"   10st 8lbs
b: Bellshill, Lanarkshire, 16 December 1964
Career: St Mirren (juniors), Queens Park (Dec 1983), Celtic (Jun 1986), Dunfermline Athletic (Oct 1987), Hamilton Accademicals (Sep 1989 - loan), Stoke City (Feb 1990 - loan), Nottingham Forest (£75,000 - Mar 1990), Reading (Dec 1990 - loan), TOWN (Mar 1991 - loan), Shrewsbury Town (Aug 1991 - loan, £25,000 - Sep 1991 - permanent).

A lightly built winger, born in the same village as Hughie Gallacher, Mark Smith moved around the Scottish scene without really settling anywhere. Brian Clough paid a sizeable sum to bring him to Nottingham, but he languished in the reserves there apart from loan spells and never got a first team outing. He appears to be more settled at Gay Meadow, having now spent four years there.

1990-91	6(1) apps	0 gls	(Loan)

SMITH Richard F
1987 Defender   5' 7"   10st 7lbs (1985)
b: Reading, 22 October 1967
Career: Wolverhampton Wanderers (1984 - appr, July 1985 - pro), Moor Green (c/s 1986), TOWN (Mar 1987).

1986-87	1(1) apps	0 gls

SMITH Terence V
1959 - 61 Half Back   5' 10"   11st 0lbs
b: Rainworth, Mansfield, 10 July 1942
Career: Woodland Imps, TOWN (1959 - am, Apr 1960 - pro)

Terry Smith was another local youngster who was only just 18 when he was "blooded" by Raich Carter in the senior team.

1960-61	8 apps	0 gls

SMITH Thomas
1915 - 30 Left Full Back   5' 8"   11st 2lbs (1924)
b: Mansfield, c1896
Career: TOWN (1915)

Tom Smith must be a strong contender for the title of most faithful servant to his club. He was connected with Mansfield Town as a player for 16 years and in other capacities for longer than that. Joining the club as an 18 year old during WW I, he turned out for them until 1930. He could not claim to have always been a first team regular, but his allegiance to Mansfield Town never faltered. In 1925 when it was considered his playing days were numbered, he was appointed Reserve Team Coach, but such was his resilience, that he came back strongly the following season and made 34 appearances in the first XI. A great club servant.

1915-16	N.K.apps		3 gls		Central Alliance	
1919-20	30	"	0	"	"	"
1920-21	21	"	0	"	"	"
1921-22	39	"	1	"	Midland League	
1922-23	0	"	0	"	"	"
1923-24	4	"	0	"	"	"
1924-25	6	"	0	"	"	"
1925-26	10	"	0	"	"	"
1926-27	34	"	0	"	Midland Comb.	
1927-28	24	"	0	"	Midland League	

Honours: Central Alliance - Subsidiary Competition Championship 1916, Central Alliance runners up 1921, Championship 1920. Mansfield Hospital Charity Cup Winners 1922 & 1927, Notts F A Senior Cup Winners 1926 & 1927, Midland Combination runners up 1927, Midland Combination Cup Winners 1927, Notts Benevolent Bowl Winners 1927 (all Mansfield).

SOMERFIELD (Alfred) George

1938 - 39 Outside Right/Centre Forward   5' 10"   10st 5lbs
b: South Kirkby, South Yorks., 22 March 1918
Career: Milnthorpe W M C, Frickley Colliery, TOWN (May 1938), Wolverhampton Wanderers (exch Flowers + £500), Wrexham (Jun 1947), Crystal Palace (Sep 1947).

Alf Somerfield was signed from Midland League side, Frickley Colliery at the same time as Ossie Collier. Originally signed as a right winger, he was tried out leading the attack and scored a hat trick on his debut in the County Cup semi final v Notts County in October 1938. After only 14 League matches, Wolves' Major Buckley was sufficiently impressed to part with his talented inside forward Ivan Flowers plus cash, to take him to Molineux - but the war was looming before he got a chance there. His best years were probably during the war when he was in demand and was a "guest" player with Doncaster, Crystal Palace, Millwall, Notts County, Queens Park Rangers, Clapton Orient, Aldershot, Ipswich and Reading, in addition to the "Stags".

1938-39	14 apps	6 gls
WW II	3 "	2 "

Honours: Notts F A County Cup Winners 1939 (Mansfield)

SPEED Frederick

1936 - 39 Wing Half/Full Back   5' 8"   12st 0lbs (1936)
b: Newcastle on Tyne, 1909
Career: Linolnshire Juniors, Newark Town (c/s 1930), Hull City (Feb 1931), York City (July 1934), TOWN (Jun 1936), Exeter City (F.T. July 1939)

Although born in the North East, Freddie Speed's father moved down to Lincolnshire in search of work when he was a child. He was originally a centre forward, but was converted into a defender during his later days at York and it was in this capacity that he joined the "Stags". His sliding tackle was renowned and effective and he usually got the ball, even if the tackle started many yards away - if he was playing today he would no doubt receive a red card every time, but he was never sent off and only once is it recorded that the referee spoke to him about it - on that occasion he missed the ball by a considerable distance! He played in one match for Mansfield as a "guest" in 1939-40 season.

1936-37	34 apps	0 gls
1937-38	39 "	5 "
1938-39	27 "	0 "
WW II	1 "	0 "

Honours: Division 3 North Championship 1933 (Hull). Notts F A County Cup Winners 1938 & 1939 (both Mansfield)

SPENCER A

1926 - 27 Left Half Back
Career: TOWN (1926 - am).

Only first XI appearance was in the Byron Cup winning team.

Honours: Byron Cup Winners 1927 (Mansfield).

SPOONER (Stephen) Alan

1991 - 93 Midfield   5' 11"   12st 0lbs (1989)
b: Sutton, Surrey, 25 January 1961
Career: Derby County (1977 - appr, Dec 1978 - pro), Halifax Town (Dec 1981 - loan, F.T. Jan 1982 - permanent), Chesterfield (F.T. July 1983), Hereford United (£7,000 - Aug 1986), York City (£29,000 - July 1988), Rotherham United (Pepper + £20,000 = £45,000 - July 1990), TOWN (exch Hathaway - Mar 1991), Blackpool (F.T. Feb 1993), Chesterfield (F.T. Oct 1993)

Steve Spooner played alongside Phil Stant with both Hereford and Mansfield, where they teamed up again. Past his best at Field Mill, he was nevertheless an important cog in the promotion machinery during the run in at the end of the 1991-92 season.

1990-91	12(0) apps	0 gls
1991-92	31(0) "	2 "
1992-93	12(3) "	0 "

Honours: Division 4 Championship 1985 (Chesterfield), Division 4 promotion 1992 (Mansfield)

STAINTON James K

1954 - 57 Full Back   6' 0"   11st 12lbs
b: Sheffield, 14 December 1931
Career: Bradford P A (Apr 1953), TOWN (Aug 1954)

Only a reserve at Park Avenue and with no senior experience there, Jim Stainton remained a part-time pro throughout his short career.

| 1955-56 | 3 apps | 0 gls |
| 1956-57 | 6 " | 0 " |

STAMPS John David

1937 - 38 Inside Left   5' 10"   11st 6lbs (1937)
b: Thrybergh, Nr Rotherham, 2 December 1918
d: Winshill, Burton on Trent, 15 November 1991
Career: Silverwood Colliery, TOWN (Oct 1937), New Brighton (F.T. Aug 1938), Derby County (£1,500 - Jan 1939), Shrewsbury Town (Dec 1953), Burton Albion (Aug 1954, June 1955 - player coach, June 1956 - general assistant, Oct 1956 - player again, May 1957 - asst manager, Nov 1957 - temporary manager, Nov 1958 - manager to Oct 1959)

Jackie Stamps is another one who slipped throught the net "and got away". After only one senior appearance, although he had netted fairly frequently in the reserves from inside left, Stamps was given a free transfer and joined up with the "Rakers" for 1938-39. They tried his weight and bustle at centre forward and the 6 goals in 13 games he knocked in for them was noted by George Jobey, a future Mansfield manager, who paid £1,500 to bring him to the Baseball Ground. There he had to wait until March for his opportunity and he took it with both feet, keeping his place to the end of the season and scoring 3 goals in 8 games. His reputation soared during the war and he returned to Derby in 1945 to win a medal in the first post war F A Cup Final, scoring 2 goals. During his time at Derby he scored a total of 126 goals including three 4s and four hat tricks and was leading scorer in 1949-50. He spent a lot of time with Burton Albion when his league career was over, ultimately becoming their manager. Sadly, in his later years he went totally blind, but he still attended the Baseball Ground and listened to the match commentary for the blind. During WW II he "guested" for Chesterfield, Rotherham, Norwich, Southampton, Fulham and Crystal Palace.

| 1937-38 | 1 app | 0 gls |

Honours: Notts County Cup Winners 1938 (Mansfield), F A Cup Winners 1946 (Derby)

STANIFORTH Christopher

1921 - 22, 1924, 1926 - 27, 1928 - 30 and 1931 - 32
Inside/Centre Forward   5' 11"   12st 0lbs (1928)
b: Carrington, Nottingham, 16 September 1897
d: Creswell or Clowne, Derbys., 24 December 1954
Career: Nottingham Schoolboys (1911-12), Notts County (1913 - am), Creswell Athletic (1915), Chesterfield Municipal (1919), Creswell Colliery, TOWN (Mar 1921), Oldham Athletic (£400 - May 1922), TOWN (May 1924), Notts County (£800 - Dec 1924), TOWN (May 1926), Notts County (£800 - May 1927), TOWN (Jun 1928), Shirebrook (Jun 1930 - player coach), Grantham (Apr 1931), TOWN (c/s 1931 - player coach), Sutton Town (Aug 1932), Worksop Town (Aug 1933), Creswell Colliery (c/s 1934 - player manager).

If Tom Smith can be considered to be one of the "Stags" greatest servants, then Chris Staniforth must surely be one of the club's greatest players - he was and still is, a legend. Just mention the name to anyone in the area born before 1920 and note the reaction it brings! He had a tremendous affection for Mansfield Town as is illustrated by the fact that he signed for the club on no less than 5 separate occasions. His goalscoring for the Stags was exceptional, scoring 109 in the league and 43 in in cup competitions, 152 in all, in only 160 matches! He scored goals in every Division of the Football League as well as many in non league competitions too. His overall tally with all his clubs was a staggering 226 in 320 outings. During the 1920s when locals asked fans leaving the match how Mansfield had got on, (remember that this was before the days of T V and Radio coverage, when one had to wait for the Sunday newspapers to discover the results,) it was always followed with, *"and how many did Staniforth score?"* He captained the club for many years including the famous "egg and milk" F A Cup team of 1928-29 which reached the 4th round before defying Arsenal at Highbury until the last 8 minutes. Perhaps, appropriately, he returned to Field Mill, scene of so many of his triumphs, for the team's inaugural season in the Football League. In 1995 he is still the club's leading overall goalscorer.

1920-21 6 apps 7 gls Central Alliance
1921-22 41 " 25 " Midland Lge. Lead.Scorer
1924-25 15 " 17 "   "   "
1926-27 36 " 30 " Midland Comb. "   "
1928-29 46 " 23 " Midland League
1929-30 8 "   5 "   "   "
1931-32 8 "   2 "
Honours: Nottingham Schoolboys. Midland League Championship 1920 (Chesterfield Municipal). Midland League Championship 1925 & 1929,

Mansfield Hospital Charity Cup Winners 1922 & 1927, Midland Combination runners up, Midland Combination Cup Winners, Notts F A Senior Cup Winners, Notts Benevolent Bowl Winners 1927 (all Mansfield). Derbyshire League Championship & Sutton Charity Cup Winners 1933 (both Sutton Town).

STANT Philip R

1991 - 92 and 1993 Centre Forward 6' 1"   12st 7lbs (1991)
b: Bolton, 13 October 1962
Career: Camberley (Army), Reading (Aug 1982 - N/C), Army - S A S (Mar 1983), Hereford United (Nov 1986), Notts County (£175,000 - July 1989), Blackpool (Sep 1990 - loan), Lincoln City (Nov 1990 - loan), Huddersfield Town (Jan 1991 - loan), Fulham (£60,000 - Feb 1991), TOWN (£50,000 - Aug 1991), Cardiff City (£80,000 + £20,000 if promoted - they were = £100,000 - Dec 1992), TOWN (July 1993 - loan), Bury (Jan 1995)

Strong powerful leader who scored some remarkable goals for the "Stags" during their promotion season, but did not do as well the following season. Cardiff forked out a big fee for him and he was in dispute with them over over financial matters and allowed to rejoin Town on loan, but he was recalled to Ninian Park when they had injury problems and did quite well for them subsequently. Moved to Bury mid way through the 1994-95 season to assist in their play off push. Leading scorer with 28 goals for Hereford in in 1988-89. Selected by the P F A for the Division 4 Representative Side in 1991-92. He and his family still live in in Nottingham. The "Stags" faithful nicknamed him "Phsyco".

1991-92   39(1) apps   26 gls   Leading Scorer
1992-93   17(0) "   6 "
1993-94   4(0) "   1 "   (Loan)

Honours: Division 4 promotion 1992 (Mansfield), Division 3 Championship & Welsh Cup Winners 1993, Welsh Cup runners up 1994 (all Cardiff).

STANTON Thomas

1967 - 68 Wing Half
b: Glasgow, 3 May 1948
Career: Liverpool (1964 - juniors, May 1965 - pro), Arsenal (Sept 1966), TOWN (Sep 1967), Bristol Rovers (July 1968)

After being rejected by both Liverpool and Arsenal, Tommy Stanton did well in his one season at Field Mill, before moving to Eastville where he enjoyed 8 very good years.

1967-68   37(0) apps   1 gl
Honours: Scottish Schoolboy International

STAPLES Arthur

1928 - 29 and 1930 - 32 Goalkeeper 5' 9"   12st 0lbs (1928)
b: Newstead, Notts., 4 February 1899
d: Redhill, Nottingham, 9 September 1965
Career: Hucknall Olympic (c/s 1920), Newstead (c/s 1923), Notts County (c/s 1925), Newark Town (c/s 1926), TOWN (c/s 1928), Bournemouth & Boscombe Athletic (c/s 1929), TOWN (c/s 1930)

Footballing wise, Arthur Staples will be best remembered for his brilliance between the sticks during the cup run of 1928-29, particularly against Arsenal when he was acclaimed by the national press for his heroics. Left for Bournemouth in 1929, but failed to get a senior game and returned to Field Mill after one season. He was more famous as the Notts C C C all rounder, who played in 353 matches for the County between 1924 and 1938. Was the younger brother of Sam Staples who was more famous even than Arthur. He played in Test Matches too.

1928-29	37 apps	0 gls	Midland League	
1930-31	38 "	0 "	"	"
1931-32	13 "	0 "		

Honours: Midland League Championship 1929, Notts F A Senior Cup Winners 1931 (both Mansfield)

STARK (Wayne) Robert

1990 - 95 Forward   6' 0"   11st 8lbs (1994)
b: Derby, 14 October 1976
Career: TOWN (1990 - assoc schoolboy, 1993 - appr, c/s 1994 - pro)

Made his senior debut for the "Stags", coming on as substitute v Walsall (a) on 7 May 1994, when he was only 17½. However he failed to capitalise on this opportunity and was released a year later, having managed only one more senior game - versus Crewe in the Autowindscreens Shield.

1993-94	0(1) apps	0 gls
1994-95	0(0) "	0 "

STATHAM Alwyn

1938 - 39 Wing Half Back
b: Mansfield Woodhouse, Notts, 1920
Career: Samuel Barlow School, Clipstone Schools (1933-34), Dukeries Schoolboys, Notts Schoolboys, Wolverhampton Wanderers (1937), TOWN (F.T. c/s 1938).

Outstanding schoolboy star, Alwyn Statham slipped through the net when he joined Wolves, but the Molineux club allowed him to leave after a year and he linked up with his home town club. Sadly, injury terminated a promising career.

1938-39   3 apps   0 gls
Honours: Dukeries Schoolboys, Nottinghamshire Schoolboys, England Schoolboy International.

STATHAM Terence

1956 - 60 Goalkeeper 5' 9"   10st 0lbs
b: Shirebrook, Derbys., 11 March 1940
Career: Huddersfield Town (am), TOWN (c/s 1956 - am, Mar 1957 - pro)

Given his first outing by manager Charlie Mitten when a month short of his 17th birthday and still an amateur.

1956-57	1 app	0 gls
1957-58	1 "	0 "
1958-59	20 "	0 "
1959-60	4 "	0 "

STEELE (Eric) Graham

1988 Goalkeeper 6' 0"   12st 9lbs (1987)
b: Newcastle on Tyne, 14 May 1954
Career: Newcastle United (am, July 1972 - pro), Peterborough United (Dec 1973 - loan, July 1974 - permanent), Brighton & Hove Albion (Feb 1977), Watford (Oct 1979), Cardiff City (Mar 1983 - loan), Derby County (July 1984), Southend United (Aug 1987), TOWN (Mar 1988 - loan), Notts County (Oct 1988), Wolverhampton Wanderers (Mar 1989), Derby County (July 1992 - goalkeeping coach), Wolverhampton Wanderers (Apr 1994 - goalkeeping coach), Manchester City (Jan 1995 - goalkeeping coach).

1987-88   5 apps   0 gls   (Loan)

Honours: England Schoolboy International. Division 3 promotion 1986, Division 2 Championship 1987 (both Derby)

STEELE (Frederick) Charles

1949 - 51 Centre Forward   5' 8½"   10st 12lbs (1949)
b: Hanley, Stoke on Trent, 6 May 1916
d: Stoke on Trent, 23 April 1976
Career: Schools football, Stoke City (c/s 1931 - am, Aug 1933 - pro), Downings Tileries (1933 - loan), TOWN (£1,000 - Aug 1949 - player manager), Port Vale (Dec 1951 - player manager, c/s 1953 - manager to 1957 & 1962 to 1965)

Freddie Steele was one of the finest centre forwards of the 1930s - Stanley Matthews himself rated him the best. His ability with his head was phenomenal and it must be doubtful if there was anyone better and many of his goals were scored through this medium, including the ones at Mansfield when he was clearly past his best, but still a force to be reckoned with. He got the "Stags" into their highest ever position in the old Third Division and they were very unlucky not to win the title and promotion that year. He also got them into the Fifth Round of the F A Cup, both feats their best up to that time. His 39 goals in 52 matches for Mansfield was no mean feat for a 36 year old. He was the uncle of Northamptonshire and England batsman, David Steele and during WW II 'guested" for Notts County, Leicester, Northampton, Sheffield United, Forest, Bradford P A, Doncaster, Leeds, Fulham, Arsenal and Swansea. Still holds the "Potters" individual goalscoring record with 33 in 1936-37.

1949-50	22 apps	18 gls	Leading Scorer
1950-51	18 "	14 "	
1951-52	12 "	7 "	

Honours: England International & Football League XI (both Stoke City), Division 3 North runners up 1951 (Mansfield)

STEELE Murray A

1919 - 20 Goalkeeper
b: Mansfield, c1890
Career: Mansfield Mechanics (Jan 1911), Notts County (c/s 1912), TOWN (Sep 1919)

By the time that Murray Steele signed for the "Stags" he was licencee of the White Hart Hotel in Church Street. In only his third match for Mansfield, a F A Cup tie versus Shirebrook, he dislocated his arm and never played again.

1919-20   1 app   0 gls   Central Alliance

STENSON John A

1969 - 72 Inside Right   5' 9"   11st 6lbs (1971)
b: Catford, London, 16 December 1949
Career: Charlton Athletic (1965 - appr, Dec 1966 - pro), TOWN (£5,000 - Jun 1969), Peterborough United (Jan 1972 - loan), Aldershot (F.T. July 1972)

Recommended to Mansfield by Jock Basford who had coached the young Stenson when he was with the "Addicks". Netted 21 goals for Town from 107 matches.

1969-70	39(1) apps	7 gls
1970-71	45(0) "	12 "
1971-72	19(3) "	2 "

Honours: England Schoolboys & Youth International. Notts F A County Cup Winners 1971 (Mansfield)

STIMPSON (George) Henry
1937 - 42 Full Back   5' 11"   12st 0lbs (1937)
b: Giltbrook, Notts., 1910
d: 1983
Career: Kimberley Amateurs, Notts County (c/s 1930), Rhyl (c/s 1934), Exeter City (c/s 1936), TOWN (May 1937), Giltbrook Villa (1942 - permit player)

George Stimpson was a strong tackling full back who was lectured by the referee on more than one occasion for his methods   - sendings off and suspensions sometimes accruing. Appointed captain at Field Mill, he retired due to injury early in the second wartime season.

1937-38	40 apps	0 gls
1938-39	42 "	0 "
1939-40	3 "	0 "
WW II	25 "	0 "

Honours: Division 3 South Championship 1931 (Notts Co). Notts F A County Cup Winners 1938 & 1939 (both Mansfield)

STIMPSON Thomas
1929 - 30   Centre Forward/Wing Half Back
b: Stanton Hill, Notts., c1910
Career: Sutton United, Shirebrook (Jan 1929), TOWN (c/s 1929)

A schoolteacher by profession, Tom Stimpson started his career as a bustling centre forward, but later converted to wing half.

| 1929-30 | 17 apps | 1 gl | Midland League |

Honours: Mansfield Hospital Charity Cup Winners 1930 (Mansfield)

STONE F
1926 - 27 Centre Forward
Career: TOWN (1926 - am)

Only senior appearance was in the Byron Cup Final. Honours: Byron Cup Winners 1927 (Mansfield).

STONE R
1919 - 20 Goalkeeper
Career: TOWN (1919)

Later associated with the management of Boston United in the early 1950s.

| 1919-20 | 2 apps | 0 gls |

STORER John Arthur
1931 - 32 Outside Right
b: Swinton, Nr Rotherham, 3 February 1908
Career: Mexborough, Barnsley (Jan 1929), Bristol Rovers (May 1931), TOWN (Feb 1932), Distillery (Aug 1932).

| 1931-32 | 13 apps | 1 gl |

STORER (Stuart) John
1983 - 84 Forward   5' 11"   11st 8lbs (1987)
b: Rugby, Warwicks., 16 January 1967
Career: Rugby Schools, Wolverhampton Wanderers (assoc schoolboy, Jun 1983 - appr), TOWN (Aug 1983 - appr), V S Rugby (Mar 1984 N/C), Birmingham City (Jun 1984 - appr, Jan 1985 - pro), Everton (£200,000 - p/exch deal - Mar 1987), Wigan Athletic (July 1987 - loan), Bolton Wanderers (Dec 1987 - loan, £25,000 - Jan 1988 permanent), Exeter City (£25,000 - Mar 1993), Brighton & Hove Albion (Mar 1995).

Young Stuart Storer was well under 17 years of age when Ian Greaves pitched him into the fray on his League debut in October 1983.

| 1983-84 | 0(1) apps | 0 gls |

Honours: Sherpa Van Trophy Winners 1989 (Bolton)

STRAW Raymond
1961 - 63 Centre Forward   6' 0"   12st 7lbs
b: Ilkeston, Derbys., 22 May 1933
Career: Ilkeston M W, Ilkeston Town (Aug 1951), Derby County (Oct 1951), Coventry City (Nov 1957), TOWN (£8,000 - Aug 1961), Lockheed Leamington (July 1963)

Ray Straw had to wait until Derby fell from grace in the First Division down to Division 3 North, before he gained a regular place in the senior team. He proved to be a revelation, scoring 37 goals in 1956-57, including three hat tricks and equalling Jackie Bowers record set up in 1931. He was equally effective at Highfield Road, but whilst the "Stags" paid a big fee to secure him, he was not as proficient at Field Mill as had been hoped.

| 1961-62 | 34 apps | 11 gls |
| 1962-63 | 11 " | 1 " |

Honours: Division 3 North Championship 1957 (Derby)

STREETS
1920 - 21 Centre Forward
Career: Leeds United (c/s 1920), TOWN (Nov 1920)

| 1920-21 | 1 app | 0 gls | Central Alliance |

STRINGFELLOW
1922 - 23 Full Back
Career: Sutton Junction (c/s 1920), Derby County (c/s 1921), TOWN (c/s 1922)

| 1922-23 | 9 apps | 0 gls | Midland League |

STRINGFELLOW Ian R
1985 - 94 Forward   5' 9"   10st 4lbs (1988)
b: Kirkby in Ashfield, Notts., 8 May 1969
Career: Babworth Rovers, TOWN (May 1985 - appr, Aug 1986 - pro), Blackpool (Sep 1992 - loan), Kettering Town (Nov 1992 - loan), Chesterfield (Dec 1993 - loan), Kettering Town (£5,000 - Feb 1994)

Another of Ian Greaves' young proteges, Ian Stringfellow had a good pedigree for a footballer as he was the nephew of former "Stags" star, Mike Stringfellow (see below). He was plunged in at the deep end in a League match in April 1986 at the tender age of 16 years 356 days and it seemed that the world was his oyster. Sadly, he never quite fulfilled this early promise and whilst he was always a good reliable player, he did not reach the starring role that was anticipated. When he had only just celebrated his 18th birthday, he played in the Freight Rover Trophy Final at Wembley, the youngest player yet to do so and scored in the penalty shoot out. However, he spent ten years with Mansfield before electing to move to Kettering and assist in their bid towards winning the Conference title and

election to the Football League. He was a substitute on 58 occasions whilst with the "Stags" which must surely be approaching a record!

1985-86	0 (3) apps	0 gls
1986-87	12(10) "	4 "
1987-88	22 (8) "	8 "
1988-89	0 (8) "	1 "
1989-90	17 (2) "	3 "
1990-91	15 (9) "	2 "
1991-92	7(10) "	2 "
1992-93	26 (4) "	5 "
1993-94	10 (4) "	3 "

Honours: Freight Rover Trophy Winners 1987, Notts F A County Cup Winners 1988, Division 4 promotion 1992 (all Mansfield)

STRINGFELLOW (Michael) David
1960 - 62 Outside Left   5' 10"   10st 7lbs (1960)
b: Nuncargate, Notts., 27 January 1943
Career: Mansfield Schoolboys (1957-58), TOWN (c/s 1958 - appr, Feb 1960 - pro), Leicester City (£25,000 - Jan 1962), Nuneaton Borough (1975)

Uncle of Ian Stringfellow (above), Mike Stringfellow was also a schoolboy star, but he went on from strength to strength and his potential was fully realised. He was pitchforked into the fray by Raich Carter on the same day as Ken Wagstaff, when he was 17½ years old and such was his progress that Leicester City paid out the record fee ever paid for an 18 year old when they signed him on 16 January 1962 for £25,000. His career with Leicester was outstanding, winning numerous honours during his 14 seasons there and even being leading scorer during 1967-68. Currently a newsagent in Alfreton. A truly great player.

| 1960-61 | 33 apps | 6 gls |
| 1961-62 | 24 " | 4 " |

Honours: Mansfield Schoolboys, F A Cup Finalists 1963, Football League Cup Winners 1964 & runners up 1965 (all Leicester)

STUBBINS Philip
1987 - 88 Midfield
b: Hull, 18 October 1962
Career: Bridlington Town, TOWN (1987)

Only senior appearance was v Scunthorpe United in the Freight Rover Trophy in January 1988

| 1987-88 | 0 apps | 0 gls |

SULLIVAN (Maurice) John

1939 - 40 Inside Forward   5' 9"   11st 0lbs (1939)
b: Newport, Mon., late 1915
Career: Ynysddu, Pontyminster United, Newport County (1936 - am, Apr 1937 - pro), Derby County (£500 - May 1938), TOWN (May 1939)

"Boy" Sullivan was a rising star as a youngster with Newport and joined the "Rams" together with Brinton, but the latter soon returned to South Wales and during the last pre war close season, Sullivan joined the "Stags". Played as a "guest" for Hull and Carlisle during WW II when not available for Mansfield.

1939-40	3 apps	0 gls
WW II	8 "	1 "

SUTTON James P

1970 - 71 Forward
b: Glasgow, 6 September 1949
Career: Newcastle United (Jun 1969), TOWN (Jun 1970)

1970-71   11(2) apps   0 gls

SUTTON (Stephen) John

1981 Goalkeeper 6' 0"   12st 12lbs (1987)
b: Hartington, Derbys., 16 April 1961
Career: Nottingham Forest (1977 - appr, Sep 1979 - pro), TOWN (Mar 1981 - loan), Derby County (Jan 1985 - loan), Coventry City (Feb 1991 - loan), Luton Town (Nov 1991 - loan), Derby County (£300,000 - Mar 1992)

Steve Sutton joined the "Reds" as a youngster a progressed through the ranks to the first team, consolidating his position for the best part of ten years at the City Ground until he was displaced by Mark Crossley in 1991. He was rescued from obsurity by Derby a year later and looked set for a new lease of life, when the up and coming Martin Taylor relegated him to the reserves once more. Taylor's unfortunate accident when he broke his leg gave Sutton yet another chance, which he took enthusiastically and his career now seems to be going from strength to strength. He is a keen member of the Thoresby Colliery Band and recently his wife's daughter, Amy has joined him in this venture.

1980-81   8 apps   0 gls   (Loan)
Honours: Football League Cup Winners 1989 & 1990 (both Forest)

SWEENEY Alfred Ernest

1939 Goalkeeper 6' 1"   11st 0lbs (1939)
b: London, 1921
Career: Fulham (trial), TOWN (Aug 1939)

Signed as cover for Biddlestone and Wright, Sweeney was released when war broke out and returned to London. Made a single appearance in the Jubilee Fund match v Walsall in August 1939.

1939-40   0 apps   0 gls

SWINSCOE Terence

1956 - 59 Forward/Defender   6' 1"   12st 7lbs
b: Shirebrook, Derbys., 31 August 1934
Career: Spalding United, Stockport County (Feb 1956), TOWN (Oct 1956 - month's trial, Nov 1956 - F.T. permanent), Ilkeston Town (c/s 1959)

After playing for 3 seasons with Ilkeston, Swinscoe successfully appealed against the club terminating his contract and went on to make over 300 appearances for the club up to 1968 Joined the "Stags" as a centre forward, but later played at full back and centre half.

1956-57	5 apps	0 gls
1957-58	6 "	0 "
1958-59	3 "	0 "

SYKES Alexander B

1992 - 94 Forward   5' 8"   11st 3lbs (1994)
b: Mansfield, 2 April 1974
Career: Westfields Hereford, TOWN (£2,000 - Jun 1992), Westfields Hereford.

George Foster had high hopes for this youngster when he brought him to Field Mill, but he failed to make the grade and was released, rejoining his former club.

1993-94   1(1) apps   1 gl
Honours: England Youth International (Westfields).

SYRETT David K

1977 - 79 Forward   5' 11"   11st 13lbs (1978)
b: Salisbury, Wilts., 20 January 1956
Career: Swindon Town (1972 - appr, Nov 1973 - pro), Wolverhampton Wanderers (Sep 1975 - loan), TOWN (£25,000 - Aug 1977), Walsall (£105,000 = Austin, valued at £30,000 + £75,000 - Mar 1979), Peterborough United (Aug 1979), Northampton Town (Jun 1982), Brackley (1984)

Signed by Peter Morris for Mansfield's first campaign in the Second Division, Dave Syrett struck up a successful partnership with Ernie Moss, but when the latter was injured the goalscoring dried up and the team slumped. His career was ended by a back injury at Brackley and he became a milkman in Towcester.

1977-78   42(0) apps   16 gls   Leading Scorer
1978-79   23(0)   "   4   "   "   "
Honours: England Youth International (Swindon).

TARRANT Brian L
1960 - 61 Inside Forward   5' 11"   11st 7lbs
b: Stainforth, Leeds, 22 July 1938
Career: Leeds United (juniors, pro - Aug 1955), TOWN (F.T. July 1960)

1960-61   3 apps   0 gls

TAYLOR Charles
1926 - 27 Inside Left
Career: North Anston, TOWN (1926)

1926-27   1 app   3 apps   Midland Combination
Honours: Byron Cup Winners 1927 (Mansfield).

TAYLOR John
1957 - 60 Centre Forward   5' 10"   11st 7lbs
b: Creswell, Derbys., 11 January 1939
Career: Mastin Moor Derbys., Chesterfield (c/s 1956 - am), TOWN (May 1957), Peterborough United (July 1960)

1959-60   5 apps   2 gls

TAYLOR Paul
1983 - 84 Left Full Back
b: Leith, 20 December 1966
Career: Scottish Juniors, TOWN (1983 - N/C)

1983-84   3(0) apps   0 gls

TAYLOR (Samuel) James
1925 - 26 Centre/Inside Forward 5' 8½" 11st 9lbs (1925)
b: Sheffield, 17 September 1893
d: Sheffield, March 1973
Career: Atlas & Norfolk Steelworks, Silverwood Colliery, Huddersfield Town (Mar 1913), The Wednesday (£2,500 - Jan 1921), TOWN (May 1925), Southampton (£950 - Jun 1926), Halifax Town (Jun 1928), Grantham (Jan 1929), Chesterfield (May 1929), Llanelli (c/s 1931), Grantham (c/s 1933).

Brilliant leader of the "Stags" attack during 1925-26, Sammy Taylor started his career before the first World War as a 19 year old with the "Terriers" and led their attack in the 1920 F A Cup Final when they lost 1-0 to Aston Villa at Stamford Bridge. The following year he was transferred to the Wednesday for a sizable sum and led their line for 4 years until he rejected their terms in 1925 and was transfer listed at £1,000 - so he joined Mansfield, where he netted 28 goals in the Midland League. Next summer he was signed by Southampton for £950 of which Wednesday received only £300, Mansfield getting the remainder. He stayed there for two seasons and finished his career mainly in the Third Division, but was still scoring goals up to retirement at the age of 41! WW I guest player for Rotherham County and Bradford P A.

1925-26 34 apps 28 gls Midland League Lead.Scorer
Honours: F A Cup runners up 1920 (Huddersfield). Midland League runners up & Notts F A Senior Cup Winners 1926 (both Mansfield).

TAYLOR (Steven) Jeffrey
1979 - 80 Forward   5' 10"   10st 8lbs (1980)
b: Royton, Lancs., 18 October 1955
Career: Bolton Wanderers (July 1971 - appr, July 1974 - pro), Port Vale (Oct 1975 - loan), Oldham Athletic (£38,000 - Oct 1977), Luton Town (£75,000 - Jan 1979), TOWN (£75,000 - July 1979, makeweight in Mick Saxby deal), Burnley (£35,000 - July 1980), Wigan Athletic (Aug 1983), Stockport County (Mar 1984), Rochdale (Nov 1984), Preston North End (Oct 1986), Burnley (Aug 1987), Rochdale (Feb 1989 - loan, Mar 1989 - permanent).

Came to the "Stags" + £150,000 when Mick Saxby joined the "Hatters", which at Luton's valuation of £75,000 was Mansfield's record signing up to this time. He was allowed to join Burnley at a substantial financial loss after only one season.

1979-80   30(7) apps   7 gls

TAYLOR William

1923 - 24 and 1925 Inside Forward
b: Co Durham, c1899
Career: Crook Town (1918), The Wednesday (c/s 1919), Doncaster Rovers (c/s 1922), TOWN (c/s 1923), Mexborough

(July 1924), TOWN (Feb 1925), Doncaster Rovers (c/s 1925), Mexborough (c/s 1927), Worksop Town (Jan 1928)

Grafting inside forward who had played First Division football with Wednesday, Billy Taylor provided much of the guile in the "Stags" attack during the championship campaign of 1923-24. He moved on the following season, but returned briefly to be involved in another title winning run.

1923-24   36 apps   18 gls   Midland League
1924-25   11 "   2 "   "   "
Honours: Midland League Championship 1924 & 1925 (both Mansfield)

THOMAS (Barrie) Ernest B

1957 - 59 Centre Forward   5' 9"   11st 0lbs
b: Measham, Leics., 19 May 1937
Career: Measham Imperial, Leicester City (July 1954), TOWN (F.T. Jun 1957), Scunthorpe United (£15,000 - Sep 1959), Newcastle United (£45,000 - Jan 1962), Scunthorpe United (£20,000 - Nov 1964), Barnsley (Nov 1966), Measham Swifts (May 1968 - manager).

Subsequent clubs made nice profits out of a player who initially joined Mansfield on a free transfer. Barrie Thomas was a natural goalscorer and netted over 200 in his career. His most fruitful period was probably at the Old Show Ground where he played Second Division football and his spell at St James's Park was marred by injuries. He was leading scorer in each of the two seasons he spent at Field Mill. Returned to his native Leicestershire upon retirement and managed a club in the Leicesterhire Senior League. Still Scunthorpe's record goalscorer with 31 in 1961-62.

1957-58   32 apps   23 gls   Leading Scorer
1958-59   34 "   21 "   "   "
1959-60   6 "   4 "
Honours: England Youth International (Leicester).

THOMAS John C

1958 - 59 Full Back 5' 10"   11st 7lbs
b: West Houghton, Lancs., 22 September 1932
Career: Wath Wanderers, Wolverhampton Wanderers (Aug 1951), Barnsley (Jun 1952), TOWN (£1,750 - Mar 1958), Chesterfield (July 1959)

Speedy full back signed as cover when Colin Toon was injured.

1957-58   13 apps   0 gls
1958-59   28 "   0 "

THOMPSON (David) Stanley

1970 - 73 Outside Right   5' 7"   10st 7lbs (1972)
b: Catterick Camp, North Yorks., 12 March 1945
Career: Otley Schools, Yorkshire Schools, Dawson, Paine & Elliott F C, Wolverhampton Wanderers (Apr 1962), Southampton (£7,500 - Aug 1966), TOWN (£6,000 - Oct 1970), Chesterfield (£5,000 - Dec 1973)

David Thompson was born at the well known Army camp in North Yorkshire where his father was stationed shortly before the end of the war. Gave the "Stags" very good service for three years, before moving to Chesterfield in a controversial manner. He returned to the family farm at Otley upon retirement and is still there.

1970-71   34(0) apps   8 gls
1971-72   40(0) "   4 "
1972-73   38(2) "   8 "
1973-74   17(0) "   1 "
Honours: Notts F A County Cup Winners 1971 & 1972 (both Mansfield)

THOMPSON G Brian

1979 - 80 Full Back 5' 10"   10st 12lbs (1980)
b: Ashington, Co Durham, 7 August 1952
Career: Sunderland (Jun 1971), York City (Mar 1973 - loan), Yeovil Town, Maidstone United, TOWN (Nov 1979)

1979-80   9(0) apps   0 gls
Honours: England semi professional International (Yeovil & Maidstone)

THOMSON Brian L

1979 - 82 Forward   5' 8"   10st 2lbs (1980)
b: Paisley, 1 March 1959
Career: Morecombe, West Ham United (Jan 1977), TOWN (Aug 1979), Kings Lynn (c/s 1982)

Rendered Mansfield useful service during 2½ seasons here.

1979-80   5(3) apps   0 gls
1980-81   24(2) "   1 "
1981-82   25(4) "   0 "

THORPE Adrian

1982 - 83 Forward   5' 7¾"   11st 6lbs
b: Chesterfield, 20 November 1963
Career: TOWN (Aug 1982 - N/C), Heanor Town (c/s 1983), Bradford City (Aug 1985), Tranmere Rovers (Nov 1986 - loan), Notts County (Nov 1987), Walsall (Aug 1989), Northampton Town (Mar 1990), Instant Dict Hong Kong, Kettering Town (c/s 1993), Arnold Town (c/s 1994)

After his League career was over, he played in local semi-pro football and joined the fire service.

1982-83	0(2) apps	1 gl

THORPE Leonard
1945 - 47 Inside Forward
b: Warsop, Notts., 7 June 1924
Career: Nottingham Forest (am), TOWN (Aug 1945), Grantham (1950).

WW II	17 apps	2 gls
1946-47	5 "	0 "

TIMONS (Christopher) Bryan
1988 onwards Defender 5' 10"   11st 2lbs
b: Mansfield, 8 December 1974
Career: Clipstone Welfare, TOWN (1988 - assoc. sch., 1990 - appr, May 1993 - N/C, pro - May 1994), Stafford Rangers (Mar 1995 - loan).

Opportunities have been few for this young central defender, but his time may well come in the future.

1993-94	15(1) apps	1 gls
1994-95	4(2) "	0 "

TODD Robert C
1968 - 69 Winger
b: Goole, East Yorks., 11 September 1949
Career: Scunthorpe United (appr), Liverpool (July 1967), Rotherham United (Mar 1968), TOWN (Nov 1968), Workington (July 1969)

1968-69	3(1) apps	0 gls

TODD Samuel J
1974 Wing Half Back
b: Belfast, 22 September 1945
Career: Glentoran, Burnley (Sep 1962), Sheffield Wednesday (May 1970), TOWN (Feb 1974 - loan), Great Harwood (May 1974)

1973-74	6(0) apps	0 gls	(Loan)

Honours: Northern Ireland International (Burnley & Sheffield Wednesday), Northern Ireland under 23 International (Burnley)

TOMLINSON
1921 - 22 Centre Forward
Career: TOWN (1921)

1921-22	2 apps	1 gl Midland League

TONES John D
1974 Centre Half Back
b: Silkworth, South Yorks., 3 December 1950
Career: Sunderland Schoolboys, Sunderland (1966 - appr, May 1968 - pro), Arsenal (F.T. May 1973), Swansea City (Sep 1974 - loan), TOWN (Oct 1974 - loan)

1974-75	3(0) apps	0 gls	(Loan)

TOON Colin
1956 - 66 Full Back 5' 9"   10st 7lbs
b: New Houghton, Derbys., 26 April 1940
Career: New Houghton, TOWN (c/s 1956 - am, July 1957 - pro).

A very young starter, Colin Toon came from a mining family and first signed for the "Stags" as an amateur in 1956, when he was just 16, becoming a pro the following year. An outstanding full back he soon secured a first team place and kept it, apart from injuries for nine seasons, in all, making 214 League appearances for the club. He had the misfortune to break a leg in October 1963 which kept him out of action for a whole year, but he returned as effective as ever. After his playing days were over, he joined a supermarket chain, eventually rising to be a warehouse supervisor. He is a cousin by marriage to the author.

1957-58	7 apps	0 gls
1958-59	17 "	0 "
1959-60	19 "	0 "
1960-61	42 "	0 "
1961-62	44 "	0 "
1962-63	42 "	1 "
1963-64	16 "	0 "
1964-65	17 "	0 "
1965-66	9 "	0 "

Honours: Division 4 promotion 1963, Division 3 - 3rd 1965 (both Mansfield)

TREHARNE Colin
1960 - 66 Goalkeeper 5' 10"   12st 0lbs (1960)
b: Bridgend, Glamorgan, 30 July 1937
Career: Army RAOC, TOWN (am, Dec 1960 - pro), Lincoln City (July 1966), Ilkeston Town (c/s 1967), Heanor Town (1970), Boston (c/s 1971), Worksop Town (c/s 1972), Ashby Institute Scunthorpe (1976 - manager), Hykeham United (1981 - manager).

Signed by Mansfield from local Army football when Treharne was doing his National Service in the area. He provided a very safe pair of hands and was highly rated by the Field Mill faithful. Managed a Scunthorpe amateur side for a time after retirement and is now living in North Hykeham on the outskirts of Lincoln, engaged in the frozen food business.

1961-62	32 apps	0 gls
1962-63	46 "	0 "
1963-64	46 "	0 "
1964-65	38 "	0 "
1965-66	29 "	0 "

Honours: Division 4 promotion 1963 & Division 3 - 3rd 1965 (both Mansfield)

TREMELLING Elijah (Solomon)
1915 - 16 and 1919 - 21 Centre Forward/Centre Half
b: Newhall, Derbys., 1885
Career: Newhall Swifts, Derby County (Nov 1905), Burton United (1909), Ilkeston United (Nov 1909), Gresley Rovers (1911), Shirebrook Forest (1912), Bradford City (Mar 1913), TOWN (1915), Gresley Rovers (Oct 1922)

Sol Tremelling was the eldest of four brothers who played football professionally and three of them played in the First Division - Sol with Derby, Dan with Birmingham and Billy with Blackpool and Preston. All of them played for the "Stags" at various times, but Sol was with the club longer than any of his brothers - 7 years in all, which included the war years when the club closed down and during this period, he "guested" with Chesterfield Town and Shirebrook. He was a centre forward in the earlier days of his career, but played mainly for Mansfield at half back.

1915-16	N.K. apps	0 gls	Central	Alliance
1919-20	29 "	1 "	"	"
1920-21	30 "	2 "	"	"

Honours: Central Alliance - Subsidiary Competition Championship 1916, Central Alliance Championship 1920, runners up 1921 (all Mansfield).

TREMELLING Josiah Jeremiah ("Jack")
1919 - 20 Centre Forward
b: Newhall, Derbys., c1899
Career: TOWN (c/s 1919), Worksop Town (c/s 1920), Staveley Town (c/s 1929).

The Tremelling parents obviously had a great liking for biblical names for their children, Daniel and Reuben also featuring! J J was always known as "Jack" and he spent several seasons with the "Tigers" after leaving Field Mill.

1919-20	23 apps	18 gls	Central Alliance

Honours: Central Alliance Championship 1920 (Mansfield), Midland League Championship 1922 (Worksop).

TREMELLING (William) Reuben
1921 - 22 Inside Forward/Centre Half 5' 8" 12st 11lbs (1935)
b: Newhall, Derbys., c1901
d: 1954.
Career: Shirebrook Foresters (1918), Shirebrook (c/s 1919), Kirkby Colliery (c/s 1920), TOWN (c/s 1921), Welbeck Colliery (c/s 1922), Retford Town (c/s 1923), Worksop Town (Jan 1924), Blackpool (c/s 1924), Preston North End (Dec 1930), Blackpool (Jan 1938 - coach).

Other than Dan, Billy was the most famous of the Tremelling brothers and as a rather wild and erratic centre forward had many clubs before reaching the "Seasiders". His career did not really take off until, in an emergency, he was tried at centre half - becoming an instant success, so much so that he played in the 1937 F A Cup Final when Preston were beaten by Sunderland 3-1. Playing in the same match were Joe Beresford (Preston) and Raich Carter (Sunderland), both having associations with the "Stags"

1921-22   2 apps   0 gls   Midland League
Honours: Division 2 Championship 1930
(Blackpool). F A Cup runners up 1937 (Preston).

TRINDER (Jason) Lee
1994 onwards Goalkeeper 6' 1"   12st 4lbs (1994)
b: Leicester, 3 March 1970
Career: TOWN (1985 - Youth), Notts County (1986 - Youth),
Friar Lane Leicester, Leicester United, Oadby Town, Grimsby
Town (Aug 1994 - trial N/C), TOWN (Nov 1994 - loan, Dec
1994 - permanent)

A former fork lift truck salesman, Jason Trinder
came to Field Mill in a deal that took Jason Pearcey
to the "Mariners". He was soon in first team action
and had the unusual and perhaps unique experience
of being substituted for the injured Darren Ward on
two occasions in three weeks - both at half time!

1994-95   4(3) apps   0 gls

TROTMAN (Reginald) Wilfred
1930 - 31 Inside Left
b: Bristol, Aug 1906
d: Bath, 5 January 1970
Career: Kingswood A F C, Bristol Rovers (1927), Rochdale (Aug
1928), Sheffield Wednesday (Jan 1929), Worksop Town (Mar
1930), TOWN (May 1930), Dartford (Aug 1931), Bath City (May
1932), Bristol St Georges (Aug 1934), Trowbridge Town (Aug
1934)

Inside forward who had experienced Third Division
football, but was only a reserve at Hillsborough.
After a lean spell initially at Mansfield, he recovered
his place and finished strongly at the season's end.

1930-31   23 apps   6 gls   Midland League
Honours: Notts F A Senior Cup Winners 1931
(Mansfield)

TURNER John A K
1937 - 39 Outside Right   5' 8"   10st 7lbs (1938)
b: Worksop, c1914
Career: Northern Rubber Works Retford, Leeds United (Oct
1935), TOWN (£150 - Dec 1937), Bristol City (£250 - May
1939)

When playing in local football, Jack Turner was
signed by Leeds United in 1935, but only managed
a handful of games for their first XI before joining
the "Stags" for a modest fee in 1937. He did well
at Mansfield for two years, before joining Bristol
City just before the outbreak of war, playing in all
three of their league games in the aborted 1939-40
season. Played a few games for the Field Mill club
as a "guest" during W W II.

1937-38   24 apps   5 gls
1938-39   34   "   4   "
WW II   3   "   0   "
Honours: Notts F A County Cup Winners 1939
(Mansfield)

TYRER Alan
1963 - 65 Inside/Wing Forward   5' 7"   10st 2lbs
b: Liverpool, 8 December 1942
Career: Everton (Juniors, Dec 1959 - pro), TOWN (£2,500 - July
1963), Arsenal (F.T. Aug 1965), Bury (Aug 1967), Workington
(July 1968)

This small and slightly built forward made 9 First
Division appearances for Everton prior to joining
Mansfield who he helped to achieve 3rd place in the
Third Division in 1965. Had his best period at
Borough Park, where he played in well over over
200 games for the Cumbrian side in six years,
before retiring in 1974.

1963-64   23 apps   4 gls
1964-65   18   "   1   "
Honours: Division 3 - 3rd 1965 (Mansfield).

UPHILL Edward (Dennis)
1957 - 59 Inside Forward   5' 9"   11st 10lbs (1957)
b: Bath, 11 August 1931
Career: Peasedown Colliery, Tottenham Hotspur (Mar 1948 - am),
Finchley (Aug 1948 - am), Tottenham Hotspur (Sep 1949 - pro),
Reading (Feb 1953), Coventry City (Oct 1955), TOWN (Mar
1957), Watford (Jun 1959), Crystal Palace (Oct 1960), Rugby
Town (c/s 1963), Romford, Dartford (Feb 1964)

Only a reserve at Spurs to Eddie Baily and Les
Bennett, Dennis Uphill nevertheless managed 6
games in the first XI whilst at White Hart Lane.
His career took off however at Reading, where he
went as makeweight in the deal that took Johnny
Brooks to Spurs, where he made nearly 100
appearances, scoring over 40 goals. His scoring
prowess continued with all his other clubs and he
finished up with 147 League goals in 344 outings,
more than acceptable by modern standards.

1956-57   13 apps   6 gls
1957-58   26   "   13 "
1958-59   44   "   19 "

UZELAC Stefan
1976   Full Back 5' 11"   11st 4lbs (1978)
b: Doncaster, 12 March 1953
Career: Doncaster Rovers (Juniors, Jun 1971 - pro), TOWN (Feb
1976 - loan), Preston North End (May 1977), Stockport County
(Mar 1980)

1975-76   2(0) apps   0 gls   (Loan)

VAUX Edward

1936 - 38 Right Full Back   5' 10½"   12st 4lbs (1936)
b: Goole, East Yorks., 1914
Career: Thorne Colliery (1932), Goole Town (1933), Doncaster Rovers (c/s 1934), TOWN (c/s 1936), Chelsea (F.T. May 1938), Peterborough & Fletton United (c/s 1949)

Ted Vaux was recruited from the Rovers reserves and never attained the first team at Belle Vue. At Mansfield he took over when Frank Perfect went to Wolves and held his place until the end of the season. Next term he lost out to the more experienced new recruit George Stimpson and was released in April 1938, whereupon Chelsea signed him and he did quite well in their London Combination side until the outbreak of war. During hostilities, he was a "guest" player for Clapton Orient, Southampton, Doncaster and Hull, apart from turning out for the "Pensioners" occasionally. He is the grandfather of Gavin Worboys (Doncaster & Notts County).

1936-37	26 apps	0 gls
1937-38	3 "	0 "

Honours: South Yorkshire Schoolboys.

VAUGHAN Terence R

1957 - 59 Inside Forward   5' 10"   12st 0lbs
b: Ebbw Vale, South Wales, 22 April 1938
Career: Ollerton Colliery, TOWN (Jun 1957 - am, Sep 1957 - pro)

Terry Vaughan's father moved from South Wales to Ollerton to work locally - hence his Welsh eligibility.

1958-59	6 apps	2 gls

VICKERS Samuel

1930 - 31 Outside Left
Career: TOWN (c/s 1930)

1930-31	2 apps	0 gls Midland League

VILLIERS Henry (George)

1922 - 23 Left half Back
b: Bedford, c1896
Career: Army, Bedford Town, Rugby Town (c/s 1919), Leicester City (c/s 1920), Hinckley United (Dec 1921), TOWN (Aug 1922).

Wing half who had gained Second Division experience with Leicester City.

1922-23	29 apps	0 gls Midland League

VINTER Michael

1984 - 86 Forward   5' 9"   11st 0lbs (1986)
b: Boston, Lincs., 23 May 1954
Career: Boston, Notts County (Mar 1972), Wrexham (£150,000 - Jun - 1979), Oxford United (£25,000 - Aug 1982), TOWN (£10,000 - Aug - 1984), Newport County (Aug 1986), Gainsborough Trinity (c/s 1987), Boston United (c/s 1988), Matlock Town (c/s 1989), Oakham United (c/s 1990 - player coach), Hucknall Town (Jun 1991 - player coach), Sutton Town (c/s 1992).

An opportunist in the goalgetting stakes, Mick Vinter netted a total of 113 during his League career, plus many more scored in non league circles. Known as the "Lincolnshire Poacher" at Meadow Lane, he was still turning out for Ashfield United, formerly Sutton Town up to 1993 and has recently been playing for Sneinton in the Notts Alliance. Left his first club when Boston - by the time he returned they were Boston United.

1984-85	31(2) apps	3 gls	
1985-86	21(0) "	4 "	

Honours: Welsh Cup runners up 1981 (Wrexham). Division 4 promotion 1986 (Mansfield).

WADDLE Alan R

1982 - 83 Forward   6' 3"   12st 12lbs (1982)
b Wallsend, Northumberland, 9 June 1954
Career: Wallsend B C, Halifax Town (Nov 1971), Liverpool (£50,000 - Jun 1973), Leicester City (£45,000 - Sep 1977), Swansea City (£24,000 - May 1978), Newport County (£80,000 - Dec 1980), Gloucester City, TOWN (F.T. Aug 1982), Hong Kong (Dec 1982), Hartlepool United (Aug 1983), Peterborough United (£6,000 - Oct 1983), Hartlepool United (Jan 1985 - N/C), Swansea City (Mar 1985 - N/C), Finland (c/s 1985), Barry Town (May 1986 - part time & Swansea commercial operations), Port Talbot, Maesteg Park, Bridgend Town (Nov 1989), Llanelli (Dec 1989)

One of football's perpetual travellers, Alan Waddle's initial promise was never quite fulfilled and he drifted from club to club. Was still playing in minor football when nearly 40.

1982-83	14(0) apps	4 gls

WAGSTAFF Kenneth

1960 - 64 Centre Forward   5' 9½"   11st 0lbs (1962)
b: Langwith, Notts., 24 November 1942
Career: Whaley Thorns, Carter Lane School Shirebrook, N E Derbyshire Schools, Langwith B C, Langwith Woodland Imps, Rotherham United (trial), TOWN (May 1960), Hull City (£40,000 - Nov 1964), George Cross Australia (May 1975 and again May 1976). Hull Minor football (Aug 1977), Goole Town, Bridlington Town (Sep 1980 - manager to Dec 1980).

One of the "Stags" biggest post-war successes, Ken Wagstaff was a local lad who had been knocking in goals galore for Woodland Imps before signing as a pro for Mansfield when 17½. Along with Mike Stringfellow and Peter Morris, he was thrown in at the deep end by manager Raich Carter before he was 18 and never looked back, scoring 93 goals in 181 outings before Hull forked out a large fee to take him to Boothferry Park. His goalscoring continued unabated and he finished there with 173 goals in 378 games - so 266 goals in 559 matches was a pretty useful record upon which to retire! Surprisingly his only international recognition was when he was a member of the F A party which toured Australia in 1971. Settled in Hull after he hung up his boots and is a respected publican in that city. Town's Second leading League goalscorer and Third overall - he is also the leading "Stags" goalscorer still living up to 1995. One of the few professional footballers to have a racehorse named after him, "Waggy" in 1968 - of this select band, two were former "Stags" players - Clarence Wonnacott being the other in 1935.

1960-61	27 apps	9 gls		
1961-62	42 "	12 "		
1962-63	44 "	34 "	Leading	Scorer
1963-64	46 "	29 "	"	"
1964-65	22 "	9 "		

Honours: North East Derbyshire Schoolboys, Division 4 promotion 1963, Divsion 3 - 3rd 1965 (both Mansfield). Division 3 Championship 1966, F A XI & F A Tour Australia 1971 (both Hull).

WAINWRIGHT (William) Thomas
1936 - 38 Right Half Back   5' 10½"   12st 0lbs (1936)
b: Worksop, c1916
Career: Worksop Town (c/s 1935 - am), TOWN (Mar 1936 - pro), Aldershot (c/s 1938).

Young reserve player recruited from the Midland League, but his opportunities were limited and he moved on to Aldershot. He played a couple of matches for the "Stags" as a "guest" player during the first wartime season.

1935-36	0 apps	0 gls
1936-37	3 "	0 "
1937-38	0 "	0 "
WW II	2 "	0 "

WAKE Henry Williamson ("Harry")
1931 - 32 Right Half Back   5' 7"   11st 3lbs (1931)
b: Seaton Delavel, Co Durham, 21 January 1901
Career: Bigges Main Colliery, Newcastle United (May 1919), Cardiff City (£200 - May 1923), TOWN (£250 - Jun 1931), Gateshead (July 1932).

Harry Wake did not manage to break through into regular First Division football until he joined Cardiff, where he held his place quite consistently until the season before he joined the "Stags". He was one of the acquisitions in a £2,000 spending spree that was embarked upon by Jack Hickling when Mansfield were elected to the the Football League. Although he played in the 1925 F A Cup Final, he missed the 1927 final due to injury, when Cardiff took the cup out of England for the first and only time, but he did play in the semi final and scored a goal - an own goal for the opposition! He was also "debited" with the mistake that allowed Tunstall to score the winning goal in 1925!

| 1931-32 | 20 apps | 0 gls |

Honours: Welsh League XI, Division 1 runners up 1924, F A Cup runners up 1925, Welsh Cup runners up 1929, Winners 1930 (all Cardiff).

WALKER Alan
1992 - 93 Central Defender   6' 1"   12st 7lbs (1988)
b: Mossley, Manchester, 17 December 1959
Career: Mossley, Stockport County (Aug 1978 - am), Bangor City (Aug 1978), Telford United (Feb 1980), Lincoln City (£50,000 - Oct 1983), Millwall (£32,500 - July 1985), Gillingham (£50,000 - Mar 1988), Plymouth Argyle (Sep 1992 - trial), TOWN (F.T. Sep 1992), Barnet (£10,000 - Sep 1993)

Centre half who George Foster signed for the "Stags" on a free transfer, but after some rather inept displays, the North Stand crowd barracked him into asking for a transfer and he departed for Barnet after only one season.

| 1992-93 | 22(0) apps | 1 gl |

Honours: F A Trophy Winners 1983 (Telford), Division 2 Championship 1988 (Millwall)

WALKER David (Clive) Allan
1969 - 75 Left Full Back   5' 8"   10st 10lbs (1972)
b: Watford, 24 October 1945
Career: Leicester City (1960 - appr, Oct 1962 - pro), Northampton Town (Oct 1966), TOWN (F.T. July 1969), Chelmsford City (F.T. c/s 1975), Gravesend, Northampton (coach, 1982 - manager to 1984, 1985 - coach to 1990), Shrewsbury (1991 - chief scout), Kettering Town (asst manager).

What an excellent bargain was Clive Walker - six years of first class service after joining the club on a free transfer! Born in Watford, his family moved to Leicester when he was still a child. A former schoolboy international, he played in well over 200 league matches for the "Stags".

1969-70	45(0) apps	1 gl	
1970-71	46(0) "	2 "	
1971-72	41(0) "	0 "	
1972-73	40(0) "	3 "	
1973-74	42(0) "	2 "	
1974-75	9(6) "	0 "	

Honours: England Schoolboy International. League Cup runners up 1965 (Leicester). Notts F A County Cup Winners 1971 & 1972 (both Mansfield).

WALKER Michael J
1969 - 70 Right Winger
b: Harrogate, Yorks., 10 April 1945
Career: Sheffield Wednesday (appr), Doncaster Rovers (Aug 1963), Bourne Town, Bradford City (Oct 1964), Rotherham United (Mar 1966), Los Angeles U S A, TOWN (Mar 1969), Altrincham, Stockport County (Aug 1970), Chesterfield (Sep 1970)

1968-69	2(0) apps	0 gls

WALKER (Richard) Neil
1995 Defender   5' 11½"   12st 7lbs (1995)
b: Derby, 9 November 1971.
Career: Notts County (1988 - appr, July 1990 - pro), TOWN (Mar 1995 - loan).

1994-95	4(0) apps	0 gls	(Loan)

WALLER Philip
1968 - 72 Wing Half Back   5' 10"   11st 5lbs (1968)
b: Leeds, 12 April 1943
Career: Derby County (juniors, 1959 - am, May 1961 - pro), TOWN (£6,000 - Mar 1968), Ilkeston Town (Jun 1972 - player manager), Boston (Jan 1973), Matlock Town (Aug 1974), Burton Albion (Oct 1974), Belper Town (July 1975 - player coach), Ilkeston Town (1976), Kimberley Town (Nov 1977), Burton Albion (Mar 1977 - manager to Nov 1978).

Another of Mansfield's long serving players, Phil Waller spent 4½ seasons at Field Mill and made over 150 appearances in the senior team. Was a member of the "Giant Killers" Cup Winning team of 1968-69. Since retiring from the game has been a partner in a prosperous motor business at Mickleover, near Derby and a general sales manager for Ansells Brewery in the Potteries.

1967-68	13(0) apps	0 gls	
1968-69	45(0) "	1 "	
1969-70	40(0) "	0 "	
1970-71	34(3) "	0 "	
1971-72	21(3) "	0 "	

Honours: "Giant Killers" Cup Winners 1969 (Mansfield). Northern Premier League Championship 1973 & 1974 (both Boston)

WALTERS Charles

1928 - 29 Centre Half Back   6' 0"   12st 13lbs (1928)
b: Sandford on Thames, Oxford, 1 April 1897
d: Bath, 13 May 1971
Career: Oxford City (am), Tottenham Hotspur (Dec 1919 - am, Apr 1920 - pro), Fulham (Oct 1926), TOWN (Aug 1928)

Charlie Walters had a glittering career with Spurs, winning an F A Cup Winners medal only a year after he became a pro at White Hart Lane. He also was selected for England v Belgium in 1923, but had to withdraw due to injury and was not chosen again. A solid stopper centre half, he was reputedly the fastest player on Tottenham's books at the time. Spent a whole season with Mansfield, but could only win a first team slot in 2 League, 2 Cup and a Friendly match, due to the brilliance of Bernard Chambers.

1928-29   2 apps   0 gls
Honours: F A Cup Winners & F A Charity Shield Winners 1921 (both Tottenham).

WARD A

1913 - 20 Wing Half Back/Inside Forward
b: c1893
Career: TOWN (c/s 1913).

Local born half back/inside forward who played for the club each side of WW I, although only in the reserves post war.

1913-14	N.K. apps	3 gls	Central Alliance
1914-15	N.K. "	0 "	Notts & Derbys League.
1915-16	N.K. "	2 "	Central Alliance
1919-20	0 "	0 "	" "

WARD Darren

1988 - 95 Goalkeeper 5' 11"   12st 9lbs (1993)
b: Costhorpe, Nr Worksop, 11 May 1974
Career: TOWN (1988 - assoc schoolboy, 1990 - appr, Jun 1992 - pro), Notts County (£100,000 + £60,000 after set number of appearances - Jun 1995)

Brilliant young goalkeeper, improving all the time. Made his debut v Hartlepool at home on 16 February 1993 at the age of 18, when he displaced Jason Pearcey and made the custodian's position his own. Was invited by Glenn Hoddle to accompany Chelsea on their 1994 overseas summer tour and performed very well for the "Pensioners". Recognition of his ability came on 28 March 1995, when he was drafted into the Welsh Under 21 squad for the match v Bulgaria at Plovdiv - the first player to be called up for under 21 international duty and also for Wales whilst on the club's books. Unfortunately the brilliance of Tranmere's Danny

Coyne kept him on the substitute's bench in this match and also when he was called on again for the match against Germany at Wuppertal a month later. Although born locally and with an English father, he was eligible for the principality by virtue of his mother being Welsh. Out of contract, he somewhat surprisingly opted to move up just one division to Notts County.

1992-93	13(0) apps	0 gls	
1993-94	33(0) "	0 "	
1994-95	35(0) "	0 "	

Honours: Bassetlaw Schoolboys, Nottingham-shire Schoolboys, Welsh U/21 International squad (all Mansfield).

WARD G E

1920 - 21 Goalkeeper
Career: TOWN (1920)

1920-21   2 apps   0 gls   Central Alliance

WARD (Thomas) Edward

1930 - 31 Goalkeeper 6' 1"   12st 6lbs (1931)
b: c1912
Career: South Normanton Colliery, Bedouins, TOWN (1930 - am), Luton Town (c/s 1931 - pro)

1930-31   1 app   0 gls   Midland League

WARD (Thomas) Edward George

1939 - 40 Centre Forward   5' 10"   11st 7lbs (1939)
b: Chatham, Kent, 27 April 1914
Career: Chatham Boys, Chatham (am), Crystal Palace (Aug 1933), Grimsby Town (Jun 1934), Port Vale (c/s 1936), Stoke City (p/exch H Davies + small fee - Feb 1938), Port Vale (Jan 1939), TOWN (c/s 1939)

Tom Ward started his career as a wing half and it was not until he reached Port Vale he was tried at centre forward with instant success, and 21 goals in 49 games. Had a short spell at neighbours Stoke City, where he deputised for Freddie Steele, but did not score at the Victoria Ground. Played in all three "Stags" matches in the aborted 1939-40 season, scoring 3 goals. Played in a few matches for Mansfield during hostilities, in addition "guesting" for Hull, Leeds and his old club Grimsby.

1939-40 3 apps   3 gls Leading Scorer (Joint)
WW II   7   "   2   "
Honours: Chatham Schoolboys.

WARNER (Reginald) Owen
1955 - 57 Half Back   6' 0"   12st 0lbs
b: Anstey, Leicester, 1 March 1931
Career: Anstey Methodists, Anstey Nomads, Leicester City (Apr 1949), TOWN (Mar 1955), Hinckley Athletic (1957)

Joined the "Stags" as a wing half, but later played mainly at centre half where his height and weight told. Returned to Leicestershire Senior League football after two years at Field Mill.

1954-55   7 apps   0 gls
1955-56   20   "   0   "
1956-57   6   "   0   "
Honours: England   Schoolboy   &   Youth International.

WATKIN Thomas (William) Steel
1955 - 56 Inside Forward   5' 11"   11st 7lbs (1955)
b: Grimsby, 21 September 1932
Career: Grimsby Town (juniors, Oct 1949 - pro), Gateshead (Dec 1952), Middlesbrough (£10,000 - Mar 1954), TOWN (Jun 1955)

Billy Watkin was brought to Field Mill by Stan Mercer for what was often described in those days as "a substantial fee". However, he did not exactly set the town alight and moved on at the end of the season.

1955-56   25 apps   4 gls
Honours: England Schoolboy International

WATSON Frank
1930 - 31 Outside Right
Career: Blackpool, Leeds United, Grantham (c/s 1928), TOWN (Feb 1931).

1930-31   3 apps   0 gls Midland League

WATSON Thomas (Sidney)
1948 - 61 Wing Half Back   5' 8"   10st 0lbs
b: Pleasley, Mansfield, 12 December 1927
Career: Palterton Welfare, TOWN (Sep 1948 - am, Jan 1949 - part time pro, Jan 1950 - full time pro), Ilkeston Town (1961 to 1965), Coalite Bolsover (- to 1978), TOWN (A and B team coach)

A former "Bevin" boy, Sid Watson worked at Pleasley Colliery, entering the mineral water industry after the end of the war. He continued in this occupation after becoming a part time pro with the "Stags", throwing in his lot with them completely a year later. He became one of Mansfield's longest serving players, post war, being with the club for 12½ years and was still playing in local soccer with Coalite when he was 51. A more thas useful cricketer, he turned out for Pleasley Colliery until he was 55 and then switched to umpiring in the Bassetlaw League - a function he was still performing in 1995. An inside forward when he first came to Field Mill, he converted to wing half in 1953 and made nearly 300 League appearances for the club. An employee at King's Mill Hospital until retirement in 1992.

1951-52	21 apps	1 gl	
1952-53	30 "	1 "	
1953-54	39 "	0 "	
1954-55	39 "	1 "	
1955-56	42 "	1 "	
1956-57	41 "	1 "	
1957-58	25 "	4 "	
1958-59	24 "	0 "	
1959-60	22 "	0 "	
1960-61	9 "	0 "	

WATSON Vaughan
1952 - 54 Centre Forward   5' 11"   12st 3lbs
b: Mansfield, 5 November 1931
Career: Mansfield West End (1949), Army Football Germany, TOWN (Apr 1952), Chesterfield (May 1954), Ransome & Marles (c/s 1955).

A big bustling leader, Vaughan Watson joined Mansfield after he had finished his Army service in Germany, where he gained experience in service teams.

1952-53   10 apps   5 gls
1953-54   4   "   4   "

WEBB A
1927 - 28 Outside Left
Career: TOWN (1927 - am)

1927-28   3 apps   1 gl Midland League

WEIGHTMAN Arthur W

1931 - 33 Left Half Back   5' 9"   12st 0lbs
b: Newark on Trent, Notts., 1910
Career: Newark Town, Torquay United (1930), TOWN (F.T. July 1931), Newark Town (c/s 1933)

Nottinghamshire born Arthur Weightman came to Field Mill for the first season in the Football League, but returned to the club where he started his career, two years later.

1931-32	28 apps	1 gl	
1932-33	17 "	0 "	

WEIR James ("Jock")

1962 - 63 Outside Left
b: Glasgow, 12 April 1939
Career: Clydebank, Fulham (July 1957), York City (Jun 1960), TOWN (Sep 1962), Luton Town (Aug 1963), Tranmere Rovers (July 1964), Scarborough.

Jock Weir had been a regular member of the "Minstermens'" team before he arrived at Field Mill and he contributed to Town's promotion during the season he spent here.

1962-63   18 apps   3 gls
Honours: Division 4 promotion 1963 (Mansfield)

WEST Alfred

1919 - 20 Left Full Back   5' 7"   11st 9lbs
b: Nottingham, 15 December 1881
Career: Ilkeston United (1900), Barnsley (1902), Liverpool (Nov 1903), Reading (Jun 1909), Liverpool (1910), Notts County (July 1911), TOWN (Sep 1919), Shirebrook (Nov 1919)

Alf West had a glittering career with both Liverpool and the "Magpies" and had all but retired when Harry Willett, the "Stag's" secretary signed him at the age of 37. Unfortunately, He found the pace of competitive football too much for him and he soon moved on to try his luck with Shirebrook. One of the oldest players to turn out for the club.

1919-20   2 apps   0 gls   Central Alliance
Honours: Division 1 Championship 1906 (Liverpool). Division 2 Championship 1914 (Notts County).

WESTLAND James

1946 - 47 Inside Left
b: Aberdeen, 21 July 1916
Career: Inchgarth, Banks o' Dee, Aberdeen (1933), Stoke City (Aug 1935), TOWN (£1,000 - Nov 1946).

Jim Westland was a regular team member with Stoke, alongside Stanley Matthews and Freddie Steele before the war, but had been unable to regain his place in 1946 when Roy Goodall signed him for what was for Mansfield, a huge fee and their record outlay at the time. He failed to achieve the desired result at Field Mill and soon drifted out of the game, returning to minor football in Scotland. WW II "guest" with Derby and Doncaster.

1946-47   10 apps   0 gls

WHATMORE Neil

1984 - 87 Forward   5' 9½"   11st 8lbs (1983)
b: Ellesmere Port, Cheshire, 17 May 1955
Career: Bolton Wanderers (Jun 1971 - appr, May 1973 m- pro), Birmingham City (£340,000 - Aug 1981), Oxford United (Oct 1982 - loan), Bolton Wanderers (Dec 1982 - loan), Oxford United (£25,000 - Feb 1983), Bolton Wanderers (Mar 1984 - loan), Burnley (£15,000 - Aug 1984), TOWN (Nov 1984 - loan, Nov 1984 - permanent), Bolton Wanderers (Aug 1987 - trial, Sep 1987 - N/C), TOWN (Oct 1987 - Res Team Coach), Worksop Town (F.T. Aug 1988), Eastwood Town (c/s 1989), Manning Rangers South Africa (Jan 1990 - manager), South Africa (coaching), Forest Town Rangers (Aug 1990), Eastwood Town (Jan 1991 - coach), Rainworth M W (Jun 1993 - manager to Nov 1994).

Much of Neil Whatmore's career was spent with the "Trotters", indeed he signed for them on no less than four occasions, making well over 300 appearances for the club. Spent a successful three years at Field Mill, the last one as reserve team coach, assisting the club to gain promotion from the Fourth Division and win the Freight Rover Trophy along the way. Settled in the area when his playing career was over.

1984-85	26(0) apps	7 gls	
1985-86	30(1) "	9 "	
1986-87	15(0) "	4 "	
1987-88	0(4) "	0 "	

Honours: Division 2 Championship 1978 (Bolton). Division 4 promotion 1986 & Freight Rover Trophy Winners 1987 (both Mansfield)

WHEATLEY Ernest

1922 - 23 Full Back
Career: Rotherham County (c/s 1919), TOWN (May 1922), Wath Athletic (c/s 1923 to 1928).

Full back who had been a fairly regular member of the "Millers" Division 2 team for two seasons before joining Mansfield.

1922-23   31 apps   0 gls   Midland League
Honours: Notts F A Senior Cup Winners 1923 (Mansfield).

WHEATLEY R

1924 - 25 Centre Forward
Career: TOWN (1924 - am)

1924-25   1 app   0 gls   Midland League

WHEATLEY William

1948 - 50 Outside Right   5' 5½"   8st 4lbs (1948)
b: Mansfield, 5 November 1920
Career: Mansfield Colliery, Nottingham Forest (am), Huthwaite CWS, TOWN (Aug 1947 - am, Aug 1948 - pro)

It is perhaps rather appropriate that Billy Wheatley should have been born on Guy Fawkes day, as he was a real little crackerjack! Although small and light, he was fast and tricky - a real handful for the opposing full back - and very reminicent of his illustrious forebear, Ron Dellow. He fell out of favour when Freddie Steele arrived and Billy Coole was converted to a right winger, so he drifted out of League Football, having spent all of his last season in the reserves. A cousin of Cyril Poole, he was still playing for Creswell Colliery in 1954. Served in the Forces for 5½ years in WW II and played a lot of cricket and table tennis in his youth.

1948-49	37 apps	3 gls
1949-50	1 "	0 "
1950-51	0 "	0 "

WHILDE Christopher

1929 - 30 Outside Right   5' 7"   10st 0lbs (1929)
b: Pleasley, Mansfield, October 1912
Career: Pleasley Hill School, Mansfield Shoe Co (c/s 1927), TOWN (c/s 1929 - am, Oct 1929 - pro), Mansfield Shoe Co (c/s 1931), Sutton Town (c/s 1932)

1929-30	12 apps	4 gls	Midland League
1930-31	0 "	0 "	"	"

Honours: Mansfield Hospital Charity Cup Winners, Byron Cup Winners & Bayley Cup Winners 1930 (all Mansfield).

WHITE Claude

1929 - 32 Full Back   5' 10"   12st 4lbs (1931)
b: Mansfield, c1905
Career: Shirebrook (Jan 1927 - am), Wombwell (1928), TOWN (c/s 1929).

Reserve full back who greatest claim to fame is that he accompanied Jack Hickling around the Country in 1931, helping to promote the "Stags" election to the Football League - very successfully too, as they were elected that June, displacing Newport County. His reward - a single appearance in the League!

1929-30	4 apps	0 gls	Midland League
1930-31	16 "	0 "	"	"
1931-32	1 "	0 "		

Honours: Byron Cup Winners, Bayley Cup Winners 1930, Notts F A Senior Cup Winners 1931 (all Mansfield).

WHITE William

1955 - 56 Goalkeeper 6' 0"   13st 7lbs (1955)
b: Clackmannan, Stirlingshire, 25 September 1932
Career: Alva Albion Rangers, Motherwell (July 1952), Accrington Stanley (Aug 1953), TOWN (May 1954), Derby County (Sep 1955 - loan), Bacup Borough (c/s 1956 to 1958)

Reserve 'keeper for two seasons at Field Mill, Willie White retired due to injury in 1958 and went to work in the mines.

1954-55	3 apps	0 gls
1955-56	0 "	0 "

WHITTAM (Ernest) Alfred

1935 - 36 Inside Forward   5' 9"   12st 4lbs (1935)
b: Wealdstone, London, 7 January 1911
Career: Deighton Council School, Huddersfield Town (Nov 1926 - am, Nov 1928 - pro), Chester (£500 - May 1933), TOWN (May 1935), Wolverhampton Wanderers (£750 - Feb 1936), Bournemouth & Boscombe Athletic (Apr 1936), Reading (Jun 1939), Rotherham United (Apr 1945), Leeds United (Dec 1947)

Ernie Whittam's family moved from London to Yorkshire when he was a boy. Joined the "Terriers" as a 15 year old when working at a local bakery and in five years there made 20 appearances in their First Division team. Commanded a "substantial" fee when he came to Field Mill and performed so well in half a season that Wolves bought him, with Mansfield making a substantial profit. It was quite remarkable that he was as successful as he was, as he only had the sight of one eye - what would he have achieved with the sight of two! Wartime "guest" with Rotherham.

1935-36	20 apps	4 gls

Honours: Division 3 North - 3rd 1935 (Chester)

WHITWORTH Stephen J

1983 - 85 Defender   6' 0"   12st 0lbs (1982)
b: Coalville, Leics., 20 March 1952
Career: Leicester City (1968 - appr, Nov 1969 - pro), Sunderland (£125,000 - Mar 1979), Bolton Wanderers (Oct 1981), TOWN (F.T. Aug 1983)

A tall full back, Steve Whitworth had an outstanding career, making over 650 League appearances for his various clubs. He also won England caps at Schoolboy, Youth, Under 23 and senior level, where he gained 7. Ian Greaves brought him to Mansfield, having previously signed him for Bolton when he was manager there. Whitworth did not find it easy to adjust to the rigours of Fourth Division football after playing for so long in the First Division, and asked to be released in May 1985 to go into business in the South.

1983-84　41(0) apps　0 gls
1984-85　39(0)　"　2　"
Honours: England Schoolboys, Youth, U/23, full international, Division 2 Championship 1971 & Charity Shield Winners 1972 (all Leicester). Division 2 runners up 1980 (Sunderland)

WHYSALL L

1922 - 23 Left Half Back　5' 8"　10st 7lbs (1924)
b: c1900
Career: TOWN (Feb 1923 - am)

Younger brother of Wilfrid Whysall, the Notts and England cricketer who tragically died after a fall at the Palais de Dance in Leeming Street in October 1930 when at the height of his career. A cricketer like his brother during the summer months, but at a somewhat lower level - for Bullcroft Colliery and by the early 1930s for Hardwick.

1922-23　2 apps　0 gls Midland League

WIGNALL Frank

1971 - 73 Centre Forward　5' 11¾"　12st 7lbs (1972)
b: Chorley, Lancs., 21 August 1939
Career: Horwich R M I, Everton (May 1958 - am, May 1960 - pro), Nottingham Forest (£20,000 - Jun 1963), Wolverhampton Wanderers (Mar 1968), Derby County (£20,000 - Feb 1969), TOWN (£8,000 - Nov 1971), Kings Lynn (July 1973 - player manager), Burton Albion (Aug 1974 - manager), Qatar (Oct 1975 - national coach to 1980), Shepshed Charterhouse (July 1981 - manager to Mar 1983)

Frank Wignall was signed for the club by Chairman Arthur Patrick immediately after he had dismissed Jock Basford and hours before he appointed Danny Williams. Wignall had been capped by England and was a proven goalscorer, but he did not save Mansfield from relegation and did not fit in as had been hoped, so after a season and a half he was released. He later managed Shepshed Charterhouse during the most purple patch in their history.

1971-72　23(2) apps　8 gls
1972-73　27(4)　"　7　"
Honours: England International, Football League XI (Nottingham Forest). Notts F A County Cup Winners 1972 (Mansfield)

WILDE H W

1927 - 28 Inside Left　5' 7½"　11st 10lbs (1927)
b: c1904
Career: Grimsby Town, TOWN (c/s 1927), Ripley Town (c/s 1928)

1927-28　6 apps　1 gl Midland League

WILKINSON (Stephen) John

1989 - 95 Forward　5' 10"　10st 12lbs (1988)
b: Lincoln, 1 September 1968
Career: Leicester City (July 1985 - appr, Sep 1986 - pro), Rochdale (Aug 1988 - loan), Crewe Alexandra (Sep 1988 - loan), TOWN (£80,000 - Oct 1989), Preston North End (£100,000 - Jun 1995).

Signed by George Foster, Steve Wilkinson was at the time, Mansfield's most expensive signing, although Foster equalled that again within a few months when he signed Fairclough from Notts County. A steady goalscorer, he had been leading scorer in five of the six seasons he spent at Field Mill and many felt that he operated better in a midfield role rather than as an out and out striker. Had only been with the club six months when he netted all 5 goals in the 5 - 2 roasting of Birmingham City. Has made his home in Eastwood with his wife and baby daughters, the second of whom was born on 6 May 1995. Was placed Sixth in the club's aggregate goalscoring list and Third in League matches by May 1995, having overtaken Ted Harston and Roy Chapman during 1994-95. The same season he also slipped into second place behind Ken Wagstaff in the post WW II list. His total goals tally in all matches for the "Stags" was 91. At the end of his most successful season to date, he was transferred to Preston for what must bave been well below the market value for a proven striker - still in his prime at 26.

1989-90	36(1) apps	15 gls	Leading Scorer	
1990-91	36(3) "	11 "	"	"
1991-92	30(0) "	14 "		
1992-93	35(8) "	11 "	Leading Scorer	
1993-94	36(6) "	10 "	"	"
1994-95	41(0) "	22* "	"	"

* (+1gl Play-offs)

Honours: Lincolnshire Schoolboys. Division 4 promotion 1992 (Mansfield).

WILKINSON Thomas
1926 - 27 Goalkeeper
Career: TOWN (c/s 1926 - am)

Young amateur whose only first team game was in the Benevolent Bowl Final, when he was in the winning side.

1926-27   0 apps 0 gls   Midland Combination
Honours: Notts Benevolent Bowl Winners 1927 (Mansfield)

WILLIAMS Charles
1933 - 34 Goalkeeper 6' 1"   12st 6lbs (1933)
b: 1913
Career: Shirebrook (c/s 1932), TOWN (May 1933)

1933-34	22 apps	0 gls

WILLIAMS (George) Robert
1957 - 62 Right Half Back   5' 10"   11st 0lbs
b: Felling, Co Durham, 18 November 1932
Career: Rotherham United (juniors, July 1950 - pro), Sheffield United (£1,000 - May 1954), Wisbech Town (c/s 1955), Bradford City (Jun 1956), TOWN (July 1957)

North Eastener George Williams' career really took off when he came to Mansfield and after five seasons he had made over 150 League appearances for the club, whereas he made only 10 for his 3 other clubs altogether. Essentially a wing half, he did play in a few matches at inside forward, before ending his Football League career in May 1962.

1957-58	12 apps		0 gls	
1958-59	29	"	1	"
1959-60	32	"	2	"
1960-61	45	"	2	"
1961-62	36	"	0	"

WILLIAMS Granville
1927 - 28 Inside Right   5' 10"   11st 9lbs (1927)
b: Hucknall, Notts., c1905
Career: Blackpool (c/s 1926), TOWN (July 1927)

1927-28	3 apps	0 gls

WILLIAMS (Michael) James
1994 onwards Midfield 6' 0"   11st 4lbs (1994)
b: Sutton in Ashfield, Notts., 3 November 1976
Career: TOWN (1993 - appr).

Micky Williams was an apprentice brought on as substitute in the final match of the 1994-95 season.

1994-95	0(1) apps	0 gls

WILLIAMS Steven B
1986 - 89 Midfield 5' 11"   10st 6lbs
b: Mansfield, 18 July 1970
Career: TOWN (Aug 1986 - appr, July 1988 - pro), Chesterfield (F.T. Oct 1989)

This young midfielder twice broke his leg early in his career before moving on to the "Spireites" where he has done well. Made his "Stags" debut when only 16 years old and still a trainee.

1986-87	3(1) apps		0 gls	
1987-88	0(4)	"	0	"
1988-89	1(2)	"	0	"

WILLIAMS (William) Thomas
1966 - 67 Centre Half Back   6' 1"   13st 0lbs
b: Esher, Surrey, 23 August 1942
Career: Portsmouth (juniors, Jun 1960 - pro), Queens Park Rangers (July 1961), West Bromwich Albion (£15,000 - Jun 1963), TOWN (£10,500 - Jan 1966), Gillingham (£7,000 - Sep 1967), Durban Celtic R S A (1972)

Bill Williams was the "Stags" most expensive player at the time he moved from the Hawthorns. A classy and commanding pivot, he was brought in to replace John Gill, but he fell out of favour the following season and languished in the reserves until the

"Gills" moved in for him and he had five good seasons with them playing in over 170 matches before leaving British football. Currently acting as Gillingham's commercial manager.

1965-66   28(0) apps   0 gls
1966-67   15(2) "   0 "
1967-68   4(0) "   0 "
Honours: England Schoolboy & Youth international (Portsmouth)

WILSON Alan A

1966 - 67 Goalkeeper
b: Bathgate, Midlothian, 10 January 1945
Career: Partick Thistle, Scunthorpe United (July 1964), TOWN (Aug 1966).

Young Scot who stood in for Alan Humphreys during October 1966.

1966-67   5(0) apps   0 gls

WILSON Albert

1938 - 39 Outside Left   5' 8"   10st 8lbs (1936)
b: Rotherham, 28 January 1915
Career: Rotherham Y M C A, Rawmarsh Welfare, Stafford Rangers, Derby County (£125 - May 1936), TOWN (July 1938), Crystal Palace (£525 - Jan 1939), Rotherham United (Jun 1946), Grimsby Town (July 1947), Boston (Jun 1948).

By dazzling opponents with his trickery at Marston Road, Albert Wilson soon attracted the attention of League clubs and was quickly snapped up by the "Rams" for whom he appeared in the First Division when Dally Duncan was injured. Picked up by Mansfield for a song two years later, he delighted supporters with his play and they were dismayed when he moved to Selhurst Park to help Palace in their promotion push - but they were pipped at the post by Newport County. Starred with the "Glaziers" during the war years and also assisted Carlisle, Clapton Orient, Arsenal, Hartlepools, Aldershot, Blackburn, Bradford City and Brighton on the odd occasions when he was away from London. Nicknamed "Cowboy" because of his rolling gait, he was later groundsman at Millmoor for many years.

1938-39   20 apps   2 gls
Honours: Notts F A County Cup Winners 1939 (Mansfield). Division 3 South runners up 1939, Division 3 South Cup Joint Winners 1939, War South D Championship 1940, War South Championship 1941 & Division 3 South - Southern Section Championship 1946 (all Crystal Palace).

WILSON James

1955 - 56 Outside Right   5' 5"   10st 0lbs
b: Glasgow, 19 December 1929
Career: Alloa Athletic, Leicester City (July 1954), TOWN (Mar 1955)

Jimmy Wilson was really a reserve at Field Mill, being brought into the senior side only when necessity prevailed. He did not make the League XI at Filbert Street, but had previously made 31 appearances, scoring 6 goals for Alloa.

1954-55   4 apps   0 gls
1955-56   15 "   1 "

WILSON James E

1931 - 33 Goalkeeper 6' 1"   12st 0lbs (1931)
b: Garforth, Leeds, c1908
Career: Rothwell Amateurs, Leeds United (Mar 1928), Halifax Town (Mar 1930 - trial), Shrewsbury Town (Aug 1930 - trial), Shirebrook (Dec 1930), TOWN (£50 - c/s 1931), Sutton Town (Jan 1933 - loan), Bradford P A (£100 - Jun 1933), Bristol City (c/s 1934), Bristol Rovers (c/s 1938).

Jim Wilson had experienced First Division football at Leeds and Third Division with Halifax by the time he joined Mansfield. When with Shirebrook was considered to be the best goalkeeper in the Midland League and subsequently did good work for Bristol City. Holds the unenviable record of being the first player to be sent off after the "Stags" election to the Football League.

1931-32   29 apps   0 gls
1932-33   12 "   0 "

WILSON Kenneth

1925 - 26 Outside Right
Career: Wombwell, TOWN (Sep 1925), Wath Athletic (Aug 1926)

Signed to understudy Lance Sheldon, but got few chances and moved on the following close season.

1925-26   7 apps   1 goal Midland League

WILSON Lee

1992 - 94 Forward   5' 10"   11st 4lbs (1993)
b: Mansfield, 23 May 1972
Career: Clipstone C W, TOWN (Oct 1992 - N/C), Telford United (Mar 1994 - loan, May 1994 - permanent).

Young striker with a tearaway style, who after many good performances in the resrves, failed to fulfill his promise when with the senior squad and was persuaded by George Foster to throw in his lot with Telford in the Conference, where he was better able to show off his talents.

| 1992-93 | 0(4) apps | 0 gls |
| 1993-94 | 9(5) " | 1 " |

WITHE Christopher

1991 - 93 Full Back 5' 8½" 11st 3lbs
b: Speke, Liverpool, 25 September 1962
Career: Newcastle United (1978 - appr, Oct 1980 - pro), Bradford City (F.T. Jun 1983), Notts County (£50,000 - Oct 1987), Bury (£40,000 - July 1989), Chester (Oct 1990 - loan), TOWN (Jan 1991 - loan, exch Kearney Mar 1991 - permanent), Shrewsbury Town (F.T. Aug 1993)

This player's most successful period was at Valley Parade where he clocked up nearly 150 appearances for the "Bantams". He was signed by George Foster in an attempt to avoid relegation, unsuccessfully as it happened. Something of a free kick specialist, he scored several spectacular goals and is still turning out for Shrewsbury. Younger brother of Peter Withe the ex England, Nottingham Forest and Aston Villa forward.

1990-91	21(0) apps	0 gls
1991-92	10(0) "	1 "
1992-93	44(1) "	4 "

WOMWELL Dennis

1945 - 46 Centre Forward
Career: TOWN (1945)

Recruited locally, Womwell only played for the club during the first half of the last wartime season, but he did play in all six F A Cup ties, scoring 5 goals.

| WW II | 23 apps | 15 gls |

WONNACOTT (Clarence) Benjamin

1929 - 30 and 1932 - 33 Inside Left
b: Clowne, Derbys., 31 December 1909
d: Nuneaton, Warwicks., 21 February 1989
Career: Clipstone Welfare, TOWN (c/s 1929), Northampton Town (Aug 1930), Shelbourne (Jun 1932), TOWN (Dec 1932), Racing Club de Calais France (c/s 1933), Kidderminster Harriers (Feb 1936), Nuneaton Borough.

Player who had two spells at Mansfield, with stints at Northampton and Shelbourne in the Irish Republic sandwiched in between. Whilst in Ireland he was selected for the Free State League XI which defeated the Welsh League at Dalymount Park, Wonnacott scoring one of the goals.

Popular whilst in France, he had a racehorse named after him. Post war Clarence Wonnacott spent many years as part time trainer to Nuneaton Borough whilst working in engineering and spending 15 years as a local councillor After his death, his ashes were scattered on the Field Mill turf.

| 1929-30 | 15 apps | 5 gls | Midland League |
| 1932-33 | 15 " | 2 " | |
Honours: Byron Cup Winners, Bayley Cup Winners 1930 (both Mansfield). Free State League XI (Shelbourne).

WOOD Ian N

1976 - 82 Defender 5' 10" 10st 7lbs (1978)
b: Kirkby in Ashfield, Notts., 24 May 1958
Career: TOWN (1974 - appr, Jun 1976 - pro), Aldershot (F.T. Aug 1982).

Another local lad who made good, Ian Wood made his debut with Mansfield when just 17 and developed into a first class defender. After just one season with the "Shots" he decided to retire at 25 and return to the family butchers' business.

1975-76	2 (0) apps	0 gls
1976-77	13 (1) "	0 "
1977-78	36 (0) "	1 "
1978-79	6(11) "	0 "
1979-80	21 (0) "	0 "
1980-81	21 (2) "	4 "
1981-82	36 (0) "	4 "
Honours: Division 3 Championship 1977 (Mansfield)

WOOD Leonard
1935 - 38 Left Half Back   5' 8"   10st 7lbs (1936)
Career: Huddersfield Town (c/s 1934), TOWN (Dec 1935)

Known to his team mates as "Danny", Len Wood was recruited from the "Terriers" in mid season to replace the out of form, Wilf Slack.

1935-36	16 apps	1 gl	
1936-37	26 "	2 "	
1937-38	4 "	0 "	

WOOD (William) Horace
1934 Wing Forward/Half Back   5' 8½"   11st 9lbs (1933)
b: Mereclough, Nr Burnley, 5 April 1910
Career: local juniors, Blackburn Rovers (Jun 1927 - am), Burnley (Apr 1930), Blackburn Rovers (Jan 1934), TOWN (Feb 1934 - trial), Chorley (c/s 1934), Darwen (c/s 1935).

Outside left, converted to wing half by Rovers, Billy Wood came to Field Mill on trial, but was not retained.

1933-34   5 apps   0 gls

WOODHEAD Simon C
1980 - 85 Defender   5' 10"   11st 0lbs (1980)
b: Dewsbury, Yorks., 26 December 1962
Career: TOWN (1978 - appr, Sep 1980 - pro), Crewe Alexandra (c/s 1985), Burnley (c/s 1986), Shepshed Charterhouse (c/s 1987), Frickley Athletic (c/s 1989), Altrincham (c/s 1992).

Made his debut for the "Stags" when 18 in the last match of the 1980-81 season, but did not establish himself as a first team regular for two years. Played mainly at full back.

1980-81	0(1) apps	0 gls	
1981-82	11(1) "	0 "	
1982-83	35(7) "	3 "	
1983-84	41(2) "	1 "	
1984-85	21(3) "	2 "	

WRAGG Douglas
1960 - 61 Outside Right   5' 8"   10st 5lbs
b: Nottingham, 12 September 1934
Career: West Ham United (Jun 1953), TOWN (Mar 1960), Rochdale (July 1961), Chesterfield (July 1964), Grantham.

In seven years at Upton Park, Doug Wragg's career never quite took off and he managed only 16 senior appearances there. He only had a year at Field Mill, before he had the most successful period of his career at Spotland, playing in over 100 games for Rochdale.

1959-60	13 apps	2 gls		
1960-61	33 "	11 "	Leading	Scorer

Honours: Nottinghamshire Boys. England Schoolboys & Youth International.

WRIGHT Dennis
1939 - 57 Goalkeeper 5' 10"   11st 0lbs
b: Boythorpe, Nr Chesterfield, 19 December 1919
d: Palterton, Nr Bolsover, Derbys., August 1993
Career: Chesterfield Schoolboys, Clay Lane Rangers, TOWN (Mar 1939, 1957 - head groundsman to 1965).

The archetypal one club man, Dennis Wright spent 18 years at Field Mill as a player and a further eight as groundsman. A truly great clubman. He did not make the first team before the war, although his chance nearly came when Jack Hughes sustained a long term injury in pre season training, but Dennis was thought to be too inexperienced and Fred Biddlestone was brought in. He was one of the first "Stags" players to volunteer for the Army in October 1939 and spent most of the war years in Northern Ireland where he "guested" for Glentoran, winning a Unity Cup medal in 1943. Later in the war he toured with the Army representative team and played in matches against Scotland, France, Holland and Belgium. When on leave he failed to secure a place at Field Mill, although on one occasion when the "Stags" were playing Leicester at Filbert Street and he was travelling as a reserve, Leicester were a man short, so Dennis turned out for them - at centre forward and scored a goal! He also turned out for Nottingham Forest during 1943-44. Made a total of 379 League appearances for Mansfield, which for a long time was a club record and he played his last senior game for the club when he was nearly 37. Darren Ward, Town's current 'keeper resembles him closely.

1946-47	32 apps	0 gls
1947-48	15 "	0 "
1948-49	27 "	0 "
1949-50	41 "	0 "
1950-51	45 "	0 "
1951-52	46 "	0 "
1952-53	29 "	0 "
1953-54	46 "	0 "
1954-55	43 "	0 ".
1955-56	46 "	0 ".
1956-57	9 "	0 "

Honours: Chesterfield Schoolboys. Irish Unity Cup Winners 1943 (Glentoran - guest player). Division 3 North runners up 1951 (Mansfield).

WRIGHT J Ernest

1934 - 37 Wing Half Back 6' 0" 11st 9lbs (1936)
b: 1912
Career: Huddersfield Town (c/s 1931), Bradford City (c/s 1933), TOWN (c/s 1934), Boston (Aug 1937).

A young reserve with his two Yorkshire clubs, Ernie Wright gave the "Stags" sterling service for three seasons before moving back to Midland League football. Only a reserve in his last season at Field Mill.

1934-35	15 apps	0 gls
1935-36	32 "	0 "
1936-37	0 "	0 "

Honours: Bass Charity Vase Winners 1935 (Mansfield).

WRIGHT Vincent

1952 - 53 Winger
b: Bradford, 12 April 1931
Career: Derby County (Sep 1951), TOWN (July 1952)

1952-53	2 apps	0 gls

Honours: England Youth international.

WROE Harold

1927 - 28 Outside Left
Career: Barnsley (1925), TOWN (Feb 1928), Sutton Town (Apr 1928 - loan), Denaby United (Jan 1929 loan), Shirebrook (Nov 1929), Welbeck Athletic (c/s 1930).

1927-28	3 apps	0 gls Midland League

WYLLIE Robinson G N

1959 - 62 Goalkeeper 5' 11" 12st 4lbs
b: Dundee, 4 April 1929
Career: Monifieth Tayside, Dundee United (1949), Blackpool (May 1953), West Ham United (May 1956), Plymouth Argyle (July 1958), TOWN (Oct 1959)

This experienced player was signed by manager Sam Weaver to plug the void that had not been satisfactorily filled since Dennis Wright retired and after an initial falter, Rob Wyllie filled the position well until displaced by the younger Colin Treharne.

1959-60	34 apps	0 gls
1960-61	46 "	0 "
1961-62	12 "	0 "

WYNN (George) Arthur

1921 - 22 Inside Right 5' 6" 10st 0lbs
b: Treflach, Llansilin, Oswestry, Salop., 14 October 1886
d: Abergele, North Wales, 28 October 1966
Career: Pant Glas, Oswestry United (Apr 1906), Wrexham (May 1908), Manchester City (£250 - Apr 1909), Coventry City (£300 - Nov 1919), Worksop Town (Feb 1920), Llandudno Town (c/s 1921), Halifax Town (Jan 1922), TOWN (Feb 1922), Mossley (Sep 1922), Oswestry Town.

This well known player was 35 years old when he joined the "Stags" and was well past his best, but he had enjoyed a glittering career when he was in his prime. Capped by Wales 12 times, 4 with Wrexham and 8 at Hyde Road - City's last ground prior to moving to Maine Road - George Wynn was a diminutive grafting inside forward who split defences with his telling passes

1921-22	4 apps	1 gl	Midland League

Honours: Welsh Cup Winners 1907 (Oswestry United) & 1909 (Wrexham). Welsh International (Wrexham & Manchester City). Division 2 Championship 1910 (Manchester City).

YATES Wilfred James ("Billy")

1929 - 30 Right Full Back 5' 9" 12st 7lbs (1929)
b: c1901
Career: Southport (c/s 1919), Preston North End (c/s 1920), Crewe Alexandra (c/s 1925), Tranmere Rovers (c/s 1926), TOWN (Oct 1929), Staveley Town (Apr 1930).

"Billy" Yates as he was known, was a very experienced full back who had made nearly 200 appearances in the Football League before reaching Field Mill - over 60 of them in the Second Division.

1929-30	2 apps	0 gls Midland League

THE NEARLY MEN

Players in this section never appeared in the senior team but are included for one of the following reasons:
1. An appearance in an abandoned or expunged match.
2. A spell on the club's books after having appeared in the Football League for a previous club.
3. A period with the club before moving on to another, where Football League appearances were made.

....

BELLAS (William) Joseph
1948 Centre Half Back   6' 0"   11st 9lbs (1950)
b: Liverpool, 21 May 1925
Career: Notts County (Apr 1945), Nottingham Forest (May 1946), TOWN (Aug 1948), Southport (Oct 1948), Grimsby Town (exch Barratt & Taylor + £1,000 - July 1951), Barry Town (c/s 1952).

No League appearances until he reached Haig Avenue.
Honours: Welsh Cup Winners 1955 (Barry Town).

BRALLISFORD Albert
1932 - 32 Centre Forward   5' 6"
b: Hartlepool, 9 October 1911
Career: Trimdon Grange, TOWN (1931), Southport (c/s 1932), Blackpool (c/s 1933), Darlington (c/s 1937), Gillingham (Oct 1937)

Made the senior XI with all his other clubs.

BRAZIL Gary N
1986 Forward   5' 11"   9st 13lbs (1986)
b: Tunbridge Wells, Kent, 19 September 1962
Career: Crystal Palace (am), Sheffield United (Aug 1980), Port Vale (Aug 1984 - loan), Preston North End (Feb 1985 - loan, Mar 1985 - permanent), TOWN (Aug 1986 - loan), Newcastle United (Feb 1989), Fulham (Sep 1990 - loan, £110,000 - Nov 1990 - permanent).

Opportunity to make his loan debut for Mansfield in the League was denied when Preston recalled him, although he did manage two senior appearances - one in the friendly match against the Canadian national team and the other, four days later, in the County Cup semi final versus Notts County. He was in a winning side on both occasions.

CHANDLER Albert
1929 Right Full Back
b: Carlisle, 15 January 1897
d: Carlisle, January 1963
Career: Carlisle Schools, Army (1915), Derby County (Aug 1919), Newcastle United (£3,250 - Jun 1925), Sheffield United (£2,625 - Oct 1926), TOWN (c/s 1929), Northfleet (Nov 1929), Manchester Central (Feb 1930), Holme Head (c/s 1930), Queen of the South (c/s 1931).

This well known and experienced full back, who excelled at the sliding tackle, signed for Mansfield during the close season of 1929, but for some strange reason did not ever pull on a shirt for the "Stags" - not even in the pre season trial matches and was allowed to join Northfleet a few months later. Assisted Newcastle to the First Division title in 1926-27, but failed to make sufficient appearances to qualify for a medal. Had earlier played in over 180 games for Derby Honours: Carlisle Schoolboys.

CHESTER (Reginald) Alfred
1921 Outside Left
b: Long Eaton, Derbys., 21 November 1904
d: Long Eaton, Derbys., 24 April 1977
Career: Long Eaton Rangers (am), Notts County (1921 - trial), TOWN (1921 - trial), Peterborough (Aug 1921 - am), Stamford Town (1922 - am), Aston Villa (Dec 1924 - am, Apr 1925 - pro), Manchester United (Aug 1935), Huddersfield Town (Dec 1935), Arnold Town (c/s 1936), Darlington (May 1937), Woodborough United (1938 to 1940 - retired)

Enjoyed a distinguished career elsewhere including much First Division football.

COOPER Stephen B
1984 Forward   5' 11"   10st 12lbs (1987)
b: Birmingham, 22 June 1964
Career: Moor Green, Birmingham City (Nov 1983), Halifax Town (Dec 1983 - loan), N A C Breda, Holland (Mar 1984), TOWN (Aug 1984 - loan), Newport County (Sept 1984 - loan, permanent - Jan 1985), Plymouth Argyle (£15,000 + Staniforth - Aug 1985), Barnsley (£100,000 - July 1988), Tranmere Rovers (£100,000 - Dec 1990), Peterborough United (Mar 1992 - loan), Wigan Athletic (Dec 1992 - loan), York City (£35,000 - Aug 1993), Airdrieonians (£60,000 - Sept 1994)

A very widely travelled player who nevertheless has commanded a couple of quite substantial transfer fees. Did not manage an appearance during his loan spell at Field Mill. Now trying his luck in the Scottish First Division.

COWLING David R
1975 - 77 Midfield   5' 7"   11st 4lbs (1988)
b: Doncaster, 27 November 1958
Career: TOWN (1975 - appr, Nov 1976 - pro), Huddersfield Town (Aug 1977), Scunthorpe United (Nov 1987 - loan), Reading (Dec 1987 - loan, Mar 1988 - permanent), Scunthorpe United (Aug 1988).

Released by the "Stags" without a single first team appearance, David Cowling went on to play in over 330 league matches for Huddersfield and a further 85 for the "Iron".

DRAPER Cyril
1921 - 22 Centre Half Back
b: Tibshelf, Derbys., c1897
Career: Derby County (1919), Chesterfield Town (c/s 1920), TOWN (Dec 1921), Shirebrook (c/s 1922), Sutton Town (c/s 1924).

Played twice in Chesterfield's senior XI 1921-22.

DYKES Donald W
1959 - 60 Inside Forward   5' 11"   10st 11lbs (1954)
b: Ashby by Partney, Lincs., 8 July 1930
Career: British Crop Driers Metheringham, Lincoln City (Aug 1947 - am, Aug 1949 - pro), TOWN (c/s 1959), Boston (Dec 1959), Ruston Bucyrus Lincoln (1961).

Made 95 League appearances for the "Imps". Honours: Southern League Championship 1960 (Boston).

EASTGATE Bernard
1930 - 32 Left Full Back   6' 1"   11st 13lbs (1930)
b: Mansfield, c1909
Career: Brunts School, Nottingham University (1928), TOWN (c/s 1930 - am), Brunts O B (1932 to 1939).

The writer became personally acquainted with Bernard Eastgate when the latter took a teaching appointment at Bull Farm Junior School in 1936 and the former was a pupil. Naturally and in view of his sporting prowess, Eastgate soon took over the sports responsibility from the very willing but aging Miss Walker, soon building the football team into a pretty useful outfit. Possessor of a powerful kick, as many youngsters could testify when they received the full force of a wet leather ball about their person from one of his clearances during training. He converted the writer from an extremely right footed player by the simple expedient of making him wear a plimsoll on the right foot, a football boot on the left and playing him at outside left - it works - and one learns quickly when a 10/11 year old and kicking with the flimsily clad foot hurts!

FERGUSON James (Brian)
1977 - 78 Midfield   5' 10"   10st 6lbs (1981)
b: Irvine, Ayrshire, 14 November 1960
Career: TOWN (1977 - appr), Newcastle United (Jan 1979 - pro), Hull City (Dec 1980), Goole Town (c/s 1982), Southend United (Aug 1983), Chesterfield (Oct 1984 - loan, Dec 1984 - permanent).

Young Scot, taken as an apprentice, but not retained.

FLEWITT Stanley
1934 - 36 Inside/Centre Forward
Career: TOWN (c/s 1934 - am), Notts County (c/s 1936 - am), Nottingham Forest (c/s 1938 - am, 1943 - pro)

Regular player for the reserves (1934-36) and for Forest during WW II. Appeared for the "Stags" again as a Forest "guest" in 1944-45 season.

FORREST George A
1935 - 36 Wing Half Back
Career: Peterhead, Plymouth Argyle (c/s 1934), TOWN (c/s 1935)

In Plymouth's Division 2 team during 1934-35.

GODWIN Robert G
1950 - 51 Inside Forward   5' 8"   11st 0lbs
b: Wootton Bassett, Wilts., 3 February 1928
Career: Swindon Town (am), Burnley (am), TOWN (Sep 1950 - am, Feb 1951 - pro), Swindon Town (F.T. Sep 1951)

Debut for Swindon as a 17 year old amateur in 1945-46 season, playing for the senior XI during his second spell there too.

GREATOREX Lawrence
1922 - 23 Centre Forward   5' 10"   11st 9lbs (1925)
b: Huthwaite, Notts., 1902
Career: Sutton Junction (c/s 1920), Lincoln City (c/s 1921), Notts County (c/s 1923), Southend United (c/s 1926), TOWN (c/s 1928)

In the "Magpies" Division 1 team of 1924-25.

GYNN Michael
1995 onwards Midfield   5' 5"   10st 10lbs
b: Peterborough, 19 August 1961
Career: Peterborough United (1977 - appr, Apr 1979 - pro), Coventry City (£60,000 - Aug 1983), Stoke City (F.T. Aug 1993), Peterborough United (Jan 1995 - trial), TOWN (Feb 1995 - trial, Mar 1995 - N/C), Hednesford Town (Apr 1995 - loan).

Micky Gynn was oustanding with the "Posh" and this persuaded Coventry manager Bobby Gould to sign him after his predecessor, Dave Sexton had been monitoring him for some time. Joined "Stags" to assist in the promotion push towards the end of 1994-95, but he was not called upon for first team duty - languishing in the reserves and on loan to Hednesford. In ten years at Highfield Road made over 200 appearances for his club in addition to 35 as a substitute, the record for a "Sky Blue". Helped Hednesford to the Championship of the Beazer Homes League in 1994-95.
Honours: F A Cup Winners 1987 (Coventry).

HAMMERTON John Daniel

1928 - 29 Centre Forward   6' 0"   12st 0lbs (1928)
b: Sheffield, 22 March 1900
d: 15 June 1968
Career: Oughtibridge, Barnsley, Rotherham County, Barnsley (£200 - c/s 1926), York City (c/s 1927), TOWN (c/s 1928)

Team regular with all his clubs, but failed to make the first team at Field Mill.

HARDWICK

1938 - 42 Goalkeeper
Career: TOWN (c/s 1938)

Pre war reserve 'keeper who managed a single senior appearance during the first wartime season. WW II   1 app   0 gls

HEYES Darren L

1986 - 87 Goalkeeper 5' 11"   12st 9lbs
b: Swansea, 11 January 1967
Career: Nottingham Forest (1983 - appr, Jan 1984 - pro), TOWN (Oct 1986 - loan), Wrexham (Jan 1987 - loan), Scunthorpe United (July 1987), Rochester (c/s 1990 - player coach), Halifax Town (c/s 1993)

Taken on loan for a month, but not used in the senior team. Appeared for Halifax in the F A Cup Second Round at Field Mill in December 1995. Honours: England Schoolboy & Youth International.

HOLLIDAY John R

1992 Defender 6' 4"   11st 0lbs
b: Penrith, Cumbria, 13 March 1970
Career: Carlisle United (Sep 1989), TOWN (Aug 1992 - trial)

Sat on the substitutes' bench versus Fulham (h) in 1992-93 but was not called upon, although he did appear in several reserve matches.   Made 19 appearances for Carlisle.

HOLLINGWORTH Reginald

1927 - 28 Centre Half Back   5' 10½"   12st 0lbs (1935)
b: Rainworth, Mansfield, 17 October 1909
d: Sparkbrook, Birmingham, 8 July 1969
Career: Rainworth School, Rainworth Church, Rufford C W (1925), TOWN (c/s 1927 - am), Sutton Junction (c/s 1928), Wolverhampton Wanderers (Oct 1928 to 1936)

Town wanted to sign him professionally in 1927, but could not afford to take another pro on the staff, so he moved elsewhere and to great heights with Wolves. Died when he sustained a heart attack whilst driving his car in Sparkbrook. Honours: Mansfield Schoolboys (1924), Division 2 Championship 1932 (Wolverhampton)

HOOKS Paul

1985 Midfield 5' 7"   10st 8lbs (1984)
b: Wallsend, Northumberland, 30 May 1959
Career: Notts County (1975 - appr, July 1977 - pro), Derby County (£60,000 - Mar 1983), TOWN (Aug 1985 - N/C), Boston United (Sep 1985), Cotgrave M W (1987)

First team player with Notts County and Derby but not at Mansfield.

HUGHES (Emlyn) Walter O B E

1983 Centre Half Back   5' 10½"   11st 13lbs
b: Barrow in Furness, 28 August 1947
Career: Roose F C Blackpool, Blackpool (1963 - appr, Sep 1964 - pro), Liverpool (£65,000 - Feb 1967), Wolverhampton Wanderers (£90,000 - Aug 1979), Rotherham United (F.T. July 1981 - player manager), Hull City (Mar 1983 - N/C), TOWN (Aug 1983 - N/C), Swansea City (Sep 1983 - N/C), Harworth Colliery (Mar 1993).

Although this famous player made himself available to the "Stags", he was only called upon in a pre-season friendly. Honours: North Lancashire Schoolboys. England U/23 & full International, Football League XI, European Cup Winners 1977 & 1978, U E F A Cup Winners 1973 & 1976, F A Cup Winners 1974, F A Cup runners up 1971 & 1977, Football League Cup runners up 1978, Division 1 Championship 1973, 1976, 1977 & 1979 (all Liverpool). Football League Cup Winners 1980 (Wolverhampton).

KING Colin

1980 - 81 Goalkeeper
b: Edinburgh, c1958
Career: Blackpool (c/s 1976), Clydebank (F.T. c/s 1977), Notts County (c/s 1979), Rotherham United (Jan 1980 - loan), TOWN (c/s 1980 to Oct 1981).

This young Scot's only first team games were with Clydebank, where he managed six in the 1977-78 season.

KNIGHT Francis

1939 - 40 Winger   5' 9"   11st 2lbs (1939)
b: Hucknall, Notts., 26 October 1921
d: Nottingham, 18 December 1993
Career: TOWN (c/s 1939), Nottingham Forest (May 1943)

Frank Knight only played in a few reserve matches before the outbreak of WW II, joining Forest a few years later and played for them in the League up to 1949.

LAGER (Ellis) Walter

1933 - 34 Centre Forward
b: Mansfield, 14 January 1918

Career: Mansfield Rovers, Old Elizabethans, Sutton Junction, TOWN (Apr 1933 - am), Coventry City (Aug 1934 - am, Jan 1935 - pro).

Ellis Lager and his brother Kenneth were both on the "Stags" books together in the early 1930s. Had a successful career with the "Bantams" both before and during the war and he retired as a player in 1943 before hostilities ended. "Guested" for Watford, Nottingham Forest and Notts County during WW II. Another brother, Frank was a Town director from 1933, but he resigned over manager Harry Martin's dismissal in March 1935. Still living in the town in 1995 at the age of 77.
Honours: England Junior International 1935 (Coventry)

LEE Frederick
1936 Outside Left
b: Yardley, Birmingham c1907
Career: Yardley White Star, Coventry City (c/s 1930), Walsall (c/s 1932), Blackpool (c/s 1935), TOWN (Mar 1936), Ollerton Colliery (c/s 1936)

Experienced winger who failed to make the League team with either Blackpool or the "Stags", having previously played in 7 games for Coventry and 85 for Walsall, where he scored 24 goals.

LONGDON Charles (William)
1937 - 38 Wing Half Back
b: Mansfield, 6 May 1917
Career: TOWN (c/s 1937 - am), Brentford (c/s 1938), Brighton & Hove Albion (May 1939), Bournemouth & Boscombe Athletic (May 1946), Rochdale (July 1947), Creswell Colliery.

Billy Longdon made only 10 League appearances, all post war, but he "guested" regularly during the war years with Bournemouth, Liverpool, New Brighton, Bristol City, Chesterfield, Southport, Swansea and Mansfield, apart from turning out over 100 times for Brighton.

LOXLEY Herbert
1964 - 65 Centre Half Back   6' 1"   12st 10lbs (1963)
b: Bonsall, Derbys., 3 February 1934
Career: Bonsall F C, Notts County (Mar 1952), TOWN (July 1964), Lockheed Leamington (Sep 1965), Lincoln City (July 1966 - trainer coach, May 1970 - manager, Mar 1971 - trainer coach to 1987)

245 appearances with County and 7 with Lincoln, but only used as a reserve at Field Mill.

MESSER (Alfred) Thomas
1922 Centre Half Back

b: Deptford, South London, 8 March 1900
d: Reading, 28 July 1947
Career: Mansfield Colliery, Sutton Town, TOWN (1922), Nottingham Forest, Reading (Jun 1923), Tottenham Hotspur (July 1930), Bournemouth & Boscombe Athletic (May 1934 - player coach to 1936)

Certainly one who got away, subsequently playing over 250 games for Reading and 50 for Spurs.
Honours: Division 3 South Championship 1926 (Reading)

MILLER J
1923 - 24 Wing Half Back
b: c1890
Career: The Wednesday (1912), Doncaster Rovers (1919), TOWN (1923)

Played for Wednesday in the First Division before WW I.

MITTEN Charles E
1961 - 62 Forward
b: Altrincham, Cheshire, 14 December 1943
Career: Newcastle United (1959 - appr), TOWN (Nov 1961), Altrincham, Halifax Town (Oct 1965)

Youngest son of Charlie Mitten, Town manager (1956-58).
Honours: Mansfield Schoolboys 1957.

MOWL William (John)
1949 - 50 Goalkeeper 6' 1"
b: Bulwell, Nottingham, 23 June 1922
Career: R A F, Notts County (Oct 1944), TOWN (July 1949)

Senior team player with Notts.

NIMMO William B
1962 - 63 Goalkeeper 5' 11"   11st 7lbs
b: Forth, Lanarkshire, 11 January 1934
Career: Heart of Midlothian (1950 - am), Edinburgh Thistle, Alloa Athletic (c/s 1955), Leeds United (£1,250 - Feb 1956), Doncaster Rovers (exch Ted Burgin - Mar 1958), TOWN (Jun 1962).

Played in first team with all his other clubs, but failed to secure a first team slot at Field Mill due to the brilliance of Colin Treharne.

POPLAR
1935 - 36 Outside Right
Career: TOWN (1936).

Young reserve winger who made a single appearance for the senior XI in a friendly v Derby County in April 1936.

PRICE Gareth

1987 - 89 Midfield/Full Back   5' 10"   11st 0lbs (1991)
b: Swindon, 21 February 1970
Career: Kirkby Centre, TOWN (May 1987 - appr), Bury (July 1989 - pro), Kettering Town (F.T. c/s 1992), Gainsborough Trinity (1994 - loan).

Ian Greaves recommended this player to Bury when he was not retained by Mansfield and he subsequently made four League appearances for them in the two seasons he spent at Gigg Lane. Had a horrendous spell of illnesses, including Crohn's Disease, epilepsy and a brain tumour, but mercifully is now fully recovered.

RANDLE Herbert Clarence ("Harry")

1930 Wing Half Back   5' 7½"   11st 2lbs (1937)
b: Stonebroom, Derbys., 31 July 1906
d: Chesterfield, 7 August 1976
Career: Shirebrook, TOWN (£25 - May 1930), Birmingham (£275 - May 1930), Southend United (Aug 1932), Gillingham (July 1934), Accrington Stanley (May 1937), Barrow (May 1939).

Harry Randle, as he was known, never kicked a ball for the "Stags" and the reason for this is somewhat unusual and worth recounting. Jack Hickling - Mansfield's part-time manager and with many other strings to his bow too, amongst which was his inside knowledge of football, having been a League referee and had his ear close to the ground - picked up the news that Leslie Knighton, the Birmingham manager was keen to sign Randle. Hickling knew that the player was pretty useful and Shirebrook would only ask a very modest fee for him, so he drove straight over to the White Swan Ground and signed him for Mansfield for a £25 fee.   The following day, Birmingham made their formal approach to the "Magpies" for Randle, only to be told that he had joined the "Stags", whereupon Knighton contacted Hickling to see if he could be tempted to sell - Hickling could - and did - for £250 profit! Randle was a Mansfield registered player for just one day.

REDDISH Shane

1987 - 90 Midfield 5' 10"   11st 10lbs (1989)
b: Bolsover, Derbys., 5 May 1971
Career: TOWN (1977 - appr, July 1989 - pro), Doncaster Rovers (F.T. Feb 1990), Kettering Town (Aug 1992 - loan), Carlisle United (F.T. July 1993), Hartlepool United (F.T. March 1995).

Released by the "Stags" without being given a first team opportunity.

RICKARDS Charles Thomas ("Tex")

1939-46 Outside Right/Centre Forward 5' 8" 12st 10lbs (1942)
b: Giltbrook, Notts., 1914

Career: Johnson & Barnes, Gilbrook Villa, Notts County (1931 - am, Jan 1933 - pro), Cardiff City (c/s 1938), TOWN (F.T. c/s 1940), Peterborough United (c/s 1946).

Had a lengthy career with Notts County pre-war. Released by Cardiff in May 1939, he returned to Nottingham and first turned out for the "Stags" during 1939-40 as a non contract player, signing for the club permanently the following Summer. "Tex" Rickards was a hefty, bustling type of player and he troubled defences with his persistence and powerful shooting, scoring a lot of goals from centre forward during the war years.   Towards the end of hostilities when not required by Mansfield, he "guested" for Derby, Chesterfield, Notts County, Crewe, Leicester and Stockport. Released in 1946, he went into the Midland League for a couple of seasons before retiring from the first class game.

WW II   124 apps   65 gls
Honours: Division 3 South Cup Joint Winners 1937 (Notts County).

ROBINSON (George) William

1931 - 33 Inside Forward
b: Kirkby in Ashfield, Notts., 15 February 1908
d: Derby, 16 July 1967
Career: Welbeck Colliery (May 1922), Alfreton Town (Aug 1924), Barnsley (Feb 1926), Sutton Town (c/s 1927), Denaby United (c/s 1928), TOWN (Aug 1929 - trial), Shirebrook (Sep 1929), TOWN (c/s 1931), Bilsthorpe Colliery (c/s 1933), Sutton Town (c/s 1935)

Only a reserve at Field Mill, but senior player elsewhere. A more than useful cricketer, playing 26 times for Notts C C C between 1930 and 1936.

SARSON Albert

1948 -49 Inside Right
b: Rossington, Nr. Doncaster, 31 December 1920
Career: TOWN (c/s 1948 - am), Doncaster Rovers (Aug 1949)

Became a pro with "Rovers" after Mansfield failed to re-sign him, but could only manage a couple of appearances in the very successful Doncaster side of this period.

SCOTHORN Gary

1974 - 75 Goalkeeper 5' 11"   11st 6lbs (1974)
b: Hoyland, S Yorks., 6 June 1950
Career: Sheffield Wednesday (July 1965 - appr, Jun 1967 - pro), TOWN (Aug 1974), Sligo Rovers (Jun 1975).

No senior appearances at Mansfield, although he had played in the "Owls" First Division eleven - oddly enough, including an F A Cup tie against the "Stags" in February 1967.

SHAW (Cecil) Ernest
1929 - 30 Full Back 5' 10"   12st 0lbs (1935)
b: Mansfield, 22 June 1911
d: Handsworth, Birmingham, 20 January 1977
Career: Mansfield Invicta, Blidworth Juniors, Rainworth Church, Rufford Colliery, TOWN (c/s 1929 - am), Wolverhampton Wanderers (Feb 1930), West Bromwich Albion (£7,500 - Dec 1936), Hereford United (Jun 1947 to 1949). West Bromwich Albion (1950s - scout), Oldbury & District League (1959-60 - referee)

Another future "star" who slipped through the net. Carved out a great career with both Wolves and West Brom., playing for the Football League against the Irish League in Belfast (1936).
Honours: Football League XI (Wolverhampton).

SHIRLEY Alexander G
1948 - 49 Outside Right
b: Milngavie, Ayrshire, 31 October 1921
Career: Dundee United (1938), New Brighton (Oct 1946), Bradford City (Aug 1947), TOWN (Aug 1948)

First team player elsewhere, but not at Mansfield.

SHOOTER Francis A
1931 - 32 Centre Forward
b: Warsop, Notts., c1906
Career: Ilkeston Town (1925), Ransome & Marles Newark (c/s 1928), Notts County (c/s 1930), TOWN (c/s 1931), Matlock Town (c/s 1932).

Could only make the reserve team at Field Mill, despite having been in the "Magpies" Division 3 South Championship team the previous season.

SMALLEY Ernest (Walter)
1931 - 32 Wing Half Back
Career: Chesterfield (1929), TOWN (F.T. c/s 1931)

"Spireites" senior player before joining the "Stags".

TAYLOR Ernest
1922 - 23 Full Back
b: Mansfield, c1901
Career: TOWN (1922), Southend United (Jun 1923), Frickley Colliery (Aug 1924).

Did not make the first team at Field Mill, but made five appearances for the "Shrimpers" in 1923-24.

THOMPSON Harry
1932-33 Inside Forward/Wing Half 5'10" 10st 8lbs (1937)
b: Mansfield, 29 April 1915
Career: Carter Lane School, High Oakham School, Mansfield Invicta, TOWN (Jun 1932 - am), Wolverhampton Wanderers (Mar 1933), Sunderland (£7,500 - Dec 1938), York City (Dec 1945), Northampton Town (Nov 1946 - player coach), Headington United (July 1949 - player manager)

Another of the many successful ex High Oakham schoolboys who made good in the football world and who cost the "Wearsiders" a very big fee indeed just before war broke out. Showed promise in the reserves and was offered a contract, but Wolves could offer him much more money and he moved on to bigger things. Ultimately moved into management with Headington United (now Oxford United).

THORPE Albert Edward ("Teddy")
1929 - 30 Full/Wing Half Back   5' 10"   10st 8lbs
b: Pilsley, Derbys., 14 July 1910
d: Langwith, Notts., 3 January 1971
Career: Shirebrook (1926 - am), Coventry City (Apr 1928 - trial), Wolverhampton Wanderers (May 1928), TOWN (July 1929), Notts County (Sep 1930), Norwich City (May 1932), Crystal Palace (exch Manders - Oct 1935), Scunthorpe & Lindsey United, Hereford United.

Fame did not arrive until he joined the "Canaries" where he made 61 appearances and won a Championship medal.
Honours: Division 3 South Championship 1934 (Norwich)

TIZARD Charles Walter
1935 - 36 Goalkeeper 5' 10½"   12st 7lbs (1935)
b: Blandford, Dorset, 1914
Career: Winchester City (am), Crystal Palace, TOWN (c/s 1935), Northampton Town (c/s 1936), Dundalk (1938)

Only 4 appearances for Palace, none for the "Cobblers" and none for Mansfield, but became a regular with Dundalk, being selected for the League of Ireland team versus the Irish League at Dublin in March 1939.
Honours: League of Ireland XI (Dundalk).

WILSON (Frederick) Charles
1935 - 36 Centre Half Back   6' 1"
b: Nottingham, 10 November 1918
Career: Mansfield Baptists, TOWN (1935 - am), Wolverhampton Wanderers (May 1936 - pro), Bournemouth & Boscombe Athletic (May 1937), Weymouth (Jun 1951).

Another local boy who made good. Found employment in Bournemouth during WW II and made well over 200 appearances for them 1939-46, apart from playing in almost 100 games both before and after the war for the "Cherries" - also "guested" for Brighton during the war.
Honours: Division 3 South Cup Winners 1946 (Bournemeouth).

1995 CLOSE SEASON SIGNINGS:

BOWLING Ian
Goalkeeper   6' 3"   14st 8lbs (1993)
b: Sheffield, 27 July 1965
Career: Frechesville C A, Staffoed Rangers, Gainsborough Trinity, (c/s 1988), Lincoln City (£2,000 - Oct 1988), Hartlepool (Aug 1989 - loan), Kettering Town (Feb 1990 - loan), Bradford City (Mar 1993 - loan, £27,500 July 1993 permanent), TOWN (F.T. July 1995).

A giant of a goalkeeper who suffered a number of injuries whilst at Sincil Bank. On his tranfer to the "Bantams" in July 1993, the fee was decided by tribunal.

CARMICHAEL Matthew
Midfield/Forward   6' 2"   11st 7lbs (1994)
b: Singapore, 13 May 1964
Career: Durrington, Salisbury Town, Wycombe Wanderers (Oct 1987), Bromley, Basingstoke Town, Lincoln City (Aug 1989), Scunthorpe United (p/exch David Hill - July 1993), Barnet (Sep 1994 - loan), Preston North End (Mar 1995 - loan), TOWN (July 1995 - three months trial).

Vastly experienced player who can play in either midfield or as a striker, where his goalscoring record is excellent. A late starter in professional football, spending six years in the Royal Artillery as a P T Instructor. Lincoln Player of the year, 1991-92.

EUSTACE Scott D
Central Defender   6' 0"   12st 4lbs (1993)
b: Leicester, 13 June 1975
Career: Leicester City (1990 - ass schoolboy, 1991 - appr, July 1993 - pro), TOWN (F.T. Jun 1995).

Young player released by Leicester and snapped up by Andy King in early June 1995 - and hence no appearances at time of going to print. Had limited senior experience at Filbert Street.

SALE Mark D.
Forward   6' 5"   13st 8lbs (1993)
b: Burton on Trent, 27 February 1972
Career: Stoke City (1988 - appr, July 1990 - pro), Cambridge United (F.T. July 1991), Rocester (Dec 1991), Birmingham CIty (Mar 1992), Torquay United (£10,000 - Mar 1993), Preston North End (£20,000 - July 1994), TOWN (£50,000 - July 1995)

Mark Sale must be one of the tallest players in the Football League - at 6' 5" he is barely 2" shorter than Keven Francis, who was transferred to Birmingham City - one of Sale's former clubs. Scored his first goals whilst at Torquay afer an unfruitful year at St. Andrews.

SLAWSON Stephen M
Forward   6' 2"   12st 6lbs (1994)
b: Nottingham, 13 November 1972
Career: Notts County (1989 - assoc schoolboy, 1990 - appr, July 1991 - pro), Burnley (Feb 1993 - loan), TOWN (F.T. July 1995).

Striker secured on a free transfer to replace Steve Wilkinson after his move to Preston a month earlier. Over 40 senior appearances for the "Magpies".

From
'YORE PUBLICATIONS'
12 The Furrows, Harefield, Middx. UB9 6AT

(Free lists issued 3 times per year. For your first list please send a S.A.E.)

FORGOTTEN CAPS (England Football Internationals of two World Wars) (Bryan Horsnell and Douglas Lamming)
A much acclaimed book written by the two leading authorities on the subject. A complete Who's Who record of every England player (including non playing reserves) - over 100. A biography and photograph of **every** player (the famous and the not so famous) has been included. Full match statistics, modern interviews with the players, the programmes feature, etc. A truly complete record! 112 large pages, price £8-95 plus £1-30 P/P.

WHO'S WHO OF LINCOLN CITY F.C. 1892 - 1994 (Donald & Ian Nannestad)
A very similar format to the Mansfield Town Who's Who book. Every Football League player is included, together with several additional sections, e.g. a brief history of the club, managers and secretaries, etc. 190 pages, price £9-95 plus £1-15 postage & packing.

DONNY - The Official History of Doncaster Rovers (Tony Bluff and Barry Watson) Written by two supporters of the Club, the full statistics (from 1879) and including line-ups (from 1901). The book is well illustrated, including many line-ups, and also contains the full written history of the Club. Hardback with full coloured dustjacket and 240 pages. Price £14-95 plus £1-80 postage & packing.

COLCHESTER UNITED - The Official History of the 'U's' (Hal Mason)
With football involvement from the 1920's, the Author - a former journalist and Colchester programme editor - is well qualified to relate this complete history of the Club since its formation in 1937 (including complete statistics and lineups from this season). Large Hardback, 240 pages, priced £14-95 plus £2-70 postage.

AMBER IN THE BLOOD - History of Newport County: (Tony Ambrosen).
The full written story of football in Newport from the pre-County days up to and including the recently formed Newport AFC club. The text is well illustrated, and a comprehensive statistical section provides all the results, attendances, goalscorers, etc. from 1912 to 1993 - the various Leagues and principal Cup competitions; additionally seasonal total players' appearances are included. Large hardback with 176 large pages is exceptional value at £13-95 plus £2-60 postage.

BREATHE ON 'EM SALOP - THE OFFICIAL HISTORY OF SHREWSBURY TOWN (Mike Jones).
Written by long time supporter and local radio broadcaster, and aided by the club's official statistician, this 256 large page hardback book tells the full story - including statistics from 1886. It is very well illustrated, and includes a 'one-liner' Who's Who section, and a feature on all the managers. Price £14-95 plus £3-50 P/P.

REJECTED F.C. VOLUME 1 (Reprint) (By Dave Twydell)
The revised edition of this popular book - now in hardback - this volume provides the comprehensive histories of: Aberdare Athletic, Ashington, Bootle, Bradford (Park Avenue), Burton (Swifts, Wanderers and United), Gateshead/South Shields, Glossop, Loughborough, Nelson, Stalybridge Celtic and Workington. The 288 well illustrated pages also contain the basic statistical details of each club. Price £12-95 plus £1-30 postage.

REJECTED F.C. VOLUMES 2 and 3 (Reprints) The revised and extended former volume 2 has now been reprinted in two volumes, and includes the rest of the 'ex-League' clubs: Accrington/Acc. Stanley, Barrow, Darwen, Merthyr Town, Thames Association plus new addition Leeds City (Volume 2), and Durham City, Gainsborough Trinity, Middlesbrough Ironopolis, New Brighton/New Brighton Tower, Northwich Vics., Southport plus new addition Wigan Borough (Volume 3). 256 pages (hardback), and each priced £12-95 plus £1-30 P/P.

(Also Rejected F.C. of Scotland: Volume 1 covers Edinburgh and The South (Edinburgh City, Leith Athletic, St.Bernards, Armadale, Broxburn United, Bathgate, Peebles Rovers, Mid-Annandale, Nithsdale Wanderers and Solway Star - 288 pages). Volume 2 covers Glasgow and District (Abercorn, Arthurlie, Beith, Cambuslang, Clydebank, Cowlairs, Johnstone, Linthouse, Northern, Third Lanark, and Thistle -240 pages). Each priced £12-95 plus £1-30 postage.

FOOTBALL LEAGUE - GROUNDS FOR A CHANGE (By Dave Twydell). A 424 page, A5 sized, Hardback book. A comprehensive study of all the Grounds on which the current English Football League clubs previously played. Every Club that has moved Grounds is included, with a 'Potted' history of each, plus 250 illustrations. Plenty of 'reading' material, as well as an interesting reference book. Price £13-95 Plus £1-70 Postage.

THE CODE WAR (Graham Williams)
A fascinating look back on football's history - from the earliest days up to the First World War. 'Football' is covered in the broadest sense, for the book delves into the splits over the period to and from Rugby Union and Rugby League, as well as Football (Soccer). Potted histories of many of the Clubs are included, as is a comprehensive index. 192 page hardback, price £10-95 plus £1-20 postage.